A History of National,
State, & Private Cooperation
by William G. Robbins

American Forestry

University of Nebraska Press: Lincoln & London

The paper in this book meets
the guidelines for
permanence and durability
of the Committee on
Production Guidelines for
Book Longevity of the
Council on Library Resources.

Library of Congress Cataloging
in Publication Data

Robbins, William G., 1935 –
American Forestry.

Bibliography: P.
Includes index.
1. United States. Forest
Service – History.
2. Forest policy – United
States – History.   I. Title.
SD565.R57   1985
353.0082'338   84-28122
ISBN 0-8032-3872-X
(alk. paper)

To the memory of Tom Hogg, who got it all started

Contents

Acknowledgments

This study originated in a contract with the U.S. Forest Service that called for the preparation of a "documented and scholarly history" of the agency's "cooperation with states and private individuals and companies." Tom Hogg, Bill Honey, Karen Starr, John Young, and Clair Younger assisted in the long cross-country search through federal and state archives and private manuscript collections. They turned up volumes of archival material, conducted oral interviews, and contributed valuable observations about their research. In keeping with the Forest Service mandate for this study, their effort has been truly a "cooperative" one.

From her hilltop sanctuary in San Francisco, Jan Newton read the entire manuscript and offered important insights about private sector influences on public policy. Her extensive experience and research interests in the economic and social substructure of rural communities have helped broaden my understanding of the external influences that shaped rural life and directed the course of forest exploitation. Jan's suggestions about organization and consistent and logical argument contributed to making this book a more coherent story. A bouquet of Oregon wildflowers for you, Jan.

Although the Forest Service supported the research and writing of this study, the direction of the research, the organization of the book, and the interpretive framework are mine. Several agency officials, past and present, reviewed the manuscript and offered the benefit of their years of "on-the-ground" practical work in some of the policies described in the study. Where we differed over the implications of cooperative programs, I revised the argument when reviewers convinced me that my conclusions went beyond the evidence. But on other debatable issues, my version of the story remained unchanged when documented sources and the public record suggested that I was closer to the truth.

I have no illusions, however, that this work will satisfy everyone; the subject is diffuse and those who were actively involved in administering field programs may see matters differently. Where the historical sources suggested that service policy aided and abetted certain groups over others, I have said so; and I have tried to point out the many occasions when powerful political influences in the federal capital limited or altered cooperative policy.

This study attempts to touch upon the more important Forest Service cooperative programs. Bug people and blister rust folks may feel shortchanged; farm forestry personnel will think they were slighted; foresters associated with the various Clarke-McNary programs will argue that they deserve an entire book (and they are probably right); regional and state foresters will make similar claims; and each of the fifty states will want its day in the sun. But the published literature and the extensive archival material give the greatest emphasis to those policy issues and programs included in this book.

Finally, a word of appreciation to the librarians, archivists, and Forest Service personnel who offered their assistance and advice during the course of research: to the staff of the National Archives and Records Service, Washington, D.C., and its regional branches in Atlanta, Georgia, San Bruno, California, and Seattle, Washington; the Franklin D. Roosevelt Presidential Library, Hyde Park, New York, and the Herbert Hoover Presidential Library, West Branch, Iowa; to Ron Fahl, editor of the *Journal of Forest History,* and the staff of the Forest History Society, Santa Cruz, California, for generously sharing their wealth of knowledge on sources in forest history; the Oregon Historical Society, Portland; the Georgia State Archives, Atlanta; the California State Archives, Sacramento; the Minnesota Historical Society and Archives, St. Paul; the Oregon State Archives, Salem; the Washington State Archives, Olympia; the National Agricultural Library, Beltsville, Maryland; and the staff of the University of Oregon Library, Eugene. And to Pat Brandt and Ed Brazee of the Oregon State University Library for their patience and assistance.

Introduction

In its long and distinguished existence as the principal forestry agency of the U.S. government, the Forest Service (and its bureaucratic predecessors in the Department of Agriculture) has been charged with three major areas of responsibility—administration (of the national forests), research, and cooperation. The latter mission has involved an extended association with state forestry bureaus and the private sector. Since the late nineteenth century, federal foresters have conducted a wide variety of congressionally mandated technical and financial assistance programs to promote forestry and to aid forest-dependent industries.

From the relatively simple tree-planting agreements under the direction of Bernhard Fernow in the 1890s, federal forestry assistance has evolved into a complex and broad range of programs that have influenced virtually every phase of public and private forestry. This extensive effort—conducted through state, county, and municipal governments and special compacts with corporations—expanded under the cooperative fire control programs of the early twentieth century and today embraces everything from fire prevention to a wide array of incentive programs for small woodland owners.

While responsibility for managing the national forests and conducting research is fairly well defined in service policy, the programs, agreements, emergency projects, and interdepartmental exchanges that fall under the rubric of cooperation are less distinct and have received little attention in historical literature to a wide array of incentive programs for small woodland owners.

While responsibility for managing the national forests and conducting research is fairly well defined in service policy, the programs, agreements, emergency projects, and interdepartmental exchanges that fall under the rubric of cooperation are less distinct and have received little attention in historical literature. In fact, federal cooperation in forestry has meant many things to many people, and government policies and programs have affected state and private forestry practice in different ways. Henry Clepper, whose association with professional forestry spans a period of fifty years, remarked recently that there are "as many contrary views about cooperative work as people you talk to."

This study attempts to provide a general description of federal forestry relations with public agencies and private enterprise. A broad and elusive theme that defies clear definition, federal cooperation has been the topic of heated congressional debates and equally divisive arguments in leading professional journals since the 1890s. And because these policies deeply affected one of the great natural resource industries of the country, they involved important social, economic, and political implications both for the general public and the forest industry.

Sharp differences between Forest Service officials and spokesmen for the forest industry have surfaced in debates over forestry policy. Heavy lobbying with the Forest Service and before Congress greeted even the mildest proposals to impose federal regulations on industrial forestry activity in exchange for cooperative assistance. The move to adopt federal requirements—which waxed and waned from the 1920s through the 1950s—involved the forestry profession, forest products officials, politicians, and conservation organizations. These factions aired their differences in public forums and before congressional committees. On these occasions, forest industry leaders accused the Forest Service of deviating from its traditional and proven forms of cooperation. The charges point to an important characteristic of cooperative programs—since their inception, these arrangements have reflected the needs and aspirations of the forest products industry.

The establishment of a forestry agency in the Department of Agriculture in the late nineteenth century was part of a broader move to create federal bureaus devoted to gathering and publishing reports about the latest scientific findings—information increasingly important to an industrializing America. The development of scientific forestry and the extension of federal assistance programs to states and private owners reflected a growing concern for the perpetuation of forests and the protection of municipal watersheds. Manufacturing organizations with a vested interest in a healthy forest resource backed a variety of programs to prevent erosion and flooding and to protect and enhance forests for industrial purposes. Their objectives were clearly commercial utility.

Industrial objectives, therefore, have deeply influenced federal policy, and both state and federal legislatures, in turn, have affected the relationship between the Forest Service and the private sector. Their collective actions have touched on virtually every phase of forest industry activity. Federal and state forestry programs also have had a considerable impact on forest-dependent communities.

All of this is to say that cooperation as a major Forest Service mission has always involved more than a linear relationship between federal and state agencies. Moreover, cooperative programs and activities were varied and complex; some were short-lived and unilateral responses to natural disaster like insect and disease outbreaks, flood emergencies, and blowdowns. But others, like cooperation in fire control, have involved federal foresters since the beginning of the twentieth century. And there was usually some form of federal assistance in fire protection, indirect aid in marketing information, and forest products research.

To make matters more confusing, cooperative policy often has mirrored changing presidential and congressional priorities. The Forest Service, for instance, has cooperated with other federal agencies in rural rehabilitation projects, many of which did not survive more than one presidential administration; others, such as the Civilian Conservation Corps, ended when wartime emergencies intervened. And Congress has periodically initiated assistance programs to increase production on small forest ownerships—and then backed off when these programs came under attack.

As was the case with other federal resource agencies, congressional political struggles and the distribution of federal funds determined the success or failure of Forest Service programs. This book is the story of Forest Service administration of congressionally authorized programs. It is also an account of policies that were never implemented because of opposition from the private sector or because Congress or state legislatures failed to appropriate the necessary money.

The study is arranged both chronologically and thematically. The first two chapters cover the beginnings of federal forestry and its association with the needs and aspirations of important segments of America's increasingly urbanized and industrialized economy. Chapter Three traces the establishment and growth of the early state forestry organizations and suggests some regional characteristics associated with the uneven pattern of development. Migrating centers of lumbering activity shaped state forestry policy during these years. This theme is traced through the experiences of selected states in different regions of the country — Georgia, Minnesota, and Oregon and Washington. Important developments in other states enter the story when they point to important changes in policy.

Chapters Four, Five, and Six trace the extension of cooperative fire protection to states through the Weeks Act of 1911 and the Clarke-McNary Act of 1924. These hallmark pieces of legislation vastly expanded federal assistance to states, although the extent of the relationship was uneven and depended on the strength and financial condition of the state organizations. But fire was the great catalyst for federal cooperation. Congressmen and senators from timber-producing sections of the country eagerly sought to expand this form of assistance.

Chapter Seven recapitulates Forest Service cooperative activities outside those mandated in the Weeks and Clarke-McNary legislation. These included working relationships with other bureaus and agencies in the Department of Agriculture, interdepartmental agreements such as those with the Bureau of Indian Affairs, a variety of research and investigative agreements, and collaboration with state and private sector agencies to promote tourism in the national forests.

Chapters Eight and Nine focus on the great expansion in cooperative assistance during the Great Depression. The economic and social crisis of the 1930s opened new avenues for rehabilitative work in forest conservation, flood control, and other emergency projects. Although Congress designed most of these programs to relieve unemployment and alleviate social discontent, many of them accomplished remarkable feats in reclaiming eroded landscapes through tree planting and other conservation measures. And they were all labor-intensive. The Forest Service had other cooperative assistance programs on the drawing boards during these years, but they never gained congressional approval.

Mobilizing the forest industry for the Second World War and then the return to peacetime relations are the subjects of Chapters Ten and Eleven. Congressional and presidential priorities forced the Forest Service to abandon many of the emergency projects initiated in the 1930s and to pursue programs that were production-oriented. Federal decisions forced the service to shift policies again with the return of peace in 1945. But in one sense there was a degree of continuity between the war and postwar era—the industry and Congress insisted that production be the major objective of assistance programs.

The debate over adequate forest resources for the future has been a point of controversy since 1945. Chapters Twelve, Thirteen, and Fourteen take up the major themes that concerned Forest Service cooperators during these years: fire protection, insect and disease control, watershed protection programs, river basin development projects, assistance to small woodland owners, the complex cooperative relationships with the Soil Conservation Service and the Extension Service, and the Great Society programs of the Lyndon Johnson years. These chapters also show the growing professionalism of state forestry agencies and their close working relationship with the forest products industry. Support for Georgia's state agency literally blossomed during the period when it became obvious that the Southeast would be the center of forest products manufacturing in the last quarter of the twentieth century.

Finally, Chapter Fifteen attempts to make sense out of the multitude of policy areas and administrative jurisdictions that have emerged in the last few years. The increased complexity in the number and scope of programs in recent years compounds the task of attempting to evaluate these in the context of the traditional federal-state cooperative relationship. The jury, of course, is still out. But there are observable trends since the 1970s that indicate a major shift of forestry responsibility to the states. If this movement continues, it will present a great challenge to the professionalism and self-direction of state forestry. And it will likely dilute further the conventional forms of federal-state relations in forestry.

Chapter One

Scientists and the Beginning of Forest Conservation

In the decades following the American Civil War, the scientific community in the United States became increasingly aware that the nation's rapidly expanding industrial and commercial base was raising havoc with the natural environment. War-related demands on forest resources, a growing industrial appetite for wood supplies, the rapid liquidation of the Great Lakes states pineries, and the increasing frequency and severity of forest fires raised questions about the effects of diminishing forest cover and timber supplies. Moreover, it was increasingly apparent that deforestation contributed to watershed deterioration, an ominous warning to the nation's growing cities.

When George Perkins Marsh published his classic *Man and Nature* in 1864, he influenced a generation of scientific thinking about the relationship between streamflow and the forest environment. The annual reports of the departments of Interior and Agriculture referred to Marsh and a small group of scientists as the preeminent authorities on the effects of timber depletion and its relation to flooding. Frederick Starr contributed a paper as part of the Department of Agriculture report for 1865 that predicted a timber famine within thirty years; he urged the government to sponsor private research to learn about proper forest management practices. Other natural scientists studied the association among soil erosion, the siltation of streams, and the disappearance of the salmon runs from New England streams.[1] Clearly, there was an abundance of evidence — widely shared in the learned communi-

ties—that something must be done to halt these destructive influences. Moreover, writers like Marsh associated the political and economic character of industrial capitalism with the destruction of natural
resources.

Although the actions of the federal government lagged behind the
recommendations of scientific investigators, there was occasional forward movement (though often for the wrong reasons). In his annual
report for 1866, the commissioner of the General Land Office recommended that homesteaders be required to plant trees, especially on
the western prairies where they were scarce. Conventional wisdom
suggested that tree planting would satisfy the need for wood, increase
rainfall, and protect watersheds. Based in part on the writings of
Linus P. Brockett ("rain will follow the plow"), this form of psuedo-
science gained credibility when Congress passed the Timber Culture
Act, which permitted a settler to plant trees as part of the residency
requirement for acquiring public land. Land speculators for wheat
and cattle interests put the law to wholesale abuse before its repeal in
1891.[2]

But for most of the last quarter of the nineteenth century, forestry
was an educational movement—an effort to impress upon the public
the need for conservation. State and federal governments slowly began
to develop a sense of forestry consciousness, and an occasional owner
began to apply forestry practices in the field. Although there were few
apostles of forest conservation, increasing numbers of publications began to focus on some aspect of forestry.

The Beginning of Federal Involvement

In the early 1870s a small group of scientists convinced the government to investigate forestry conditions in the United States. William
Brewer, a Yale University professor of agriculture, prepared a synthesis of the prevailing knowledge on woodlands in the United States for
the *Statistical Atlas* of 1874. More significant for the future of forestry
was the work of Franklin B. Hough, a physician with wide intellec-
tual interests in the sciences. Hough directed the New York census
for several years with an expertise that led to his selection to assist
with the 1870 census of the United States. Through his work Hough

became aware of a sharp decline in northeastern lumber production and the finite nature of the timber resource. In his famous address to the American Association for the Advancement of Science (AAAS) in 1873, "On the Duty of Governments in the Preservation of Forests," Hough pointed to the "economical value of timber" and "our absolute dependence on it." He advocated the establishment of forestry schools, state legislation to promote better forest use, and the need for Congress to consider "the subject of protection to the forests, and their cultivation, regulation, and encouragement."[3]

The AAAS recognized the importance of forests to the national economy when it memorialized Congress to investigate forest conditions. A dilatory federal legislature finally authorized the commissioner of agriculture in 1876 to appoint a person "acquainted with the methods of statistical inquiry" to study the condition of the nation's forests. The president appointed Hough as the government's first forestry agent in the Department of Agriculture.[4]

Hough made use of his contacts with eminent scientists: Asa Gray, the compiler of the classic *Manual of Botany*; William Brewer; George B. Emerson, a Harvard botanist and writer; and Josiah D. Whitney, a California geologist. Hough corresponded with public officials in nearly every state; with lumbermen, botanists, and horticulturalists; and with the agencies of foreign governments. He traveled by rail during the spring and summer of 1877 to observe forestry conditions in different parts of the country. The result of Hough's investigation—the lengthy three-volume *Report upon Forestry*, published between 1878 and 1882—contained most of the available information on American forests (including the forest products industries) and on European forestry. The first volume recommended leasing federal timber to private operators for harvesting, prohibiting illegal trespass on public timberlands, and curbing the great waste of timber resources.[5]

Congress rewarded Hough by elevating the forestry agent's position to chief of the Division of Forestry in 1881. The third volume, published after a tour of European forests, convinced Hough to add to his recommendations for American forestry. The volume included an extensive account of forest fires and recommendations to reserve public timberlands, to establish forest experiment stations, to employ

European-trained foresters to manage public timberlands, and it advised the federal purchase of suitable private lands under certain circumstances.[6]

Hough's contributions were notable. Largely self-educated in forestry, he had compiled in three massive volumes what Bernhard E. Fernow termed the "most useful publication of its kind . . . in this country."[7] Ten years after he began to inform himself about the condition of American forests, Hough was undoubtedly the most knowledgeable American on the subject. His pioneering work laid the foundation for federal forestry, and his recommendations anticipated future developments in both public and private forestry.

The establishment of scientific bureaus in the federal government indicated the increasing importance of natural resources to the economic health of the United States. And the educational work and lobbying activities of private groups contributed to a growing interest in sciences like forestry. The oldest (and still existing) conservation organization in the United States, the American Forestry Association (AFA), was organized in 1875 for the purpose of "protection of the existing forests of the country from unnecessary waste," and to promote the "propagation and planting of useful trees." John A. Warder, a trained physician like Hough, arranged the first meeting and served as president of the organization for its first seven years. Warder announced that the association would foster the "interests of forest planting and conservation."[8]

Although the AFA was not very visible at first, it became more active when it merged with another Warder organization, the American Forestry Congress, in the 1880s. The first congress, which met in 1882, passed resolutions urging states and the federal government to appoint "Commissioners of Forestry" and to "enact such laws as will serve to protect existing forests and stimulate an interest in forest culture." The membership of the merged organization included lumbermen from every major producing region, prominent railroad and coal entrepreneurs, and some of the leading politicians of the day. Along with the AAAS, the AFA pressed Congress to establish permanent forest reserves in the American West. Fernow, who drafted the constitution for the organization, cited as its objectives: (1) spreading knowledge about tree planting, (2) the study of climate and other influences that affect forests, (3) collecting forest statistics, and (4) the "advancement" of forestry-related educational and legislative measures.[9]

Published literature about forest conditions in the United States continued to multiply. In 1884 Charles Sprague Sargent published his monumental *Report on the Forests of North America*. Sargent's study, the first scientific survey of forestland in the United States, called attention to the rapidly diminishing white pine stands in the Great Lakes states.[10]

Meanwhile, Nathaniel Egleston, a Congregational minister, replaced Hough as chief of the Forestry Division in 1883. Political differences were obvious in Hough's dismissal; he had difficulty getting along with George B. Loring, President James Garfield's new commissioner of agriculture. When Egleston began his three-year stint as chief, the Division of Forestry employed three field agents and operated on an annual budget of $10,000. But federal forestry did not languish under Engleston's leadership for long. In 1886 President Grover Cleveland appointed Fernow, a graduate of the Prussian Forest Academy at Munden, to head the forestry division.[11]

Fernow's appointment underscored the federal government's increased awareness of the importance of forests and forest products to economic development. Although Fernow's division was small and without a forest to manage, the new chief was thoroughly educated in scientific forestry. During his twelve years as head of the division, Fernow published studies on forestry research, cooperated with state agricultural stations, and drafted forestry legislation for both state and federal governments. He nurtured the agency's cooperation with private associations like the AFA, the AAAS, the National Grange, and other groups interested in scientific forestry. He promoted federal forestlands "as practical schools of forestry, as object lessons, as forest experiment stations." By successfully managing its forests, Fernow believed, the federal government could encourage scientific timber-management practices.[12]

In his first report the new chief listed the most important objectives of federal forestry. The division's earlier studies, Fernow said, were sufficient to "show the deplorable condition of our forestry." But because of its limited appropriations, he recommended that the government successfully manage its own forestlands and that it offer private forest owners "the advice and guidance of well-qualified forestry officials." The individual states, he argued, should inaugurate similar policies through the establishment of forestry organizations.[13]

Fernow also urged the government to withdraw its timberlands from further entry and to limit the annual harvests to "not more than what grows yearly or during certain periods." His rationale for setting aside forest reserves established the basic arguments used by federal officials for the next twenty years: (1) the reserves would protect watersheds, (2) they "would form a nucleus and an example for American forestry," and (3) they would preserve land that was "principally more valuable for the timber on it." Fernow's recommendations included a "Plan for a Forest Department," which outlined an organization for administering the reserves.[14]

But the historic conditions under which the government disposed of its public domain, Fernow said, posed even greater difficulties. Enormous waste accompanied the clearing of land in the eastern portions of the country; then the "rapid development of our railway system" led to the settlement of the trans-Mississippi West, a "spirit of speculation" in public timberlands, and "enormous profits." The low prices of government timberland "have excited such competition in the lumbering industry" that mills can turn a profit "only when driven to their utmost capacity of production." This tendency, Fernow warned, was not conducive to "proper forest management."[15]

Fernow's recognition of the lumber industry's economic difficulties established a precedent for understanding between the federal government's forestry agency and lumbermen. As future heads of the forestry bureau learned, economic conditions were directly related to forest management. Moreover, government programs that ran counter to the industry's economic needs were doomed to failure. The requirements of the forest products trade would be the essential feature of federal cooperation with private timberland owners. "To induce any forest owner to adopt rational and conservative forest management," Fernow pointed out, "we should have to show him that it is directly profitable."[16]

Origins of the National Forests

While Fernow established a working basis for forestry, private associations sought to expand federal jurisdiction to protect public timberlands. The AFA adopted a resolution in 1886 urging the federal government to grant public lands "at the sources of streams" to the states, to be "kept by such States in perpetuity" for purposes of watershed protection. By the late 1880s the AFA, the AAAS, and the American Forestry Congress supported Fernow's proposal to establish a system of national forest administration and to withdraw all public lands from entry until they were surveyed.[17] This was not a new idea.

Secretary of the Interior Carl Schurz (1877–1881) repeatedly had advised Congress to withdraw all federal timberland from public entry and to provide for its protection and management. Edward A. Bowers, a lawyer in the General Land Office, prepared a measure in 1887 to provide for the reservation and administration of public land "valuable in any degree for timber or their forest growth." Finally, Bowers collaborated with Fernow in drafting the forest reserve legislation of 1891. Under the measure, the president had the authority to withdraw forested land from public entry and to establish forest reservations. The new policy marked a dramatic change in the land policy of the United States. President Benjamin Harrison, with little public opposition, created six forest reserves in 1891 and 1892, the meager beginnings to the millions of acres in the present national forest system.[18] This reserve act addressed one concern of the private forestry associations, but it did not specify the function of the reserves; it failed to provide for the protection and administration of the reserves; it failed to establish procedures for the sale of timber; and it did not end timber theft and overgrazing on the reserves.[19]

The move to adopt a management policy for federal timberlands quickened in 1896 when the Cleveland administration requested the National Academy of Sciences to recommend a management policy for the reserves. The academy appointed an advisory committee, commonly referred to as the Forest Commission, to tour the western forests and to offer suggestions for their management. After visiting most of the public timberlands in the West, the commission recommended the creation of thirteen new reserves amounting to 21 million acres. President Cleveland complied and set off a storm of protest.[20]

As cattle- and sheepmen and mining and lumber interests angrily expressed their objections, the ever-cautious Fernow thought the president had made a mistake. Cleveland, he observed, had neither consulted with westerners in creating the new reserves nor had he proposed a management policy for them. The "storm broke loose," the forester reflected, when a large block of the West was withdrawn from private settlement.[21]

One of the more outspoken opponents of the federal reserves, John Minto, an Oregon fruit grower and sheepman, thought that the government had suspended "the general land laws against landless citizens." The recommendation of the National Academy of Sciences to expand the reserves, he feared, would eventually contravene the rights of the states. The forest commission had acted "imperiously" and was infringing on the rights of the citizen.[22] Like many small landowners in the West, Minto thought the reserve system was an eastern conspiracy to keep public lands from the common citizens.

With the inauguration of President William McKinley in March, 1897, supporters of the federal forests feared that the entire system might be in jeopardy. Consequently, groups like the AFA and the newly founded Sierra Club advised the new president to approve a measure for managing the federal reserves. The legislation provided the main statutory basis for the management of the federal forests for the next sixty-three years. And it was popular—western senators supported the measure because it made clear that the purpose of the reserves was "to furnish a continuous supply of timber." According to the biographers of the Weyerhaeuser story, the measure promoted sound public policy because the formula for the reserves "would be utilization, not hoarding." Fernow, still without a federal forest to manage, thought the 1897 act made it clear that the function of the reserves would be one of economics.[23]

Lumbermen from every forest region in the country supported the management measure. Moreover, when the national forests came under attack, organized lumbermen often were the first to defend the system. Federal forestry embraced a myriad of activities and policies; among these is the long tradition of mutual support and cooperation between federal forestry officials and the leading lumber organizations in the management policies for the national forests.

The Division Expands Its Activities

The Division of Forestry, of course, was concerned with much more than the single-minded pursuit of reserving and managing the federal timberlands. While he headed the division, Fernow promoted the establishment of state forestry agencies and scientific forestry practices among farmers and small woodlot owners. Farmers, he believed, were the most desirable of forest owners because they were the "most stable class of our population, and can devote the most care and attention to the management of their wood lots." But he feared that the increasing value of forestland offered farmers "great inducements to part with it prematurely." Still, the forestry head praised farmers: "Whatever attempt at rational forest management exists in the United States is found among the farmers."[24]

In his first annual report Fernow recommended the use of military reservations to establish experimental forests. These would demonstrate scientific forest management and provide a means for distributing seedlings, "either gratuitously or at nominal rates," to prospective tree planters. Although he favored tree planting on the western prairie, he thought the Timber Culture Act was ineffective. In his 1889 report he stated bluntly, "The timber culture act has been a failure, so far as the creating of forests is concerned."[25]

But the forestry division's most vexing problems under Fernow were inadequate facilities and appropriations. The lack of funds limited the division's activities to that of a "simple corresponding bureau." Fernow argued that there were important interests the division could serve, but much of this had to be deferred because of the inability to attract "competent co-workers." Still there were successes — a cooperative investigation with railroads; a cooperative survey into the needs of the cooperage industry; the publication of several pamphlets on eastern pines; the mailing of seeds to agricultural experiment stations; and the publication of statistics on the export and import of forest products.[26]

Most of the requests to the division during these years concerned the industrial uses of forest products. Railroad companies requested information about the strengths of woods for trestles and cross ties and for advice on the lasting qualities of wood under different climatic conditions.[27] Occasionally companies interested in acquiring timberland made inquiries to the division. Others wanted information on the woods best adapted for making pulp, paper, and other wood-based products. By the early 1890s these requests were burdensome; Fernow complained about the time involved in answering correspondence and of the need for a trained staff to carry on technical inquiries.[28]

The forestry division's policy of offering information to industrial users of wood products was not a one-way affair. Railroad companies provided free transportation of wood test materials. Fernow mentioned this reciprocal relationship in his annual summaries. Despite "the always scantily measured appropriations," he reported in 1891, the division accomplished a great amount of work through the cooperation of the railroads in transporting materials and men "free of charge," and through the "economical work" of others in supplying testing apparatus and "collecting and examining the material." Two years later, he paid tribute again to the railroad companies "whose generosity . . . has made it possible to handle much larger amounts than our funds would otherwise have permitted."[29]

Fernow also used his position to build a closer relationship with agricultural colleges, state forestry associations, and commercial organizations. Despite his perennial complaints about budgetary constraints on the division's work, Fernow's office turned out an impressive array of bulletins and circulars. Twenty-five thousand copies of the bulletin, *What Is Forestry,* were printed in 1891. The publication emphasized the importance of forest products to the American economy and listed the "principles which underlie proper management of forest resources."[30]

When Congress increased Fernow's budget during his last years as chief, the division pursued three principal lines of research: (1) experiments in tree planting on the Great Plains, (2) examinations of timber physics, and (3) biological investigations. The division cooperated with experiment stations in its tree-planting research. Fernow reported in 1897 that the projects had been successful "and have attracted much favorable attention from the people . . . they were designed to benefit." And in cooperation with an early urban forestry project, the forestry division head delegated his assistant, George B. Sudworth, to assist the tree and park commission of Savannah, Georgia, in selecting plants for the city's streets and parks, "although the subject is not exactly germane to the work of the division."[31]

Fernow also proposed a scheme of fire protection that required private cooperation when the properties involved "private interests." Because "the State has an economic interest" in forest protection, its

10

cooperation would be necessary as well. Under "the Canadian plan," as Fernow termed the proposal, the government would assume half the costs of protection and private holders the other half.[32] Fernow's advocacy of the Canadian plan was the clear forerunner to the cooperative programs developed under the Weeks Law of 1911 and the Clarke-McNary Act of 1924.

When he left the division in 1898, Fernow had established the scientific basis for federal forestry. With a fledgling staff, he directed dendrology research projects, tree-planting experiments (mainly in the Plains states), and conducted investigations into the physical properties of wood. Industrial users praised Fernow's work and provided the support that enabled the division to expand its activities beyond the constraints of limited budgets. By the end of the century, it was clear that federal forestry programs provided a valuable service to the requirements of a rapidly expanding economy. The forestry chief intended the incipient cooperative relationships worked out in the 1890s to meet the needs of the producers and consumers of forest products. There was nothing romantic or sentimental in Fernow's advocacy of forestry.

The annual reports of the division reveal an agency sensitive to the relationship between forests and forest products and economic development. Because of his keen understanding of the lumber industry, Fernow recognized the lumbermen's need for statistics to conduct rational and efficient business activity. He reasoned that such action could only "be based upon carefully obtained and digested statistics" that would aid in "estimating and comparing present supplies and future requirements." In this respect, Fernow initiated federal forestry's long-standing policy of providing the lumber industry with the information it needed to make investment decisions. In his reports to the Department of Agriculture and in his speaking engagements, Fernow emphasized the need for more statistics on lumber production and for inventories of forest resources because industries required accurate data to make intelligent decisions. His biographer put the case accurately: "Businessmen had confidence in Fernow."[33]

A New Era

The appointment of the energetic Gifford Pinchot to head the Divi-

11

sion of Forestry in 1898 marks the beginning of a new era in federal policy. The changes that took place during Pinchot's tenure have shaped the administration and jurisdiction of federal forestry ever since. In 1898 Pinchot headed a small staff without a forest to manage. Three years later Congress advanced the Division of Forestry to bureau status, thus strengthening the agency's position and giving it more prestige in the Department of Agriculture. Then in 1905, the most significant move of all — the transfer of 63 million acres of federal forestland to the Department of Agriculture. In recognition of its new status, the bureau was renamed the Forest Service (July, 1905), and two years later the federal timberlands were designated as national forests. These expanded responsibilities entailed a dramatic increase in staff—from eleven employees in 1898 to 821 in 1905.[34] The modern Forest Service bureaucracy was born.

Pinchot is an intimate part of federal forestry. Born to wealth and comfortable living and amidst a family overly solicitous for his welfare, Pinchot established a reputation for spartan energy and hard work. He was more than six feet tall, slim, and sported a thick moustache (the latter a delight to cartoonists). Despite a sheltered upbringing, the Yale graduate was a man of strong personality who attracted great loyalty from his supporters and equally strong opposition from those who disagreed with him. William B. Greeley, whose influence on the Forest Service ranks second to that of Pinchot, remarked that Pinchot brought to forestry "a religious intensity and a magnetic personal leadership that have rarely been equalled in the American drama."[35] Magnanimous words about a man he often disagreed with.

Pinchot both created and inspired the modern Forest Service. He established a model of efficient agency management. He demanded that subordinates respond immediately to requests and had a special fetish for answering letters on time. An independent study of the Forest Service administration in 1908 paid high tribute to Pinchot's administrative ability. "Rarely, if ever," the report concluded, have we "met a body of men where the average of intelligence was so high, or the loyalty to the organization and the work so great." The study added that the agency had conducted a volume of business "worthy of the highest commendation."[36]

Pinchot was an avowed publicist for "practicing Forestry in the woods." He criticized the old forestry division for its failure to produce "any forest management whatsoever," and demanded that the Washington office spend time in the field observing the practical problems of bringing forestry to the woods. The potential for this work was virtually limitless—"The world was all before us," he exclaimed. "I could pick my own trail." And there was little doubt about the direction he would choose. Just as the "business" of farmers was to manage farms, the "business" of foresters would be to manage forests.[37] It was in pursuit of these objectives that Pinchot vastly expanded and extended federal forestry cooperation with the private sector.

Only four months after his appointment, the office published Pinchot's famous Circular No. 21, which offered advice "to farmers, lumbermen, and others" in managing their forestlands. The service was free to woodlot owners, but the division charged traveling expenses and subsistence costs "in the case of large tracts." Nine months after the publication of "our major offensive," the division was "totally unable to meet the public demand upon it." And by 1902 requests continued "to outstrip more and more the ability of the Bureau to meet them."[38] This was the first federal program that was universally popular among timberland owners.

But Circular No. 21 was more; it was the first federal program to offer assistance in the field. Before the program was cut back in 1909, federal foresters had examined approximately 8 million acres, mostly in large holdings. These landowners included William G. Rockefeller, Abram S. Hewitt, E. H. Harriman, the St. Regis Paper Company, the Great Northern Paper Company, the Weyerhaeuser Timber Company, and the Kirby Lumber Company.[39]

Despite the popularity of Circular No. 21, the Bureau of Forestry devoted most of its energies to government work, even before the transfer of the forest reserves to the Department of Agriculture. In 1903 Pinchot noted that "a very large proportion" of the bureau's activity involved federal lands. But the agency could neglect the needs of private holders only at the risk of "seriously endangering the object of its existence." Pinchot then outlined what was to become a central theme for increased federal assistance. In meeting private requests for aid, he observed, "it is the public rather than any private interest which is at stake."[40] This refrain anticipated industry arguments before congressional committees in the 1920s, the appeals for increased aid to lumbermen in the 1930s, and especially the testimony calling for the expansion of federal forestry programs after the Second World War. Pinchot was a thoroughgoing modernist in recognizing the principal argument for government-industry cooperation.

The government intended Circular No. 21 assistance as a temporary arrangement to prepare the way for the private forester. J. Girvin Peters told the Society of American Foresters that the federal bureau did not intend to compete with private forestry. But because the bureau had to create a "working field," it sought cooperation with private owners and "offered very generous terms." At first the government carried three-fourths of the costs, but this share diminished as the demand for assistance increased. By 1904, Peters pointed out, owners were paying for all "the expense of the cooperation" except the salaries of bureau officials and office work. The government, he said, was making an effort to transfer every expense to the timberland owner.[41]

But for "the holders of small parcels of land," Peters outlined a different approach. Because hiring a private forester was not practical for this class of owner, the Bureau of Forestry would continue to offer free preliminary examinations. Government aid to small holders, he concluded, "will always be a cardinal feature of the Bureau's cooperative work."[42] The federal agency continued direct assistance to individual landowners for several years but disbanded the practice when federal legislation opened the way for greater aid through the individual states. But the most important reason for the cutback in direct cooperation with private holders was the Forest Service responsibility for managing the national forests after 1905.

Because of the broadened scope of the cooperative programs, the Pinchot administration continually struggled with policy memoranda outlining cooperative agreements. The Service Committee, a policy-making group organized in 1903 and comprised of the head forester and the division heads, debated and then drafted the administrative directives for the cooperative programs.[43] The committee's deliberations were sometimes lengthy, and the record reveals considerable disagreement about the appropriate federal role. The committee's responsibilities were broad. It negotiated cooperation between forestry and other divisions and bureaus within the Department of Agriculture. The committee tendered a request from the Division of Agrostology for cooperation in the reclamation of sand dunes. In this instance (April 25, 1903), Pinchot advised accepting the offer "for diplomatic reasons." Such a move, he said, would leave the bureau "more at liberty to carry on its work along this line."[44]

One of the more important cooperative relationships during the early Pinchot years was the bureau's working association with the Department of the Interior. Because Interior had jurisdiction over the federal forests, and because the foresters were in the Department of Agriculture, the two departments drafted agreements for the management of the forest reserves. For Pinchot's staff, the work load was heavy. Pinchot repeatedly mentioned the Interior Department's demands upon his staff for the preparation of "working plans" similar to those drafted for private owners.[45] When President Theodore Roosevelt signed the transfer act into law, the management of the federal forests became a major housekeeping responsibility rather than a negotiated commitment of technical expertise.

The federal agency also continued some of the cooperative agreements initiated under Fernow.[46] Pinchot provided small sums of money for "collaborators" — persons "of established reputation in forestry" but not associated with the division — "who have knowledge of special value to it." Dispersed across the country, these "collaborators" wrote authoritative pieces "at a very moderate cost." This form of cooperation, Pinchot related in his autobiography, was an effort to gain the expertise of people with training in the sciences.[47]

Although Pinchot's policies differed from those of his predecessor, he continued the practice of making cooperative agreements in tree planting. He replaced Fernow's practice of cooperating with state agricultural experiment stations by providing advice to tree planters similar to that offered under Circular No. 21. The cooperative tree-planting program, outlined in Circular No. 22, had its greatest impact in the Plains states. The planting program again distinguished between large and small tracts. Federal foresters provided owners of fewer than five acres with free advice and assistance, but the program did not include the expenses of planting and caring for the trees. On larger acreages the preliminary inspection was free, but landowners were responsible for all subsequent expenses.[48]

15

Under Fernow's administration, the division's planting program had serious problems. When newspapers announced that the government was giving away trees, people applied for seedlings with little knowledge about proper planting techniques. To make matters worse, the government made contracts with private growers who often palmed off their unsalable inventories to the applicants. On one occasion a private supplier provided an applicant with wild stock pulled from the ground with the bare roots exposed.[49] For these reasons the division discontinued its free distribution of seed stock and adopted the policy described in Circular No. 22.

But problems persisted. A Bureau of Forestry investigation in the summer of 1903 revealed that applicants had planted only 50 percent of the acreages agreed to. When the bureau revised and tightened the requirements, the move created even greater difficulties. George L. Clothier, a bureau assistant involved with cooperative tree planting, thought the 1903 revision bristled with "threats of charges to the landowner." The new policy, he claimed, "was made in the spirit of hostility to the landowner," as though the bureau was prepared "not to be again 'taken in' by imposters." Clothier warned that it would frighten away farmers "who never rode in sleeping cars." Despite the clearly stated offer that the Department of Agriculture still provided free preliminary examinations, the number who applied for farm planting declined. Clothier thought he knew why; it was the abuses of private nurserymen who sold farmers deficient stock. The Forest Service subsequently issued another revision of Circular No. 22 with an "entirely new outline" for planting cooperation.[50]

By 1906 the Forest Service had extended its planting assistance to large landholders whose motives, according to Pinchot, were "purely economic." At the same time the Forest Service increased its work with the Bureau of Reclamation; most of these projects involved planting along government-financed canals in the arid West. But when Congress transferred the forest reserves to its jurisdiction, the service lost interest in tree planting. The Office of Dry Land Agriculture continued experimental planting in the Plains states with some success for the next few decades, but the Forest Service did not take up cooperative planting again until the expanded authorization under the Clarke-McNary Act of 1924.[51]

During the Pinchot years federal foresters also conducted field work with the U.S. Geological Survey (USGS), especially to gather information for the proposed Appalachian forest reserve. Pressure to establish an eastern reserve gathered momentum in 1900, when Congress authorized the forestry office and the USGS to conduct a joint study of the southern Appalachians. The exhaustive report, completed in 1901, formed the basis for the eventual establishment of national forests in the region. The annual reports also mention cooperative work with the Department of War, assessing timber sales on military reservations, and drafting working plans for the improvement of timber stands.[52]

The federal government also expanded forestry research in the first decade of the new century. The Pinchot staff conducted field investigations of commercially valuable trees to determine their distribution and reproduction characteristics, and in 1903 Pinchot established the Section of Silvics "to contribute to ordered and scientific knowledge of our forests." At the same time the bureau cooperated with the Bureau of Entomology to study "remedies" for combating insect damage.[53]

Although these investigations were important, there was no plan for coordinating the research findings until Raphael Zon, a Russian immigrant and graduate of Cornell, suggested the establishment of experiment stations. Zon, who visited Germany, Austria, and France in the winter of 1908, recommended separate branches for research and administrative work. The Forest Service implemented this strategy in 1915, when it created the Branch of Research. As head of the Section of Silvics, Zon was chiefly responsible for setting up the first forest experiment station on the Coconino National Forest in Arizona in 1908; and with McGarvey Cline, he established the Forest Products Laboratory at Madison, Wisconsin, in 1910.[54]

The function of research, according to Zon, was practical—to "supply technical facts." Forestry research should solve "immediate practical problems" encountered in daily industrial activity. Through the influence of Zon and others, Forest Service research developed as an integral part of federal cooperation with the producers and users of forest products. The investigations embraced a wide array of activities—studies of lumber industry economics, market inquiries, and the compilation of statistics on lumber prices (the agency began the latter practice in 1908 with the cooperation of wholesale lumbermen).[55]

By the time William Howard Taft dismissed Pinchot in January, 1910, the Forest Service had established the general outlines of a cooperative policy. Fernow's programs and the vastly expanded activities of the Pinchot administration both emphasized the importance of private forests to the national welfare. And both men directed their appeals to the acquisitive side of timberland ownership. Pinchot's Circular No. 21 advised owners to "understand that it pays better . . . to protect a forest, in harvesting a timber crop, than to destroy it."[56] Thus, the government packaged its cooperative program in the form of federal advisory assistance to assure future timber supplies.

Although the Forest Service curtailed its forest management and tree-planting assistance after the transfer of the forest reserves to the Department of Agriculture, the agency became involved in several other cooperative commitments with federal bureaus and departments, colleges and universities, and, more important, with a growing number of state agencies. But Pinchot recognized a continued responsibility to the private sector when he organized the Division of State and Private Forestry in 1908. The new division immediately undertook a study of forest taxation in cooperation with individual states. Federal forestry officials also had to work out procedures for cooperating with the Reclamation Service, the USGS, the General Land Office, and the Indian Office.[57]

Summary

The early cooperative programs established a precedent for federal forestry. They offered federal outreach assistance to landowners, processors, and consumers of forest products and gave public visibility to Forest Service officers. The government's cooperative assistance programs also opened up employment opportunities for an increasing number of graduate foresters. As a profession with close ties to the lumber industry, forestry came of age in the first decade of the twentieth century. The groundwork for this advance, however, lay in the last thirty years of the nineteenth century when an astonishing growth in public consciousness about the importance of the forest resources took place.

But the activities of scientists and federal foresters explain only part of the development of cooperative forestry assistance. As with virtually all federal resource programs, industrial conditions determined policy. In this case, lumber industry spokesmen and their allies in the Forest Service defined and molded federal programs to meet the requirements for a modern lumber economy. That many of these individuals moved easily from public to private employment underscores the congeniality and common purpose that characterized many of the federal assistance programs.

The Lumber Industry and
the Federal Government

Chapter Two

Paul Bunyan notwithstanding, the woods products industry has played an important part in the growth of the American economy. Indians had skillfully used forest resources for a variety of purposes, but their impress upon the environment was light. When Europeans came to North America, however, they began to exploit the forest warehouse to provide energy for cooking and heating and material for the construction of houses, ships, and a multitude of other structures. Forest products were also important to an expanding international trade that included naval stores, ship masts, and related wood-based products.

There was good reason for looking to the forests to satisfy both subsistence and commercial needs. First, the awesome timber stands in eastern North America were the most conspicuous feature of the landscape. And the record shows that colonials viewed the endless woodlands as an impediment to cultivated agriculture and to the building of transportation arterials. In this view and others, forested land symbolized savagery — the antithesis of civilization. Clearing the forests, therefore, meant progress and obedience to the biblical command to subdue the earth. [1]

The great variety of forest resources and their broad distribution across North America were important to westward expansion and to commercial and industrial development. Hence the lumber industry from the eighteenth century to at least the 1950s witnessed a steady move through successive logging frontiers. By the time the westward-moving white population pressed upon the Great Plains in the mid-nineteenth century, the best and most accessible of the northeastern forests had been logged. The industry moved on—first to the Great Lakes area in the 1840s and 1850s, then to the great southern pine forests after the Civil War, and finally to the dense forested slopes of the Douglas-fir region in the early twentieth century.

The lumber trade came of age between 1890 and 1910. During this period the industry reached its peak in the production of sawed lumber, engaged in a frenzy of speculation in southern and western timberlands, and adjusted to the federal government's policy of establishing permanent forest reservations in the West. The lumber business also was part of the expanding industrial capitalism of the period; it experienced mercurial price fluctuations, cutthroat competition, and periodic overproduction. The consequences of these unstable market conditions were extravagant waste, devastated forest environments, and disrupted communities—symbols common to other resource-based industries in the United States.

Bernhard Fernow, whose grasp of forestry conditions surpassed that of most of his contemporaries, summarized the reasons behind the industry's expansive and itinerant nature: "It would be difficult to set a date or mark an event from which the change in the methods of the lumber industry, which is now such a stupendous factor in forest decimation, might be reckoned. It came as gradually or as fast as the railway systems expanded and made accessible the vast fields of supply in the Northwest, while the supplies of the East were being exhausted."[2] But these practices characterized most industrial activity in the late nineteenth century. In the case of the lumber industry, easy access to capital and the continued opening of cheap sources of virgin timber well into the twentieth century brought new mills into production, encouraged waste, and acted as a deterrent to forest conservation. These conditions helped shape industrial practice and private and public policy and gave birth to the ideas and programs associated with resource conservation.

At this point material conditions in the lumber industry made forest conservation uneconomic and exploitation a necessity. During these years the Forest Service played a central role in explaining these conditions and in supporting legislation and policies favorable to industry. At the same time there was a growing public sentiment against the abuses of monopoly capitalism and a conviction in some quarters that the Forest Service was serving as a handmaiden to industry.

As one strategy to meet uncertain business and industrial conditions, lumbermen organized trade associations, a voluntary and cooperative attempt to resolve the industry's economic problems. Beginning in the 1880s and then with greater momentum in the 1890s, modernists in the industry formed collective trade agreements to lessen the strains of competition and to achieve a more stable economic environment. By the 1890s regional associations were beginning to appear, and they were gaining increasing credibility.[3]

Lumbermen with huge capital investments in timberland and mill equipment — businesses that were particularly vulnerable to fluctuating markets because of their large fixed investments and heavy bonded indebtedness — led the move to form trade associations. These early collective trade groups attempted to control production through "curtailment programs"; but as the associations became more cohesive, their activities included other issues important to lumbermen.[4] The overriding purpose, however, was a commitment to industrial cooperation as an antidote to overly competitive business conduct.

By the turn of the century the completion of several transcontinental rail links had contributed to an increasingly integrated lumber economy. Producers from the South and Far West now vied with each other for eastern and midwestern markets, developments that convinced progressive-minded lumbermen to move from regional trade groups to nationwide organizations like the National Lumber Manufacturers Association (NLMA) organized in December, 1902.[5]

During its first years of existence, the NLMA handled railroad issues, compiled and distributed statistical information, investigated insurance and credit programs, promoted the adoption of uniform grades and sizes of lumber, and argued for more equitable taxes on timberland. But most of its attention centered on what the NLMA believed was the excessively competitive nature of the lumber economy. A period of rapid industrial expansion had contributed to an increase in lumber prices (because of a greater demand) and to frantic speculation in western forests.

The availability of cheap timberland and in many instances the abuse of federal land laws fueled the speculation. The annual production of lumber in the United States reached an all-time high in 1906 and 1907, then conditions worsened. The tremendous capacity of the mills and the increasing availability of substitute building materials combined to glut the lumber market. While the federal government launched an investigation of the industry for suspected antitrust activity, stumpage and lumber prices plummeted downward and the trade entered a prolonged depression.[6] Such boom-and-bust cycles characterize the industry to this day.

Convergence of Interests

Lumber groups sought to bring order to their world in other ways, some of them consistent with federal forestry objectives. Eastern lumbermen, for instance, supported the establishment of eastern forest reserves—assuring future timber supplies meant survival for many of them. The National Wholesale Lumber Dealers Association sent a resolution to Congress in 1903 supporting the creation of an Appalachian forest reserve "for economic reasons"; it would assure a perpetual supply of timber. The American Forest Congress of 1905, where the influence of important lumbermen was apparent on every hand, also passed a resolution in support of eastern reserves. And the NLMA backed a move to expand the entire reserve system.[7] Despite the introduction of bills in virtually every session of Congress after 1900, the eastern reserve idea waited until passage of the Weeks Act in 1911 to gain legislative authorization.

The NLMA also established a good working relationship with the Bureau of Forestry and Gifford Pinchot. The trade group established a committee on forestry that pledged cooperation with the bureau and urged its membership to support the passage of state laws to promote forestry. In 1905 Pinchot went before the directors of the NLMA to seek support for bureau programs and to solicit financial backing for an endowed chair of "applied forestry and practical lumbering" at Yale University. With Frederick E. Weyerhaeuser leading the way, the NLMA made a sizable endowment to the university.[8]

The sense of reciprocity and good will extended throughout the ranks of federal foresters. When Henry Graves left the Pinchot staff in 1901 to accept appointment as the dean of the forestry school at Yale, a lumber trade journal praised Graves for relating "forest theories" to "practical commercial ideas." Two years later Pinchot told the

23

National Wholesale Lumber Dealers Association that forestry was a business and had no practical application if it did not pay. After the establishment of the Section of Lumber Trade in 1906, Pinchot reported that lumbermen were much interested in the statistical work of the Forest Service. The published statistics included data on forest ownership, fires, taxes, production and consumption patterns, and other matters of interest to the industry.[9]

The confidence and good will between the NLMA and the Forest Service increased as cooperative programs expanded under the Weeks and Clarke-McNary legislation. Forest Service personnel appeared at association meetings to share and discuss issues of importance. The beginnings of this atmosphere of trust and common interest dates to the founding of the American Forestry Association (AFA) and the Division of Forestry in the mid-1870s and gained momentum when Fernow was chief. But it achieved its greatest boost during the administration of Pinchot.

Lumber trade journals, some of them dating to the late nineteenth century, provide one of the most accurate barometers of industry opinion. The trade press editorialized about the policies of the federal government and published comprehensive reports of association meetings and congressional hearings. The journals supported the general thrust of federal forestry policy — its research and cooperative work, the creation of additional forest reserves, the advancement of the Division of Forestry to bureau status, and a host of other issues important to federal foresters.[10]

Both the lumber journals and the trade associations provided significant support for the forest reserve policy. The *Timberman,* published in Portland, Oregon, praised the forestry division in 1900 for its studies of the reserves in Oregon and Washington. And following President Theodore Roosevelt's additions to the national forests in 1907, the paper applauded the president's action and said the "future will demonstrate the wisdom of the reserve policy." The Chicago-based *American Lumberman* lauded the president's move and added, "The people at large will stand back of the President in this matter."[11]

Industrial Influence and Conservation Policy

Despite the popular belief that the John Muirs, the Sierra Clubs, and the Izaak Walton Leagues determined the character of the conservation movement in the early twentieth century, recent scholarship clearly shows that economic and political issues defined conservation arguments and policies. [12] Because it was more closely associated with the conservation movement than with other enterprises, [13] the lumber industry provides the classic example of industrial influence in shaping conservation policy. As early as the 1890s, lumber spokesmen defined conservation in terms of the industry's economic problems — forest fires, timberland taxes, duties on forest products imports, railroad rates, reforestation, varying sizes and grades of lumber, and the inefficient utilization of wood.

Fernow was the first federal forestry official to recognize the relationship between economic conditions in the lumber industry and forestry conservation. Forest owners, he reported in 1892, failed to practice forest conservation because it did not pay. The costs of management showed that the profitable exploitation of timber and conservation "are at present more or less incompatible." [14] J. E. Defebaugh, the veteran editor of the *American Lumberman,* expressed a similar view in an address to the AFA in 1893. Timber owners had no interest in forest preservation, he stated, because these issues were economic; therefore, the pecuniary needs of the private operators would determine the course of practical policy. The heavy burden of timberland ownership, transportation, and milling costs, Defebaugh claimed, had forced lumbermen to liquidate their forest holdings as rapidly as possible: "It is evident that little can be expected from the lumberman or timberowner who depends upon that business for his livelihood in the direction of conserving the forests, simply because it does not pay him." [15]

Pinchot also understood the relation between forest conservation and the economic health of the lumber industry. On one occasion he told an audience of lumbermen that it would be fruitless to discuss forestry unless it was profitable: "We must show first that forestry will pay." Royal S. Kellogg, one of Pinchot's subordinates, made the same case in an address to the Southern Lumber Manufacturers Association in 1906. Lumbermen would continue "in the same old wasteful, extravagant way" until the bulk of the virgin timber was gone, he thought, and then they would turn to "the now commonly despised 'second growth' as their source of supply." The forests "will not be handled rationally until they become valuable." [16]

25

Two years later the *American Lumberman* declared that forestry would come to the woods when it became profitable practice. And in 1910 the *Timberman* noted the relation between forestry and the control of production. The journal added that lumber interests were gaining "a saner and more just appreciation of the real viewpoint of the conservation movement." Conservation meant that the "market will not be glutted and gorged with a tremendous output."[17]

Lumbermen also argued that burdensome taxes were an impediment to forest conservation. Although Fernow had raised the question earlier, timberland taxation did not become an important public issue until the Pinchot years, when some lumber spokesmen began to blame inequitable tax systems for causing the rapid liquidation of the forests. Finally, when Pinchot established the Division of State and Private Forestry, he directed the division to offer assistance to states in studying timberland tax policies.[18] The issue gained even more attention when the industry plunged into a prolonged depression after 1907.

The clamor for tax reform was heard at all levels. At its first meeting in 1909, the Western Forestry and Conservation Association (WFCA) proposed a program to convince the public that high timberland taxes "stimulate the removal of timber and consequently decrease the taxable valuation of the counties." The NLMA joined the fray in 1910 when its president, Edward Hines, told the annual meeting that timberland taxes must be "considered with the national conservation movement." Everett G. Griggs, the association's president in 1912, warned that properly adjusted tax laws were a prerequisite to reforestation.[19]

In a penetrating essay, "Forestry on Private Lands," published a few months before his dismissal from office, Pinchot argued that excessive taxation was the principal deterrent to forest conservation. The fear of burdensome taxes caused timber owners to liquidate their stands irrespective of market conditions.[20] During the next eighteen years his first two successors, Henry Graves and William Greeley, also emphasized that enlightened tax policy was a prerequisite to reforestation.

The industry's perception that taxation and conservation were interrelated was not lost on federal officials. The Forest Service cooperated in several state tax studies to determine the extent to which excessive taxes led to the premature cutting of timber. For its part, the industry's effort to reform tax laws placed lumbermen in conflict with state tax reformers. That discord persists to the present day.

While he was chief forester, Pinchot supported a variety of conservation-related programs, most of them directed at issues of vital economic concern to the lumber industry. And lumbermen, in turn, linked many of the legislative bills at the state and federal level to their financial needs and to the question of forest conservation. Government cooperation in seeking tax policies more favorable to the lumber trade was only one palliative to alleviate economic distress.

The Forest Service and the Tariff

The Forest Service contributed to the public discussion of another matter vital to the lumber industry—the tariff. After more than 100 years of protection, Congress began to equivocate in the early twentieth century on the tariff issue. During the first decade of the century, groups who wanted to promote conservative use of forest resources and lumbermen with cutting privileges to Canadian timber made an effort to remove the duty on lumber.[21] Although majority sentiment wanted to maintain the tariff, the debates of 1908 and 1909 indicated that the wood products industry was not of one mind.

Regional trade associations, especially those in the West, argued that the introduction of cheap Canadian lumber to an already glutted market would depress prices even further and perpetuate wasteful practices. By contrast, a duty on lumber imports would lead to the more efficient use of logs. The *American Lumberman* argued that forest conservation would begin when it ensured a profit to the investor.[22]

Trade leaders emphasized the relation between a lumber duty and forest conservation during the winter of 1908–1909. The WFCA, in a resolution to Congress, feared that removing the tariff would hamper efforts at reforestation. And most trade journals cheered when Pinchot testified in favor of the lumber tariff before the House Ways and Means Committee. The industry achieved a partial victory when Congress voted to retain the lumber duty.[23]

The Roosevelt-Pinchot years marked the peak of the Progressive conservation movement. Muckrake writers like Lincoln Steffens and Ida Tarbell investigated urban corruption, business monopoly, and a host of related evils and wrote exposés to rouse the public to action. Progressive tax reformers agitated in Wisconsin and in other states where crusaders like Robert La Follette rose to smite entrenched politicians from power. And at the federal level a few journalists and politicians (not all of them progressive reformers) accused the Forest Service and the lumber industry of acting in conspiratorial fashion to thwart the interests of the public.

An unprecedented rise in lumber prices finally prompted Congress in 1906 to order the Department of Commerce and Labor to investigate the lumber industry. Lumber trade associations that had openly promoted agreements to maintain uniform prices and to limit production ended these activities as the "lumber trust" rumors mounted and the government increased its efforts to curb illegal trade practices. The federal antitrust investigations, which coincided with the onset of the depression in the lumber industry, angered trade leaders who were attempting to cope with the vagaries of a mercurial market.[24]

Antitrust crusaders and free-market opponents of the federal land system made the Forest Service an object of attack. Politicians assailed the agency before the annual appropriations hearings in Congress. While the responsibilities of managing the national forests is one reason for the decrease in cooperative work with private individuals, it should be recognized that these were difficult times for the Forest Service. Congressional attacks challenged the agency's image of selflessness and public service and made its yearly budget battles sometimes torturous affairs.

Idaho's Senator Weldon E. Heyburn, a strident critic of the reserve system, opened the attack against the Forest Service in March, 1907. By promoting the "vicious system of forest reserves," he thundered, the Forest Service was acting in collusion with the major lumber interests; timberland owners who already held large acreages wanted the remaining federal timber withdrawn from the market to eliminate additional competition. The AFA, the Weyerhaeuser combine, and the Forest Service, Heyburn charged, were cooperating with each other to the detriment of "common people."[25] There is obvious bluster here, but the Idaho senator's remark alarmed Pinchot, who feared that the entire edifice of the national forest system might be disassembled.

The on-going Bureau of Corporations investigation of the lumber industry continued to fuel congressional debates over Forest Service appropriations, and muckrakers like Charles Edward Russell made public charges of collusion between lumbermen and government agencies. And Senator Heyburn, in an attack on the 1911 appropriations for the service, likened the agency's employees to common thieves who could gather seeds for their nurseries only by "robbing the squirrels' nests." But Washington congressman William E. Humphrey made one of the strongest denunciations against the Forest Service which, he said, encouraged monopoly and worked in collusion with major lumbermen and the AFA to promote conservation in the name of the people.[26]

There was more to these attacks on the Forest Service than the ruffled feathers of a few cantankerous westerners or the lively barbs of progressives reveal. When Pinchot was fired in 1910, both the federal agency and its dismissed chief stood at the center of public attention. Although the Pinchot-Ballinger controversy is beyond the scope of this study, it provided worrisome problems for an agency already accused, on the one hand, of being too aggressive in its pursuit of forest conservation and, on the other, of working in collusion with the lumber industry.

The Forest Service was not without effective means to counter these charges; the agency used great skill in molding public opinion, and it put forth cooperative work as its favorite stalking horse. Pinchot's administration used press releases and printed materials to establish a favorable climate with newspapers. Indeed, Pinchot's frequent use of newspapers to publish "educational work" on conservation matters rankled Congress to the point that it explicitly prohibited the use of federal appropriations for the preparation of newspaper or magazine articles. However, both of Pinchot's biographers note that congressional admonitions did little to hinder the work of "popular education" in forest conservation.[27] The chief forester also urged his staff to write letters to senators and representatives telling them about Forest

Service accomplishments. And when he appeared before congressional committees, Pinchot required his subordinates to furnish him with "important facts which should be brought to the attention of the Committee." Forest Service programs probably would have accomplished little without these extended efforts to publicize its activities.[28]

Forest Service officials also appeared regularly before meetings of the NLMA and its regional affiliates to promote government-industry cooperation. Early in his administration, Pinchot asked lumbermen to eliminate "the differences in points of view between lumbermen and foresters." His successor, Henry Graves, immediately proposed to make Forest Service cooperation "as extensive and efficient as our organization will permit," and a subordinate and future head of the service, Earle Clapp, told a lumbermen's gathering the Pacific Northwest that their "spirit of cooperation" would be difficult to improve upon.[29]

For their part, trade leaders provided the Forest Service with valuable support in the agency's annual struggle to obtain congressional appropriations for its work. E. T. Allen, the principal executive officer of the WFCA and a man with a growing reputation in industry circles, believed that the inability of the service to gain long-term commitments from Congress prevented it from establishing a consistent and clear-cut policy. Every session of Congress, Allen remarked, repeated the same debates without "any real knowledge of forest economies." Most frequently, however, lumber trade officials protested reduced appropriations for Forest Service cooperation in fire protection activities.[30]

This atmosphere of mutual cooperation persisted through the second and third decades of the twentieth century. Chief Foresters Graves (1910–1920) and Greeley (1920–1928) expanded on the working relationships established under Pinchot and insisted, as their predecessor had, that government-industry cooperation was in the public interest. A healthy lumber industry required mutual trust between the government and the private sector and, in turn, would redound to the general welfare. Lumber trade and Forest Service spokesmen both emphasized this theme, and it provides a thread linking the early years of the twentieth century with the present day.

Cooperation and the Lumber Economy

Organized lumbermen struggled to cope with the demoralized conditions that spread throughout the trade after 1907. This economic turbulence convinced modernists of the need for trade association cooperation with government agencies. In the South and the Pacific Northwest, where overproduction was rampant, trade leaders tried to adjust legislative and regulatory policy to lessen the strains of what they called excessive competition. One trade journal editor pleaded for closer coordination between producing regions: "In a commercial sense we are undergoing a revolution in thought in regard to the method of doing business. It is the battle of cooperation against competition and cooperation must prevail. Competition carried beyond a reasonable point is industrial death." Allen added his voice to this charge — the public should seek the repeal of the Sherman Antitrust Act to permit sensible cooperation. [31]

A series of Federal Trade Commission (FTC) hearings in 1915 and 1916 show that lumber industry sentiment for repealing the Sherman Act was widespread. John Henry Kirby, an important southern lumberman, told the FTC officials that antitrust statutes hindered industrial mergers and thereby prolonged depressed conditions in the lumber market. A northwestern investor told the hearing officials that lumbermen should be allowed to limit production and recommended that the government compel cooperation to "force the consolidation of now small, independent producers" into bigger, more efficient organizations. [32]

While the FTC conducted hearings on the lumber industry, the Forest Service, at the urging of Greeley, was in the midst of its own "constructive" investigation of the lumberman's problems. Published in 1917 and largely the work of Greeley, the Forest Service study focused attention on the lumber trade and "particularly how forest conservation is affected by economic conditions." The greatest cause of instability in the lumber business was the heavy burden of timberland investment, which made it difficult for owners to adjust production to the requirements of the market. "Competition," the report exclaimed, "is not only keen but often destructive."[33]

The source of the difficulty, the Greeley study pointed out, was historical. Beginning in the 1890s and continuing into the first years of the twentieth century, the acquisition of timber went beyond the requirements for practical use. Timber purchases were made with borrowed capital, and then the owners bonded the timber to finance mill construction. According to Greeley, the problem was not limited to one region, because the southern pine manufacturers were not "far behind their western competitors in the capitalization of their industry with borrowed funds." The root problem, therefore, was the timberland owner's need to liquidate his stands to meet "carrying charges" in taxes, interest on bonds, and the costs of fire protection.[34]

Greeley's sympathetic appraisal of those who had to borrow against their land to acquire the capital to build mills obscures the fact that some purchasers, like Weyerhaeuser, bought vast acreages of timberland in the Pacific Northwest at very low prices. Although these were speculative purchases, they were designed for long-term gain, and for the larger capitalists they proved to be sound investments. But Greeley had made his mark with the industry, and he remained a favored and respected friend for the rest of his life.

The 1917 Forest Service report was the most significant assessment of the national lumber economy until the publication of the Copeland report in 1933. The study assessed the peculiar economic conditions associated with the lumber business, and because it had wide appeal to lumbermen, the report was frequently cited when industry leaders went before Congress to seek relief. Its principal author — Greeley — was the commanding figure in federal forestry policy during the 1920s, and he continued to wield great influence as a trade association executive and conservation spokesman for the next fifty years. Greeley, more than any other Forest Service official, articulated the agency's philosophy of cooperation in the twentieth century, and he said it all in the 1917 study.

The achievement of an adequate national forest policy, Greeley pointed out, "rests mainly upon cooperation between the public and the lumberman." Public programs, therefore, should strive to make timberland ownership more stable and assist lumbermen in achieving more efficient business operations. But the greatest need, Greeley said, was for the industry and the public to approach the problem "in a cooperative spirit rather than a divided or antagonistic one."[35]

Under Greeley's influence, the direction of Forest Service cooperative policy was no longer a unilateral venture; the legislative and regulatory programs that followed invariably originated through the collaborative effort of industrial leaders and federal forestry officials. When the service attempted to act alone and develop policy without the approval of the forest products industry, such programs usually died in legislative subcommittees. At times, Greeley's figure looms larger than that of Pinchot in shaping Forest Service policy, and certainly his philosophy of cooperation and voluntary action has dominated state and private programs.

Summary

With the publication of the Forest Service study in 1917, the lumber industry had come of age. By the turn of the century, its migratory propensity had taken it to the Pacific edge of the continent where the opening of vast stands of virgin timber created conditions of endemic overproduction. As lumbermen became aware of these conditions, they sought to rectify their unstable business and industrial environment through a variety of organizational, legislative, and regulatory approaches. They achieved some limited legislative successes in tax and tariff policy and in the Weeks Act of 1911, but not until Greeley provided them with a broad historical synthesis, did lumbermen have before them a comprehensive analysis that offered a way out of their difficulties.

Although the broadening of assistance programs under the Weeks and the Clarke-McNary acts marks the maturing of the cooperative relationship, Forest Service and industrial leaders had established the basic working philosophy even before Congress gave it legislative legitimacy. But there is much more to this story, namely, the activities that took place at the state and regional level in the thirty or forty years prior to the passage of the Weeks legislation. These developments are a necessary supplement to understanding the emergence of federal forestry cooperation.

Chapter Three

Although legislatures had expressed concern for the forest environment as early as the colonial era, there were no practical and enforceable state laws regulating forest use until long after the Civil War. And then the same issues that stimulated forestry consciousness at the national level — the ravages of fire, the waste and destruction of timber, eroded mountainsides, and silt-clogged rivers — convinced a few states to establish boards of inquiry and forestry commissions and associations and finally to appoint formal bureaus and departments of forestry. Once again, the pioneering work of individuals like George Perkins Marsh and Franklin B. Hough influenced the organization of the first state chapters of the American Forestry Congress and the American Forestry Association (AFA).

An awareness on the part of industrialists that forests affected streamflow, a leisured class interest in forests for their aesthetic qualities, and the traditional concern for future timber supplies spurred the formation of forestry organizations in eastern states like New York and Pennsylvania. In the Pacific Northwest, where different settlement patterns prevailed and where industrial development was still at an early stage, the first forestry associations focused largely on protecting valuable timber from fire. Material conditions, therefore, were powerful factors explaining the establishment of relatively progressive forestry agencies in some states and their absence in others.

Writers who trace the "real beginning" of American forestry to the states[1] ignore the fact that the movement's origins at this level were sporadic at best. Rather, the accomplishments of a few "progressive" states paralleled that of the federal government and the names of some of the prominent leaders appear in both ledgers.[2] There was, however, a gentle stirring of forestry interest throughout the land that undoubtedly created an atmosphere favorable to the establishment of state forestry agencies.

The First State Forestry Agencies

During the 1860s and 1870s a few states established temporary commissions to inquire into the destructive effects of forest exploitation. Although few of these early investigations led directly to the formation of state forestry agencies, the commissions inquired into the relationship between forests and streamflow and spurred a few states to pass tax exemption laws to encourage timber planting. After extensive investigations in the 1870s and early 1880s, the New York legislature established the first state forest, the Adirondack and Catskill preserve, in 1885.[3]

The formation of state affiliates of the AFA paralleled the appointment of the forestry inquiry commissions. Minnesota was the first to establish a state association in 1876 and several others followed suit in the 1880s; the Pennsylvania Forestry Association, the most active of the early organizations, succeeded in committing that state to one of the most progressive forest policies in the country. And when Congress gave permanent statutory rank to the Division of Forestry in 1886, the nation's forestlands gained official recognition as important factors in the national economy. At the same time several states (California, Colorado, New York, and Ohio) passed legislation creating forestry agencies; except for the New York venture, however, the other organizations did not last.[4]

In New York Charles Sprague Sargent headed a fact-finding commission that issued a report emphasizing the need to protect and preserve state lands; in quick order, Bernhard Fernow modified several legislative bills into one measure that was signed into law in 1885. The New York law provided for the establishment and management of the Adirondack and Catskill preserve, recommended that state educators promote forestry in the public schools and colleges, and directed the state's new agency to distribute circulars offering advice on the proper care of forestland.[5]

The California attempt to establish a state forest policy was short-lived. The 1885 measure authorized the governor to appoint a forestry board to investigate activities common to most of the early state agencies—to collect and distribute statistics on forestry and to make inquiries about the protection of watersheds. The board inventoried California's forest resources as one of its first tasks; acquired a staff of competent specialists; conducted experimental plantings in newly established nurseries; and busied itself with frequent appearances at horticultural society meetings.[6] But personality differences between board member Abbot Kinney and the governor's office prompted legislators to repeal the law establishing the California Board of Forestry. A penny-conscious governor and, according to Fernow, a "perversion of the moneys appropriated" were the key reasons for its dissolution.[7] The state legislature did not act again until 1905, following a series of disastrous fires.

Although Colorado and Ohio were among the first states to organize forestry agencies, their experiences, too, were brief. Colorado, the first state to provide for the protection of forests in its constitution, failed to establish an effective forestry program, and its Office of Forest Commissioner was left vacant when the federal government began to set aside forest reserves in the state. The embryonic forestry movement in Ohio, the brainchild of John A. Warder and the Ohio Forestry Association, succeeded in getting the legislature to establish a three-member state forestry bureau in 1885. But, as in California, the Ohio effort suffered from dissension and lack of commitment and came to an end in 1900.[8]

These early forestry commissions and state agencies asked the federal Division of Forestry for assistance in conducting surveys of forest resources. In return for the federal government's advice and expertise, the states provided the division with information on the distribution and density of standing timber, the effects of denuded hillsides on streamflow, and other data of great value. Fernow recognized these findings in his voluminous *Report upon the Forestry Investigations,* published in 1899. For their part, the state agencies sought the division's assistance in drafting legislation to protect forest property against fire.[9]

State Forestry Agencies and Centers of Lumber Production

The development of forestry commissions and bureaus at the state level coincided with a tremendous boom in lumber production in the Great Lakes states and the South and in the opening of the immense Douglas-fir stands along the North Pacific slope. Although the Great Lakes states led the nation in total lumber production in 1890, the social costs were also readily apparent—debris-filled streams, eroding hillsides, and annual fires that raced across cutover areas and virgin timber stands. Perceptive observers noted that fire and the woodsman's ax were rapidly diminishing the once seemingly inexhaustible forests.

Both Michigan and Wisconsin appointed special commissions in 1867 to report on the effects of forest destruction. Although these commissions came away empty-handed, another Michigan commission in 1887 recommended the establishment of a state forestry agency, a measure the legislature finally adopted in 1899. The Wisconsin legislature ordered another inquiry that eventually led to the creation of a forestry agency in 1903.[10] But the most progressive forestry development in the Great Lakes states took place in Minnesota.

Christopher C. Andrews, who became interested in forestry during a stint as U.S. minister to Sweden and Norway, had a great influence on the development of forestry in Minnesota. In 1880, in conjunction with the St. Paul Chamber of Commerce, Andrews petitioned Congress to grant land to the state to establish a school of forestry. He continued to write and speak about forestry matters until his adopted state finally passed a modified version of the New York statue in 1895.[11]

The Minnesota law authorized the state auditor (acting as forest commissioner) to appoint a chief fire warden with the authority to prevent and suppress "forest and prairie fires." Under the provisions of the law, the chief fire warden appointed village, town, and city officials as local wardens, the state to compensate them for their services. The great Hinckley forest fire in 1894, which took 418 lives, undoubtedly spurred the legislature to act and was responsible for the heavy emphasis on fire prevention and suppression.[12] The law also called for a survey of the state's forests and a study of the methods used to promote the regrowth of timber. In 1897 the state legislature appropriated $3,000 to the Minnesota Forestry Association (the oldest of all the state organizations) to encourage tree planting on the prairies and for watershed protection. At the same time the legislature created a nine-member Minnesota State Forestry Board with the authority to manage state lands "as shall be set aside by the legislature for forestry purposes."[13] The establishment of the board was the beginning of a more effective forestry policy for the state.

While the Great Lakes states groped slowly toward the adoption of mandated forestry standards, Pennsylvania, under the able leadership of Joseph Rothrock, moved much more aggressively. Rothrock, an internationally known botanist, was instrumental in founding the Pennsylvania Forestry Association in 1886, which recommended the creation of a state division of forestry, the acquisition of land for a state forest, fire protection measures, and the reforestation of cutover lands. The Pennsylvania legislature finally established the Pennsylvania Bureau of Forestry in 1895 with Rothrock as its first commissioner. In 1897 the state adopted a modified version of New York's fire law and began a policy of setting aside state forest preserves.[14] The expanded authority of the state's forestry agency paralleled the development of similar policies at the federal level.

In the great southern pine belt stretching from Virginia south and west to Texas, state forestry programs developed at a much slower pace. Louisiana was the first southern state to create a forestry unit, in 1904, and three others followed suit in the same decade. By the mid-1920s Georgia and Mississippi had joined the ranks, and finally, following a series of disastrous fires in 1931, Arkansas became the last state in the region to establish a forestry commission.[15] Both in the Great Lakes region and in the South most of the state legislatures established forestry agencies *after* the peak years of timber harvesting had passed.

In a series of articles published in a commercial weekly in 1892, Fernow warned southerners about the future direction of the forest products industry. The center of lumber production, he pointed out, was gravitating toward the South as the stands in Michigan, Wisconsin, and Minnesota were being depleted. Although the region still possessed a rich resource, he hoped it would "be utilized in a more rational manner." He appealed for an "associated effort" to bring "social and commercial changes" to assure a more promising future for southern forests. But for the present, Fernow observed, forestry practices in the South were bleak. [16]

At the onset of the twentieth century the production of the southern mills was awesome. Southern lumber production amounted to 45 percent of the national cut in 1909, 47 percent in 1919, and still totaled 42 percent in 1929. Henry Clepper, a student of the development of professional forestry, provides an accurate assessment of the boom and bust cycle that characterized the southern lumber economy in the first three decades of this century: "From birth to decay, the average sawmill town lasted about two decades, rarely three. Most companies, after cutting off their timber, liquidated their operations and either quit or moved on, usually to the relatively untapped forests of the West. Meanwhile, the end of the South's inexhaustible timber was in sight. As the tide of logging swept onward, it left in its wake hundreds of thousands of acres, cutover and burned over, that nobody wanted at any price. The little sawmill towns disintegrated among the charred stumps." [17]

The enactment of forestry legislation in the southland, like that of the Great Lakes states, took place in the midst of a charred and ravaged forest environment. But forestry in the South had earlier, more casual beginnings. None other than Gifford Pinchot claimed that George W. Vanderbilt's Biltmore Estate in North Carolina was "the nest egg for practical Forestry in America." Pinchot was hired in 1891 to establish working plans for the 7,000-acre Biltmore forest. During his brief stay at the estate, Pinchot worked closely with North Carolina officials who were conducting a survey of timber resources. These investigations produced three publications detailing the economic value of the state's forest resource, the destructiveness of forest fires, and a comprehensive survey of the state's standing timber. [18]

The Biltmore estate's foresters, first Pinchot and then German-born Carl A. Schenck, kept the federal division chief informed about their work. Fernow, who was skeptical when Pinchot first accepted the job, reported in 1893 that it was the only place in the country where forest management was being practiced. Although Pinchot strived mightily to place the Biltmore forest on a sound financial basis, it was clearly Vanderbilt money that made the operation possible. [19] The estate served as one of the country's first private reforestation efforts, but as a precedent to encourage forest conservation at the state level, the Biltmore work remained one of a kind.

With the exception of California's brief experience with its first forestry board and the equally short-lived one in Colorado, the formation of forestry agencies in the western states and territories lagged behind those in the Northeast. And when California and Colorado dissolved their fledgling organizations, Fernow fumed that forestry in the West had become "rather a retrograde movement."[20] State chapters of the AFA were either weak or nonexistent in the Rocky Mountain and Pacific states, and until the turn of the century conservation groups such as the Sierra Club were interested primarily in the handling of federal lands.

Early Federal and State Forestry Relations

Fernow had a considerable influence on the activities of state forestry associations. In his extensive report to the Department of Agriculture in 1899, he said the division's first achievement was to popularize "forestry" and to make it "a matter of daily conversation, a topic of public lectures." The division, Fernow enthused, "has been the most potent influence in bringing about this change." Although other agencies influenced these changes, "as a fair historian," Fernow concluded, it was "necessary to assume the position of seeming self-glorification."[21]

Fernow was correct. Through his executive position with the AFA and as head of the Division of Forestry for twelve years, he corresponded with the most influential state forestry leaders: Abbot Kinney in California, Joseph Rothrock in Pennsylvania, Christopher C. Andrews in Minnesota, William Gladstone Steel in Oregon, Abram S. Hewitt in New York, Charles E. Bessey from Nebraska, and George P. Ahern, who was doing forest "missionary" work "in the enemy's camp" in Montana. The division was the nerve center for distributing information and sharing the wealth of data that came to Washington from the state inquiries.[22]

Despite the efforts of the Division of Forestry and its friends, only nine states had active forestry administrative units in 1900, and most of these operated without technically trained foresters and with only skeletal enforcement staffs. State forestry practice was limited and confined mostly to the northeastern states. Moreover, where the lumber industry was in the ascendence, as in the South and the far West, there was little forestry activity. Two states had initiated a land purchase system, New York and Pennsylvania, but elsewhere plans for state forests were ineffective. In the South the acquisition of land for state forests was never a major objective, and today the region has only a small acreage of state-owned forestland.[23]

But the appointment of Pinchot to the Division of Forestry in 1898 and the public clamor associated with the conservation movement increased the interest in forestry. Fernow's earlier prediction, that the turn of the century "would see the first phase in the history of forestry development in the United States ended," proved prophetic.[24] Although there was little uniformity in policy until the passage of the Weeks Act in 1911, twenty-five states had some kind of forestry organization by 1910, but both in the existing agencies and in the new ones formed after 1900, fire protection was the major objective.

The first state forestry agencies relied on the federal office for more than circular information. In 1900 the New York commission asked the Division of Forestry to prepare working plans for its 1.25-million acre forest preserve (a request that Pinchot termed "a gigantic task"). Other states made similar requests for professional guidance in managing state lands. By 1903 Pinchot noted that "a large and constantly increasing share of the attention of the Bureau" involved state forestry problems, time that "could be given to a few more profitable lines of work."[25]

But the bureau spent a great amount of energy helping states carry out studies of forestry issues. One of the more important of the new efforts involved inquiries about forest fires. The bureau conducted cooperative investigations with states as a preliminary step to drafting recommendations for a forest policy, and the agreements usually were drafted in a formal contract.[26] Although most of these investigations involved eastern states, federal officers became more active in other sections of the country as interest in forestry spread. As was the case during the Fernow years, states wanted information on forest law — to encourage tree planting, to promote fire protection, and to establish and administer state forests.

And distant places made requests for cooperation. When the Territory of Hawaii created a Board of Agriculture and Forestry in 1903, the board immediately sought the advice of Pinchot's office. A bureau employee, assigned to inquire into the condition of the Hawaiian forests, recommended a policy that the board quickly adopted. The Hawaiian officials then appointed Ralph S. Hosmer, a Bureau of Forestry nominee, as its first superintendent of forestry. Hawaiian sugar cane growers provided strong support for the first Board of Agriculture and Forestry to protect and develop "the springs, streams, and sources of water supply."[27] The Hawaii case is a good example of the economic motives that usually spurred the adoption of state or territorial forest policy.

Two years before the state reinstituted its forestry board in 1905, the California legislature provided matching funds to conduct a joint survey in cooperation with the Bureau of Forestry. The California Water and Forest Association, formed in 1899, initiated the survey that permitted the state to enter agreements with federal agencies to conduct investigations of streamflow and potential sites for reservoirs and canals. To underscore the importance of the survey, Pinchot traveled to California to outline the Bureau of Forestry's part in the project.[28] The progress reports and summary findings of the California survey extended over several years and covered a variety of forestry issues. While the survey in southern California concentrated on watershed problems, in the north it centered on fire protection — the drafting of fire plans, the use of phone communication, the employment of fire crews and patrols, and the construction of firebreaks.[29] Pinchot referred at some length to the studies in his annual reports and placed special emphasis on the findings concerning forest fires. In 1904 he brashly predicted that the California project would lead to the "organization of a fire service which will reduce to the minimum the state's losses by fire."[30] One result of the joint survey was the reestablishment of a state forestry board and the appointment of a professional forester to head the new department.

The influence of E. T. Allen, California's first state forester, in shaping federal cooperative policy ranks second only to William B. Greeley. And in 1906 Allen reported that the survey findings of greatest significance were those relating to fire; all of the state forester's energies, he reported, "were directed to this end." At this early period in California's forestry work, Allen singled out fire as the major thrust for forestry in the state. Raymond Clar's comprehensive two-volume history of California forestry reiterates the same point — the dominating influence of wildfire in shaping the use and preservation of the state's mountain vegetation.[31] The concern for fire led directly to the creation of an official forestry agency and the entry of the state into forest and watershed protection.

But the significance of the joint survey extended beyond its immediate accomplishment; it was a major precedent for cooperation between the federal government and the states. At the peak of the federal commitment there were twenty-eight men in the field mapping and surveying millions of acres.[32] The federal government readily committed itself to the joint survey, an accomplishment that took place before the organization of the California Forest Protective Association (itself a major force after 1909 in lobbying for greater federal-state cooperation in fire protection).

The joint survey ended in 1906 when the state's executive branch determined that no more funds would be spent for cooperative work. But the board also predicted that "with adequate provision" the state could "better and more properly" carry on these activities, the importance of which "cannot be over-estimated."[33] In the case of the joint survey, however, a private group, the California Water and Forest Association, had convinced state officials to assume some responsibility for the forest and watershed environment.

The Forest Service also conducted cooperative work in other states. In cooperation with North Carolina officials, federal foresters studied the effects of timber harvesting on state-owned swamp lands. The service worked in Kentucky to investigate forest conditions and to draft a forest policy for the state. Federal and state foresters made these inquiries after states had established organizations to conduct cooperative work with the federal government.[34] In 1908 the Forest Service cooperated with the New Hampshire Forestry Commission to study the taxation of forestland to determine which laws would best promote "the conservative cutting of timber." The federal agency observed that forest taxation was "a legislative problem of first importance." Wisconsin also participated in a cooperative study of forest taxation, a major thrust of the federal agency's new Division of State and Private Forestry. And it produced results. In the wake of the tax investigations, several states, most of them in the East, adopted variations of a yield tax, the idea that forest owners would pay taxes when they realized an income from their property.[35]

Cooperation in the Pacific Northwest

Except for California, most far western states responded slowly to federal initiatives. Moreover, when states began to develop forestry policies, as in Washington and Oregon, forest fire protection was the dominant issue. When a small group of naturalists, meeting jointly with a lumbermen's association, formed the Washington Forestry Association in 1897, the organization's first president cited the protection of forests from fire as the "most pressing problem" of the day. The fire issue demanded attention since some "of the finest timber on earth" was being "destroyed by needless fires."[36]

Despite this expression of concern, it took Washington's version of the great Hinckley fire—the Yacolt burn of 1902—to spur the state to adopt a forest policy. In 1903 the legislature appointed the commissioner of public lands the ex-officio forest fire warden and the county commissioners deputy wardens, a system that failed badly when the county officials failed to designate their own deputies, "not caring to incur the expense." To compound matters, the state's first fire warden reported that "organization was lax and wanting in effectiveness."[37]

However, in 1905 the state legislature repealed the 1903 measure and provided for a board of forest commissioners with the power to appoint a state fire warden and deputy wardens. The state appropriated $7,500 to pay the wages and expenses of the warden and his deputies for two years. The appointment of J. R. Welty as the first "State Fire Warden and Forester" marked the modest beginnings of Washington's move toward a forest policy, the first northwestern state to do so.[38]

Forestry policy in the Pacific Northwest developed in tandem with the expansion of the region's lumber industry. Investors from the Great Lakes states and the South purchased huge acreages of Northwest timber between 1890 and 1910, and these new owners, in turn, wanted to protect their sizable investments from being consumed in fire. The smoking ruins of 1902 encouraged some lumbermen to begin patroling their own lands and, in a few instances, to join with adjacent owners to form protective associations.[39]

In the spring of 1906 Washington's forest commissioners asked timberland owners to contribute to the costs of forest protection for the coming fire season. The Weyerhaeuser groups contributed $4,000 to this effort, and the board was able to raise an additional $3,976 after mailing out letters to more than 600 landowners. But this scheme, which raised the protection fund to $10,000, proved grossly inadequate when the state experienced an uncommonly long and dry fire season.[40]

At the same time the forest protective associations made a concerted effort to get states to increase their contributions to the protection of private lands. Timberland owners north of the Columbia River formed the Washington Forest Fire Association, whose expressed purpose was more "liberal appropriation" for fire protection. George S. Long, superintendent of the Weyerhaeuser operations in the region and president of the fire association for several years, advised the association's membership to bring pressure on the legislature to "make more liberal appropriations for forest fire protection." This, he said, was one of "the state's duties to its citizens."[41] In the next few years the Washington Forest Fire Association worked closely with state forestry officials and with the Forest Service as its budget and activities increased.

The threat of incendiary holocaust also lurked behind the efforts in Oregon to establish a state forestry agency. As in Washington, timberland owners who wanted to protect their virgin stands from fire organized local protective associations well in advance of legislative action. Finally, both the legislature and private organizations acted when disastrous fires in 1902 burned over thousands of acres of the state's timberland. Timber owners formed several protective associations in the next few years, and these groups combined into a statewide lobbying organization, the Oregon Forest Fire Association, in 1910.[42]

While private protection organizations extended their activities in Oregon, lumber representatives introduced legislation to establish forest protection districts. The measure passed both houses of the legislature, but Governor George Chamberlain vetoed the bill because it placed the burden of protection on all taxpayers. The region's most popular trade journal, the *Timberman,* was outraged and accused the governor of ignoring the public value of Oregon's forestland.[43] It was clear that lumbermen needed to refine their arguments and emphasize the public benefits of such a policy if they were to gain support for their fire protection legislation.

The forest protective associations achieved a modest improvement in 1907, when the Oregon legislature created a board of forestry (to serve without pay) to investigate forest conditions in the state. During the four years of its existence, the board appointed voluntary fire wardens, issued press releases, and wrote biennial reports.[44] But the state still lacked a paid forestry official and appropriations for fighting fires. Another disastrous fire season in 1910 and the recommendations of the Oregon Conservation Commission, however, led to the establishment of the modern board of forestry in 1911.

Lawrence Rakestraw, an authority on early conservation activities in the Pacific Northwest, claims that the Oregon Conservation Commission was "the strongest single force for conservation in the state." The commission reported in 1909 that both California and Washington were ahead of Oregon in establishing progressive forestry practices. The commission and its chairman, Joseph Nathan Teal, a Portland lawyer with close ties to the lumber industry, were major forces along with the Western Forestry and Conservation Association (WFCA) and the Oregon Forest Fire Association in passing the 1911 law that created the Oregon State Board of Forestry.[45]

Although the Forest Service assisted in the passage of forestry laws in Oregon and Washington,[46] it was not until the Weeks Law in 1911 that federal cooperation became an important part of forest policy in the region. And the organization in 1909 of the WFCA, a group destined to play an important part in federal-state forestry policy for the next half century, prepared lumber interests in the Northwest for the expanded opportunities of federal cooperation.

The WFCA, like the Washington and Oregon Forest Fire Associations, originated with a group of lumbermen who wanted to promote cooperative fire protection. The association, in a brief period, extended its membership to include most of the protective associations in Oregon, Washington, Idaho, Montana, northern California, and British Columbia. William B. Greeley and Edward Tyson Allen, two young Forest Service officials, attended the organizational meeting of the WFCA. Before the year was out Allen resigned from the Forest Service to accept an appointment with the new association, a position he held until 1942.[47] Greeley, of course, soon advanced to the center of federal forestry activity in Washington, D.C.

The WFCA, designed to coordinate fire protection on the varying classes of landownership in the Pacific Northwest, used skillful publicity to convince the public of the importance of forest protection. Although it was a business-oriented association, Allen used every opportunity to emphasize WFCA cooperation with federal and state governments in forest policy. Twenty years after he joined the association, Allen summarized its purposes:

The association acts as a clearing house and service bureau affording central facilities for all organized forest agencies; private, state and federal; in Montana, Idaho, Washington, Oregon and California, with British Columbia in nearly as close co-operation. State and federal forest officers are associate members and serve on several committees. Deans of forest schools of the five states serve similarly on appropriate technical committees. Otherwise there is no individual membership, the Association being rather a sort of grand lodge for some thirty private co-operative protective associations.[48]

Although the "grand lodge" was interested in other forestry matters, its initial focus was fire protection. The 1910 conflagrations that burned uncontrolled for several weeks throughout the Northwest gave added emphasis to organized protection against fire. One Forest Service report cited the work of protection associations in the Northwest as "the largest progress thus far made toward the practice of forestry on private lands." Despite the lavish praise for cooperative work in 1910, the effort was still woefully inadequate to effectively cope with the menace of fire.[49] The Weeks Law was one remedy to meet this deficiency.

Summary

Despite the expansion of its cooperative programs by 1910, the Forest

Service still had no clear legislative mandate to pursue particular lines of activity. Rather, the pressing issues of the hour seemed to direct cooperative work—first the extension of technical advice and the drafting of working plans for individual owners; then, with the transfer of federal timberlands to the Department of Agriculture in 1905, the service deemphasized individual assistance programs and expanded its cooperative work with states.[50]

Cooperative projects with other government departments increasingly took up much of the bureau's time, and the 1905 transfer gave the agency vast new responsibility. But congressmen also wanted the Forest Service to pay attention to forestry interests in the states, a matter that may have convinced the diplomatic-minded Pinchot to create the Division of State and Private Forestry in 1908. Nevertheless, when Pinchot left the Forest Service, the agency was clearly channeling its cooperative work through state agencies rather than directly to private parties. The growing list of state forestry bureaus and commissions made this shift a feasible and practical alternative.

In his last annual report Pinchot pointed to the "wide field for cooperation" in states with large acreages of federal timber. The national government and the states had a true "partnership of interests," especially in the West, to serve the public welfare through a "spirit of hearty cooperation for a common end." These mutual "interests" included joint action to control forest fires, to enforce game laws, and to eliminate stock diseases. "Indeed, the field is capable of almost indefinite expansion," the soon-to-be-dismissed forester concluded.[51] Forest Service heads who followed Pinchot used these opportunities and others to expand vastly the agency's activities, an indication that the modern forestry bureaucracy grew more by conscious design than accident.

Henry Graves, Pinchot's successor as chief, moved quickly to clarify Forest Service responsibilities outside the national forests. Cooperative work, he said, fell into three categories: (1) advising states in establishing forest policies, (2) assisting with state surveys of forest resources, and (3) helping forest owners with practical forestry problems. Whereas the service formerly sent its men into the field to give advice, now "many states have foresters, and applicants in such states are referred to them." However, where these opportunities were not available, the Forest Service was willing to assist applicants through "correspondence or conference."[52] In effect, Graves had outlined a shift in federal cooperation—the institutionalizing of state agencies as the proper administrators of forest policy on state and private lands. The Weeks Act was the first legislative step to codify this change.

Chapter Four

Even before Congress passed the Weeks Law in 1911, the Forest Service was engaged in a wide array of cooperative fire agreements, many of them initiated in the field. In this and in its other cooperative work, agency officials wanted to take political advantage of the favorable publicity associated with these activities. Forest Service funding depended to a large degree on the popularity of its cooperative programs, and congressmen were more likely to approve increases in the agency's appropriations if they represented a "cooperating state." Because the Forest Service had no congressional mandate for cooperative agreements until 1911, administrators skillfully devised other means to augment their annual operating budgets.

Shortly after his appointment as chief, Henry Graves ordered his subordinates to establish a specific policy to assure public recognition for cooperative activity. The Forest Service, he said, should reserve the right of first publication of the results of cooperative studies and states should give proper credit to the service in their own publications. Graves also urged the immediate publication of these studies, especially if the dissemination of such literature might favorably influence legislative action.[1] Obviously Graves was no dawdler in the game of congressional politics.

Initiatives from the Field

Cooperative agreements before the Weeks Law did not always originate in Washington. Because of the decentralized administrative structure of the Forest Service, district officers were free to initiate policies and programs especially suited to the states within their jurisdictions. In the Great Lakes states, the West, and the South, district officials made cooperative agreements with railroads to reduce the fire hazard; they cooperated in joint research projects with agricultural experiment stations; they administered grazing regulations through livestock associations; and they offered technical assistance to states to conduct surveys and to formulate forestry policy.

Gifford Pinchot recognized the central role of fire in promoting cooperation. "The heavy loss from fire," he wrote in a brief article in 1910, "has led to the largest progress thus far" in the adoption of progressive forestry practices on private lands. Pinchot pointed to "large tracts" in the Pacific Northwest and smaller parcels in the East and the South that had been placed under organized protection. In a companion piece Graves looked forward to the "prospect that a policy of state assistance and cooperation with private owners will soon be general."[2] With legislation pending in Congress to expand Forest Service cooperation in forest fire protection, Graves had good reason to be optimistic.

The federal agency had stepped up its interest in fire protection in 1908, when it issued notices to states requesting information on forest fires. The return was discouraging. A few states forwarded carefully prepared reports, others sent irrelevant information, and some did not reply at all. But in the Pacific Northwest state officials and associations provided the Forest Service with systematic information on fire losses for the 1909 season. The Oregon Conservation Association, the Oregon State Board of Forestry, and the Washington Forest Fire Association worked with District Forester E. T. Allen to compile data on the occurrence and location of forest fires.[3]

And the most advanced forms of fire cooperation before passage of the Weeks measure took place in the interior Northwest. District Forester William Greeley, stationed in Missoula, Montana, reported in January, 1909, that he was working with protective associations in his district to gain legislative support for an efficient fire protection system. The protective associations and the Forest Service established cooperative fire districts and agreed upon a pro rata share per acre for the protection costs.[4] Although neither party allocated a specific fund for cooperative work, they agreed to match material and men on an acreage basis.

Greeley, the architect of the cooperative fire agreement with the northern Idaho protective associations, told a lumbermen's conference later in 1909 that the step was a most important one "in the conservation of forest resources." Because the fire danger was general and did not respect boundaries, Greeley said that it was wise for federal and state authorities and the private owner to cooperate. The threat from forest fires was "too great for anyone of us to undertake alone"; therefore, all forest owners should "join forces and pull together" to reduce the fire risk.[5]

The well-traveled Pinchot, on one of his frequent jaunts through the West, told the same gathering that the Forest Service would like to match the Idaho associations' contribution, but its funds were limited. But he offered the lumbermen a carrot: "You can help us to get larger appropriations for this purpose, and we can help along the idea that cheaper lumber injures conservation," the latter an obvious reference to the recent tariff fight in Congress.[6]

The Forest Service used these early cooperative arrangements to make political capital with organized lumbermen. In a message to the annual meeting of the Western Forestry and Conservation Association (WFCA) in 1911, Graves praised timberland owners for their cooperation with the Forest Service. The agreements with timber protective associations in northern Idaho, he said, were "the best illustrations of cooperative fire protection of a specific, detailed, and administrative character." The chief forester also referred to the liabilities of the work, the greatest of which "is the limit upon our financial resources." Most western timber owners, he acknowledged, had "spent more money . . . per unit of area" than the Forest Service, and in some western states the service was unable to meet private cooperators half way.[7]

To the annual meeting of the National Lumber Manufacturers Association (NLMA) the same year, Graves applauded the work of the fire protection associations in the Northwest, the Great Lakes states, New Hampshire, and Maine. But, he warned, more work was needed "in those localities where cooperative fire associations have not yet been formed." Lumbermen should not wait for states to pass legislation on taxation and fire protection before "making a beginning in forestry."[8] The ever-cautious Graves urged lumbermen to undertake voluntarily forestry practices on a trial basis.

Cooperative protection arrangements with lumbermen were not the only agreements the Forest Service made before the Weeks mandate. Before his transfer to Washington, Greeley pioneered negotiations with the Great Northern and Northern Pacific Railroad companies to protect national forest lands traversed by the transcontinental lines. Although the chief forester rejected some of the Greeley proposals, Graves approved other cooperative fire protection work. And to upgrade forest protection, the service urged states to secure the "maximum" cooperation from the railroad companies, an effort that often ran afoul of the powerful lobbying influence of the railroads in state legislatures.[9]

Even in the Pacific Northwest state forestry organizations were still in their formative period and poorly funded when Congress passed the Weeks Law. But the existence of influential private organizations dedicated to protecting timber from fire placed the region in an advantageous situation when the federal government offered its cooperative incentive. Moreover, the WFCA worked hard to increase the federal appropriation for Weeks Law cooperation, an indication that lumbermen wanted to take full advantage of the opportunity to expand state protection to include all of their virgin timber stands.

The Weeks Law

The fires that wreaked havoc in the Pacific Northwest in the late summer of 1910 cleared legislative smoke from congressional corridors and opened the way for passage of the Weeks Law — an act permitting federal cooperation with states to protect private forestland on the watersheds of navigable streams. And congressional debates make it clear that cooperative fire protection was not the major objective; rather, Congress considered the clause authorizing federal land acquisition to form eastern forest preserves more important. Western opposition to this feature of the bill dissolved when reports of the awesome conflagration in northern Idaho filtered into Washington. The promise of federal assistance inherent in Section 2, although it was not deemed controversial at the time, has had a far greater influence than other provisions of the act.

The background to the Weeks legislation dates to the 1880s, when the idea of setting aside blocks of eastern land through government purchase first surfaced. But it was not until the formation of the Appalachian National Park Association in 1899 that the movement gained substantial support. A New England group, with designs on a reserve for the White Mountains in New Hampshire, merged with the southern group in 1906, and when the influential American Forestry Association (AFA) added its support, the combined forces stepped up their efforts to get a bill through Congress.[10]

At first, debate centered on the eastern reserve issue and followed sectional lines — the South and the East supported the move and the West opposed it. But by 1908 clauses amended to the eastern reserve bills also provided federal assistance to states to protect forestlands bordering navigable streams. One of these early measures even required states to adopt cutting regulations before they could be eligible for federal cooperation. Finally Congressman John Weeks of Massachusetts introduced a modified bill that passed both houses of Congress and was signed into law on March 1, 1911.[11]

The Weeks Law authorized Congress to appropriate $200,000 annually for federal assistance to protect private and state lands on the watersheds of navigable streams; Congress also could appropriate up to $11 million for a five-year period to purchase land in the watersheds of such streams. To be eligible for cooperative funds, the act required states to have a forest protection agency and to provide matching expenditures.[12] Thus, the 1911 legislation, designed in part to protect forests from fire, provided the first major incentive for the expansion of federal cooperation with states. The law permitted the Forest Service to extend a fire protection policy that it was already practicing on a limited basis at the regional and local level.

Armed with this new congressional mandate, the Forest Service had to prepare plans for administering the Weeks Law. In a memorandum to Graves, one staff member recommended that the service use the funds in the eastern and central states because the national forests already protected the watersheds of navigable streams in western states. But in his letter to the secretary of agriculture, Graves avoided any discussion of regional favoritism. His proposal outlined what became standard procedure for administering the law: (1) a state must first apply to the department, providing that it had already established a system of forest fire protection, (2) the funds should be used for fire patrols, (3) the state and the federal government would draft a plan of cooperation, and (4) the field work would be subject to inspection. [13]

In administering the act the Forest Service announced that it would broadly interpret what constituted a navigable stream. To make the most effective use of the available funds, the service limited the maximum allotment to individual states to $10,000. And it established criteria for determining state grants: (1) the likelihood of assistance from private owners, (2) the amount of the appropriation from the state, (3) the importance of the watersheds to be protected, and (4) the value of the forests and the relative fire risk. In each case the Forest Service required "a reasonable effort on the part of the private owner." [14]

The Forest Service used the initial $200,000 appropriation conservatively. [15] In the first year eleven states qualified for matching funds and of these only Maine and Minnesota received the full allotment. Table 1 shows the federal allotments and state expenditures for 1911. [16] By 1913 four states—Maine, Minnesota, Oregon, and Washington—qualified for full allotments, and the number of cooperating states had increased to fifteen. [17] From the first year the Weeks Law had a greater impact in states with well-organized forestry agencies or equally strong protective associations. Usually the two went together.

J. Girvin Peters, the federal forester in charge of cooperative fire protection, praised the "practical results" of the new law. Cooperating state agencies, he noted, had quickly extinguished hundreds of fires and made permanent improvements in building trails and lookouts. A less measurable but equally important part of the cooperative work, according to Peters, was its educational value. And there were other intangibles: the federal government acted as a "clearing house" for publicizing the fire-fighting methods of efficient state organizations; and there was a move to standardize fire organizations, their

Table 1: Weeks Law Expenditures, 1911

State	State Expenditures	Allotment to States	Unexpended Balance of Allotment	Balance of $200,000 Fund, Jan. 1, 1912
Maine	$23,557.07	$10,000	$ 8.20	—
New Hampshire	13,876.21	7,200	980.50	—
Vermont	2,243.90	2,000	782.00	—
Massachusetts	400.12	1,800	1,435.00	—
Connecticut	513.96	1,000	994.00	—
New York	3,837.59	2,000	—	—
New Jersey	1,241.51	1,000	10.00	—
Maryland	262.85	600	339.00	—
Wisconsin	20,841.87	5,000	562.75	—
Minnesota	25,675.77	10,000	—	—
Oregon	8,758.89	5,000	1,695.00	—
Total	101,209.74	45,600	6,806.45	$161,206.45

equipment, lookouts, and other technical aids.[18] The only barrier to extending protection was the failure of noncooperating states to enact forest fire legislation and to appropriate enforcement funds.

To assure that cooperators were kept abreast of Weeks Law activities, the Forest Service arranged collaborators' conferences to discuss problems in administering the law. Representatives from eastern states dominated the first collaborators' conference in January, 1913, a point Pacific Northwest District 6 forester, George Cecil, brought to the attention of the Washington office. It would seem prudent, Cecil complained, that state forester Francis A. Elliott of Oregon and E. T. Allen of the WFCA be added to the program because of their broad experiences in state and private protection work.[19]

Much of the discussion at the first Weeks Law conference centered on the failure of southern states to make significant progress in forest protection work. J. H. Finney of the Southern Commercial Congress, a business organization with a deep interest in forestry, wanted to convince "legislatures throughout the South" to cooperate in federal fire protection. J. S. Holmes, North Carolina's state forester, was optimistic that a bill to fund a fire protection system for his state would soon enable North Carolina to cooperate under the Weeks Act. But Virginia's representative admitted that "practically nothing" had been accomplished in his state. Assistant forester Greeley praised the new cooperative arrangement for its "primarily educational" accomplishment. By educating and encouraging local interests, the youthful forester said, the government could "double or triple" every dollar spent in fire protection work.[20]

"Cooperation," Peters told a New England collaborators' conference in 1914, was fundamental to "effective fire protection." And there was room for improvement, especially in a small region like New England. Because no systematic plans for cooperation had been devised, Peters recommended future meetings to coordinate common action in case of emergency, the objective to "be one of mutual helpfulness." He pointed to a need for cooperation of a "more fundamental character"—the adoption of uniform forest protection legislation in common forest regions.[21]

Because the question of determining "navigable streams" continued to bother Forest Service administrators, they finally sought an opinion from the solicitor general's office. At first the service had restricted its assistance to the headwaters of streams navigable for interstate trade. In the solicitor's opinion, however, the use of a stream "for floating logs would be very good evidence that the stream is navigable." The solicitor further suggested that streams "susceptible of being used for the floating of logs . . . may be considered navigable," especially if a state requested cooperation in the protection of its watersheds. In any event, the question of navigability was left to the Forest Service.[22] Henceforth, the only real restrictions on Weeks Law cooperation were the inability of states to form protection agencies and to fund their operation, and the limits of congressional appropriations.

There were other difficulties in administering Weeks Law allocations. After three years with the program, Peters complained that protective associations had merely used federal money to lessen their own expenditures. The associations had not increased the scope of their fire control activity, he claimed, but had shifted personnel and adjusted their cost ledgers to take advantage of Weeks funds to lessen their protection costs. Peters charged that this practice was especially noticeable in Idaho, Montana, and Michigan and was "nothing more than a subsidy to the Associations." Peters urged the adoption of a definite policy in the allocation of funds.[23]

As chief of state cooperation, Peters circulated letters to state collaborators warning them to accept free railroad passes only if it were an explicit part of a cooperative agreement with the railroad company. In other words, Peters concluded, "there must be a clear case" of reciprocal obligation. He feared charges that "might prove embarrassing" to the Forest Service. While he did not want every plan of cooperation with the railroads "put in writing," he asked state foresters to send him their policy procedures.[24] Like his chief, Peters was wary of favoring the railroads at a time when the atmosphere still was charged with rumors of influence-buying and corporate corruption.

The Forest Service also tried to coordinate its publicity on a regional basis. In a circular mailed to state foresters in August, 1914, the office of state cooperation asked that conventional fire prevention publicity be supplemented to include "posters, leaflets, blotters, drinking cups, and similar devices." E. T. Allen had pioneered this technique in the Pacific coast states, but it had not been "systematically developed" elsewhere. The Forest Service advised cooperating states to adopt common poster designs that could be changed every year and that states contract with one company to save printing money. The key to the success of its publicity work, the agency claimed, was regional cooperation to cut expenses and to use "standardized" material.[25]

Promoting standardized publicity proved difficult because many state laws restricted expenditures to resident printers. Although the Forest Service did not press the issue of coordinating regional publicity for fire prevention, the effort to do so marked a shift of emphasis in Weeks Law programs. Because the state and private contribution to fire protection was much greater, the Forest Service designed its funds to bring "together the various protective agencies—Federal, State and Private—into closer relationship." Federal money, officials reasoned, should serve as an educational incentive "toward furthering the protective movement" in the United States.[26] As states expanded their protection capabilities, the Forest Service increased the emphasis on the federal program's educational qualities.

After four years of cooperative work under the Weeks Law, the Forest Service set forth two general objectives: to promote forest fire protection in states and counties and among private landowners, and to develop closer cooperation at all levels for a more "efficient, organized system." Protecting against forest fires was a national problem, it said, and "required the continued participation of the Federal Government" because of the large public interest involved. And then, in a statement that soon became inoperative, the agency said, larger appropriations were "unnecessary and not anticipated."[27] The increasing number of states qualifying for Weeks Law funding, however, quickly strained the small allocation to the point that it was becoming ineffective.

E. T. Allen and the Industry's Rationale for Cooperation

Despite the heavy lobbying of the NLMA, AFA, and WFCA, the Weeks Law appropriation was not substantially increased until 1922 when Congress raised it to $400,000. Although Forest Service statistics showed that state and protective associations had tripled their contributions, the agency considered the support inadequate. Material changes in American industrial and social life were taking their toll—a burgeoning and increasingly mobile population and the more frequent use of mechanized equipment in the woods created an even greater fire hazard.

The industry leader who spoke most eloquently for increasing the cooperative fire protection fund during these years was E. T. Allen. The WFCA economist frequently referred to public ignorance and misunderstanding of the lumber industry. It was a travesty, Allen told a retail association in 1912, that a state whose lumber income was a hundred times greater "than from wool growing would . . . appropriate (only) $500 for fire prevention and $20,000 for coyote scalps." The "great need," he charged, "is for teaching the principles of the business from start to finish." When the public recognized its stake in perpetuating forests and creating a healthy economic environment, Allen was convinced it would ask for legislation to improve these conditions.[28]

Forest preservation, Allen argued on another occasion, was "a mutual cooperative enterprise" that required a widely accepted forest policy. And some progress had been made — the United States had an efficient federal forestry administration, forest legislation existed in many states, and some legislatures were "fairly liberal" with their funds. But, he warned, there were serious problems — the Forest Service still had "to fight for existence in every congress," and the federal legislature appropriated less money "than private owners spend to protect adjoining lands." The "stupendous task" ahead was to protect existing timber stands and to reforest denuded areas "so as to best serve the people."[29] To accomplish this task, Allen believed, required the expenditure of public funds on a scale commensurate with the public interest.

Even before William Greeley became the preeminent spokesman for an expanded federal obligation, Allen had articulated a wide-ranging cooperative philosophy for lumbermen that included public solutions to private industrial problems, a trade association program to educate the public about its responsibilities for forest conservation, and improved cooperation between foresters and lumbermen. He urged lumbermen to shed their suspicions of state legislatures, and the law-making bodies, in turn, should encourage "good private management" through improved fire protection and more equitable taxation of forest properties. Throughout his long career, Allen argued tirelessly that the public and private sector shared common ground: "In my opinion forestry will never succeed in the United States until it is so closely allied with lumbering that neither forester, lumberman nor public makes any distinction."[30]

Neither Graves and Greeley in the Forest Service nor their counterparts in the major lumber trade associations provided a better synthesis of what cooperation meant to the lumber trade. Industry representatives like Allen defined cooperation and gave it meaning in the public press and legislative halls. The proper role for government policy, in this view, was to integrate itself fully with the designs of the private sector. If these ends were achieved, they believed, the public would be served well.

Funding and Other Problems

While trade associations and state forestry agencies expanded their efforts to gain a larger appropriation for cooperative fire protection, the Forest Service had to allocate a fixed sum of money to an increasing number of states. By 1915 the federal contribution was less than one-fifth of the state appropriations. More important, the Forest Service claimed, the expenditures of about forty timber protective associations equaled that of the federal and state agencies. And two years later the Forest Service estimated that private owners contributed more to forest protection than government agencies.[31] By this time, the Forest Service was deeply involved in an effort to draft a national forestry policy that included a much larger annual fund for forest fire protection.

While the agency struggled with funding problems, it was also giving greater attention to state and private forestry matters in the South. Although the region was slow in responding to the initiative of the Weeks Law, several southern states and private agencies had requested assistance in drafting forestry bills. With its potential for rapid forest growth, the Forest Service pointed out, no section of the country was "in greater need of forest conservation."[32]

But a mere statistical listing of cooperating states and their expenditures for forestry does not indicate the true dimensions of the problem, especially in regions with tremendous acreages of logged-off, burned, and denuded lands. The persisting economic difficulties of the industry and the growing number of impoverished towns and counties in the Great Lakes states and the South were behind the move to adopt a national forest policy. The prolonged forest policy debate that preceded passage of the Clarke-McNary Law involved an extensive discussion about the kind and form of government cooperation.

While the Forest Service groped toward a national policy, eyewitness reports from the field underscored the need for an expanded federal presence. Shortly after he replaced Graves as chief forester, Greeley made inspection trips to the Great Lakes states and the Far West. In the Great Lakes region he cited the need to require private timber owners to contribute to protection costs. Michigan and Minnesota, two states with large areas of forestland, had inadequate protective organizations. This continued inattention, he warned, was costly, especially in the repeated burning of new forest growth. [33]

Peters, who spent a month inspecting the Great Lakes states in 1924, reached a similar conclusion. The greatest obstacles to effective fire protection in the region were public indifference and the failure to appreciate forest values. Foresters in the Great Lakes states, Peters noted, were struggling against huge odds, the most serious being inadequate appropriations. But despite the inadequacy of state protection work, he thought the government was getting good return for its cooperative expenditures. [34] As the archival record reveals, however, Peters was more critical of cooperative work in private conversations than he was in his public statements.

Another Greeley inspection trip, this time through the South, also unsettled the chief forester. He reported to the Service Committee that there was little sentiment in Mississippi for forestry. To make matters worse, large lumber operators, many of them opposed to any forestry program, dominated state politics. Meanwhile, a Southern Pine Association survey indicated that 50 percent of Mississippi's lumber industry would be gone in ten years. The state needed fire protection, state forests, and an educational program to develop a positive public attitude. Greeley told the Southern Forestry Congress in Jackson that it was time for them to get in line before the public seized the issue. [35]

But there were bright examples of leadership in the South — Henry Hardtner in Louisiana, J. A. Holmes and Joseph H. Pratt of North Carolina, and E. O. Siecke in Texas. Greeley noticed that better conditions prevailed in Texas than in Mississippi; the Texas Forestry Association strongly advocated improved forest practices, and the state had an efficient and nonpartisan forestry agency. Despite these exceptions, the forester's report for 1922 estimated that 58 percent of all the land burned in the United States during the previous year was located in the southern tier of states. Of these, North Carolina was the only state with a forest protection agency. For the rest of the southern states, the Forest Service reported, the meager funds for protection compounded their forest fire problems. [36]

Part of the problem during these years, as Stephen J. Pyne properly notes in his study *Fire in America,* was the agency's obsession with eliminating *all* fire from the nation's woodland. And in the South with its peculiar fire heritage of random prescribed burning, the Forest Service undoubtedly believed it was confronting the devil itself.[37] Moreover, because the agency's programs depended on congressional appropriations, it tended to quantify its programs, including fire protection, on a dollar basis.

Despite what it saw as failure in the South and elsewhere, Forest Service officials still believed that federal contributions had a positive influence. Weeks Law funds encouraged backward states to begin programs in fire protection, and the promise of cooperative money enabled federal forestry personnel to speak to state legislatures about progressive protection policies.[38] But problems persisted — states refused to comply with Weeks requirements and the Forest Service still lacked a clear mandate to withdraw funds if states failed to meet federal guidelines.

When the federal government increased the appropriation for the Weeks program in 1921 to $400,000, it required states to expand protection to burned and cutover lands and acreages supporting second growth. Correspondence between Washington and federal district foresters indicates that some states failed to provide satisfactory evidence that all lands would be protected on an equal basis. Peters informed one district forester that states must submit "a definite statement on these points," and that the district inspector should certify that the state was complying with the requirement.[39] The evidence suggests that compliance may have been more a paper necessity than the application of practices in the field.

At a meeting of the Service Committee in late 1923, Peters complained that the Forest Service had no regulatory authority for its state and private work. It could educate and cooperate; it could continue its aid or withdraw its funds. He doubted that the secretary of agriculture would be willing to pursue the latter course. The effectiveness of the agency's leadership, Peters told his colleagues, depended upon its ability to maintain satisfactory relations with states and private owners and to deal with them sympathetically. In a memorandum to the files, Peters complained that congressional authorizations limited the ability of federal bureaus and departments to withhold funds from a state when the law mandated that they cooperate.[40]

Peters, who was closer to the field work than anyone else, probably was the best judge of state cooperation, and his correspondence and memos show that he was fully aware of the program's weaknesses. In addition, the state and private office had to adjust to changes. Beginning in 1922, cooperating states could qualify for federal funds for any legitimate fire protection function as long as they met federal requirements. This allowed state agencies greater latitude in determining where federal funds were needed the most.[41]

Scholars who have studied federal cooperation with states in fire protection have ignored the issue of compliance with Forest Service guidelines. State protection systems varied greatly, both within common geographic areas and between regions. States with strong private associations differed considerably from states where public agencies carried on all protection work. Moreover, states with large virgin forests continued to give most of their attention to their merchantable timber stands.

As for the Weeks Law, its greatest effect was to encourage fire protection work as a legitimate field for federal and state forestry agencies. It encouraged states with forestry departments to devote attention to the problem of fire, and it encouraged other states to form protection agencies. As the Copeland report summarized in 1933, the Weeks Law also strengthened state forestry departments and asserted a national interest in state and private forestry matters. And it also established a common ground between public foresters and the industry they were so closely associated with.[42]

Summary

Except for a few isolated (and well-publicized) examples, the private sector still showed little enthusiasm for reforestation or caring for its cutover lands. Organized lumbermen devoted their energies to the efficient production and marketing of lumber. But a persistently glutted market caused great concern and tested the organizational skills of trade leaders like Wilson Compton. To industry spokesmen, these economic issues overrode all other considerations, including those of fire protection and reforestation. In their public statements and in testimony to Congress, lumber officials argued that federal policy had to recognize this fact. For his part, Compton made it clear that the lumbermen's sole obligation to the public was to produce lumber; if the public wanted future timber supplies, it should carry some of the burden. [43]

A number of influential forestry leaders shared Compton's views, and they strived mightily to shape cooperative programs in the 1920s. The future would show that proposals that were inconsistent with the industry's economic needs made little legislative progress. But measures that offered some prospect of increased federal assistance and avoided excessive restrictions found the going easier. The leadership of the Forest Service and influential spokesmen in the lumber trade had supported the cooperative principle expressed in the Weeks Law. When proposals were made to expand this form of cooperation, a broad consensus emerged to press Congress for action.

Chapter Five

The view from Washington provides only part of the early history of federal and state cooperation in fire protection. Equally important to the successes and failures of cooperative programs were the developments that took place in individual states. Some were more progressive in promoting state forestry, while others with traditions that were highly suspicious of bureaucratic structures established forestry departments only when economic necessity forced the issue. But any assessment of state forestry must consider the influence of federal policy at that level. And lurking behind the scenes was a troubled lumber industry struggling with economic problems common to other natural resource trades.

To illustrate the differences in the development of state forestry programs, this chapter examines the establishment and evolution of agencies in different forested regions of the country. The evolution of forestry policy at the state level was uneven, a reflection of several factors — commercial and industrial wealth, the extent and condition of a state's timberland, the degree to which forest owners accepted responsibility for the health of private holdings, and unique cultural influences of regions like the South. The states of Minnesota, Oregon and Washington, and Georgia serve as representative examples.

Minnesota, once a great center of lumbering activity, established one of the earliest and most progressive forestry agencies. Oregon and Washington, where timber harvests have dominated national production for much of the twentieth century, have been forerunners in establishing commercial forestry policies. The evolution of these two agencies illustrates the parallels and policy differences in contiguous states in a common forest region. Georgia's forestry agency, weak and ineffective until after 1945, shares much of the tradition of other southern states in the slow development of its forest policy.

Minnesota

When Congress passed the Weeks Law in 1911, the Minnesota legislature had just created a new forestry organization the same year. The old forestry board, established in 1899, was limited to the management of state-owned lands and to the promotion of forestry in the state. Minnesota law did not commit the state to protect against forest fires, and the legislature failed even to appropriate money to allow the board to fulfill its primary function — expanding the state's forests. [1] But following the disastrous Baudette-Spooner Fire in 1910, several legislators introduced bills to upgrade the state's forestry agency.

Although Minnesota's legislature ignored the recommendations of its forestry commissioner, Christopher C. Andrews, for a progressive forestry code and larger appropriations, it passed several measures in 1911 that strengthened state forestry. The legislature made the forestry board responsible for reforestation and protection against forest fires, and it authorized the appointment of a technically trained forester and assistant. The board subsequently appointed William T. Cox, a Forest Service employee and native Minnesotan, as the first state forester. [2] The appointment of Cox was fortuitous; he organized a model state protection system that served the state of Minnesota for several decades and was widely copied elsewhere.

Cox appointed state district rangers who directed the work of a small staff of state and private patrolmen. The state forester's interest extended beyond fire protection; Cox began an extensive survey of the state's forest resources, established a herd of elk in the 7,000-acre Itasca park, and created an examination system for hiring employees. [3] Cox introduced modern forestry to Minnesota.

Although fire protection was his greatest concern, Cox said it was "erroneous" to believe that the work of the Minnesota Forest Service concerned only the fire danger. He advised the state to reforest cutover and burned areas and urged "a more conservative utilization" of forest resources. But the fire problem occupied most of his attention during his years as chief forester. It was not until 1920 that Cox believed there was reasonable assurance that fire losses could be kept down "with proper funds" from "the State and other cooperators."[4]

Minnesota's first forester was an articulate proponent of cooperation in forestry work. In his first annual report he praised the Weeks Law for permitting the state to hire sixty-one patrolmen during the fire season. And personnel assigned to the national forests in Minnesota cooperated to protect state lands within the federal forests and assisted with the construction of lookout towers and trails. "The two organizations," Cox concluded, "work in harmony at all times to their common benefit." He commended the Weeks Law as the most important legislation for protecting forests from fire. Its aim of cooperation between the states and private owners "'hit the nail on the head.'"[5]

Under Cox, Minnesota used the Weeks Law fund to keep an adequate force of patrolmen in the field during the fire season and employed its own personnel "to do the general construction work." The latter entailed the building of firebreaks, lookout towers, and other fire protection devices.[6] In his annual reports Cox lauded federal cooperation, especially the coordinated fire protection plans for areas where the national forests were intermingled with state and private lands.

J. Girvin Peters of the Forest Service recognized Cox for his progressive leadership when he prevailed upon the Minnesota forester to lead a discussion on state cooperation at the Weeks Law conference in 1913. According to Peters, Cox was the ideal person to address the issue, because "you have done a great deal in securing the cooperation and good-will of lumbermen in Minnesota."[7] The accolade was both appropriate and accurate.

Under Cox's leadership the Minnesota Forest Service was an aggressive publicist for cooperative fire protection. With improved enforcement of the fire laws, the state forester made progress in eliminating railroad-caused fires. He required companies to patrol their rights-of-way when the fire danger was high. Cox appointed William M. Byrne in charge of railroad fire protection, a position he held until he retired in 1949. Byrne slowly forced the railroads to take greater precautions with spark-arresting devices, to organize systems of patrols, and to keep their lines clear of burnable materials.[8]

In order for forest preservation to work in Minnesota, Cox asked for "the good will and active support of everyone." His cooperative fire protection network involved railroad and lumber companies, patrolmen in the organized towns, and the watchful eye of rural mail carriers. Beyond these, he also relied on Indian department personnel, the Weather Bureau, local fire-fighting organizations, rural fire brigades, and the Minnesota Forestry Association.[9]

Cox made a special effort to encourage organized townships to establish "fire funds," a legal step permitting them to levy a small tax to prevent and fight fires. These funds supported patrolmen who worked under the jurisdiction of the district rangers and were a valuable auxiliary to Minnesota's fire protection system. Cox frequently wrote to companies who paid a large share of a town's taxes to encourage them to promote local "fire funds" where none existed.[10]

The early Weeks Law inspection reports for Minnesota praised the state's "very liberal" forestry laws and the extensive power granted to its forester. These reviews commended the state forest service for the competence of its district rangers, a type "difficult to secure in some of the more eastern states." Although one report urged Cox to get into the field more often, it also noted that Minnesota forestry was "on a firm foundation" with "very little antagonism from the railroads or the large private owners."[11]

Federal inspectors also made suggestions for new methods of organizing fire protection. When the Forest Service drafted plans to upgrade its protection work on the national forests, it urged states to adopt similar procedures. In 1916 the Weeks Law inspector advised Minnesota to prepare fire plans for each ranger district "so that no time will be lost and no false moves made."[12] But when Minnesota suffered another wildfire disaster in 1918, the Cloquet–Moose Lake fire, there was no mention of the state's fire plan.

At this point Cox suddenly fell out of favor with the Forest Service district office in Denver. Whether the differences were personal and political or Cox suddenly became lackadasical in his administration of the Minnesota forestry agency is not clear. The recriminations between the state and district office eventually reverberated to Washington, where Cox enjoyed a reputation as a first-rate forester. And even here the Minnesota forester was found wanting (although the criticisms were based on district inspection reports).

Shortly after the 1918 fire, John McLaren, the Weeks Law inspector for the district, wrote a scathing criticism of the administration of the Minnesota Forest Service. His report referred to the lack of inspection work, the failure of the agency to establish a uniform policy for all of its ranger districts, and the low morale of field personnel. To eliminate these problems, McLaren recommended a more regular inspection of district activities, better supervision and written instructions for district patrolmen, and a firm administrative plan for coordinating directives from the state forester's office.[13]

As can be expected, Cox reacted strongly to the criticisms. To a colleague, he complained about the "accumulated regulations and instructions" that accompanied Weeks Law cooperation. Cox suspected that the extra red tape began when the Forest Service shifted the responsibility for administering the Weeks program from Washington to the district office in Denver. In a letter to the district office, he pointed to inadequate state appropriations for the inability of his office to provide satisfactory inspection and field supervision.[14]

Denver officials refused to accept the Minnesota forester's reasoning "that these things will be done if the legislature makes necessary provision for their accomplishment." In his inspection report McLaren argued that changes could be made despite a lack of funds. "These points do not appear to hinge on an increased appropriation," the district informed Cox; they "are matters of organization and administration" and could be accomplished "within your present limitation." For his part, the state forester thought the Denver people did not understand the intricacies of state work, which involved more "delicate" politicking than administering the national forests.[15]

One year after the Cloquet–Moose Lake fire, the district inspector reported "considerable improvement" in the supervision of the rangers and patrolmen, and in 1920, even more progress. Forest Service examiner J. A. Mitchell reported that fire protection in the state was "much better organized and administered than previous inspection reports would indicate." Minnesota's effort compared favorably with other states and was "considerably in advance" of that in neighboring Wisconsin and Michigan. But Mitchell also reported "friction and lack of harmony" and "dissatisfaction" in the state forest service. One year later, Mitchell again pointed to *"inadequate central office supervision"* as the agency's most serious shortcoming. [16]

The criticisms directed at the Minnesota agency were probably inherent in a decentralized organization that granted great autonomy to the district rangers. What state forester Cox and Weeks Law inspectors had praised at first, federal officials now found wanting. [17] By the early 1920s, however, more charitable Forest Service officials realized that Cox labored under severe financial constraints and that he was attempting to rectify the situation. Although Cox may have been lax in the management of his agency, the Denver office never fully appreciated his predicament as administrator of protection programs in a state with one of the worst fire problems in the country.

Minnesota joined with other Weeks Law cooperators in a coordinated effort to gain an increase in the federal government's contribution to fire protection. In a widely circulated letter, Cox pointed out that the Weeks Law contribution amounted to only $8,000 a year, whereas Minnesota was spending much more. Because of the government's interest in protecting the headwaters of the Mississippi River, Cox recommended an annual allotment of $40,000. [18] The Denver office reprimanded Cox for the request.

Several other states made similar requests to the Washington office. Oregon's state forester, Francis A. Elliott, wanted the federal allocation increased to $500,000, a figure Henry Graves cited to show that the government was not meeting its responsibilities. Because cooperating states were constantly asking for more money, Graves proposed an increase to $850,000, a figure he considered the absolute minimum to protect private and state forests adequately from fire. [19] State foresters like Elliott and Cox worked hard in the congressional lobbying campaign that finally convinced Congress in 1922 to increase the annual appropriation to $400,000.

Meanwhile, Cox survived a governor's attempt to emasculate the forestry agency, wrangled constantly with the state legislature for a larger fire protection fund, and conducted a running skirmish with the Forest Service over the efficiency of the state's administrative procedures. And unlike the states of the Pacific Northwest, Minnesota lacked strong protective associations. The vast cutover pinelands in the region simply did not offer the financial inducement to convince landowners that protection was worthwhile. In a letter to Gifford

Pinchot, Cox referred to a "conservative bunch of old lumbermen" who were "enemies of forestry" and opposed all progressive forestry legislation.[20]

Despite these handicaps, his peers thought of Cox as a leader in the state forestry movement, a fact recognized in his election as the first president of the Association of State Foresters in 1920. He had established the Minnesota Forest Service on a sound basis and (with meager salaries) had attracted a competent staff of field men. His system of decentralized administration and allocating great responsibility to the district rangers remained intact for several decades. And Cox made adjustments in reorganizing Minnesota's fire protection system, a point William Greeley recognized in a lengthy letter in 1922.[21]

During his tenure as state forester, Cox corresponded regularly with western forestry's E. T. Allen, the American Forestry Association (AFA), and the Society of American Foresters (SAF). With both the public and private sector, Cox emphasized the virtues of cooperation in forest protection. But in his native state he had created powerful enemies, even while he tried to keep "politics" out of the Minnesota Forest Service. His running battle with J. A. O. Preus, a former state auditor who was elected governor, resulted in his dismissal from office in 1924.[22]

Oregon and Washington

Like Minnesota, Oregon began its Weeks Law cooperation under a revised forestry code passed in the wake of the destructive fires of 1910. The new measure provided for an appointed board of forestry, a state forester, county fire wardens, the establishment of a regular fire season, and the regulation of burning permits; it also required operators to burn slash and to install spark arrestors on all logging equipment.[23] The law directed the state forester to make every effort to reduce the fire danger and to perpetuate the forest industries of the state. The main object of forest fire work, the state forester reported in 1912, "is to safeguard the present stands of timber until such time as they are cut or harvested."[24] The emphasis on fire in Oregon's forestry code was typical of most early legislation in heavily forested regions like the Pacific Northwest. Owners of the great virgin stands of

Douglas fir, cedar, ponderosa, and white pine wanted to protect that investment until harvest.

Oregon's forestry law also required the appointee to gather information about forest conditions, to encourage reforestation, and to seek improved methods of timber management. Under forester Francis A. Elliott's leadership, however, the state devoted nearly its entire biennial budget for forest protection work. The state forester's reports reflect the heavy presence of the timber industry's need to protect its property from fire.[25]

Elliott's summaries also underscore the importance of cooperative patrol associations in fire protection. The contribution of private landowners to forest protection proved, the Oregon forester said, that cooperation was essential, "the key note" to effective fire patrol. Elliott praised the Oregon Forest Fire Association as the central clearinghouse for patrol work. Beginning in 1912, the state forester's office and the Oregon Forest Fire Association coordinated their efforts to organize protective associations on a county basis.[26]

The forces that pushed the state of Washington to adopt modern forms of forest fire protection were similar to those in Oregon. Washington ranked twenty-first among the states in lumber production in 1869, sixth in 1899, and first for most of the next three decades. William Greeley once remarked that the people of Washington were "in the lumber business in the same way that all the citizens of Iowa are dependent upon corn, and the folks of the South are subjects of King Cotton." And this prodigious output underscored the importance of forest resources to the state. The value of its forest property stimulated an early interest in fire protection, and beginning with organizations like the Washington Forest Fire Association, the state slowly expanded its public and private protection system. Responding to the threat of fire to the great stands of merchantable timber, the state legislature enacted laws requiring logging railroads to provide patrols during the fire season. Similar measures, extended to passenger and freight rail systems, required spark arrestors and ash pans, and logging operators had to hire watchmen for a certain number of hours after work each day.[27]

The Washington Forest Fire Association was a much more centralized organization than its Oregon counterpart, which served as an umbrella organization for county protective associations. When Congress passed the Weeks Law, the Washington association's field personnel included a chief fire warden and district inspectors. Each of the district heads coordinated the work of rangers who patroled specified areas. As in Oregon, the private associations taxed themselves and provided a field force for fire protection.[28]

Washington's State Board of Forest Commissioners and the state forester used the first Weeks Law payment of $10,000 to place thirty-three additional patrolmen in the field during the 1911 fire season. These extra men divided patrol areas with district rangers and, according to the Washington fire association, maintained "a closer patrol . . . than ever before in the history of fire-fighting in Western Washington." And to improve protection work, the state agency, the fire association wardens, railroad officials, and lumber company representatives held joint meetings to coordinate their work for the fire season.[29]

Most of Washington's state forestry personnel served in supervisory capacities as deputy wardens at the county level. But the whole system could be jeopardized, as happened in 1913, when political changes occurred; in this case a newly elected governor placed his own appointee in the state forester's office. For the most part, however, cooperation between the fire association and the state was exceptional. In the spring of 1914 the state forester called a meeting of fire cooperators — county wardens, Forest Service personnel, and the Washington Forest Fire Association inspectors — to discuss mutual problems and to map a coordinated strategy for the coming fire season.[30]

Protection systems in both Oregon and Washingon had glaring weaknesses. In Oregon patroling private land was voluntary and many of the "backward timber owners" refused to join associations, reasoning that forest fires were an unavoidable evil. Then, in 1913, the State Board of Forestry and the Oregon Forest Fire Association successfully backed a measure to make it obligatory for timber owners to patrol their property. Its supporters intended Oregon's compulsory patrol law to persuade reluctant timber owners to join fire patrol organizations and to encourage landowners to form new associations. It worked. Within two years the acreage contributing to protection had more than doubled and landholders had formed eight new associations.[31]

74

Weeks Law funds also measurably aided the quality of forest fire protection in Oregon. Even with the limited allotment the state received in 1911, the state forester's office was able to place 32 additional patrolmen in the field during the critical part of the fire season, and in 1913 the department hired fifty-eight patrolmen with Weeks money. To stretch the federal contribution further, the state forester's office ordered county wardens not to hire patrolmen paid with Weeks funds until the most critical part of the fire season. "This plan," the forester reported in 1914, "made it possible to greatly increase the field force maintained by the private owners."[32]

Until the Washington legislature passed a compulsory patrol law in 1917, there also were repeated complaints in that state about timberland owners who did not contribute to the protection associations. Even in the western part of the state, where the Washington Forest Fire Association held sway, about one-third of the owners did not pay protection costs in 1915. As for the association, it avoided asking for compulsory patrol legislation, for it hoped that owners would voluntarily contribute to the protective associations "and thus avoid the necessity of compulsion." Eventually the state did adopt a compulsory patrol law that, in turn, spurred the formation of several new protective associations, most of them in eastern Washington.[33]

Washington's compulsory patrol law broadened the state's ability to extend is work to unprotected land. The patrol measure authorized the state to contract with the private fire associations to protect all properties within their areas, "whether owned by members of the association or assessed by the state." Increases in state appropriations and the growth of the protective associations made it possible to double the number of patrolmen in the field.[34] Protection was still uneven, however, and both the state and the associations had difficulty collecting assessments from uncooperative owners.

Washington's forest protection agencies cooperated extensively with the Forest Service in the construction of telephone lines and lookouts and eventually in sharing the expenses for air patrol. State and federal foresters joined with the Western Forestry and Conservation Association (WFCA) in 1919 to establish uniform procedures for reporting fires, to instruct patrolmen, and to agree on standard tools and equipment for fire-fighting crews. In that same year the legislature granted the state forester more authority in fire control work and slash burning.[35] But most of the state's protection still concentrated on keeping fires out of merchantable timber stands. The combined agencies fought fires on burned and cutover lands only when such fires threatened valuable standing timber.

In the early 1920s Washington timberland owners stepped up their appeals to state and federal officials for more adequate funding. In his annual report for 1921, Washington's forester pointed out that the state and federal appropriations had not kept pace with the increased costs for fire protection nor with the contributions of the private associations. The state forester cited spiraling wage and travel expenses for using up a larger percentage of the state's budget and forcing a shift in patrol responsibilities to the associations. Therefore, he recommended a larger patrol force, "particularly if we are to afford protection to young, growing timber," and an increase in Washington's share of the Weeks allotment from $8,000 to $75,000.[36] The congressional discussions about expanding the national fire protection program must have heartened the Washington forester.

Because Weeks Law expenditures contributed to only a small percentage of its total protection costs, Oregon also joined the growing chorus of states seeking a larger federal appropriation. The state's protection system, Elliott pointed out, extended only to merchantable stands of timber. What about the large acreages of cutover and burned-over lands, "the 'no man's land' in fire protection?" he asked. The state protected these areas only when fires threatened to spread to valuable standing timber, yet much of this land would produce a second crop of timber merely "for the price of adequate protection." He recommended an increase in the Weeks Law appropriation for the country to $500,000 annually and urged Oregonians to impress upon their congressmen the importance of protecting the state's resources.[37]

In the effort to increase federal assistance for fire protection on private lands, Oregon forestry officials took advantage of the growing influence of Republican Senator Charles McNary. Oregon and the Pacific Northwest also turned out many of the more prominent lumber industry spokesmen—individuals like E. T. Allen—who readily offered their expert testimony to congressional committees. This informal but influential group, representing the fastest growing lumber-producing region in the nation, wielded an increasing amount of power both in private and public affairs at the national level.

But Oregon's protection system was not without serious weaknesses. State forestry appropriations sometimes fluctuated wildly, and the protective associations on occasion had difficulty meeting their patrol obligations. In addition, there were numerous cases where timber owners failed to patrol their land or to contribute to a protective association. In at least one instance, a county protective association went to court to force a lumber company to pay its share of protection costs.[38]

The Weeks Law inspection reports for Oregon's forest protection system were favorable. While this may reflect an uncritical examination, the reports still suggest that the Oregon Department of Forestry was a moderately progressive organization and that the state had the most advanced forest protection requirements of its time. The annual commentaries praised the state forester's office for its field supervision and for hiring "experienced woodsmen" to fill the district warden positions. In Oregon's last inspection report under the Weeks Law, the investigator recommended better law enforcement in "changing the attitude of prosecutors, justices and juries, who often regard carelessness or incendiarism as trifling offenses."[39]

In addition to their Weeks Law program, the Oregon Department of Forestry and the Forest Service provided fire protection for the vast timber stands of the revested Oregon and California (O & C) railroad land grant. The Southern Pacific Railroad Company was responsible for these lands prior to 1913, but they were revested to the federal government in that year under a congressional order that directed the liquidation of the timber and the opening of the lands to settlers (with the Department of the Interior to administer the directive). The Forest Service protected the O & C lands lying within the boundaries of the national forests, and the Department of the Interior contracted with the state forester for the acreage outside the national forest boundaries.[40]

But the state's involvement in O & C cooperative protection work proved troublesome, mostly because of the congressional mandate requiring that the nontimbered lands be opened to settlers under the homestead law. Although only a small percentage of this acreage could be classified as agricultural, settlers filed entry with the hope that they would eventually prove up their claim. In their efforts to clear land of stumps, brush, and second growth fir, settlers set fire to their claims to burn the debris; many of these fires burned at will and destroyed reproduction on adjoining acreages. Wardens were reluctant to require burning permits because most of the settlers had no means to pay the fee and would wind up in jail.[41]

More critical than the destruction of reproducing timber, according to Oregon forestry officials, was the "moral effect this practice is having on the cooperating agencies." The failure to care for reproduction contradicted federal policy that advocated the protection and conservation of growing timber. While the Weeks Law and the O & C agreement required cooperators to protect all types of forest land, the federal government's policy of opening the grant to settlement encouraged the destruction of the forest.[42] The O & C lands remained a source of contention between federal departments and the state until Congress passed a management act for the former grant in 1937.

In the meantime, the Washington legislature had reorganized the state's administrative agencies in 1921, creating a new Department of Conservation and Development, which supervised five administrative jurisdictions, one of them the Division of Forestry. The new supervisor of forestry (formerly the state forester) was responsible to the department director. The supervisor coordinated the state's fire patrol work, administered the assessments against private timberland, disposed of logging slash, managed state-owned timber, and conducted investigations into reforestation.[43]

Before the legislature abolished the old Board of Forest Commissioners in the administrative reshuffling of 1921, the board issued a statement calling for the national forests to be ceded to the states. The request, a popular one at that time in Washington, prompted the legislature to pass a law permitting the Department of Conservation and Development to acquire cutover lands valued chiefly for growing timber, and in 1923 the state established a forest board to expand and manage Washington's state-owned lands.[44] This step marked the beginning of an aggressive expansion of the state's forest system, one of the largest in the United States.

Thus, before Congress passed the Clarke-McNary Act, timberland owners in Washington and the state's forestry agency had made considerable advances in fire protection, and some progress was made in protecting and reforesting burned and cutover lands. But before landowners could take on such a long-range investment, they argued, the state and federal government had to provide an incentive to do so. Miserly state budgets and the small Weeks contribution, lumbermen claimed, hampered adequate attention to nontimbered lands. Moreover, the protection association still labored under inefficient collection procedures that allowed large acreages to escape assessment.[45]

As part of the national move to adopt a forestry policy, Oregon officials also proposed a comprehensive program for the protection and management of its state and private lands. The thrust of the argument was that private enterprise could not carry the burden of fire protection and reforestation. Because the public had an interest in promoting forestry on private land, it should share the responsibility for protection costs and make it possible for timber owners to reforest their lands.

State forester Elliott also wanted the state to assure that the lumber industry had an adequate supply of timber for the future. His report for 1919 asked the federal government to investigate and classify all lands in the state as to their suitability for either agriculture or timber production. While the Forest Service was doing a commendable job of managing the national forests, Elliott warned, there were large acreages of private timber "being rapidly mined . . . and then left unproductive." Because this "logged-off, unproductive land" was a total economic loss, it was the state's responsibility to take action. "Private enterprise," he noted, "cannot be expected to . . . [grow] a crop which will not mature for sixty or more years." Interest rates were too high and the risks too great, therefore, "it is a state problem."[46]

In 1920 the Oregon State Board of Forestry adopted the "fundamental principles" of a forest policy to extend and perpetuate the state's forest industries and to provide adequate timber supplies for the future. Its recommendations were wide ranging, but "forest fire prevention and control" were the key features.[47] Because the future of forestry involved the public interest, lumber spokesmen argued, the state and federal government should provide a more favorable economic environment for private enterprise and contribute more to protect forests from fire. Oregon's forest policy statement of 1920 set the tone for the congressional testimony that preceded the passage of the Clarke-McNary Act in 1924.

When Congress increased the Weeks Law appropriation in 1922, it allotted each applicant a fixed percentage of the state's estimated cost for complete protection. Under the new formula, the federal government granted Oregon $28,000 and directed the state to use the fund to extend protection to burned, cutover, and other unprotected lands. The state forester's office, in turn, allotted most of the money to the contracting forest protection agencies (a practice begun in 1920 when the Forest Service simply reimbursed the state for part of its total protection costs rather than paying patrolmen directly from federal funds).[48]

The Oregon Department of Forestry was a mature, well-managed agency by the mid-1920s. Although the department devoted most of its attention to fire prevention and protection, its annual reports make increasing reference to insect infestations, the "depredations" of pine beetles, and preliminary investigations of white pine blister rust. And its fire protection work, which at first focused largely on merchantable timber, had become more efficient and better coordinated. The department gradually extended protection to burned and cutover areas, a recognition that these lands were valuable for timber production. Other states copied Oregon's compulsory patrol law, considered by many the most advanced forest protection law at the time. The state's progressive legislation and its relatively efficient forestry department can be attributed to the close cooperation between public leaders and the powerful influence of private timber owners who wanted to protect valuable forest property from fire.

Georgia

At the turn of the century, Georgia's forests still constituted the state's greatest natural resource, despite a dramatic increase in lumber production in the state in the last quarter of the nineteenth century. In fact, Georgia ranked second behind Arkansas in 1899 in the volume of lumber produced in the South. During these years cotton plantations replaced the diminishing stands of timber as the production of cotton fiber rose dramatically in the state.[49]

The sharp drop in lumber output and the dismal condition of forestlands in Georgia eventually prompted a few scattered attempts at conservation. The University of Georgia, with a private endowment, established a school of forestry in 1906, the first southern institution to grant forestry degrees. At the same time university faculty organized the short-lived Georgia Forestry Association. But with the exception of a very small number of private owners, Georgia forestry remained dormant until after the First World War. And except for purchases under the Weeks Law to establish national forests in the state, federal cooperation made no impact upon Georgia.[50]

Meanwhile, Georgia's lumber production declined by more than one-third in the first two decades of the twentieth century. To make matters worse, the Forest Service reported 23,000 forest fires in the state between 1916 and 1921. Conservative estimates suggest that these fires burned almost one-third of the state's forestland. The statistics, of course, are incomplete, as Georgia had no agency or protective organization to gather such data.[51]

But there were stirrings of change across the southland, stimulated in large measure by the work of the Southern Forestry Congress, an organization devoted to the establishment of state forestry agencies in the southern states. The Georgia Forestry Association, moribund for several years, was "reorganized" in 1921. The association subsequently was successful in getting the legislature to establish the Georgia State Board of Forestry in 1925. But even then, the state's first forest officer, B. M. Lufburrow, went without pay for eight months and his office was located in space made available by the Atlanta Chamber of Commerce.[52] Participation in federal forestry programs was a later development.

Forestry Agencies in the Northeast

While fire protection in the western timbered states had a slow and fitful development, organized protection in the more populous northeastern states did not move much faster. In New York and Pennsylvania an expanding state forest and park system occupied most of the time and money of forestry officials. Following a series of railroad-caused fires in 1903 and 1908, the New York legislature established procedures for regulating trains in the state's forest preserves. Although New York consistently spent more money than most states for its forestry work, it is difficult to compare its accomplishments with states having strong private protective associations. In addition, New York spent an increasing amount of money for mountain parkland adjacent to urban areas, and the forestry agency initiated a progressive tree planting program in 1908 when it began distributing nursery stock to landowners at cost.[53]

Despite the pioneering forestry efforts of Joseph Rothrock, Pennsylvania's commitment to fire protection was limited at the beginning of the twentieth century. But in other ways the state moved ahead. Like New York, it distributed nursery stock at cost to private owners, and its forestry commission directed an aggressive planting program on state lands. Pennsylvania also made a significant effort to expand its state forests, and it was the first state to appropriate funds to fight the chestnut blight when the general assembly provided $275,000 to begin research on the disease in 1911. Finally, when the state's forest commissioner, Gifford Pinchot, established an effective fire protection network in 1920, Pennsylvania had one of the most progressive forestry agencies in the country.[54]

Maine and Massachusetts also developed modern state forestry programs early in the twentieth century. In Maine, where lumber and pulp interests were influential, the legislature allotted $10,000 to protect the vast interior forests when severe fires hit the state in 1903. Six years later the state's lawmakers established the Maine Forestry District, which taxed landowners to support a fire control program. Despite the development of a low-cost sharing arrangement in fire control work and its qualification for Weeks fund assistance, Maine's forestry activity was limited until the late 1920s.[55] The state's industrial forestry groups restricted the agency's work to keeping fire from the woods.

In 1904 the Massachusetts legislature established its first office of state forester, whose duties included assisting landowners, issuing publications, and establishing a state nursery. The state also purchased planting stock from Germany that introduced the white pine blister rust organism to the United States, a situation where a seemingly progressive idea led to catastrophe. Massachusetts also served as the point of entry (this time from France) for the gypsy moth, and the legislature first appropriated funds to fight the pest in 1890. When the legislature placed the state's "moth superintendent" under the state forester in 1909, its appropriations for moth control surpassed the budget for the entire forestry agency.[56] The broader responsibilities of the Massachusetts forestry agency reflect the state's more diversified economic base and its growing urban population. The gypsy moth threatened the parks and tree-lined streets of Boston as well as the timber stands in the western parts of the state.

Summary

The development of state forestry programs in the United States was an uneven process, and its initial focus in most sections of the country was fire protection. The record shows that states with large volumes of standing timber were among the first to organize protection systems. Lumber entrepreneurs who purchased large acreages of virgin forestland in the Pacific Northwest pioneered these private and state efforts in an attempt to protect their properties from fire. State agencies and private organizations paid less attention to burned and cutover lands until long-range investment opportunities had improved. By 1920 the more progressive of the state agencies had broadened their work to include reforestation and efforts to control diseases and insect infestations.

In the South, where forest liquidation was in full swing in the early twentieth century, timber owners and state legislatures were slower to act. Social and economic forces deeply embedded in southern culture hindered state action and cast deep suspicion upon any form of federal activity. To be sure, there were impressive examples like Henry E. Hardtner's reforestation work at Urania, Louisiana, the showcase plantations of the Great Southern Lumber Company around Bogalusa, and the tireless efforts of the forest-missionary, Austin Cary; and several southern states qualified for Weeks Law cooperative funds. But most public and private foresters agreed that the South lagged behind other regions in the development of forestry policies. By the 1920s, however, some southerners began to realize the tremendous productivity of their forests. Clarke-McNary provided a valuable opportunity to assure the protection of that investment.

The forestry situation in the Great Lakes states was mixed. Either agricultural or industrial activity had surpassed forest products in economic importance in Michigan, Wisconsin, and Minnesota by the 1920s. But the region still possessed a sizable land base suited only for forest growth. Its major problems were to prevent forest fires from destroying reproduction and to reforest the vast burned and cutover acreages in all three states. Clarke-McNary offered a federal subsidy to encourage reforestation and to improve the region's fire protection capability.

Chapter Six

According to William Greeley's biographer, the Clarke-McNary Act was the forester's "greatest personal monument." And Greeley, who sat in the Republican cloakroom during the final arguments over the measure, remarked that after "four years of controversy, it was a great thrill to be in at the kill." The act, he said, "opened up new fields of cooperation between federal and local agencies, ended a prolonged controversy, and launched an era of good will and joint effort." David T. Mason, a young forester from Oregon, told Senator Charles Mc-Nary that the act would "be considered in future years a turning point in the history of American forests." And Wilson Compton of the influential National Lumber Manufacturers Association (NLMA) called the legislation a wise "approach to permanent forestry settlements."[1] These expressions indicate that, except for a dissident voice or two, a broad consensus of foresters and lumbermen supported the measure.

The four years that preceded the passage of the Clarke-McNary Act were the beginning of a prolonged debate over the issue of federal regulation that lasted into the 1950s. The principle of federal cooperative assistance to states and private forest owners, however, was not the subject of disagreement. Henry Graves had sketched the outline for a national forestry program in 1919, and in the ensuing years William Greeley of the Forest Service, E. T. Allen of the Western Forestry and Conservation Association (WFCA), and prominent lumber industrialists debated the issues and eventually settled upon the measure passed in 1924. The Clarke-McNary Act expanded federal assistance to states for fire protection, provided matching funds to establish nurseries, authorized the enlargement of the national forest system, and appropriated federal funds to study state forest tax policy.

Issues behind the National Forest Policy Debate

Although the main story here is the background to the Clarke-Mc-Nary Law, the debate that took place between 1919 and 1923 gave rise to a wide-ranging discussion of forest policy that centered on cooperation versus regulation. The four years of dialogue served as a forum for addressing important social and economic considerations related to forestry and the proper role of federal and state governments in forestry policy. The issues raised in the discussion were only partly resolved when Congress, under heavy lobbying pressure from the forest industries, opted for a program of federal forestry assistance to states without any regulatory strings attached. Industry officials argued that such a policy would strengthen the lumber business and ultimately benefit the public. Others, like Gifford Pinchot, were more skeptical.

The experiences of the First World War helped shape and direct the forest policy debate. Organized lumbermen feared emergency wartime measures that had the potential to place restrictions on the lumber trade. L. C. Boyle, legal counsel for the NLMA, warned that war conditions might "precipitate legislation" that would involve the natural resource industries. Boyle urged the NLMA to avoid propaganda that would prejudice the public against the industry. For the most part, however, lumbermen found the war relationship with the federal government lucrative and positive. Federal agencies and trade associations cooperated to channel labor agitation for higher wages and shorter hours into "acceptable" directions; lumber organization leaders like John Henry Kirby of the Southern Pine Association (SPA) served as administrators of government procurement efforts; and enlarged federal appropriations to the Forest Products Laboratory in Madison, Wisconsin, led to dramatic advances in wood products research.[2]

The war also deeply influenced the restless mind of young Wilson Compton, who formulated his own plan to resolve the lumber industry's problems with overcapitalization and declining profits. Shortly after the armistice of November, 1918, Compton, now the secretary-manager of the NLMA, urged lumbermen to use the cordial relationships established with government agencies during the war as a precedent for shaping future legislative policy.[3] The Forest Service loomed large in Compton's scheme.

Although Henry Graves initiated the Forest Service discussion for formulating a comprehensive forest policy, other members of the agency preceded him in calling for a broad federal commitment to forestry. In an interoffice memorandum in 1917, J. Girvin Peters pointed out that the Weeks Law recognized a federal obligation to participate in the protection of the forested watersheds of navigable streams because of the enormous public interest involved.[4] In the same year, the self-trained forestry consultant, Austin Cary, observed that economic conditions would determine forest policy. And, far away in the Pacific Northwest, Burt Kirkland of the University of Washington's school of forestry called for a larger subsidy to the private sector to encourage forest management. But, he insisted, such a policy should be locally designed and administered, thus avoiding the "new imperialism" characteristic of most federal programs.[5]

These proposals addressed a variety of issues—forest fire protection, taxes on timberland, and reforestation. In the South, where timber harvesting had denuded forestland, some owners formed organizations to sell the cutover areas for farmland. Kirby, president of the NLMA in 1918, argued that the rapid liquidation of southern forests called for a federal policy that included purchase of cutover lands, creation of new national forests, and reforestation.[6] Industry spokesmen from virtually every forest region in the country testified to the need for a greater federal role. Thus, when Henry Graves initiated the dialogue in 1919, he usually addressed informed and receptive audiences.

Like other government agencies, the Forest Service experienced an "unsettled period" when the war ended. It had to readjust to peacetime conditions, resuming conventional research and meeting its cooperative obligation to the states. Although these adjustments were not as dramatic as those following the Second World War, the agency still had major problems. Despite this, chief forester Henry Graves chose the immediate postwar period to outline a national forest policy. In the spring and summer of 1919 he addressed several lumbermen's groups and stressed the need to extend the practice of forestry to private lands.[7]

Graves first mentioned the potential for an expanded federal role in an address to the American Lumber Congress in the spring of 1919. The lumberman's problems of overproduction, excessive mill capacity, and lack of organization, he pointed out, had persisted for some time. For its part, the government could not overlook these conditions, nor could it ignore "the relation of the forest and its industries to the . . . communities in which they are located." Graves proposed that the public and the timber owners share "the burden of securing the objectives that are essential to safeguard the public welfare." He outlined a program of federal and state legislation that involved extensive cooperation between lumbermen and public agencies.[8] Although the proposal lacked detail, it established the framework for the ensuing public debate.

Graves also hinted at regulatory measures that would require protection against fire, the "conservative production of lumber, and right methods of removal." These requirements, he suggested, should be tailored to each region and might include "a combination of several methods of cooperation." Public support, in other words, meant some form of accountability. Graves anticipated a form of sustained yield production when he proposed a far-reaching cooperative scheme for the West, "where public and private lands are intermingled and economically interrelated." A broad policy of forest development would contribute to "permanent mills and all that means to the employment question."[9]

But the centerpiece to the forester's argument was his request that lumbermen cooperate in "laying the groundwork" for a national forest policy. And, in a refrain that became familiar in the 1930s under the National Recovery Administration, Graves proposed that the Forest Service delegate authority to the lumber industry to assist in formulating solutions to "our present forest and lumber problems."[10] In his public statements, Graves hinted at requirements for proper forestry practice in exchange for federal assistance, but he never made explicitly clear whether these were to be federal or state requirements.

The NLMA joined Henry Graves in supporting the "early development of an American forest policy," and the industry journal, *Lumber*, urged "a practical program of reforestation of areas, denuded either by the saw or by fire." The trade paper also pointed to the obvious— lumbermen "should have an active interest in its wise solutions." The perpetually active E. T. Allen proposed that each of the regional trade associations appoint committees to confer with local, state, and federal authorities to determine "needful and practicable" approaches. But no "general regulations" should be imposed through a federal program, Allen argued, because "forestry problems are largely local." Kirby stated publicly that existing tax laws prohibited timber owners from reforesting their lands; therefore, he declared, the federal government had a responsibility to pay the costs for reforestation because it "acts for all the people." [11]

Lumbermen from most of the timber-growing regions supported an expanded federal policy. W. R. Brown, of the Berlin Mills of New Hampshire, cited the need for a more accurate timber census, federal and state purchase and reforestation of burned and cutover lands, a permanent fire protection policy, and reasonable taxation of forest land. At a meeting in Portland, Oregon, Allen told Graves that the public "should pay most of the bills" for federal fire protection and reforestation programs; lumbermen should not be required to make an "unbalanced sacrifice." Allen urged the Forest Service, "as the leader of the public interest," to present the industry's side intelligently and sympathetically. Finally, he noted that all else was "secondary to our greatest forest problem — fire"; its resolution was "the outstanding demand upon all of us." [12]

The forestry policy debate eventually involved the *Journal of Forestry* and *American Forests,* two of the major sources of information on current forest issues. Royal S. Kellogg, the principal organizer of the National Forestry Program Committee (NFPC), an industry-oriented political action group, wrote an essay for *American Forests* outlining a program of federal and state responsibility for reforestation, a census to determine timber supplies, federal purchase of cutover lands, and more federal assistance for fire protection. Compton followed Kellogg with a call for a greater public responsibility for fire protection and reforestation. [13]

But in the *Journal of Forestry,* the official publication of the Society of American Foresters (SAF), the public debate reached a feverish pitch. An SAF committee chaired by Pinchot published a report in late 1919 urging the federal government to regulate cutting practices on private timberland. Because lumbermen could not be expected to change their ways, "the lines are plainly drawn"; the choice was between "the convenience of the lumbermen and the public good." The Pinchot report cited the "nonproductive wastes of blackened stumps and bleaching snags" as justification for federal regulation. [14] Industry leaders immediately saw the Pinchot proposal as a threat to their version of harmony and "cooperation."

The Debate Moves to the Legislative Arena

In the midst of the furor over the Pinchot report, the Woodrow Wilson administration appointed William Greeley to head the Forest Service. The new chief, of course, had already established himself as a proponent of federal cooperation to help alleviate the lumber industry's critical economic problems. Beginning with his work as district forester in Missoula, Montana, and later as principal author of the 1917 report on the lumber industry, Greeley had attempted to lessen the hostility and suspicion between lumbermen and the public. The proper route to practical forestry, he said, was close cooperation between industry and public agencies. Greeley also opposed public controls to encourage the practice of forestry. [15]

The supporters of "cooperation" were better organized and more influential than the advocates of federal regulation. Pinchot, the leader of the proponents of regulation, became involved in the Pennsylvania governor's race in 1922, a period when Greeley and the NFFC were consolidating their move for a federal program of cooperative assistance channeled through the states. That process involved extensive collaboration between the chief forester and prominent industrial leaders like Allen, Kellogg, and Compton.

The Pinchot report, which predicted a timber shortage, prompted Senator Arthur Capper of Kansas to introduce a resolution in the Senate ordering the Forest Service to investigate the nation's forestry situation. Known as the Capper report, the study bore Greeley's trademark — federal and state agencies and the private sector should cooperate to stop timber depletion. It argued that the public had a responsibility to share the costs of fire protection and to provide an equitable system of taxation. The study recommended six proposals for consideration: (1) increased cooperation with states in fire protection, (2) expansion of the national forests, (3) restocking burned and cutover federal lands, (4) a study of forest taxation and insurance, (5) a survey of forest resources, and (6) larger appropriations for forest research.[16] The recommendations in the Capper report were subsequently embodied in the Clarke-McNary Law.

Although chief forester Greeley feared that some lumbermen opposed the Forest Service proposal, he told a meeting of the Service committee that most lumbermen supported "our program." Greeley persistently hammered away that the issue was a national one requiring federal leadership and a large measure of assistance to states. But the key issue and the one on which there was "practical unanimity of agreement," Greeley insisted, was the need for a national program of forest fire protection.[17]

To broaden support for the Forest Service proposal, the chief forester requested all state foresters to meet in Atlantic City, New Jersey, in November, 1920. J. Girvin Peters asked Minnesota state forester William T. Cox to attend, because the proposed legislation "will really mean much more to the States than to the Forest Service." Cox assured Peters that he supported "the big things that you and Greely [*sic*] and the others are shaping up." For his part, Pinchot suspected that the purpose of the Atlantic City meeting was "not to consider which is the best plan, but how the Forest Service plan can be carried out." He accused Greeley of pushing state control "over a problem which is distinctly the concern of the whole nation." But state forestry officials subsequently endorsed the Forest Service recommendations despite Pinchot's admonitions.[18]

The Pennsylvania commissioner's suspicions were correct. Greeley told the state foresters that he favored extending cooperative assistance to states "not only in fire prevention but in any phase of forestry or forest research, including planting." But reducing the fire hazard and "bringing all classes of forest lands" under systematic protection were the first priorities. The purpose of federal policy in fire protection, he told the gathering, was "to influence the course of State legislation toward imposing specific obligations upon the land owner."[19] When lumbermen, mostly from the South, objected to any form of federal requirement, Greeley dropped even this modest prerequisite for assistance.

After the Atlantic City meeting, the state foresters regrouped in Harrisburg, Pennsylvania, at the invitation of Pinchot to form the State Foresters Association (the name was changed to the National Association of State Foresters in 1964). At this gathering Pinchot and Greeley "drew the battle line" and aired their differences from the same rostrum—Pinchot demanding federal regulation and the chief forester opting for state requirements. In January, 1921, Greeley told the New York Lumber Association that he sought to integrate state forest organizations into national policy without imposing federal regulations on private forestland. In his judgment, the government could "best lead the movement for reforestation not by dictation to the forest owner but by cooperation" and financial assistance.[20]

While the Forest Service carried the banner for federal cooperation, the NLMA appointed a forestry committee in 1920 that backed most of the Forest Service recommendations, including the proposal to increase appropriations for research. And Allen, who disapproved of the "extreme Pinchot doctrines," worked hard for the association's congressional campaign and kept his watchful eye on federal legislation that might include "regulatory requirements."[21]

The two alternative forest policy proposals were the subject of intermittent legislative debate for nearly three years. The Pinchot program, requiring federal regulation of private forestland, never achieved the congressional backing to pose a serious threat to the Greeley plan. The chief forester worked closely with the industry-oriented NFPC and its most prominent members, Kellogg and Allen. In his autobiography, Greeley referred to Kellogg as the committee's most "indefatigable worker" and Allen as "its master strategist." For his part, Allen thought Greeley should "be given much consideration" in planning strategy.[22] Although Allen and Greeley differed over technical aspects of the legislative proposal, they agreed on the broader outline of the committee's forestry legislation.

Although some lumbermen disapproved of state regulation, they supported most of the elements of the Forest Service program—the fire protection subsidy, studies of state tax systems, increased appropriations for forest research, and an expanded national forest network. Finally, to speed congressional work on forestry legislation, Allen convinced Greeley to drop any reference to state regulatory requirements and to focus on a broad program of fire protection.[23] From this point, the chief forester emphasized federal cooperative assistance in fire protection as the central feature of his legislative proposal.

In January, 1923, the Senate established the Select Committee on Reforestation to conduct hearings and draft a national forest policy. Oregon's Senator Charles McNary chaired the committee, and Kellogg assisted with scheduling arrangements and established a close working relationship between the Senate investigators and the NFPC. As chief forester, Greeley provided the committee with expert counsel at its hearings in the different forest regions of the country.[24]

At the close of the hearings in the fall of 1923, John W. Blodgett, president of the NLMA, warned the committee against placing restrictions on federal cooperation in fire protection. The government, he said, "should have the right to withhold, but not the right to prescribe." Allen, who recalled in later years that the Senate committee valued "our neutral expert reputation," cautioned that the government should not act as "the prescriber of rules and regulations," but should cooperate on an equal basis. And in a verbal slap at Pinchot, Allen criticized forest reformers who masqueraded as "crusaders," but who had not been "informed on the economics of the situation." The solution to the forest problem, he told the committee, was a larger appropriation for fire protection and federal support for reforestation.[25]

The bulk of the testimony to the McNary committee created the impression that foresters and lumbermen shared a broad consensus on forest policy. Except for one or two appeals for federal regulation, including those of Pinchot, Pennsylvania's new governor, Kellogg and Greeley had skillfully arranged witnesses who persistently stressed the association between the industry's economic health and the "public interest." The Clarke-McNary Law, Kellogg confided late in life, established "the principle of federal cooperation" and routed the proponents of federal regulation.[26] The issue of federal controls over private timberland did not become a public issue again until the mid-1930s, and then under vastly different circumstances.

The Clarke-McNary measure passed both houses of Congress, and President Calvin Coolidge signed the bill into law in June, 1924. The main thrust of the legislation was to increase federal assistance to state and private forestry programs. Section 2 offered expanded federal aid to states in fire protection and removed the Weeks Law restriction that limited the use of federal funds to the forested watersheds of navigable streams. Section 3 authorized the use of federal funds to assist states in studying tax laws and their influence on forest management. To encourage the growing of windbreaks and farm forests, Section 4 of the act provided assistance to states for nurseries. Other Clarke-McNary features included federal cooperation with states to assist with farm forestry projects, an expanded national forest system, and a survey of timberland in the United States.[27]

The Chicago-based *American Lumberman,* the most widely circulated lumber journal in the country, hailed Clarke-McNary as "one more step toward sound forestry." Wilson Compton told the annual meeting of the American Forestry Association (AFA) that the Clarke-McNary Law pointed the "way to a complete forestry solution." But George Long, the veteran manager of the Weyerhaeuser Timber Company, cautioned Allen to let "the constructive work and the suggestions" come from the Forest Service, "we having, of course, much to do with helping them arrive at conclusions."[28]

Forest products leaders had assured that the Clarke-McNary Act prescribed no silvicultural practices for private timberlands, nor did it limit lumber business activity. They had done their lobbying well. Trade officials hoped that the cooperative assistance programs would help stabilize the lumber market and protect the valuable stands of merchantable timber.

Greeley's Professionalism Challenged

The fact that lumbermen overwhelmingly supported the Clarke-McNary legislation is evidence that they had achieved their objective in the prolonged forestry policy debate. The "socialistic" proposals of Pinchot had been swept aside and the policies of Greeley had emerged triumphant. But while Greeley and his cohorts were herding the legislation through Congress, there were rumblings of discontent, some coming from the ranks of the Forest Service.

During the long public debate, some professional foresters, including members of the Forest Service, thought Greeley was being too friendly with lumber industry leaders. Pinchot had criticized the chief forester and the Forest Service legislative proposal in his several testimonies to congressional committees. And Pinchot's supporters in the service, like Raphael Zon, were convinced that Greeley had sold out to big lumbermen.[29] These accusations apparently bothered the chief who took pride in his professionalism.

With the passage of Clarke-McNary assured, Greeley circulated a lengthy memorandum in which he reviewed past policy and suggested a redirection for future work. In its early years, he noted, the Forest Service offered forestry assistance to landowners, but after Congess transferred the national forests to the Department of Agriculture, the agency devoted less attention to timber growing on private land. Because "the conditions affecting the feasibility of private timber growing . . . [had] materially changed," Greeley urged service heads and supervisors "to make it clear that assistance to private land owners . . . is just as much a part of the job of the Forest Service as it ever was." "The Forest Service," the chief made clear, "must be the foremost leader in this movement."[30]

Greeley warned the staff that the Forest Service could "no longer expect to hold the distinctive and largely unchallenged position of leadership" that it enjoyed in the past. But this challenge should encourage federal foresters to "be alert and aggressive" in offering assistance and advice to landowners; this was "part of the job" of every Forest Service employee.[31]

But most interesting in his long message was Greeley's call for a renewed professionalism. For some time, he said, the Forest Service had worked closely with lumbermen and timberland owners, and in its approach, the agency "deliberately sought to be 'practical.'" Then, in words that sounded much like his professional critics, Greeley cautioned the federal foresters:

I frankly fear that too many members of the Forest Service have absorbed the "practical" point of view so far that they have partially lost their professional vision and their professional punch as foresters. I fear that we have been overawed by the compound interest bugaboo and have too often accepted, without challenge, the common reaction of timberland owners that "it can't be done."

We must of course keep our feet on the ground. We must understand the conditions and limitations of the business. . . . But let us not lose our vision. Timber growing on private lands . . . is bound to come. And in this . . . the men who keep their foresight unclouded and attack their own problems in the light of the big controlling economic factors are the men who succeed.[32]

The chief's circular had both the hint of a confessional and a confusing and ambiguous charge to service personnel. The term "practical" was a Greeley trademark, a reference that he employed regularly in talks before lumbermen's organizations and other commercial groups. The word appears frequently in his 1917 study, *Some Public and Economic Aspects of the Lumber Industry*. To be "practical" meant to understand "the big controlling economic factors" and to act in accord with them. It meant government "cooperation" with industry to promote timber growing, and it meant a "public" responsibility to assist the industry to achieve these ends.

Clarke-McNary Guidelines

Although the Clarke-McNary Act established broad outlines for cooperative work, the Forest Service still had to establish the administrative details and formal requirements. And when it became apparent that changes were in order, Congress amended the act to include fire protection assistance for nontimbered lands "or watersheds from which water is secured for domestic use or irrigation." This modification extended cooperative protection to the chapparal-covered slopes of southern California.[33] The chief forester and district heads resolved most of the other questions that arose in administering the law.

In an effort to clarify protection requirements and to obtain the views of western operators, Greeley forwarded a tentative policy statement to the annual meeting of the WFCA in December, 1924. He listed three requirements as the basis for cooperation with states: (1) they must be organized on a permanent basis, (2) protection must be statewide and required by law, and (3) states must provide protection for all classes of land—"timbered, cut over and burned."[34] The federal carrot, therefore, would extend to states with properly accredited forestry agencies that could guarantee protection for all state and private lands.

States with private protection associations but lacking a formal protection agency were not eligible for Clarke-McNary funds. And the federal government allowed private expenditures to be included with state protection costs only where they were required by law. To assure that federal funds were properly matched, the protection had to be "permanent in principle and based upon a written agreement between the state and the private agency."[35]

But the Forest Service was flexible; for a limited time it accepted voluntary matching funds in cases where state requirements and compulsory patrol laws did not exist. In an explanatory memorandum to state forestry officials, Greeley pointed to the compulsory patrol laws in Oregon and Washington as the "ideal basis for private participation" in the costs of protection. As a rule of thumb, the chief forester envisioned landowners and the public each contributing half of the protection costs (with state and federal agencies providing an equal share of the public's responsibility).[36]

As the next few years proved, the administration of the Clarke-McNary Law reflected changes in the field and the needs of state forestry agencies. The extensive correspondence and memoranda in the Forest Service files show that Greeley sought the advice of district foresters, state forestry agencies, and private protection organizations like the WFCA. For its part, the western forestry group was confident that federal policy was "broad enough" to permit modification. This confidence was well placed. In his annual report for 1925, Greeley modified the requirement for "permanency" of state protection systems to "reasonable assurance of permanency."[37] In other words, the system permitted great latitude to states in their protection systems.

Implementing Clarke-McNary

The Clarke-McNary Act was the first federal law to offer substantial assistance to the owners of small farm forest properties. Although federal interest in farm forestry can be traced to the Division of Forestry and its famous Circular No. 21, most of this assistance went to large landholders and mill owners. But the Smith-Lever Act of 1914, which permitted large-scale federal-state cooperation in agricultural extension work, was the first real boost to farm forestry. By 1922 ten states had forestry specialists on their extension staffs, although many of these worked on a part-time basis.[38] Farm forestry, therefore, made little progress until it was included as part of the Clarke-McNary program.

Despite its heavy work load in administering the national forests, the Forest Service had taken an active interest in advancing forestry on small ownerships. In 1912 chief forester Henry Graves appointed Wilbur R. Mattoon as the first extension forester. And when the Department of Agriculture established the States Relations Service, Mattoon became its forestry extension specialist.[39]

As part of its push for a national forest policy in the early 1920s, the Forest Service stepped up its interest in extending assistance to small holdings. The Service Committee discussed the issue of restoring the productivity of eastern forestlands in January, 1922. W. W. Ashe proposed three approaches to encourage small owners to practice forestry—establishment of exemplary forests, demonstration work with large landholders similar to Austin Cary's efforts, and extension activity. Ashe suggested that foresters be placed under county agents as the most feasible way to reach small owners.[40]

Mattoon told the committee that the extension branch of the States Relation Service was the best way to assist woodlot owners. But, he said, the Forest Service had shown less interest in extension work than most of the other bureaus. Mattoon suggested that the Forest Service should improve its cooperation with other federal and state agencies. Claude R. Tillotson thought the Forest Service should ask for $200,000 for extension work with large landholders; the service, he said, had not paid enough attention to the owners of large tracts of timber. E. E. Carter observed that even though county agents were not forestry specialists, their work could be beneficial.[41]

Greeley supported extension assistance for farm woodlots in his annual report for 1923 because they had developed a valuable "educational machine" for reaching small woodland owners. Finally, when the passage of Clarke-McNary was assured, Greeley issued a policy statement on cooperation between the Forest Service and the Extension Service. He noted that "forestry education would seem to depend . . . upon the existence and cooperation of an effective State Forestry Department and a strong State Extension Service." Greeley urged the forestry agency and the extension service in each state to work out a plan of cooperation for farm forestry programs.[42]

But cooperation proved difficult to implement because state forestry departments and the Extension Service vied with each other for similar programs. When the Forest Service attempted to implement

Section 5 of the Clarke-McNary Law, the secretary of agriculture issued a memorandum dividing responsibility for extension forestry between the two agencies. Under the agreement, state agricultural colleges employed the extension forester who served as a representative of the Department of Agriculture. However, problems continued to plague the program in many states and the old jurisdictional jealousies persisted.[43]

The Clarke-McNary Act was the first important federal measure to move from the field of public to private forestry. Its authorization for assistance in tree planting and farm forestry opened new fields of cooperation to the Forest Service. Although fire protection still received the greatest share of federal and state appropriations, the 1924 law established the principle of management assistance to farmers.[44] The effectiveness of the farm forestry programs depended on economic conditions, the generosity of federal budgetmakers, and the powerful influence of the NLMA.

Section 4 of the Clarke-McNary Act applied to the nursery part of farm reforestation. The requirement for federal cooperation was similar to that for fire protection — federal expenditures could not exceed state appropriations and the Forest Service limited the program to farms. As a general rule the Forest Service carried out its Section 4 work through state forestry departments. But federal officials agreed to tailor cooperation to "whatever policy may be in effect in a State."[45] Meager appropriations, however, limited the effectiveness of these early farm forestry programs.

Most of the Section 4 work took place in the Northeast and in the shelterbelt region of the Great Plains. Because state agencies in New England, New York, and Pennsylvania had active nursery programs, they were able to take advantage of the token $2,000 federal matching funds in their tree distribution activities. Reports from the Plains region, however, show that tree planting was still at the experimental stage. Moreover, the Plains states were tardy in providing matching funds to qualify for the federal contribution. Wilmon Droze, an authority on tree planting in the Plains states, concludes that Clarke-McNary "was not the solution to the problem of tree planting."[46]

The distribution of Clarke-McNary funds underscores the importance of fire protection to organized lumbermen. During the fiscal year 1927, federal expenditures for fire protection totaled $710,000, while Congress allocated $75,000 for distributing planting stock to farmers. The government appropriated an even smaller amount, $50,000, for farm forestry extension. In the next few years these differences widened.[47] Although there were small increases for farm forestry, appropriations for fire protection far surpassed the modest funds designated for distributing planting stock and conducting extension work.

The powerful influence of major lumber trade groups, especially those from the Pacific Northwest, explains much of the story. For several years E. T. Allen led the protests and plotted strategies to gain increases in cooperative fire protection funds. He worked closely with Greeley in arranging the testimony of major lumber producers and state foresters before congressional budget committees. Allen cited statistical reports to show that the federal government had failed to carry out the Clarke-McNary agreement. And, on occasion, he hinted that the failure of cooperation might reopen the debate over national policy.

When the Coolidge administration proposed a $660,000 budget for "fire work" in 1925, Allen told Greeley that the amount was "so little more than the present $400,000 that it gives the appearance to the McNary program of being little more than new verbiage to gouge a little more money out of Congress." He thought the states could qualify for $1 million. Although he understood that the chief forester was "not as free to act as I have been [led] to think," he warned Greeley that people expected much more from the new program.[48] In this instance, the budget item remained the same, but in subsequent years Allen had more success.

When the House budget committee added $50,000 to the Clarke-McNary fire fund for 1927, Greeley told Allen that he appreciated the "assistance which you gave on these questions." And when the tight-fisted Coolidge administration attempted to prevent increases for the Clarke-McNary fund in 1928, Allen thought the proposed budget "would kill the Clarke-McNary law as a national policy standing for Federal cooperation instead of Federal police power." He proposed that a "delegation of businessmen" travel to Washington "and make the whole picture entirely clear" to the president.[49]

Allen also sent the chief forester a series of tables "to show that national forests, by having less money for prevention, actually spent

Table 2: Appropriations for State Cooperation, 1927–1929

	Amount Appropriated for Fiscal Year		
Item	1927	1928	1929
For the prevention and suppression of forest fires and for the forest taxation inquiry (secs. 1–3 of the Clarke-McNary Law)	$710,000	$1,000,000	$1,200,000
For the distribution of forest planting stock to farmers (sec. 4 of the law)	75,000	75,000	75,000
For farm forestry extension (sec. 5 of the law)	50,000	60,000	60,000

more in emergency funds to fight fires." Finally, a lumbermen's delegation met with President Coolidge in October, 1926, to ask the administration to "hold up its end" in fire protection. The Clarke-McNary Law, they pointed out, assumed that fire prevention was the "foundation step" to reforestation, and that state and private agencies had responded well to the challenge.[50] Their request detailed funding increases for fire protection on the national forests, for Clarke-McNary fire cooperation, and for weather forecasting; it made no reference to appropriations for tree planting or farm forestry extension activity.

These efforts eventually were successful. Greeley confidentially informed Allen late in October that the president and the budget director had agreed to increase the cooperative fire fund to $1 million, "a liberal treatment of the fire requirements." The chief forester thought the lumbermen's presentation to the president "had very much to do with the favorable action," and he thanked Allen for his "part in bringing it about."[51] Table 2 offers a comparison of the appropriations under the first five sections of the Clarke-McNary Law.[52]

The Clarke-McNary Law firmly established federal assistance as the main feature of the Forest Service effort to promote forestry in the states. Henry Graves thought it made "an effort to remove the more important obstacles to private forestry," and it provided security against "destruction and serious injury by fire." But to make Clarke-McNary a success, Graves urged the public "to cooperate in a liberal spirit with private owners." The sometimes skeptical forestry dean warned, however, that fire protection did not constitute the sole issue. In the South and the Pacific Northwest there was "a feverish haste to cut the choicest of the last remaining bodies of timber" with little effort to restock the lands.[53] Although Graves liked the thrust of the Clarke-McNary program, he was less hopeful about its success than the chief forester.

For his part, Greeley believed that the Clarke-McNary programs "had passed the ball back to the States." Because forestry was a localized activity, the legislation provided states with the opportunity to carry out that mission. But, as practical men, Greeley warned his staff that it would "take a long time for a great economic movement of this nature to work itself out." The chief forester thought the public would carry out its part because of the "genuineness and mutuality of the cooperation."[54] Until the awesome depression of the 1930s began to tear at the social fabric, there were no serious challenges to Greeley's version of cooperation.

When the Forest Service updated its cooperative manual in 1927 to include the Clarke-McNary programs, assistant forester E. E. Carter drafted a memorandum that juxtaposed two alternatives for federal forestry. One he called "the leadership of the big stick," in which the Forest Service would dominate state forestry departments. This line of activity, he contended, would "make the offices of the State Foresters inhospitable ground for Forest Service officials" and very likely bring an end to cooperation. On the other hand, the service could continue its present "cooperative program," which provided states with "the utmost freedom to work out their own problems" without the dictation of the federal government. The Forest Service, Carter concluded, could "point with pride to a record of legislative achievement and of patient and cooperative fair dealing with the States. Shall we scrap it?"[55] The large volume of correspondence between the Forest Service and state agencies argued for a continuation of the Clarke-McNary formula.

When Greeley resigned from the Forest Service in 1928 to accept an executive position with the West Coast Lumbermen's Association, his ideas were firmly established in legislative and agency policy. There were no strong challenges to his policies of integrating public and private sectors in forestry work until the economic collapse and social demoralization of the 1930s. Greeley's supporters pointed to the "splendid" accomplishments "through cooperation with local agencies under Federal leadership." The number of cooperating states had grown from eleven under the first Weeks Law allotment to thirty-eight at the end of 1927. During the same period, federal expenditures had increased from $37,000 to $710,000 and state and private expenditures from $220,000 to $3,450,000.[56]

While the Forest Service paraded statistics to prove the benefits of federal cooperation, its internal memoranda and annual reports make clear that the practice of forestry was a matter of economics. Although fire control was basic, most foresters viewed protection as merely a preliminary step to forest management. Greeley's successor, Robert Y. Stuart, reported that private owners seldom practiced forest management beyond the effort to control fire. Regional trade groups, although they thought reforestation desirable, argued that the depressed market for forest products hindered such practices. A Forest Service staff member reported that lumbermen in the South had little interest in what happened to the land once the timber was harvested.[57]

Summary

The lumber industry's problems increased as the decade of the 1920s advanced. Substitute building materials and a decline in construction contributed to a drop in lumber consumption after 1925. Wilson Compton noted that the "ill-adjusted production in the lumber industry" required attention before forestry practices could be implemented. Ward Shepard, a professional forester, chastised the industry for practicing "economic fatalism," an argument, he said, that furnished "an automatic, all-inclusive, and awe-inspiring alibi to the long tale of forest destruction and waste." The once lofty hopes for a national forest policy resulted only in cooperative fire protection, and when the timber was gone, Shepard warned, even this program might be compromised.[58]

As it did in agriculture, the Great Depression came early to the lumber industry. And when economic decline spread to other sectors of the American economy, national lumber consumption fell even more dramatically. The Clarke-McNary programs, of course, were not intended to meet a national emergency of the kind that developed in the 1930s. Therefore, many of its provisions were buried in an avalanche of forestry-related emergency programs designed to put people back to work and to aid a faltering economy. The Great Depression was not the first time the Forest Service was involved in emergency programs, nor would it be the last.

Chapter Seven

Since the days of the old forestry division, federal foresters have participated in a variety of cooperative activities ranging from collaborative research with universities and colleges to joint surveys with state
agencies. To add to this workload, presidential administrations and
the Congress frequently turned to its "scientific" bureaus, including
the Forest Service, to provide the federal government with information. These responsibilities underscore the fact that widely disparate
circumstances gave rise to Forest Service programs. Although other
departments and bureaus might have primary responsibility for a particular line of work, the Forest Service frequently served as coinvesti-
gator when its expertise was involved.

As these responsibilities increased, the service added to its staff
range management and water resource specialists, experts in silvicultural research, lumber economists, personnel trained in tropical
forestry, and wood products researchers for its Madison, Wisconsin,
laboratory. The programs that enabled the Forest Service to expand its
fields of operation included: (1) cooperation with the Bureau of Indian
Affairs, (2) regulating grazing on the national forests, (3) interagency
efforts to control insect and disease infestations, (4) recreation policies, (5) cooperative research programs, (6) gathering statistics, and
(7) responding to national emergencies like the First World War.

The Forest Service used its expanded workload with great skill.
The Washington office encouraged its researchers and coinvestigators
to cooperate fully in liaison work beyond the agency, but it wanted

full credit for these activities, undoubtedly with future appropriations battles in mind.

A *Grab Bag of Cooperative Activity*

Until the Bureau of Indian Affairs established its own forestry agency in 1910, the Department of the Interior contracted with the Department of Agriculture for assistance in managing timberlands on Indian reservations. Gifford Pinchot enjoyed free rein in handling reservation forests until he crossed swords with Interior Secretary Richard Ballinger in 1909. Ballinger quickly abrogated a 1908 agreement between Agriculture and Interior, President William Howard Taft fired Pinchot, and the Forest Service was no longer responsible for Indian forests.[1]

But Ballinger's decision did not preclude cooperative fire protection agreements between the two departments. From all indications, however, the Forest Service was cautious in asserting itself in Indian forestry matters. When he was district forester in Missoula, Montana, William Greeley advised the service not to offer assistance to reservations "until it is requested by them." Assertive action, he contended, "would be likely to make them feel that the Forest Service is taking action in affairs outside its immediate province."[2] Despite Greeley's caution, the Forest Service signed several cooperative protection agreements in areas where Indian and national forest lands intermingled.

Federal relations with western grazing interests have provided one of the longest and most hotly contested forums between the public and private sector. While western sheep and cattlemen wanted cheap and easy access to federal forestlands, government foresters attempted to control both access and the number of grazing animals. Although a court decision in 1911 gave the Forest Service the right to charge grazing fees, stockmen resisted. When the service raised the grazing fee—a matter of great concern because grazing was the dominant use of the national forests during the early years—western interests threatened to dilute the agency's authority. Despite scandalously low fees, grazing receipts surpassed timber income for most of the years between 1905 and 1921.[3]

Grazing policy has always been a major responsibility in the management of the national forests. The minutes of the Service Committee, the extended references in annual reports, and the influence of grazing administrators in the Forest Service heirarchy all point to the importance of grazing. To lessen potential friction Pinchot directed the Branch of Grazing, established in 1908, to coordinate its work with state boards of agriculture and the Department of the Interior.[4] And the Forest Service worked out compromises with groups like the National Wool Growers' Association and the American National Livestock Association.

To improve its relations with grazing permittees, the Forest Service also cooperated with local advisory boards. On some occasions, the district forester granted local associations responsibility for enforcing management of the ranges. And to improve its relationship with grazers, heads of the Branch of Grazing regularly attended meetings of the stockmen's associations. In 1922 federal foresters and western livestock representatives revised the Forest Service grazing manual, a feat the service called one "of the outstanding examples of cooperation" for the year. And in times of economic distress, service personnel suggested that better range management would help stabilize the industry.[5]

Despite its sometimes contentious relationship with western grazing interests, the Forest Service strived to establish an equitable arrangement with stockmen. The Washington office had to balance the powerful congressional influence of cattle and sheepmen against other users of the national forests—urbanites who wanted healthy watersheds, preservationists who favored an untrammeled forest environment, and, of course, lumbermen.

One of the least-heralded Forest Service projects, but an activity increasingly important to the lumber business, was the agency's work in collecting and publishing statistics on the forest products trade. Trade leaders reasoned that knowledge about market conditions would assist lumbermen in business decisions and bring about a more orderly lumber economy. Trade journals praised the Forest Service for its statistical compilations, criticized congressional efforts to limit the activity, and urged trade associations to cooperate with the federal agency.[6]

Although both Bernhard Fernow and Pinchot published annual statistics on the production and consumption of lumber, no one appreciated their significance until the second decade of the twentieth century. Finally, under Secretary of Commerce Herbert Hoover, the Forest Service established regular procedures with the Department of Commerce for publishing this information. Actually, forestry officials had published lumber price lists as early as 1907, and they had furnished data to the Bureau of Corporations in its great study of the lumber industry. Between 1914 and 1917 the service cooperated with the Bureau of Foreign and Domestic Commerce and the Federal Trade Commission to gather statistics for a study of the lumber business. Secretary of Agriculture D. F. Houston argued that this form of cooperation would promote "the right kind of constructive relationship between public agencies and an important group of industries."[7]

When the Bureau of the Census threatened to discontinue its annual reports on lumber production in 1913, the Forest Service fought hard to maintain this service. At a meeting of the Service Committee Greeley suggested that state foresters and lumber associations cooperate in gathering the data; another staff member proposed that the Department of Agriculture's Bureau of Statistics handle the job. Finally, the major trade associations offered their assistance in gathering data, and the agriculture bureau promised to publish the figures.[8]

Samuel Dana reported to the Service Committee in February, 1916, that the National Lumber Manufacturers Association (NLMA) had contributed $1,000 to assist in the collection of lumber production statistics. When the Justice Department began investigating lumber associations for antitrust activities in the early 1920s, Forest Service statistical reports became even more important to lumbermen. The Department of Commerce under the active Hoover also joined the reporting network with its monthly, *Survey of Current Business*.[9] Thus, despite prohibitions against some trade practices, two friendly government agencies continued to provide lumber associations with vital services.

Cooperation in Insect and Disease Control

In the early twentieth century Forest Service personnel initiated a series of cooperative ventures to fight insect and disease infestations. The service cooperated with the Bureau of Entomology and its Division of Forest Insect Investigations. The federal study of forest entomology began when the Division of Entomology appointed D. A.

Hopkins to investigate the forests of the Pacific coast during the summer of 1899. Soon afterward the division established its Office of Forest Insect Investigations and appointed Hopkins as its first director.[10]

For several years the Division of Entomology (elevated to bureau status in 1904) directed most forest insect investigations with the financial assistance and cooperation of federal foresters. The federal agency used the same cooperative procedures in forest pathology work. The Bureau of Plant Industry investigated forest diseases with assistance from federal forestry officials.[11]

The Service Committee discussed the possibility of assigning forest pathologists from the Bureau of Plant Industry to each Forest Service district in 1909. The bureau already operated several stations that were actively engaged in forest investigations. In one instance, the Forest Service and the Bureau of Plant Industry reported that the only way to destroy the gypsy moth was to cut down every infected oak tree.[12] In light of recent failures in gypsy moth control, the 1911 report has a startlingly modern ring to it.

The Forest Service cooperated closely with the Bureau of Plant Industry's Office of Blister Rust Control. When New York foresters discovered an outbreak of white pine blister rust in 1909, a group of foresters and pathologists met regularly to plan methods to control the disease. When the disease spread to the white pine forests of the Great Lakes states and the Far West, the Office of Blister Rust Control and the Forest Service drafted a formal memorandum of understanding. To speed the fight against the fungus, the Forest Service offered its facilities to house personnel from the blister rust control office, as was the case when the disease spread to the Pacific Northwest in the early 1920s.[13]

Because the Forest Service already had working relationships with state forestry offices, it initiated many of the federal insect and disease control programs. The Bureau of Plant Industry and the Bureau of Entomology provided the expertise and direction for field activities. And the intermingled federal, state, and private ownership patterns in the West invariably made pest and disease work a federal responsibility.

A bark beetle infestation in southern Oregon and northern California provides a good example. The Bureau of Entomology began investigating the beetle infestation in 1915. Because the outbreak involved private, state, and national forests, an Indian reservation, and Oregon and California railroad grant land, the Oregon Department of Forestry and the Forest Service requested federal support. Congress appropriated $150,000 for control work on government land providing that other ownerships cooperated. The Forest Service reported in 1922 the "gratifying cooperation between the Department of the Interior, the State of Oregon, the owners of private land, the Bureau of Entomology, and this service" in the beetle control effort. [14]

State forestry agencies in New England organized the earliest and most effective control program to combat disease and insect infestations. Forest pathologists cooperated with large timberland owners, urban parks commissions, and state and federal agencies to devise control techniques. But despite these early beginnings in insect and disease control, the activities remained a scattered responsibility until 1947, when Congress passed the Forest Pest Control Act in an effort to unify private, state, and federal programs.

Recreation and National Parks

Although timberland management was the major Forest Service responsibility, the agency adjusted policy to embrace changing public attitudes toward the national forests. When automobiles provided a means for middle-class urban Americans to travel to the federal forests, recreation potential became a major issue. Because the Forest Service considered recreation a lesser use, the agency responded slowly to this new public interest in the national forests. Supporters of the national parks, like the Sierra Club, accused the service of opposing the park system. There was truth to this charge, because both Pinchot and Henry Graves opposed the strict preservationist creed of park supporters. [15] Finally, the establishment of the National Park Service in 1916 put the Forest Service on the defensive and forced it to reevaluate its recreation stance.

A recent study of Forest Service recreation policy argues that the agency's interest in recreation grew out of its desire to prevent the creation of a parks bureau in the Department of the Interior. The lengthy discussions at Service Committee meetings and the increase in Forest Service news releases devoted to recreation support this claim. Herbert Smith shrewdly predicted in 1915 that the automobile would enhance the recreational value of the national forests; the service, he said, should take advantage of this opportunity to improve its public image.[16]

Confronted with strong public support for a national park system, the Forest Service grudgingly cooperated with the new bureau on its proposals for additions to the parks. At the same time, federal foresters pushed their own recreation programs more aggressively. In 1917 Graves appointed a professional landscape architect, Frank A. Waugh, to develop recreational facilities for the national forests. Waugh's reports emphasized the growing importance of outdoor recreation and recommended that all national forest land was suitable for such use.[17]

Graves also began to exploit the recreation theme for its publicity value. In January, 1917, he went before the American Forestry Association (AFA) to praise the "superb scenery and unexcelled recreation attraction" of the national forests. He cited the number of visitors who "came in automobiles and used the roads built by the Forest Service" and told the association that the service was "planning systematically and far ahead" to develop its recreational resources.[18] The Forest Service finally established an administrative program for recreation after the First World War.

When hostilities in Europe ended, the Forest Service hired a young landscape engineer, Arthur H. Carhart, to develop a recreation plan for the Rocky Mountain district. During the next two years Carhart worked with recreation associations to promote public use of the district's national forests. The collaboration between commercial groups and the Forest Service to promote recreation in the Rocky Mountain district proved to be Carhart's most significant contribution to developing recreation policy on the national forests.[19]

The Forest Service took full advantage of the growing commercial interest in recreation. Carhart and others wrote articles for business publications to promote the "municipal playgrounds in the forests." One journal announced that the Forest Service was "bringing the great outdoors to the city dweller," another that all roads "lead to the National Forests." A southern magazine noted that the "isolation and remoteness" of the southern Appalachians were being eliminated and urged its readers to take to the mountains as "New England's pleasure seekers" had been doing for years.[20] These commercial journals provided an ideal outlet for Forest Service public relations personnel who wrote most of the articles.

As chief forester, Greeley carried on a close working relationship with the National Park Service, although he opposed the transfer to the parks of scenic national forest lands. As a matter of practical politics he ordered district foresters to cooperate with the National Park Service to promote the idea that the two agencies complemented each other in recreation policy. But some of the old Forest Service jealousy toward the new agency persisted, as in the case of a Forest Service map of California forests that left the national parks as blank spaces. And Stephen Mather, director of the Park Service, ruffled federal foresters when he opposed appropriations for Forest Service recreation programs.[21] These abrasive relations persisted for decades, reflecting the conflicting jurisdictions and competition for congressional appropriations for outdoor recreation.

And congressional support for Forest Service recreation was grudgingly slow. When Congress approved only $10,000 for sanitary facilities in the national forests in 1922, Carhart resigned. Although Greeley requested more money for recreational facilities in the national forests, Congress appropriated only small sums. Forest Service recreation activities remained at a low level until the 1930s and the unemployment relief programs of Franklin D. Roosevelt.[22] The magnificient structures built during the Depression years made recreation an important priority, a tendency that gained momentum with the growing affluence of the 1950s.

Research

While Forest Service planning for recreation labored under meager budgets and without lumber industry support, one of the agency's major program areas — research — fared much better. From its inception under the German-trained Bernhard Fernow, federally funded forest research expanded in the first two decades of the twentieth century to include several regionally based forest experiment stations, the Forest Products Laboratory, and finally the establishment of the Branch of Research in 1915. The major trade associations and professional forestry organizations supported the expansion of the agency's research capability.

The more progressive trade leaders understood the value of government research. One liberal-minded executive urged the government to conduct research "requiring special equipment or specially trained men for researches of an elusive character which may require considerable expenditure and a long period of time." The regional trade associations, he thought, would complement federal work with their own specialized investigations. By the 1930s the regional experiment stations were investigating state and private forestry problems as well as those important to the management of the national forests.[23]

The Branch of Research conducted economic studies, an increasingly important avenue of research to the forest products business. The research branch also gathered most of the information for Greeley's study of economic conditions in the lumber industry, in which the Forest Service undertook the technical investigations to determine the "more profitable utilization of timber and better methods of manufacturing." But the major objective was to secure "more stable and healthy conditions" for forest industries.[24] Thus, from its inception Forest Service research embraced issues of vital economic importance to lumbermen. And when appropriations bills came before the Congress, the service could always call upon influential trade leaders like E. T. Allen or Wilson Compton for support.

Lumber trade leaders also supported reforestation studies on the national forests. And for their part, Forest Service personnel investigated artificial methods of extracting seed from lodgepole pine cones; the relation between seeds germinating in the greenhouse and in the field; the effects of seed source on the growth of trees; and other reforestation experiments of value to lumbermen. Fire research, of course, was an ongoing federal activity that had its beginnings early in the Pinchot administration and eventually evolved into a complex system with great regional variation.[25]

Both of the major twentieth-century wars had a dramatic effect on Forest Service research. In his annual report for 1918 Graves remarked that the European war had made "numerous and important demands on Forest Service technical knowledge," and he reported that the agency had halted all investigations not associated with the war effort. The most important war-related research activity concerned wood products — studies of specialized materials used in wagons and other vehicles, rifle stocks, airplanes, and shipping containers. To meet these needs, the Forest Service placed "practically the entire research organization . . . on special war investigations."[26] The evidence indicates that the service labored hard to cooperate with military departments and the war industries.

Cooperation with the War Department enabled the Forest Service to expand its research capability. The department channeled appropriations to the Forest Products Laboratory in Madison to examine wood materials used in airplane construction and to conduct box tests. Earle Clapp, who headed the Branch of Research, reported that these investigations would have been impossible without War Department funding. And to accommodate the need for more space, the University of Wisconsin provided the laboratory with an additional large building.[27]

When the war ended, congressional cutbacks in military expenditures sharply reduced money for Forest Service research. But war-related research did not end with hostilities because the War Department commissioned new studies of wood properties for airplane construction. And as part of its peacetime conversion, the service sought to disseminate its new research information to wood-using industries. After a decade of operation, the Madison laboratory proudly announced that its investigations were saving industry $30 million annually.[28] However, frugal congressional budgets continued to hamper the work of the Branch of Research during the 1920s.

In an effort to neutralize fiscal conservatives in Congress, the Forest Service enlisted the support of lumber trade leaders to obtain adequate appropriations for its experiment stations and the Forest Products Laboratory. When Congress threatened to cut the budget for the forest experiment station at Berkeley, California, in 1925, a California lumberman asked Allen to use his influence to secure the original appropriation. And one trade official told Greeley that the activities of the Forest Products Laboratory were "the most constructive aid that the lumber industry has ever had for working out a solution of these economic questions." He urged Congress to make a larger appropriation "so that further scientific research may be made by the laboratory."[29]

The National Forestry Program Committee (NFPC) and its chairman, Royal Kellogg, remained active after the passage of the Clarke-McNary Law and worked with the NLMA and the Forest Service to support forest research. Compton pushed hard for more funds for the Madison laboratory, suggesting in 1925 that "several key men in the industry" should go before Congress and request better facilities for forest products research. One year later both Compton and Kellogg met with Senator Charles McNary to plot strategy to restore a budget item for the Forest Products Laboratory.[30] In addition, the NLMA office advised its members to write their senators and representatives about such matters.

With the support of the lumber industry, the Forest Service launched a major effort in the mid-1920s to gain permanent statutory status for its research activities. Led by Clapp, service personnel worked with professional foresters and industry leaders to push for a larger Forest Service research program. Clapp's proposal, outlined in detail to the Service Committee in April, 1926, embraced four classes of research: (1) silvicultural, (2) grazing, (3) forest products, and (4) forest economics. Clapp argued that his program would serve private forest landowners, state agencies, lumber manufacturers, and consumers and would redound to the conservation needs of the country and a healthy and permanent lumber industry.[31]

Although Clapp's research plan included benefits for nearly everyone, the leading forest products groups stood to gain the most. The receptiveness of trade associations to the proposal indicates its industrial thrust. The scheme also anticipated the expanding Forest Service research programs of the post–World War II era—cooperation with the Bureaus of Plant and Animal Industry, Agricultural Economics, and the Biological Survey. But, the overriding need, Clapp said, was an organic act covering forest research.[32] Clapp himself had a genius for detailed program development, an ability clearly apparent in his contributions to the Copeland report seven years later.

The Forest Service and its artful research head gained their objective when Congress passed the McSweeney-McNary Act in 1928. The measure authorized $3 million for an expanded forest and range experiment system and research in forest products, a nationwide survey of forest resources, and a study of future requirements for forest products. As the bill made its way through Congress, the leadership of the NLMA and its regional affiliates lobbied hard for its success. Royal Kellogg thanked C. S. Chapman, the Weyerhaeuser Timber Company forester, for "doing all that is necessary" on behalf of the bill. And Clapp worked behind the scenes to coordinate strategy with Kellogg on the selection of people to testify before Congress. Clapp was confident that the two of them could arrange "a very influential and representative group" for the hearings.[33]

A broad consensus of support contributed to the passage of the McSweeney-McNary legislation. A recent writer points out that the measure "was based on the cooperative principle and provided a broad charter for forestry research." It established for forest research what Clarke-McNary did for fire protection—an integration of private needs with public policy and a program of public assistance to achieve private ends. The major benefits of the act would accrue to the industrial groups that had lobbied hard for its passage; the measure leaned toward Raphael Zon's earlier prophecy that most scientific research was "utilized by those who controlled the economic power of the country."[34] For the next several decades the Forest Service and leaders of the forest products industry pressed congressmen for the full appropriation authorized under the measure.

Cooperation in Wartime and Other Emergencies

The First World War influenced Forest Service cooperative programs other than research. The war-related demand for forest products caused a sharp increase in lumber production and a corresponding neglect of forestry practices in the field. Lumbermen speeded up logging activity in the southern pineries, circumstances that brought an unaccustomed and short-lived prosperity to otherwise beleaguered backcountry mill towns. In the Pacific Northwest an equally impressive increase in production occurred. Greeley related later that war demands took "as much as a full year of peacetime production."[35] Both the industry's production needs and the military conscription programs affected the work of the Forest Service; personnel shortages curbed fire protection on the national forests, and some of the agency's top officials, like Greeley, joined the military and served overseas.

The Forest Service worked closely with the War Department's Spruce Production Corporation to speed the harvesting and milling of spruce in the coastal forests of the Northwest. Although the spruce corporation never produced a single piece of wood that found its way aloft during the war, its complement of 30,000 officers and men represented a sizable part of the logging and lumber workforce in the region and played a major role in breaking strikes led by the Industrial Workers of the World. At war's end, some of the corporation's timber holdings were transferred to the Forest Service; other timber properties, mills, and railroads were sold on the open market.[36]

The Forest Service was involved in war mobilization in more informal ways. Shortly after the United States declared war, the agency's chief of state cooperation, J. Girvin Peters, issued a circular to all state foresters calling for "surveillance and intelligence work in connection with national defense." Peters requested protection personnel to report to the Department of Justice or the local law enforcement officials the operation of wireless apparatus, "remarks directed to affect enlistments," efforts at property destruction, seditious or treasonable remarks, firearms "held by alien enemies," and "suspicious persons."[37] Clearly, this exercise in snooping, conceived as an agreement between the Justice Department and the super patriotic American Protective League, reflected a government move to counter antiwar sentiment.

In cooperation with the Federal Fuel Administration, the Forest Service joined in a publicity campaign to increase the use of wood fuel in forested districts, a move that presumably would increase the availability of coal and oil for war-related needs. In a related move Graves enlisted the aid of the Boy Scouts of America to conduct a census of the black walnut, a wood well adapted for airplane propellers and gunstocks. The forest resources of the country, he observed, "will undoubtedly be a very important factor in the winning of the war."[38]

Graves also requested state foresters to help with the black walnut survey. The chief forester asked them to inform farmers about the government's need for black walnut, its market value, and where it could be sold. Because the job was "impossible" for the Forest Service to handle alone, state foresters "can be of real service to these owners." Evidently there was confusion in the hectic chase after black walnut, because the War Industries Board also asked William T. Cox, Minnesota's state forester, for information about the availability of the wood and hinted that it was conducting its own survey.[39]

Forest Service cooperation during the war was, in some respects, an extension of its liaison with state foresters and the lumber trade organizations. In 1917 the Forest Service already cooperated through well-established programs in the Northeast, the Great Lakes states, and in the Far West. Therefore, the agency's war-related work in these regions was more extensive than in the South, where there was little federal land and where state forestry agencies were relatively undeveloped.

Other emergencies influenced Forest Service programs. When the lower Mississippi River turned into a raging torrent in the spring of 1927, critics charged that the destruction of forests on headwater streams was solely responsible for the floods. The Forest Service Office of Information issued a news release stating that flood control of the Mississippi was *both* an engineering and a reforestation problem, and Greeley met with representatives from the Mississippi valley to discuss the flood issue.[40]

In his annual report, the chief forester said that stopping floods on the Mississippi was "fundamentally an engineering problem," but in the upper reaches of its major tributaries good forest management could measureably slow runoff and lessen the potential for flooding.[41] The Mississippi flood of 1927 was a major catalyst for congressional action on flood control programs that involved extended cooperation between the Forest Service, other federal bureaus, and state agencies.

Early Cooperation with Local Governments

Although urban forestry is a phenomenon of the era after World War Two, the Forest Service has a long record of cooperative work with municipal governments. In the days of the old forestry division, urban conservation leaders supported the establishment of forest reserves to protect metropolitan watersheds. The Oregon Alpine Club lobbied successfully in the early 1890s for the creation of three federal reserves—the Bull Run timber reserve to protect the city of Portland's water supply, the Ashland watershed reserve, and the Cascade Range Reserve. Today the Bull Run and Ashland reserves are special units in the national forests managed under cooperative agreements between municipal governments and the Forest Service. In southern California civic leaders provided a broad consensus of support for establishing reserves to protect watersheds for the population growth taking place in the Los Angeles lowlands.[42] This common bond between federal foresters and local governments to protect urban watersheds carried over into the twentieth century.

While the Forest Service was willing to cooperate in managing municipal watersheds, it opposed urban efforts to secure title to these forests. When the city of Seattle floated the idea of gaining title to national forest lands east of the city, Forest Service leaders thought it would set a bad precedent and encourage other urban governments to make similar moves. In a Service Committee meeting staff members argued that the federal agency was best fitted to manage forests to assure maximum conditions to sustain water flow. Graves concurred with staff sentiment—there was no reason to transfer these areas to the jurisdiction of cities.[43] Forest Service officials feared the precedence of the Seattle case, but its opposition to such transfers was not always successful.

In a related case in 1919 the Forest Service signed a cooperative agreement with Salt Lake City to manage its watershed lying within the boundaries of the national forests. The contract specified that the federal agency would maintain full control over the area and manage the timberland. Albert Potter, a member of the Service Committee, thought the agreement was a satisfactory one for the Forest Service.[44] The Salt Lake City arrangement was one of several the agency signed with municipal governments whose watersheds were within the boundaries of the national forests.

Federal cooperative programs assisted community forestry in still other ways. In the New England states, where municipal forests were more numerous, the Weeks Law provided assistance in fire protection. These town forests often served as community watersheds, and sometimes they provided a modest revenue from timber sales. The expansion of federal assistance under the Clarke-McNary programs speeded the reforestation of community forests and enhanced the states' abilities to offer technical assistance to local governments.[45]

According to Greeley's report for 1925, town forests covered more than 500,000 acres, most of them located in the New England states, New York, and Pennsylvania. The chief forester praised this advance in forestry for protecting municipal water supplies and providing local recreation areas and revenue from timber sales.[46] The system of community-owned forests continued to expand, especially in the 1930s when urban and county governments took over large acreages of tax-delinquent land. And the Forest Service consistently supported the municipal forest movement because it was another way to increase the nation's timber production.

Summary

At the onset of the Great Depression, the Forest Service had both statutory and indirect channels for cooperation with states, county and local governments, and the private sector. And as one of the government's natural resource agencies, it assisted other federal bureaus and departments in times of national emergency. Its decentralized administrative network, which provided considerable autonomy to branch chiefs and regional foresters, gave the service a flexibility that other federal administrative bodies lacked. The economic and social crisis of the 1930s severely tested this administrative flexibility and created a situation of near chaos because of the great expansion in cooperative work.

But the service was well equipped for these increased responsibilities. It enjoyed a full complement of dedicated career officers with years of policy and administrative experience. Many of these were principled men of broad vision who strived mightily to establish a social basis for forest policy. Robert Y. Stuart, successor to William Greeley and chief forester until his tragic death in 1933, had an abiding concern for the stability of lumbering communities. Ferdinand A. Silcox, who followed Stuart, was even more forceful in stressing the social relationship among forestry, industrial life, and community stability. If the lumber industry did not meet its social responsibilities and obligations, Silcox believed, the government must force it to do so. Earle Clapp, who had been close to policy decisions in Washington for more than twenty years, finished out the decade as acting chief and served until 1943.

There were other veteran officers who provided wise counsel during these years. Raphael Zon, director of the Lakes States Experiment Station since 1926, was closely involved in the research and planning for the shelterbelt project; Earl Peirce headed up the Division of State Cooperation in the late 1930s and directed the salvage work after the New England hurricane of 1938; Robert Marshall, young, radical, and abrasive, wrote the recreation component of the Copeland report and served in several influential positions until his untimely death in 1939; Ward Shepard, former assistant to Clapp, worked for the Indian Forest Service, served as a research fellow at Harvard University, and had close ties to the Roosevelt administration; others important in policy decisions were E. A. Sherman, Ed Munns, Fred Morrell, and regional heads like Lyle Watts in the Pacific Northwest. And operating on the fringes of service policy through his incessant letter writing and close friendship with Marshall and Zon lurked the ageless figure of Gifford Pinchot.

Chapter Eight

Reflecting upon his years as a public and private forester at the close of
the turbulent 1930s, William Greeley offered some candid observations to his son, Arthur. Businessmen, he said, should have primary
responsibility for changing forest enterprise from a process of speculation and quick liquidation to a system of continuous production. But,
he suggested, "the Government has got to help in a number of important ways," and federal foresters and "professional conservationists"
need to consider the problem "in their thinking and planning."[1]
Greeley's summary was at the heart of a running debate during the
1930s between federal foresters and leaders of the forest products industry. The matter concerned fundamental political differences about
the relationship between federal forestry programs and the private
sector.

When the dramatic market collapse of the early 1930s disrupted
established forms of cooperation and created discord, federal foresters
and lumber industrialists were sharply divided over proposals to stabilize business activity and lower unemployment. Some forestry officials wanted to require improved forestry practices from the industry
in exchange for government assistance; others (both in public and private employment) argued that the government should merely provide
conventional incentives with no strings attached.

The Depression was a complex and shattering experience for American capitalism. Industrial leaders played fast and loose with a variety
of syndical-like solutions to their problems. And with equal vigor
they fought social programs that threatened to undermine their au-

tonomy. Some of the lumber industry's favored proposals went sour when they became public policy, and when members of Congress or the Forest Service countered with measures that would exact regulatory concessions in exchange for assistance, the lumber trade lobbied heavily to defeat them.

The discussion here focuses on early moves to alleviate contracting markets in the lumber trade through the Timber Conservation Board; the debate at the onset of the Depression for solutions to the crisis; the recommendations of the Copeland report; the establishment of the National Recovery Administration (NRA) and the continuing argument over cooperation versus regulation; the controversy surrounding chief forester Ferdinand Silcox; the proposals of the Joint Congressional Committee on Forestry at the end of the decade; and, finally, the industry's effort to defeat what it called "socialist-inspired" legislation, the Cooperative Forest Restoration bill.

The Debate Heats Up, 1928–1933

Conditions in the lumber industry worsened in the late 1920s when annual production fell from a postwar high of 41 billion board feet in 1925 to 36 billion in 1928, 26 billion in 1930, and finally a low of 10 billion board feet in 1932. The dramatic contraction in the lumber market brought forth a variety of nostrums from industry and federal spokesmen that became more radical as the economic crisis deepened. Chief forester Robert Stuart informed the agriculture secretary in 1929 that the "making over of the industry" from a migratory to a steady business "was more than an internal problem"; it involved the public as well.[2]

At a meeting of the board of directors of the National Lumber Manufacturers Association (NLMA) in August, 1929, Wilson Compton proposed a "Timber Conservation Board" to investigate the economic problems of forest-dependent industries. This "fact-finding and . . . educational agency" would gain the public's confidence, a necessary ingredient to the success of any industrial stabilization plan. The *American Lumberman* called the Compton proposal "the best possible answer to the . . . discredited government-control enthusiasts of the Pinchot type."[3]

Finally, both the NLMA and the American Forestry Association

(AFA) requested President Herbert Hoover to appoint "a fact-finding agency for purposes of public education." When Hoover appointed the Timber Conservation Board and a twenty-one member advisory committee in late 1930, the Society of American Foresters (SAF) added its support to the industry-sponsored effort. The SAF urged the public to meet its responsibility through increased appropriations for fire protection and revision of forest tax laws.[4] Before the board held a single meeting, it had the support of every major forestry organization.

The board conducted hearings, commissioned studies on taxation and sustained yield proposals, and issued quarterly reports for several months. Fred Morrell, who presented a critique of David Mason's sustained yield management proposal, did not believe cooperatively managed public and private timberlands would work. Stuart cited the industry's failure to reforest its lands, and he told the board that the "abnormal economic conditions" cast doubt on the ability of private owners or public cooperative policies to remedy the situation.[5]

But in its final report, the Timber Conservation Board ignored Stuart's and Morrell's objections and endorsed the Mason proposal. Its other recommendations focused on ways to stabilize the lumber industry—an expanded public acquisition program; limits on federal timber sales; increased Clarke-McNary appropriations; adjustments in state forest taxes; redirecting forest products research to help resolve "emergency needs" of the lumber industry; implementing sustained yield management; more liberal antitrust laws; and merging timber ownerships into larger units.[6]

Except for an item or two that reflected the immediate crisis, the recommendations were familiar industry proposals. The Timber Conservation Board, a clear predecessor to the Lumber Code Authority under the NRA, advocated the further integration of public and private policy. Supporters of these initiatives called for greater government-industry cooperation to stabilize the forest products business and to promote the conservation of the nation's timber resource.

While trade leaders pressed the Hoover administration to investigate the nation's forest problems, professional foresters also debated a variety of proposals to stabilize industry. George P. Ahern, a retired army officer with a lifelong interest in forestry, precipitated the public discussion in 1928, when he published *Deforested America,* a sharp attack that accused the lumber industry of forest destruction. A *Journal of Forestry* editorial feared that Ahern's pamphlet would divide public and private interests at a time when the two groups were attempting to resolve lumber and forestry problems. The SAF publication regretted that Ahern wanted to scrap "the present cooperative method" for federal regulation.[7]

It oversimplifies the problems of the forest products industry to explain differences in terms of regulation versus cooperation, but Compton and several professional foresters used that argument in attacking Ahern's pamphlet. Greeley, the new secretary-manager of the West Coast Lumbermen's Association (WCLA), advised the organization's directors to draft their own program to ward off "radical proposals for federal control of private timber." The association subsequently adopted Greeley's recommendations, all firmly rooted in the "cooperative principle."[8] The WCLA proposals set the tone for the Depression years when the troubled Pacific coast lumber industry initiated most of the calls for federal action.

The SAF forest policy committee also released a report that called for a "clear-cut nation-wide program of action" involving public and private agencies. John B. Woods, forester whose career bridged both the public and private sector, supported an increase in Clarke-McNary appropriations, adequate funds to complete the national timber survey, and greater cooperation between government agencies and private industry.[9] Woods, who worked as a forester with the NLMA for a few years, was a leading advocate of increased government-industry cooperation in the 1930s.

Federal foresters also suggested remedies to resolve the industry's problems. Some, like William Sparhawk, argued that the difficulties were fundamentally economic: "The economic feasibility of private forestry may be influenced . . . favorably or unfavorably by the policy of public forestry, depending on whether the public undertakes forestry as a supplement to private enterprise or in competition with it." For private forestry to succeed, Sparhawk contended, public forestry had to supplement, not compete with it.[10]

Stuart agreed that waste and inefficiency in the trade were due to "certain economic maladjustments that the lumber industry can not alter." But the situation could be alleviated, he suggested, through a greater public and private effort to promote forestry—expanding the government's research activities, completing the forest survey, providing statistics to lumbermen, expanding the federal forests, and withholding national forest timber from the market. [11]

Herbert A. Smith, of the Forest Service public relations department and a close friend of Gifford Pinchot, supported assistance for privately owned forestland because "the ownership of real property carries with it various obligations" that affect the public interest. He argued that the public should provide tax relief in addition to its cooperation in fire protection. [12] He also urged that federal agencies should be responsible for research, provide cheap planting stock, conduct taxation and tariff studies, and carry its traditional share of fire protection costs. State governments, on the other hand, had an obligation to stop the "denudation" of private forestland. Smith thought there would be constitutional problems if the federal government regulated private lands. [13] Smith's break with Pinchot on the regulation issue probably was realistic; neither the president nor Congress supported the federal regulation of forest management at this time.

Compared with Smith's conventional strategy, Ward Shepard proposed a grand scheme to stabilize the industry and to encourage good forestry practices—the establishment of a system of forest boards, associations of forest owners and producers, and loan boards and banks. Because state action to prevent deforestation would be "difficult to attain," federal safeguards would be needed to require forest owners to follow certain forest practices. And the public had a right to exact management requirements, because forest destruction meant the confiscation of "social capital" and could be replaced only at great public costs. [14] Shepard's proposals gained support in the early discussions over the NRA when the Roosevelt administration attempted to place restrictions on the lumber industry in exchange for suspending the antitrust laws.

Meanwhile, the economy continued to deteriorate. As part of an economy move, Compton advised the NLMA in 1930 to disband its recently created forestry department and to give a notice of termination to its forester, Franklin W. Reed. Reed thought Compton's move unwise, because it would give the "radicals who demand mandatory legislation . . . strong ammunition for their guns." E. T. Allen agreed—the forestry department was valuable to the industry "as good advertising." Greeley feared that Compton's decision would "bring down upon the industry a critical public sentiment," because so much publicity had surrounded the creation of the department two years earlier.[15]

Most of the industry's suggestions to stabilize the lumber market centered on greater business cooperation and structural adjustments aimed at cutting back on production. These industrial resolutions called for public action—the time-worn panacea of increased appropriations for fire protection, studies of forest taxation, and the completion of the timber survey.[16] But lumber associations also requested federal assistance in trade extension work, permission to conduct merger negotiations, and the right to join in stabilization agreements. And most federal foresters supported the industry's request to remove obstacles to business practice. Stuart called for "wisely directed public and private effort" to stabilize production and conserve the forest resource.[17] Stuart, who supported Greeley's "cooperative" approach during the 1920s, was moving toward a much more aggressive federal program.

For their part, lumbermen began to look increasingly to the nation's capital for solutions to their problems. One trade journal noted that business leaders were ready to adopt any measure that promised relief, and as unemployment lines lengthened in the spring of 1932, a Weyerhaeuser executive called the recommendations of the Timber Conservation Board ineffective, "stop-gap" measures[18]—a remark showing the extent to which the economic crisis caused lumbermen to reexamine their relationship with the federal government.

Shortly after Franklin D. Roosevelt's presidential inauguration, the Forest Service submitted its report, *A National Plan for American Forestry*, in response to Senate Resolution 175. In his letter to the secretary of agriculture, Stuart said it was time "for another great forward step" in forestry, and a large part of that move "should be the public assumption of a much larger part of the enterprise." The Copeland study, directed by Earle Clapp, was an encyclopedic account of American forestry and the industrial conditions that had contributed to its difficulties. Henry Clepper characterized the report as "the most important document on forestry policy up to that time."[19] The assessment was appropriate. Any discussion of American forestry must reckon with its impressive analyses of past policy and its recommendations for the future.

The Copeland report sharply criticized state and private commitments to forest management. While the federal government had extended aid to private owners to encourage them "to shoulder a major part of the job of timber growing," timberland holders willingly accepted the aid but rarely did anything on their own. The study pointed out that federal aid provided some form of assistance to nearly all states. However, the inability of states to match federal funds had diminished the significance of cooperative programs, especially in the South where the need was greatest.[20]

But having pierced the mantle of success that usually characterized descriptions of federal cooperative programs, the Copeland report still contended that the assistance was worthwhile. It recommended an increase in appropriations for fire protection; an expansion of public forests; greater public expenditures for insect and disease detection and control; the distribution of planting stock to industrial and farm owners at one-half cost; an expansion of federal and state research programs; an increase in farm forestry extension work, and the offer of similar aid to industrial owners. The report also recommended public loans to private owners, and federal authorization for mergers and the right of producers to make production curtailment agreements.[21] The latter proposals were incorporated in the Lumber Code Authority under the National Industrial Recovery Act (NIRA).

Compton praised the recommendations in the report, because they would help grow trees "for commercial purposes" and steady the market. Henry Graves liked the federal acquisition item and believed that an increase in assistance to the lumber industry would remove "economic obstacles" and promote the cause of forestry. Some foresters, however, took issue with the emphasis on public acquisition. Shepard, for one, told Stuart that the nation's forestry problems required a more comprehensive approach than mere "nationalization."[22] Despite the general acclaim greeting the Copeland report, it was soon lost amid even headier proposals for federal cooperative assistance.

The National Recovery Administration

The Roosevelt administration's decision to adopt a broad industrial recovery program excited trade association leaders and business groups. The architects of the plan intended the NIRA and its administrative agency, the NRA, to institutionalize trade association work in government policy to control prices and production. The "partnership in planning" was based on the principle of industrial self-regulation with the state serving as an enforcement agency. Compton called the recovery scheme a "bold effort" in planning and regulation to avoid further "economic degeneration."[23]

While government and industrial leaders debated the details of the Lumber Code Authority, a group of professional foresters urged the president to use the recovery act to force private owners to adopt sustained yield forestry. Shepard wanted Roosevelt to demand proper cutting practices in exchange for the industry's right to control prices and production. Raphael Zon recommended that the industry be required to practice specified cutting methods in exchange for its freedom to circumvent the antitrust laws.[24] What followed was a long series of negotiations to define the forest conservation requirements of the lumber code. Compton bargained hard for a repeal of "confiscatory" timberland taxes, adequate protection against fire, a tariff on lumber imports, and credit agencies like those in agriculture. Zon, Robert Marshall, and Ed Munns wanted enforceable cutting requirements tied to the code provision, referred to as Article X.[25]

The final agreement, approved by the president on March 23, 1934, called for expanding public assistance to control fire, disease, and insects; modifying forest taxes; providing fire insurance and extending credits to forest industries; and better cooperation between private owners and public agencies. For their part, the regional trade associations (organized into divisions under the Lumber Code Authority) agreed to guarantee the "conservation and sustained production of forest resources." The agreement emphasized, however, that real accomplishment in conservation depended on "public cooperation."[26]

Because the private sector defined the federal responsibility under this arrangement, it assumed the position of judge and jury in determining the success of the agreement. Compton informed the president on one occasion that the failure of the government to fulfill its commitment meant that industrial conservation would be "largely a gesture."[27] For the rest of the decade industry leaders like Woods and Greeley repeatedly accused the government of failing to keep its part of the bargain.

After the U.S. Supreme Court declared NRA unconstitutional, lumber spokesmen continued their quest for federal assistance. Although the NRA scheme failed, industry leaders praised lumbermen for fulfilling their responsibilities. A Weyerhaeuser forester, Clyde Martin, concluded that the lumber code had improved forestry practices and created closer relations between the lumber industry and the Forest Service. J. J. Farrell of the Northeastern Lumber Manufacturers Association urged lumbermen to pursue the public support promises of the Article X agreement.[28]

To convince Congress to pass the "public" measures in the old Article X promise, trade leaders kept alive a committee that had functioned under the Lumber Code Authority. Known as the Joint Committee of the Article X Conference and dominated by trade spokesmen, the committee served as a quasi-public body to present the industry's viewpoint.[29] The joint committee maintained a paper existence for several months after the demise of the NRA, acting mainly as a public relations adjunct of the NLMA.

Silcox and the Regulation Issue

When legislators or public figures like Pinchot raised the issue of regulation in the early 1920s, the industry charged that such proposals were coercieve and would negate cooperation. The Clarke-McNary Act, by contrast, favored the principle of federal cooperation with states and private owners, and for nearly a decade the issue seemed resolved. Then in January, 1935, chief forester Ferdinand Silcox called for public controls over private timberland practices.[30] The resulting debate lasted until the early years of the Second World War when President Roosevelt ordered all regulatory proposals shelved for the duration of the crisis.

When Silcox was appointed chief forester in October, 1933, he brought to the office a reputation for public activism and a commitment to social change. At his first meeting with the Service Committee, Silcox told his colleagues that the Depression offered "great possibilities" for the Forest Service. But the agency's most important commitment, he said, was the need "to consider forestry in its social relation to our industrial life."[31] His 1935 speech to the SAF elaborated the same theme — that the government must assure that lumbermen conducted themselves in a socially responsible manner. Although he had been a district head, Silcox was appointed chief after fifteen years of work in the field of labor relations. Clepper described Silcox as "handsome, personable, articulate, and withal a forester's forester." At the time Greeley believed the new chief was open-minded and "not wedded to any fixed theories." In his autobiography, however, Greeley saw matters differently — there was "a colder atmosphere" in the service and the "warmth of cooperation present in the early Clarke-McNary days was missing."[32]

Self-serving or not, Greeley's later perspective accurately characterized the industry's reaction to Silcox. The chief forester's talk about federal regulation spurred trade leaders like Woods and Mason to reassert the industry's influence in federal policy and to pressure Congress to pass industry-sponsored bills. Despite industry suspicions, association officials sought the chief forester's support for their legislative program.

If one looks beyond the rhetorical haze surrounding the chief forester's public statements, it is obvious that the Forest Service and the lumber industry continued most of their conventional forms of cooperation. Mason, Woods, Compton, and Silcox worked together to plot strategies to seek appropriations for fire protection and funds for the forest survey, to fight blister rust, and to support Forest Service research programs. Industry leaders urged their congressmen to provide adequate funding for the cooperative activities of the Forest Service.[33] Clearly, cooperation was still working well during the Silcox administration.

Despite his occasional reference to federal regulation, the chief's public addresses to lumbermen were congenial and conciliatory. To the Western Forestry and Conservation Association (WFCA) in late 1935 Silcox expressed "a desire to cooperate" with industry "in every way possible." A few months later Silcox told Woods that progressive lumbermen, particularly the kind he met at the WFCA conference, were attempting to bring an end to the industry's migratory propensity. The recognition that there was an inherent responsibility in private ownership, the chief forester observed, would "redeem the industry's social obligations." If the private sector carried out its part, that would help the Forest Service "gain additional public support" for lumbermen.[34]

Hostility toward the chief forester was most intense in the South. In one issue the *Southern Lumberman* raged that Silcox "burns with the unquenchable fire of the zealot" in his effort on behalf of federal control over the nation's timberlands.[35] Yet when Silcox addressed the Southern Pine Association in the spring of 1939, the title of the chief forester's speech, "The Co-operative Approach between Industry and Government in Forest Conservation," was more accommodating, the journal observed, than "some of his more radical declarations." The *Southern Lumberman* told its readers that Silcox had put the industry on the spot: "The lumbermen have urged the co-operative approach to the problem; Mr. Silcox endorses that view. If they ignore the opportunity for co-operation, it may be construed by him as evidence that federal regulation is the only alternative."[36] But the chief forester made it clear that the initiative in forest conservation did not rest solely with the private sector.

Woods wondered if lumbermen and the Forest Service were "chasing each other around in circles" but not always being frank with one another. He reminded Silcox that "a wise government" would promote sound forest management without extending control over private timberlands. And shortly before Silcox died from a heart attack in late 1939, the *Southern Lumberman* again warned of a "strong bloc within the Forest Service of decidedly radical views." Although the chief forester's public statements were conciliatory, the journal believed that Silcox was still "strongly under the influence of this radical fringe."[37]

Greeley probably spoke the truth in his autobiography when he characterized Silcox as a "master of verbal fencing" who offered only vague and general proposals for forest regulation. In his last two annual reports Silcox recommended a three-point program, including "cooperation," to attain the "managed use" of the forest resource. The forms of cooperation included public aid for fire protection and basic research and work in taxation, forest credits, and forestry extensions. While some forestry progress had been made through public and private cooperation, Silcox concluded that more was needed to adequately protect the public interest.[38]

The chief forester's proposal for regulation called for *"some form* (italics mine) of public regulation to cutting practices on private forest land." And when he asked Congress to expand public ownership in

1939, he cautioned that it "should be determined by the extent to which public interests are protected by private owners."[39] The brief space in the report devoted to regulation suggests that the chief forester was using a carrot-and-stick approach to encourage private industry to meet its responsibility to the public.

The Joint Congressional Committee on Forestry

Because of the persisting problems in the lumber trade, President Roosevelt asked Congress to investigate the present conditions and future prospects of forestry in the United States. Compton told Secretary Henry Wallace that the industry would cooperate fully, and in a confidential note Compton advised the NLMA's conservation committee to avoid attacking Silcox. Rather, he said, the industry should focus on "research, cooperation, extension of markets, [and] economic stability for forestry." Allen, writing from his secluded home on the northern Oregon coast, also advised the WFCA to stay away from Silcox and emphasize practical problems.[40]

The Joint Congressional Committee on Forestry, headed by Alabama Senator John H. Bankhead, conducted hearings in every major forest region in the United States at which public and private forestry interests rehashed most of the old arguments. Compton made one concession to the push for regulation—it should be applied at the state level but only as experience and need dictated. Clapp, the acting head of the Forest Service after Silcox's death, also favored state regulation, but he wanted the federal government to establish minimum guidelines.[41]

The joint committee's report, published amid the growing international crisis in 1941, cited private woodlands as the country's most critical forestry problem. The joint committee recommended: (1) an increase in the Clarke-McNary fire authorization to $10 million; (2) more money to fight insects and diseases; (3) assistance in reforestation; (4) financial support for research; (5) the formation of cooperative sustained yield units; (6) forest credits; and (7) additions to the national forests.[42] Only one of the committee's recommendations mentioned regulation, and that in convoluted fashion.

As the United States moved toward war, Forest Service and industry leaders continued to grapple with the regulation issue. Compton

counseled his colleagues to work for state regulation of forest practices. Greeley also thought lumbermen should move quickly to adopt
"grass roots" state cutting regulations. And the aging Allen advised
states "to assume more responsibility" over forestry practices within
their jurisdiction. He added that it was the federal government's obligation "to help bear the cost."[43]

Finally, Senator John Bankhead introduced a multifaceted bill to
implement the recommendations of the Joint Congressional Committee on Forestry. The measure (and a companion bill introduced in the
House) was never reported out of committee. The lumber industry
opposed it, because the bill prescribed regulation under federal guidelines. Congress also was preoccupied with urgent war legislation, and
the complex nature of the forestry bill probably precluded its serious
consideration. When the measure failed to make headway in Congress, the Forest Service and Secretary of Agriculture Claude Wickard
made occasional efforts to attach regulatory features to emergency
wartime orders.[44] The president's opposition doomed these to failure
as well.

Although the forestry bill failed, Congress passed important elements of the joint committee's recommendations in the next few
years. It raised the Clarke-McNary authorization to $9 million and
passed the Sustained-Yield Forest Management Act of 1944 and the
Cooperative Forest Management Act of 1950.[45] Greeley and the
proponents of cooperative forestry finally had obtained most of the
legislative program they had sought since the days of the Lumber
Code Authority. Moreover, they had defeated attempts at regulation
and pressured Congress to table another measure that did not fit the
industry's prescription for federal cooperation.

The Cooperative Forest Restoration Plan

For every modest New Deal proposal that Congress approved, the
law-makers turned down an equal number of truly progressive measures. This was especially true in the case of social programs to assist
the more destitute sectors of rural America. Progressives in the Forest
Service devised several schemes of this sort, but most of the proposals
lacked the approval of district heads and the Washington office. One
such measure, the Cooperative Forest Restoration Plan, garnered the

semblance of a public hearing and then was ripped asunder—most of the criticism coming from professional foresters and lumber industry spokesmen.

The forest restoration scheme—designed to provide farmers with an income from their woodlands to offset a declining cotton economy —was a grass-roots proposal that grew out of the impoverished southern back country. A group of farmers and state foresters from the South met in late 1937 and drafted the restoration plan—a cooperative woodland management and employment program. Earl Tinker forwarded the proposal to the chief forester with the recommendation that federal funds be used "for unemployment relief" and to rehabilitate commercial timberlands.[46]

The restoration measure proposed to coordinate private forest rehabilitation with the "social problem of employment." Subsequently, the Forest Service expanded the idea to include every forested region in the country. But there were problems ahead. Tinker wrote Shepard that the plan was a "step in the right direction," despite the "destructive comments" that had been made. Because of "intraprofessional criticism," however, Shepard advised Tinker to limit the proposal to specific "submarginal farm regions with an acute relief problem."[47]

When Tinker asked regional and state foresters for suggestions in order to build support for the forest restoration plan, the responses were mixed. The director of Georgia's forestry division reported that landowners feared the plan because it would permit the government to "control private forestry activities." From within the Forest Service, Edward I. Kotok argued that existing legislation would accomplish the same objectives.[48] Elsewhere the forest restoration plan fared better. An Iowa forester liked the idea because it would introduce forest management to "small privately owned tracts of land." The Association of State Foresters endorsed the proposal; the Joint Congressional Committee on Forestry showed an interest in the plan; and the Works Progress Administration added its approval. By the end of 1938 the plan included a provision for the federal leasing of private land.[49] The proposal required the cooperation of federal departments, the Forest Service, state forestry agencies, and private woodlot owners.

There were complex cooperative features to the restoration plan:

(1) the Works Progress Administration would pay wages to farmers needing a supplemental income and to people on relief; (2) the Forest Service would administer the program through state forestry agencies; (3) administrative units would conduct the field work, and no unit could be formed unless more than 50 percent of the acreage in the area was committed to the program; (4) long-term cooperative agreements would authorize the Forest Service to manage the land and draft cost arrangements; and (5) the agreement would remain in effect until the property had repaid the government an agreed percentage from the sale of forest products. Landowners would maintain title to the property and pay taxes on it.[50]

Despite the endorsement of the Association of State Foresters and other prominent individuals, many foresters objected to the proposal, especially those with ties to the lumber associations. Greeley wanted a definite expiration date for the lease agreements to prevent the government from gaining a "perpetual lien upon the property." He also lectured the agency about misstatements in the proposal, which had the effect of a "rabblerousing sort of window dressing." The Forest Service, he said, should "deal with the facts."[51]

When Congressman Hampton Fullmer introduced the Cooperative Forest Restoration bill in Congress, there were even more fireworks. Clyde Martin, a former Weyerhaeuser forester now with the Western Pine Association, blasted the restoration plan because it would allow the government to log, mill, and sell forest products; because cooperating farmers would be political assets; and because small farmers would be getting a free ride. The *Journal of Forestry* called the restoration bill misguided. Supporters of the bill, it said, were being "somewhat opportunistic" in emphasizing its employment aspects, and the measure would give the government "rather direct control" of a large forest area.[52] Herman H. Chapman of the Yale School of Forestry delivered the most severe indictment of the bill. Writing in the *Journal of Forestry*, Chapman said the measure involved "prohibitive expense, accompanied by the destruction of private ownership of the forest lands affected." Then in bold print he listed his objections: (1) "*It is class legislation*," (2) "*It is disguised public acquisition of private property*," (3) "*The program will kill the incentive of the owner and reduce him to the status a tenant dependent on federal aid*," and (4) "*The program is unnecessary and the expense unjustified*." Chapman's

Yale colleague, the economist Fred Rogers Fairchild, stated in the same issue of the journal that the bill was "a gigantic subsidy to a favored class."[53]

These arguments undoubtedly impressed a profession heavily influenced by industry and already suspicious of the regulatory strings attached to federal programs. Congress, increasingly concerned with issues of security and national defense, buried the bill. For their part, the government and the forest products industry were about to enter more far-reaching cooperative ventures associated with the war.

Summary

Crucial economic, social, and political issues shaped federal forestry cooperation with the private sector, a tendency most evident during the years of the Great Depression. Henry B. Steer, a Forest Service economist, put the case bluntly in the midst of the social disruptions of 1932—economic considerations should guide "the application of forestry and the formulation of forest policies."[54]

The social crisis of the 1930s deeply affected federal cooperation. A shaken industry looked to Washington for cooperative arrangements that would alleviate economic distress and restore industrial order. Lumber trade leaders successfully fought proposals requiring federally prescribed rules of forest practice, but Congress continued to implement the more conventional forms of cooperative assistance. The industry, in short, had "weathered the storm."

The Depression influenced federal forestry policies in other ways. In a move to provide unemployment relief, lessen the potential for social disruption, and stabilize the economy, the Roosevelt administration initiated several emergency forestry and conservation programs. Because many of these schemes required the expertise of professional foresters, the Forest Service became deeply involved. These emergency measures demanded close cooperation between federal departments, the Forest Service and state and regional agencies, and between the government and the private sector.

Chapter Nine

Changing political fortunes, a demoralized economy, and a need for rehabilitative work on public and private forestlands combined in the 1930s to create ideal conditions for establishing publicly supported forestry programs in the United States. The New Deal administration of Franklin D. Roosevelt, although without a detailed framework for economic recovery, was, nevertheless, committed to putting people to work and determined to use a variety of conservation-oriented projects, including forestry, to accomplish its end. But New Deal policymakers were not alone in providing an agenda for economic and environmental rehabilitation. Federal agencies, like the Forest Service, and several state governments already had established fledgling programs of this sort.

The new president's interest in forestry also was not new. As a member of the New York legislature, Roosevelt had chaired a committee on forestry; he gained practical knowledge about forest management from handling his estate at Hyde Park, New York. During his tenure as governor, Roosevelt established a state-supported program in reforestation, and in his election campaign he advocated the creation of more national forests in the eastern United States to provide forestry-related work for the unemployed. [1]

All of this provided New Deal "brain trusters" with an abundance of information for shaping new proposals. The programs that seemingly emerged in helter-skelter fashion in the late spring and summer of 1933, therefore, had precedence both in the president's personal political world and in emergency projects in the states. But the vast expansion of these efforts at the federal level was unprecedented—and it pushed the Forest Service into new areas of cooperation.

As the economic crisis worsened and the unemployment lines lengthened, the Forest Service received inquiries about the potential for using the national forests to put people to work. The suggestions included projects to remove dead timber and underbrush from the forests; to improve forest stands adjacent to highways; to carry out planting and thinning programs; to construct fire lines and fire breaks; and to expand the system of forest roads and trails.[2]

Chief forester Robert Stuart dismissed the suggestion to remove dead timber from the national forests because it would have little permanent value, and the daily wage costs "would attain vast proportions." But he proposed other work projects that would have "permanent value" and help reduce unemployment—constructing roads and trails, building fire lookouts, installing telephone lines, and clearing fire lines and fire breaks.[3] These proposals clearly anticipated some of the fundamental work of the Civilian Conservation Corps (CCC).

A few state governments already had practical experience with some of these projects at the time of Roosevelt's inauguration. Wisconsin's conservation department provided jobs for 4,260 men during the summer of 1932; California expanded its forest work camps to accommodate 7,000 unemployed; and during the spring of 1932 New York's conservation department employed more than 10,000 men in forestry work.[4] Although state budget constraints limited public relief work prior to the New Deal, these early programs provided temporary employment for thousands of people.

The state programs also had an uneven quality, most of it attributable to differences in the ability to finance such projects. Fred Morrell, a Forest Service official familiar with state activities, noted that wealthier states were able to take advantage of the Clarke-McNary programs and could afford to employ people in a variety of forestry projects. But in the South, where fire protection and other Clarke-McNary incentives lagged, there was little forestry work-relief before the New Deal.[5] In both a social and technical sense such regions had the greatest need for federal assistance.

The most popular and perhaps the most successful of the New Deal unemployment relief programs was the CCC. Enshrined in popular literature for its work in soil erosion, reforestation, fire protection, flood control, and a myriad of other activities, the CCC was the best known of all New Deal agencies.[6] Rexford Tugwell's remark nearly twenty-five years after its founding spoke the truth—the agency sometimes became "too popular."[7] Senators and congressmen vied with each other for camps to service their constituents, and newspapers were unstinting in their praise for the CCC. The popularity of the CCC makes it difficult to separate fact from fancy and reality from romance.

The beginning of the agency, however, is no mystery. Shortly after his inauguration Roosevelt moved to implement his work-relief plans for conservation. With the assistance of chief forester Robert Stuart and members of the president's cabinet, the administration drafted and submitted to Congress a bill to establish the CCC. Stuart testified on the need for conservation work on the national forests and argued successfully to amend the bill to include state and private activities as well. After debating portions of the bill, Congress passed the measure and the president signed it into law on March 31, 1933.[8]

Although popularly referred to as the CCC, the initial designation for the new agency was Emergency Conservation Work (ECW). Because organized labor had criticized the proposal, the administration appointed Robert Fechner, a conservative labor leader, to head the ECW. The president assigned specific functions to each of the government departments involved—the Department of Labor would select the enrollees; the War Department would operate the camps; and the departments of Agriculture and Interior would handle the work projects.[9] These responsibilities remained essentially unchanged throughout the life of the corps.

The Forest Service was heavily involved in CCC projects, mainly in forest protection and improvement work. A *Journal of Forestry* editorial in May, 1933, looked forward to great advances in fire protection on the public forests and said federal foresters were counting "on the undertaking to stimulate greatly the forestry movement."[10] These hopes were slowly realized in the coming months as the number of camps engaged in forestry-related activities increased.

The forest conservation activities of the CCC and the quick expansion in forestry-related work dramatically increased the demand for professional foresters. Forestry schools, unlike most college programs during the Depression, were filled to capacity. When the government terminated the CCC in 1942, more than 50 percent of its 2.5 million enlistees had worked on national, state, and private forests under the supervision of the Forest Service. The CCC "boys" thinned trees, battled spruce sawflies and "Mormon" crickets in western forests and gypsy moths in the East and Northwest, constructed lookout towers, roads, and trails, and fought forest fires and planted trees.[11] The last two tasks were the most highly praised.

But the agency also had its critics. E. T. Allen thought the CCC was "wasteful of money and results," especially in areas like the Pacific coast where there already existed a "highly perfected" cooperative organization for doing the same work. The New Deal had crippled Clarke-McNary protection and substituted "expensive untrained forces" whose effectiveness was "conspicuously spotty." The Forest Service praised the CCC, Allen reflected, "because it got all the best of the allotment of help."[12]

Allen's criticism struck a note of truth because Clarke-McNary fire protection funds increased very little during the 1930s. C. S. Cowan, forester for the Washington Forest Fire Association, thought that the CCC served as a strong fire suppression unit, but he pointed out that it lacked permanent existence and drained money from the Clarke-McNary protection fund.[13] Despite occasional criticisms, most state foresters and lumber industry officials valued the fire protection work of the CCC.

Despite the heavy politicking in locating CCC camps, the Forest Service attempted to place camps in areas already under protection or where there was at least local support for fire protection. In some instances, however, overzealous state foresters were too aggressive in ordering CCC camps to assist in fire protection. In one case, Christopher Granger assured a local director that the camps "are entirely under your jurisdiction and final decision rests with you." But Granger cautioned the official that the position of the service should always be one of "helpful cooperation."[14]

141

The Forest Service CCC camps fought fires on the national parks and the public domain and assisted in suppression work on state and private lands. The service made mutual assistance agreements with federal and state agencies and the Bureau of Biological Survey, which operated a few CCC camps. But it did not sign a cooperative agreement with the Division of Grazing because of "rather delicate relations"; instead, it allowed regional foresters to make their own agreements. [15] In most cases these guidelines left the regional officers with a great deal of autonomy.

At the end of 1933 Fred Morrell estimated that state forestry organizations were directing 60 percent of the CCC camps. He warned the Service Committee that CCC "improvement work" required more funds and organization than the normal Clarke-McNary appropriations. Moreover, because the camps confined their activities to areas already protected, there still were vast areas in need of fire protection, especially in the South. [16]

The American Forestry Association (AFA) and the National Lumber Manufacturers Association (NLMA) shared Morrell's concern about the temporary nature of CCC funding. George Harris Collingwood, a forester with both the AFA and the NLMA, feared that the conservation program would be in jeopardy until it was "returned to a permanent financial basis." [17]

Interagency cooperation was critical to the success of CCC work, and the emergency agency sought Forest Service help in its public relations activities. Guy D. McKinney, the artful director of CCC publicity, urged regional foresters to ask camp officials to explain their programs to the local press to assure "first rate publicity" to both agencies. Henceforth, the cooperating agencies and the ECW administration provided the public with a steady diet of positive news about the CCC. [18]

McKinney and the Forest Service issued news releases extolling CCC work in tree planting and fire suppression. They pointed to the benefits the camps pumped into local economies through the purchase of food and supplies and money returned to dependent families. The Forest Service usually provided the topic and the technical details and the ECW staff handled the news releases. After two years of operation the ECW also issued short releases to specialty publications in addition to its regular news items for the local press. [19]

The Forest Service and the ECW staff worked well together. An agricultural experiment station director praised the erosion control efforts of the emergency agency and asked that it remain "under the supervision of the Forest Service." For its part, the Forest Service applauded CCC projects with the U.S. Bureau of Fisheries and state fish and game departments. And McKinney was effusive in his praise of Forest Service public relations work. In correspondence he referred to the "splendid" cooperation of the Forest Service in "giving publicity to important . . . phases" of CCC activity.[20]

This aggressive public relations work was necessary and self-serving. The ECW (and after 1937 the CCC) needed favorable publicity to survive as an administrative agency. Moreover, these programs greatly increased Forest Service cooperative work, and the agency obviously wanted to see these activities continued. It behooved the service, therefore, to publicize CCC accomplishments at the grass-roots level. Thus, when budget cuts forced Fechner to close several Forest Service camps, he asked the service to prepare local news stories listing their accomplishments.[21]

Despite the scheming and politics necessary to keep the CCC alive, its accomplishments were substantial. Under its decentralized administration the Forest Service gave great flexibility to regional officials in determining local conservation needs, with an occasional bow to political necessity. At a time when state finances were badly strained, the CCC enabled the Forest Service to continue its cooperative fire protection and to expand other conservation activities. For their part, state foresters were virtually unanimous in their praise of the CCC. Grover Conzet, director of Minnesota's forestry department, pointed out that the forest improvements "done by the boys" were "worth many times the cost of doing it." But in a confidential letter to a Minnesota congressman, Conzet complained that federal officers sometimes acted "superior to state employees." Despite these reservations he thought Minnesota CCC camps had "gotten along better" than camps in other states.[22]

Because of the need for conservation work, Minnesota officials requested camps for erosion control and for help in constructing dams for urban water supplies and recreational facilities. While the CCC accomplished considerable work in this line, the Forest Service made most of its Minnesota camps available for fire work. In 1937 CCC activities in fire protection still constituted about 70 percent of its workload.[23] Still, the CCC spurred a multitude of forest-related activities in Minnesota. The state enacted legislation in 1933 that permitted it to acquire tax-delinquent lands, primarily to provide an arena for CCC conservation projects. Before the CCC was disbanded, Minnesota had established thirteen new state forests.[24] It is obvious that the state's well-established forestry agency enabled it to take full advantage of emergency conservation programs during the Depression.

The CCC made a similar contribution to California, where relief and job programs brought a 45 percent reduction in the forestry budget for 1933. The use of CCC crews and workers from other camps eventually enabled the forestry division to meet its fire protection responsibilities. There were still problems, however, because state supervisory personnel complained that some of the men were too old, irresponsible, or not physically fit for the job.[25]

But the California CCC camps made lasting contributions to forest conservation. By 1935 CCC fire fighters were increasingly important to the state's suppression force. The success of the CCC, Raymond Clar's study of California forestry indicates, "was obvious and accepted." Clar notes that the 165 Forest Service camps and the thirty-four assigned to the state forestry division were important in upgrading California's fire protection capability during the 1930s.[26] Equally significant, according to Clar, is the fact that the Forest Service and the California agency wanted their accomplishments to be "of lasting public value." As a consequence, the CCC forest camps in California made impressive contributions in the construction of ranger residences, lookout towers, crew houses, garages and warehouses, bridges, firebreaks, roads, and telephone lines.[27] The California forestry division, Clar concludes, "experienced its 'golden years' during the Civilian Conservation Corps period." He points out that projects like the great Ponderosa Way firebreak along the Sierra range pushed the division's physical goals "at least 20 years ahead of schedule." All this was accomplished despite the fact that the CCC was never a part of the division, although it was "always welcome and appreciated."[28]

Forest Service CCC camps also made substantial accomplishments in forest conservation in the South, where the need for fire protection and reforestation was greater than in any other part of the country. To make matters more difficult, most forestland in the southern states was privately owned, yet the private sector contributed only 10 percent of the estimated costs of fire protection. This became a liability when emergency programs became available after 1933, because the government distributed ECW funds according to the ability of the states to pick up the permanent costs.[29] Under this formula southern states did not fare as well as other regions in the number of CCC camps allotted.

The state of Georgia is a good example of the slow progress of southern forestry. Declining rural income in the early years of the Depression drove people to the cities in search of employment. Then, disaster—declining state tax revenues, a prolonged drought, devastating fires, and negative Clarke-McNary inspection reports.[30] The CCC was the catalyst for forest fire protection in Georgia. Federal officials located camps on the holdings of the state's several timber protective associations, enabling Georgia to obtain more CCC camps than any other southern state. The camps accomplished the usual tasks of building telephone lines, firebreaks, lookout towers, bridges, mapping of forestland, and helping with timberland improvement. But the major thrust of CCC activity in Georgia was improving the state's fire protection capability.[31] For their part, state officials were quick to acknowledge this contribution. But the burden of coordinating CCC work taxed the energies of Georgia's woefully understaffed forestry division. State forester Elmer E. Dyal reported in 1936 that the agency had worked hard "to carry on the expanded program called for in cooperation with the Federal government." In turn, he praised the federal agencies for their "splendid cooperation" in advancing forestry.[32]

Although the national forest CCC camps in Georgia were organized first, those located on state and private lands eventually outnumbered them. For the first four years of ECW activity in Georgia, state foresters worked long hours to take advantage of the expanded federal cooperation. Finally, in 1937, following legislative recommendation, the forestry division reorganized its field personnel, relocated its district offices, and upgraded requirements for district foresters. With the aid of CCC funds the forestry division constructed a new district headquarters, and the division's director, Frank Heyward, proudly reported "outstanding progress" in the state's fire protection program.[33] The most significant factors in the expansion of Georgia's forestry work were the CCC camps located on timber protective organization land. And the prospect of obtaining additional CCC camps prompted timberland owners to establish new protective associations. These organizations, in turn, pressured the legislature to increase the state's match for federal protection money. Heyward put the case bluntly: "The backbone of Georgia's protection activities is . . . the Civilian Conservation Corps."[34]

Forestry problems in Georgia and the South, however, were still immense. A study published by the Georgia forestry division and the Forest Service in 1939 reported that fire protection remained the state's "most pressing problem."[35] But the CCC helped reduce fire loses during these years and contributed to the state's ability to provide more adequate protection.

Although Louisiana's forestry agency was better funded, the CCC camps also gave the state's protection system a boost. The camps allotted to Louisiana made the usual physical improvements and aided in fighting fires. By the time the CCC was disbanded, according to one authority, Louisiana forestry "compared favorably with that of other states." In Mississippi, where the extension of forest protection was slower, the CCC contributed to "real progress," heightened interest in forestry, and contributed to the formation of the Mississippi Forestry Association in 1938.[36]

Even in the Pacific Northwest, with its long tradition of private protection associations, CCC forest camps significantly improved the region's protection capability. Oregon's forester reported in 1935 that the CCC allowed the state to complete work plans that otherwise "would have required from 10 to 15 years of state and private effort." As with other states, fire fighting was the most significant CCC activity; CCC contributions, the state forester said, "cannot be too highly commended."[37]

Forest improvements, including the construction of conventional protection facilities, accounted for much of the CCC work in Oregon. Because the state had a well-established fire organization by the 1930s, CCC forest camps devoted more time to construction and forestry work. With the aid of CCC labor the state also expanded and improved its nursery.[38]

The major thrust of CCC forestry work in the Northwest, however,

146

involved the national forests. Because private timberland owners already contributed heavily to protection costs, the Forest Service reasoned, it was unlikely that federal cooperation would significantly increase protection on private land. Oregon's forester, J. W. Ferguson, reacted angrily to this policy, pointing out that state and private camps did not have "proper recognition in previous allocations of CCC camps," despite the fact that the acreage under state and federal protection was virtually the same. Ferguson told Senator Charles McNary that the public responsibility "in the perpetuation of our forests in this area is just as essential as with the National Forests."[39]

The government granted Washington a larger complement of state camps than its southern neighbor because a large percentage of its forestland was in state and private ownership. In his annual report for 1936 the state forester mentioned the CCC camps which did "most of the fire fighting." This was a slight exaggeration, because the CCC spent only a few more "man-days" on fire suppression than state and private personnel.[40] And there were minor problems. In 1937 regional forester C. J. Buck reported that Washington officials were reluctant to use CCC men on "operator caused" fires because of the "labor question." Well-paid logging crews resented the use of "low paid labor on relief"; therefore, the state used the CCC only in fire emergencies.[41] The evidence suggests, however, that the camps were significant as a protection force through the 1940 fire season. As elsewhere in the country, CCC support for forest protection in Washington ended in 1941. Washington's forestry supervisor, T. S. Goodyear, complained that it was difficult to recruit fire-fighting crews, because "for the first time since 1933 there was practically no help available from the CCC camps."[42] This, of course, was only the beginning of the manpower problem.

The Forest Service also employed its CCC camps in the effort to control the spread of tree diseases and forest insects. CCC "boys" worked on the white pine blister rust eradication programs; whole camps scoured the countryside pulling up by hand the small bushes (*Ribes*) that acted as "alternate hosts" for the spread of the disease. When emergency control work ended in 1941, considerable progress had been made in halting the spread of the disease.[43]

CCC enrollees also fought bark beetle infestations, gypsy moths, grasshoppers, and the Dutch elm disease.[44] The Forest Service coordinated these activities with the Bureau of Entomology and Plant Quarantine, the Soil Conservation Service (SCS), the Bureau of Animal Industry, and other federal departments. The Forest Service negotiated the details of the cooperative work and which government agency should provide the financial support. In most instances, federal and state foresters and cooperating agencies signed formal agreements before undertaking a project.

But the primary function of CCC forest camps was to supplement the Clarke-McNary fire protection program. All physical improvements that enhanced protection, whether they were on state or private land, remained after the CCC was gone. E. W. Tinker, who was associated with these programs in the 1930s, told a state forester that everyone had the same objective—"more and better fire protection—and I can see no reason why we cannot satisfactorily work out the problem."[45]

The Forest Service could be determined, however. On one occasion field personnel wanted Ferdinand Silcox to discontinue CCC camps in West Virginia unless the state agreed to maintain the projects. But Silcox refused to sign such a letter to the state's governor and thought the matter should be decided in council.[46] In the vast literature of Forest Service cooperation in CCC work, however, these incidents were rare.

The Forest Service threat to terminate camps when state cooperation lagged was tied to the agency's assumption that CCC work on state and private lands complemented Clarke-McNary programs. It considered lookout towers, trails, and other improvements the property of the state. If the state did not maintain the improvement, then technically Clarke-McNary assistance could be withdrawn. But the threat to close CCC camps existed mainly in correspondence between the office of the Forest Service and its regional foresters; letters exchanged between regional and state foresters were far more conciliatory.[47]

The Forest Service also had serious problems with the War Department over the responsibility for the CCC camps, especially in handling complaints that the army was overstepping its prerogatives. And the service lectured Fechner's office for burdening its staff with requests for reports "some of which seem rather trivial." Fred Morrell told the ECW office that the Forest Service and its regional affiliates should handle CCC correspondence without having to respond through the ECW. "Such a procedure," Morrell pointed out, "would save a great deal of typing and considerable time on our part."[48] These rejoinders were rare, however, and relations with Fechner's office remained cordial.

The opportunity to expand its conservation work during the 1930s was a heady experience for the Forest Service. Because of its longstanding liaison with other federal departments, state governments, and private associations, the service enjoyed advantages that other government agencies lacked. The statistical compilations of work accomplished tell only part of the story of the extensive network of Forest Service cooperation through the CCC. Its work with the Tennessee Valley Authority, the Prairie States Forestry Project, and the SCS expanded the traditional forms of cooperation offered through the Clarke-McNary programs. But the volume of archival material on CCC forestry work clearly shows that its chief focus was fire protection.

Shortly before the government disbanded the CCC, Compton praised its forest protection work and urged that the CCC be continued "on a limited basis" for the duration of the war. And Greeley, speaking on behalf of Northwest lumbermen, applauded the CCC for its "efficient service to forest protection." Morrell noted that the Forest Service always considered CCC "work on state and private land as a complement to regular Clarke-McNary activity"; therefore, Congress should extend the agency's programs. Earl S. Peirce, who spent a career with state and private programs, told Harold Steen in 1975 that the CCC provided for the first time adequate manpower for certain kinds of activities.[49] Although the agency was liquidated after the bombing of Pearl Harbor, the manpower requirements for fire protection remained.

The New England Hurricane of 1938

Forest Service cooperative programs during the Depression embraced natural as well as human disasters (although the two often overlapped as was the case in the Dust Bowl). When a tropical hurricane swept into New England on September 21, 1938, it left in its wake destruction to property and damage to resources unparalleled in the region's history—and an unprecedented opportunity for forest rehabilitation work on approximately 35 percent of the six-state area. Congress immediately appropriated $5 million to reduce the fire hazard on state, municipal and private land.[50] This was only the beginning.

Before the end of September the Forest Service had assumed direction of the fire-reduction and salvage operations from its Washington office. The Region 7 office cooperated with state officials to adopt a plan for handling the emergency, and Silcox appointed Peirce, who headed the division of state and private forestry, as his personal representative in New England. In a memoir prepared years later, Peirce drew special attention to the second phase of the operation: "timber salvage was something entirely new to the Forest Service, a project without a modern prototype, one so large and hazardous that no individual, corporation, or state could undertake it, and one that demanded the stabilizing influence of a competent and experienced Federal agency."[51]

While enroute to Boston, Peirce and his staff prepared a tentative program for the fire reduction and salvage operations. The emergency organization was divided into two divisions (hazard reduction and timber salvage), with state direction of programs, and district directors coordinating activities within each state. President Roosevelt authorized the cooperation of the Works Progress Administration (WPA) and the CCC; these emergency crews were put to work immediately to reduce the fire hazard.[52]

The program proceeded with remarkable speed considering the enormity of the task. The New England Forest Emergency Organizations (NEFE) operated on the plan Peirce and his staff proposed—with headquarters in Boston and branch offices in six states. By the spring of 1939 more than 14,000 laborers, mostly from WPA and CCC crews, had made remarkable progress in the fire hazard reduction program.[53] There still remained, however, the task of salvaging the enormous amounts of down timber before it deteriorated.

To accomplish this job, the agencies cooperating with NEFE formed the Northeastern Timber Salvage Administration (NETSA). The chief of the Forest Service, acting on behalf of the Federal Surplus Commodities Corporation (a subsidiary of the Reconstruction Finance Corporation), directed the new agency, which established log prices and provided cash payments for logs delivered to designated places. To facilitate the purchase of logs, NETSA asked each of the towns in the devastated areas to appoint committees to coordinate local activities. Earl Tinker, in charge of the program, ordered state directors to give town salvage committees "as wide publicity as possible."[54]

To spread information about the timber salvage program, NETSA flooded radio stations and newspapers with press releases. The publicity emphasized the need to reduce the fire hazard and provided the public with the names and addresses of state and federal officials in charge. And, in the early stages of the hazard reduction work, NETSA frequently called for more CCC camps and WPA crews.[55]

The salvage operation was so immense that NETSA had problems locating enough logging trucks and contractors to haul and mill its log purchases. To overcome these difficulties the agency contracted with operators outside the hurricane zone to set up business in the districts where salvage operations were underway. Despite these problems Tinker reported in the spring of 1939 that the salvage work had made "creditable accomplishments" and that its progress was "satisfactory."[56]

The Forest Service also worried over the continuity of its salvage effort. On one occasion Tinker informed the governor-elect of Rhode Island that it was important for "technically qualified" officials to "be assured of reasonable continuity in their positions."[57] Clearly, Tinker wanted a friendly working relationship with the state's forestry agency to continue with a minimum of disruption.

One of NETSA's most delicate problems was the disposal of lumber milled from hurricane-salvaged timber. To formulate sales policy and to avoid glutting the lumber market, the Forest Service arranged a conference to discuss a course of action. Because the disposal of salvaged timber was the source of a great deal of "anxiety within the trade," Wilson Compton urged all NLMA affiliates to attend. He pointed out that the Forest Service had "shown a cooperative attitude" by calling the conference.[58]

The problem of disposing of the large volume of New England lumber disappeared, of course, with the outbreak of war in Europe. A Department of Commerce official told the gathering that his office "was being flooded" with requests for lumber from England and France. Under these conditions, the *American Lumberman* reported, the conference "took on new aspects and importance." After the conference adjourned, Compton praised the Forest Service for being "considerate of the possible adverse effects on the normal competitive lumber markets." For his part, J. F. Campbell, director of the NETSA, expressed his appreciation for Compton's "cooperation" and advice.[59]

When the agencies had completed the hazard reduction work in the summer of 1941, the Forest Service transferred the remaining staff to the salvage program. Within a year this operation was cut back and early in 1943 the remaining work was turned over to the Region 7 office. At the peak of its activity the NETSA operation directed the work of 241 sawmills and enabled approximately 13,500 landowners, mostly farmers, to receive fair prices for their timber.[60] Its task completed, the agency closed shop and disbanded.

Campbell praised the Forest Service and its "good cooperative relations" for the "outstanding" success of the program, and he applauded the responsiveness of state foresters for cooperating with NETSA. But the most direct beneficiaries of the combined programs, according to Peirce, were the thousands of timber owners who participated and the large number of unemployed people who found jobs in clean-up and salvage work; this, he said, "gave the economy of New England a boost at a time when business was at a low ebb." Harold C. Hebb, a forester with the NLMA, thought the Forest Service deserved recognition for "noteworthy accomplishment" and "doing the job as best they could."[61]

All accounts agree that the Forest Service functioned well in organizing and coordinating the clean-up operations. Although the hurricane disaster was unprecedented in the scale of destruction, the emergency presented little that was new to the service. Amicable relations between state and federal foresters, a ready workforce in the CCC and WPA crews, and the willingness of Congress and the Roosevelt administration to provide emergency assistance made the New England salvage operation successful and unique.

Shelterbelt Cooperation

Other emergency relief and conservation programs of the 1930s proved far more controversial than CCC work or the New England

152

hurricane clean-up. One of these, the Roosevelt administration's shelterbelt scheme, involved planting strips of trees at regular intervals through the prairie states from Canada to Texas to abate the prevailing winds and lessen soil erosion.[62] Like other emergency programs, the shelterbelt project offered the Forest Service the opportunity to expand its cooperation with federal and state agencies.

The point of this discussion is not to detail the history of the shelterbelt project, because Wilmon Droze's excellent book, *Trees, Prairies, and People,* is undoubtedly the definitive study of this New Deal project. The purpose here is to point out the importance of the work to Forest Service research programs and to its relationship with state and other government agencies. Until 1942, when Congress transferred the project to the SCS, shelterbelt work was an important element in Forest Service cooperation with states. Although congressional budget cuts nearly killed the project in 1936, it struggled on until Congress officially approved the Depression-born project in the Cooperative Farm Forestry Act of 1937.[63]

The shelterbelt program was embroiled in controversy from its inception. Foresters debated the utility of planting trees on the arid plains, and even when they agreed, they argued about appropriate planting methods. Some, like Ed Munns, thought the project was "a vast experiment" both in tree planting and as a relief measure. And before he died, the ever-cautious Robert Stuart advised a scaled-down version of Roosevelt's original idea.[64]

The shelterbelt project became an action program in the summer of 1934 when the president approved the measure. While newspapers ridiculed the plan and the Society of American Foresters debated the issue, the Forest Service began the tedious process of growing planting stock for the project area. Fred Morrell and Raphael Zon set up procedures to establish a scientific base for the work.[65]

Paul Roberts, who was director of the project, established relations with the Agricultural Adjustment Administration, the Soil Erosion Service, Office of Dry Land Farming, the Biological Survey, and the state extension offices in the project area. Zon, who headed the research adjunct of the plan with the assistance of Carlos Bates, cooperated with the Bureau of Plant Industry to gather information about tree planting on the Great Plains.[66] And Silcox handled his small but dedicated staff of project foresters with great success.

The shelterbelt project employed thousands of WPA and CCC workers who planted trees on nearly 19,000 miles of the arid plains in cooperation with 30,000 farmers. Because the plan was part of a broad Department of Agriculture effort to rehabilitate the economic life of the Great Plains, project leaders integrated their work with the SCS, the Bureau of Agricultural Economics, and the region's agricultural colleges. Cooperation with the WPA was difficult, and the whole scheme always limped along uncertain as to when the next pay check would arrive. But its most ardent supporters—Munns, Roberts, Bates, and Zon—never lost the faith. In 1942 a departmental reorganization transferred Forest Service responsibilities to the SCS. Thereafter, the Forest Service limited its role to tree distribution to state forestry and extension agencies.[67]

Summary

By 1942 war-related activities were making greater demands on the Forest Service. War priorities circumscribed traditional forms of cooperation, altered conventional forest research investigations, and sharply curtailed funding. The war also brought an end to unemployment relief programs. Congress terminated virtually all emergency conservation agencies and diverted the money to defense purposes. Roosevelt's grand objective to make the CCC a permanent agency ended abruptly when Congress voted to liquidate its remaining assets.

But the Depression years were exhilarating for Forest Service administrators. The emergency programs of the New Deal offered federal foresters opportunities for extensive liaison with other federal departments and bureaus and with state agencies. Forest Service administration of the CCC forestry camps, the New England hurricane clean-up program, and the shelterbelt project, although not without some bickering, was carried out with a minimum of friction. Certainly the popularity of the CCC looms large today, in part, because the Forest Service, in charge of a majority of the camps, conducted important and prideful conservation work in the field.

Chapter Ten

When Germany invaded Poland in the late summer of 1939, the Roosevelt administration ordered all federal agencies to inventory their resources for national defense purposes. Acting chief Earle Clapp, with a wealth of experience as head of Forest Service research during the First World War, discussed the importance of wood products to national defense in his annual report for 1940. In Clapp's view, it was prudent to use resources wisely if the country was "to be truly prepared," and despite the increasing use of steel and aluminum, wood products would still fill many requirements.[1]

The major point in Clapp's report was to show that the war crisis would accentuate the traditional problems of protecting and managing the national forests, conducting forest research, and cooperating in state and private forestry. While domestic conditions had shaped federal activity during the 1930s, there were new demands on federal resource agencies during the Second World War. Never before had a federal administration seized so thoroughly the nation's economy to pursue a single objective. For their part, industry leaders skillfully used the rhetoric of patriotism to promote their own policy objectives in the war administration.

Clapp probably underestimated the extent to which the war would affect the Forest Service. For he was one of the old guard, a diminishing breed in the service, and a group to whom the war-induced changes must have presented a dizzying spectacle. Harold Steen's history of the Forest Service speaks to the issue: "The war was the last hurrah for many forestry pioneers and brought a change of direction for American forestry."[2] But the Second World War also saw a great deal of continuity with previous experience, especially in the number of corporate executives and trade leaders who flocked to Washington to direct the mobilization and resource procurement programs.

On the Rhetorical Front

Immediately after the bombing of Pearl Harbor, the Roosevelt administration vastly stepped up the conversion of civilian industries to meet the huge production requirements of war. On January 16, 1942, the president established the War Production Board, with corporate executive Donald Nelson as head, to direct production and to "exercise general responsibility" over the economy. Under the Second War Powers Act of March 1942 the board limited nonessential production, prohibited the use of certain materials, offered lucrative incentives to boost industrial production, and initiated cost-plus contracting (with the government assuming all the risks).[3] It was in this environment that Forest Service and lumber industry leaders jockeyed for positions of power and influence.

The debate over federal cooperation, a matter of contention during the 1930s, was still a major point of controversy between industry officials and the leadership of the Forest Service at the onset of the war. Both groups vied for advantage with the president of the War Production Board. Spokesmen for the National Lumber Manufacturers Association (NLMA) criticized the Forest Service for attaching regulatory strings to its cooperative assistance proposals.

G. H. Collingwood, a forester with the NLMA, told Clapp in March, 1942, that the industry hoped the Forest Service would "undertake a cooperative program" and join in a common front to achieve "an early victory"; trees were less important than human lives, and the country might "have to sacrifice future needs for immediate demands." Clapp disagreed; he thought the issues were joined because of the contribution of "continuously productive forests" to social and economic well-being. In winning the war, the Forest Service head argued, it was "wholly unnecessary . . . to destroy or depreciate the future productivity of our forests."[4] Clapp's letter inquired further. Did Collingwood mean that the Forest Service should adopt the industry's view, assume that all was well on private forestlands and join

156

with lumbermen in their effort to gain a larger appropriation for fire protection? The acting chief thought it would be difficult for any responsible public official to comply with the industry's terms.[5]

While Clapp parried publicly with industry representatives, he urged the president to impose federal cutting regulations through his special powers as commander-in-chief. But this move failed when forest products leaders convinced Nelson that increased federal authority would slow production. Finally, after Bureau of the Budget officials also discredited the regulatory proposals, the president directed that there would be no administration action or legislation on the matter until the war was over. But differences between the Forest Service and industry leaders persisted.

At one point, some lumber trade executives proposed a truce in their verbal battles with the Forest Service. But Weyerhaeuser forester Clyde Martin opposed an "armistice" with Clapp, because it would "be almost impossible for him to reverse his policy." Stuart Moir, speaking for the Western Pine Association (WPA), also questioned the utility of a "truce" and said the Forest Service should "strive to develop a feeling of mutual confidence between the industry and the service." Collingwood thought the Forest Service report for 1941 was "a reply to my letter" and indicated that the agency would make "every effort to secure federal regulations."[6]

In a public attempt at conciliation William Greeley urged lumbermen and the Forest Service to shed their adversarial roles and join in the common effort to win the war. The pressing issue of the day, he wrote in *American Forests,* was to protect the nation's forests from enemy incendiarism. In his autobiography Greeley reflected that it was "distressing to witness the partial breakdown of cooperation" and that lumbermen became alarmed when the Forest Service "veered away from its constructive functions and set its sights on domination."[7] These observations make it clear that industry leaders associated federal controls over cutting practices as a move away from the agency's traditional policy of cooperation. And it also indicates a fear of losing control over their economic and political world.

On the War Front

Meanwhile, the Forest Service readied itself, in Clapp's words, "to make the maximum possible contributions to prosecution of the war effort." To facilitate efficient administrative procedures, the Forest Service head established a defense liaison group with a full-time coordinator in each regional office.[8] By the early summer of 1942 the Forest Service was promoting its own scheme—a far-reaching cooperative program designed to boost mill production in the East and South—the Forest Products Service Plan.

Clapp's proposal, submitted to the War Production Board, would allot a revolving fund to the Forest Service to purchase lumber, build up stockpiles, and to market the products to the appropriate national defense sector. The Forest Products Service was designed "to stimulate and facilitate" production units "now idle or only partially used." A confidential Forest Service memorandum emphasized that the plan would "supplement rather than supplant" private production. The proposal advised federal purchase of small but important tracts of timber, subsidizing "submarginal production," and extending credit to boost output. The plan also would require "satisfactory woods practices in connection with purchase contracts."[9]

The greatest potential for the Forest Products Service plan was in the East and the South, where most private timberlands were located and where there were many idle and submarginal mill operations. The War Production Board approved the plan and sent it to the president for his acceptance. At this point lumber trade groups released a storm of letters and petitions opposing the scheme.[10] Their objections prevailed, indicating again that Forest Service proposals that ran counter to the wishes of powerful interests in the forest products trade would fail.

The Lumber and Timber Products War Committee, the NLMA's national defense lobbying arm, asked the president to reject the plan. The Forest Service proposal, the committee pointed out, would greatly affect the "conditions of war production," influence the "status of private forest industry," and stir "misgiving, mistrust and resentment." Equally important, the NLMA committee observed, the plan would subsidize small, inefficient mills to the disadvantage of "more highly mechanized plants."[11] A truly cooperative federal policy, forest products leaders argued, would avoid federal regulatory "bottlenecks," protect the labor force from military conscription, and revise the timber depletion tax provisions so that lumbermen would not

158

be penalized for the extra timber cutting the war required. This might not be good forestry, the NLMA admitted, "but it is necessary war practice." In a February 1943 policy statement, the organization advised that "controversial and explosive issues" like regulation be deferred until the war was over. [12] Cooperation, in effect, meant getting on to the main task of war production with a minimum of restriction.

Faced with major opposition from the wood products trade, the president dumped the Forest Products Service proposal for a "more generally acceptable plan." J. Philip Boyd of Weyerhaeuser suggested the "acceptable plan" to the new Forest Service head, Lyle Watts, which included advice for small operators, aid to mills in securing timber, and assistance in obtaining contracts. The president authorized the War Production Board to carry out these assignments, directed the Forest Service to offer its "full cooperation," and appointed Boyd to head the Lumber and Timber Products Division of the War Production Board. This move pleased Wilson Compton, who disliked the "original obnoxious proposal," and he advised the industry to offer its full cooperation. [13]

Franklin Roosevelt's decision to modify the original Forest Service proposal led directly to the establishment of the Timber Production War Project (TPWP). Boyd, now firmly in charge of lumber production, outlined the kind of "cooperation and assistance" the Forest Service would be asked to provide for the duration of the war—advisory, technical, and cooperative service. [14] These responsibilities touched virtually every phase of Forest Service activity.

Nelson ordered the Forest Service to provide industry with technical assistance, including the planning and development of logging roads, advice about efficient logging and milling techniques, and supervision of timber marking. As part of its "cooperative service" responsibility, the Forest Service assisted the forest products industry in locating labor, encouraged the employment of women, made patriotic appeals to attain better production, and presented draft deferment needs to local selective service boards. [15] These arrangements swept away any semblance of Forest Service autonomy; the material demands of the War Production Board and the production objectives of the forest products industry prevailed in every respect. In effect, the state and private branch of the Forest Service became an administrative arm of the board for the duration of the conflict. Executive decree rather than legislative mandate directed most Forest Service activity.[16]

Because lumber production fell behind military requirements, the War Production Board ordered the Forest Service to develop a program for the eastern United States where labor shortages had closed thousands of small mills, thereby creating a critical drop in lumber production. To implement the "action project," the War Production Board directed the Forest Service to cooperate with "all interested agencies, both public and private."[17] Although the TPWP placed an additional burden on an already overworked staff, the Forest Service drew upon its experience with emergency projects to put the plan into effect.

The state and private forestry branch of the Forest Service directed the field work through the three eastern regional offices at Philadelphia, Atlanta, and Milwaukee. One state and private forestry administrator called the TPWP "the biggest war production job in which foresters have ever participated."[18] The remark accurately gauged the scope of the project, especially in its far-reaching opportunity for liaison with public agencies and the private sector.

When the project finally got underway in mid-summer 1943, Boyd assured lumbermen that "neither the War Production Board nor the Forest Service would "enter the cutting and milling business." The Forest Service appointed Howard Hopkins of the state and private office to direct TPWP, and he immediately ordered work to begin in the Southeast, where small mill production lagged badly. When the first field reports showed significant increases in production, the War Production Board expanded the plan to include most of the eastern states. Because labor problems (both a shortage of labor and a striking degree of job itinerary) were responsible for many of the production difficulties, most TPWP activity involved efforts to provide an adequate work force for mills.[19]

To speed production and to reduce worker absenteeism, the Forest Service showed army films and sponsored caravans of wounded war veterans through the timber-producing eastern states. And early in 1944 the army allowed the use of prisoners-of-war to assist in the production of forest products. To speed production Hopkins emphasized field over office work, and despite some industry criticism, he kept personnel costs to a minimum. The project employed 181 full-time Forest Service employees and approximately 700 personnel from other federal agencies on a part-time basis. [20]

In his quarterly reports to the War Production Board, Hopkins warned policy-makers not "to translate TPWP activities into specified volumes of products." Yet the project's own reports claimed that it had helped to increase output in the first six months of 1944. But the most significant contribution of TPWP in Hopkins's estimation was the elimination of mistrust between the forest industry and public agencies. The program, he said, demonstrated that federal, state, local, and private forestry agencies "can cooperate effectively in the attainment of a common objective." [21]

W. S. Swingler, project director in the eastern region, thought the field contacts would be of lasting value in gaining "experience and knowledge" about the lumber industry. There were cynics, too — in the Far West Corydon Wagner of the St. Paul and Tacoma Lumber Company thought the project was top-heavy with supervisory personnel and that this might "be one of the most important reasons why . . . we are having such a time keeping up with production." [22]

Others were less skeptical. According to Wilson Compton, there was a general consensus in the industry to "give it a trial." He noted that Boyd had asked for the project, and he was "in a better position to know than most of the critics." Collingwood pointed out that the production problem was primarily one of "labor shortage," or not providing "sufficient incentive" to get workers into the woods. But the executive secretary of the Northeastern Lumber Manufacturers Association told Collingwood that TPWP personnel were using "an enormous amount of money" gathering statistics and writing articles "to justify their existence." [23]

To address these complaints Harold C. Hebb, an assistant forester for the NLMA, spent a week inspecting project work in Kentucky. His report praised the organization for helping resolve labor and other problems and "rendering a definite and valuable service" to small mill operators. But another trade group investigation in Wisconsin reported that small mills were producing an inferior quality of lumber and that the Forest Service had made "a rather extravagant estimate" about production increases. [24]

The NLMA sent another of its junior foresters, Wellington Burt, to inspect TPWP activity in the Great Lakes states. His report applauded the "cooperative project" for assisting small operators to increase production. TPWP personnel were doing a "conscientious job and should be highly commended for their cooperative efforts." Burt's only criticism was that TPWP personnel spent too much time "figuring out how much credit they should take for lumber produced."[25] The NLMA forester thought they should be in the field assisting small sawmill operators.

For its part, the Forest Service kept the NLMA and its regional affiliates informed about TPWP activities. This probably reflected the policies of the new chief forester, Lyle Watts, and the fact that the TPWP was an arm of the War Production Board. The service kept trade leaders informed of its field work and solicited advice from the industry in formulating policy.[26]

For the duration of the war the Forest Service avoided controversy. It emphasized that the TPWP was "war forestry" and would end with the conclusion of the war. Hopkins applauded state forest services that, in some instances, provided the entire field personnel for the project. When the government disbanded the TPWP at the end of the war, Hopkins pointed to the good relations established between owners and operators and project personnel.[27] Whether this spirit of cooperation would carry over to the postwar era, however, was yet to be determined.

The executive committee of the NLMA passed a resolution in May, 1945, directing its staff to assure that the government terminated the TPWP when the war ended in the Pacific. And when an Ohio congressman attempted to revive the wartime project, the NLMA successfully opposed the measure.[28] Henceforth, the industry became more assertive in opposing "subsidies" for small and "inefficient" operating units.

The War and Fire Protection

Because of the huge drain of experienced personnel to the military services and to war industries, the Forest Service faced a major task in forest fire protection during the Second World War. To compound matters, the Civilian Conservation Corps (CCC), the "front line of defense" in fire control, was also gone. And protection officials feared that enemy agents would put the torch to the nation's woodlands.[29] But, as it had done in other emergencies, the Forest Service was able to organize an impressive fire protection capability that involved a broad spectrum of the community.

One of the more important protection schemes during the war was the Forest Fire Fighters Service (FFFS). Under the general supervision of federal and state forestry agencies, the FFFS established a nation-wide fire protection service that included farmers, ranchers, social and recreation groups, and high school and college students. In time, the FFFS became a valuable supplement to the public protection agencies.[30] But this volunteer force was only part of the wartime effort to keep forest fire loses to a minimum.

To strengthen fire protection, the Office of Civilian Defense ordered the Civilian Air Patrol to provide personnel and aircraft, and the Forest Service signed a cooperative agreement with the army to fight fires near training locations. And to raise the public's consciousness, the Forest Service cooperated with the Advertising Council, state foresters, and civic and conservation groups. And toward the end of the war Congress appropriated a special fund to employ and train special standby crews that would be ready to deploy quickly to extinguish fires.[31]

Another fire protection scheme, the War Forest Fire Cooperation Program (WFFC), was designed to strengthen fire protection on state and privately owned forestlands of strategic national importance. The Forest Service administered the program through state forestry agencies to meet "unusual hazards growing out of the war." The objectives of the program included protecting military districts from forest fires, reducing the smoke blankets around airfields, protecting lines of communication and transportation, and minimizing the diversion of manpower to fight forest fires.[32]

WFFC funds supplemented the regular Clarke-McNary grants and did not require states to provide matching funds. Most of the money was spent to employ strategically located seasonal fire crews.[33] Because of the great variety in topography and vegetation and the dispersed location of military facilities, the WFFC programs differed from one region to the next.

The Forest Service concentrated its Region 1 WFFC crews within a thirty-five-mile radius of Spokane, Washington, an area with vital transcontinental railroad lines and other strategic facilities. In California funds went to Los Angeles, Ventura, Santa Barbara, and San Mateo counties, all highly militarized and industrial areas. Region 6 centered its activity in the "coastal dimout area" and the heavily timbered region of the Cascade Mountains. The Great Lakes states used the emergency fire protection money to employ fire guards and to purchase and maintain fire fighting equipment.[34]

The Southeast region located its emergency suppression crews near military installations or in strategic areas along the coast. Some states allotted WFFC funds to strengthen existing Clarke-McNary protection, while others used the money to extend assistance to lands outside regularly protected areas. Region 8 inspection reports indicate that many southern states had great difficulty recruiting and keeping WFFC personnel for their protected areas because the emergency crews were tied to existing Clarke-McNary wages.[35]

The WFFC program had its greatest impact in the Pacific Northwest, particularly along the heavily timbered slopes west of the Cascade Range. Because of the region's acute labor shortage, high school boys made up most of the WFFC crews except for the supervisory personnel. The crews generally began work in June and spent considerable time training for the rigorous activity of fighting fires. After the program had been in operation for a year, several school districts offered training classes as part of their regular curriculum.[36]

Both state and federal forestry officials in the Pacific Northwest reported that the WFFC crews performed well — a tribute, undoubtedly, to the training programs. The greatest difficulty was locating competent foremen for the crews, as acute manpower shortages and high industrial wages made it difficult to hire good crew leaders. "A few good men were obtained," the Oregon state forester reported in 1944, "but as a general rule the crew foremen were only mediocre."[37] But in Region 6 there was no difficulty in recruiting crews or keeping them through the fire season, as was the case in the South.

Despite the problems of training adolescent males for the rigors of fire fighting, the WFFC program in the Northwest was a great success. The emergency crews served as initial attack forces and in many cases were able to contain forest fires before they spread out of control, and they did other protection-related work. One of the last WFFC reports underscores the contributions the crews made to fire protection: "Most crews in the West were comprised of high school boys who gave the most excellent account of themselves and a large degree of the cooperative fire control efforts may be attributed to the contribution made by the federal funds used on the WFFC program."[38]

The FFFS and the WFFC were emergency projects that filled the manpower requirements for fire protection, a critical need after the Japanese attacked Pearl Harbor on December 7, 1941. The CCC crews were no longer available, and military and defense industry manpower requirements had taken many of the experienced fire protection personnel. To make matters worse, neither Congress nor the states had measurably increased their Clarke-McNary contributions during the 1930s. Therefore, after Pearl Harbor federal and state forestry agencies made appeals to patriotism and self-sacrifice through the FFFS to assure that the nation's forests did not go up in smoke.

Finally, Congress raised the annual authorization for Clarke-McNary protection to more than $6 million for 1945 and $9 million by 1949. The Society of American Foresters, the American Forestry Association, and Roosevelt's tight-fisted Bureau of the Budget supported the amendment to the 1924 law.[39] The increased authorization still required states to provide matching funds before the federal government extended its offer, which rankled some state foresters.

State Forestry and the War

Because of the proximity of the powerful Japanese navy to the Pacific coast, the states of Washington and Oregon established forest defense councils to meet emergencies. In Washington the Forest Service, National Park Service, Bureau of Indian Affairs, and state and private protection agencies organized a joint council to pool fire fighting forces and equipment, and the Washington council met with its Oregon counterpart to coordinate strategy.[40]

Oregon's forest defense council included all protection agencies and was authorized to coordinate manpower and equipment, and to serve as a liaison between the army and the civilian defense office in the case of a fire emergency. Under this arrangement, the Oregon forester reported in 1942, state and private lands had never before "been so efficiently policed and protected."[41]

Forest Service and military cooperation in the Pacific Northwest extended beyond their designated roles in the WFFC program. Fire officials used military aircraft to drop smokejumpers and to transport Forest Service personnel to the scene of major conflagrations. H. J. Andrews, the regional forester, thought that the availability of military transport was "a contributing factor" in limiting the size of many forest fires. In Washington forestry division officials cooperated with the War Department's Interceptor Command to construct, maintain, and operate seventy-nine aircraft warning observation posts until the summer of 1944 when they were abandoned.[42]

And armed forces personnel in the Pacific coast states provided a reserve manpower pool to be called upon in the case of major forest fires. The military also worked closely with forestry agencies, because fire weather conditions were important to the security and defense of the coastal region.[43] In the end, the availability of military aircraft and the access to a large manpower pool contributed to diminished fire losses during the war.

The incendiary threat to the heavily timbered north Pacific slope was a major concern to national leaders. But other Pacific coastal areas also required increased attention to contend against dangerous fire conditions. Southern California, with its parched and brushy hillsides and heavy concentration of defense industries, was the object of intense protection effort. California's forestry division developed civil defense projects, constructed aircraft warning stations, and was responsible for protecting new industrial installations and military bases from fire. Wildland fires, one of the division's major problems, decreased sharply during the war.[44]

Protection forces in the South confronted different problems. In Georgia the state forestry agency faced its perennial menace—rural incendiarism—in addition to new protection responsibilities associated with five large military installations. Emergency protection funds probably did more to advance fire control work in Georgia and the other southern states than anywhere else in the country. By the end of the war, the fire threat in rural areas, much of it incendiary in origin, had diminished.[45] And the emergency programs enabled these states to extend their work to unprotected lands.

Both the Georgia and Louisiana legislatures passed measures to enforce their forest fire laws, singling out for special punishment perpetrators of incendiary fires. Although Louisiana's new fire law allowed parishes to tax acreage for fire protection, the great expansion in Louisiana cooperative fire protection came after 1945.[46]

Emergency fire protection funds permitted South Carolina to extend minimum fire protection to every county. Mississippi also made its first measurable progress in limiting damage from forest fires during the Second World War. In Arkansas budget cuts and the disbanding of the CCC crews reversed the slow development of forest protection, a fact made clear when fires burned uncontrolled in the southern part of the state in 1943. The Arkansas legislature did not provide reasonable financing for fire protection until 1947.[47]

Two important factors also limited the southern contribution to lumber production during the war—inadequate supplies of quality second-growth timber and a shortage of rubber tires. Despite the publicity efforts of the War Production Board and the hard work of the Southern Pine Association war committee, the output of southern pine lumber actually decreased during the war. At the end of the war southern lumbermen continued to struggle with the same problems.[48] But the advances in forest protection during the war years made the transition to peacetime forestry much easier.

Research and the War

One of the more extensive Forest Service war projects was a scheme to make the United States self-sufficient in rubber production, a foreign import that was cut off when Japan gained control of Pacific ocean lanes. Because the guayule plant, a native to the American Southwest, produced a latex extract required in the manufacture of rubber, the War Production Board ordered the cultivation of guayule on a massive scale. Forest Service personnel worked with the Bureau of Plant Industry and the Bureau of Agricultural Chemistry and Engineering in "a race against time" to grow the plant.[49] After an auspicious and ambitious beginning, however, the project ran into trouble.

The government curtailed production in the spring of 1943 when scientists made dramatic advances in the synthetic production of rubber. By 1944 project directors had confined the operation to California; finally the nurseries were shut down, the guayule plants sold to

Mexican buyers, and the entire project liquidated.[50] What began as an effort to keep the American war machine mounted on rubber tires fell victim to advances in the synthetic production of rubber.

But in other ways Forest Service research contributed significantly to advances in wood technology during the war. The agency revised its research objectives at the beginning of the war to grant priority to those projects directly related to national defense. It postponed all other projects except for the maintenance necessary to prevent deterioration or loss of investment. Drastic budget cuts closed down the Northeastern Forest Experiment Station and curtailed lines of work at other stations that were not war-related.[51] And, repeating the experiences of the First World War, the government ordered the Forest Products Laboratory at Madison, Wisconsin, to supply technical information about wood materials to war agencies.

The Madison laboratory published reports on the properties and uses of wood, plywood, and paper base and wood base plastics in aircraft; it designed containers for packaging ordnance equipment; and it assisted other war agencies with packaging and shipping problems. Madison researchers conducted training courses for armed forces packaging inspectors and offered instruction in repairing, maintaining, and inspecting wooden aircraft.[52]

Although the Forest Service willingly carried out its war-mandated investigations, Lyle Watts warned that curtailing regular research did not serve the "long-time public interest." He said the country was "sacrificing long-range values" in forest research to meet the war crisis. The chief forester's word of caution was part of a broader concern in the Department of Agriculture to establish a planned strategy for the postwar era.[53] Despite this concern, industrial and congressional priorities would be the most important factors shaping Forest Service research in the postwar era.

Summary

The Second World War slowed some Forest Service programs, pushed others to the front, and created new opportunities for cooperative action. Farm forestry, a fledgling program with meager appropriations at the onset of the war, was put on hold; extension foresters turned their attention solely to production problems; and, of course, when

Congress shifted its priorities to war matters, the lawmakers terminated cooperative programs made possible through the CCC and the shelterbelt project. The government also dropped smaller, less conspicuous cooperative projects in the rush to increase the production of war materials.

Both Earle Clapp and Lyle Watts attempted to use war emergency programs to place regulatory controls on private forestry practices. When the agency failed to achieve these objectives, it settled for industry programs to increase lumber production and to protect timberland from fire. Forest products officials like Weyerhaeuser's J. Philip Boyd exercised a powerful influence in determining policy, and this, in turn, shaped the character of Forest Service cooperation. Production was the name of the game whether it be boosting the output of small mills in the South or growing guayule in California. Under these conditions, federal programs to promote good forestry had to await the end of the war.

President Roosevelt, who exercised a powerful influence in mediating the differences between industry and Forest Service proposals during the war, was reluctant to back programs that did not have the support of major industrial groups. In the case of the TPWP, the president ordered the Forest Service to cooperate fully with the War Production Board, much to the satisfaction of Wilson Compton and the NLMA. War and profit needs, not forestry requirements, dictated Forest Service cooperation during the Second World War. For his part, Wilson Compton thought the war experience had benefited lumbermen: "Lumber is no longer an unpopular industry, and it is emerging from this war, on the whole, with a fine performance record, a cooperative relationship with the war agencies, and a heightened prestige. That did not happen in the last war."[54]

Chapter Eleven

When hostilities ended in Europe and in the Pacific, the government began dismantling its war agencies and disposing of surplus material and equipment. Both public forestry agencies and the forest products industry, anticipating a postwar building boom, began to make adjustments to civilian market conditions. The experiences of the Depression years—overproduction, high unemployment, and government relief programs—offered only a faint blueprint for the future, but few anticipated the expansiveness of the economy after 1945.

The tremendous volume of wood materials consumed during the war and the dramatic increase in cutover acreages placed a large responsibility on federal and state forestry agencies. As the war in Europe was winding down, Lyle Watts noted that there would be a great demand for lumber to supply the European reconstruction effort. The United States, he warned, "must take stock of its present and potential forest productivity" if it was to satisfy European requirements for lumber.[1]

In addition to these words of caution, Watts suggested that the government provide emergency employment to restore cutover or abandoned land, to reduce the fire hazard, and to carry on insect and disease eradication programs. For private lands Watts proposed programs to restore their productive capacity. In 1945 he reported that the Division of Private Cooperation had directed its efforts at the larger operators where "a small amount of work would exert the most far-reaching influence," but the greatest need, he said, was to extend forestry to small forest owners who received no government assistance.[2]

The chief forester also called for greater assistance to farm woodlands, an ownership class whose productive potential was vastly underestimated. While farmers struggled to produce cotton and other agricultural crops for a glutted market, they neglected the contribution that timber growing could make to a balanced farm economy. Although William Sparhawk, a Forest Service economist, had outlined a program for planting trees on marginal cropland at the onset of the Depression, the agency lacked a legislative mandate to become involved in farm forestry until 1937 and then the war eliminated appropriations for the program.[3] Watts's 1945 report, therefore, kicked off a protracted political debate on the issue.

The most influential support for the Watts's proposal came from the nation's oldest conservation organization, the American Forestry Association (AFA). Its two-year Forest Resource Appraisal in 1946 reported that future increases in the production of forest products "must come from growth"; this situation provided great opportunities for "encouraging planting" on private lands and providing small landholders with technical assistance. The productive potential of small forestlands was "so striking as to suggest the desirability of increasing it manyfold."[4] For the next few years the annual reports of the Forest Service echoed the AFA appeal.

Shaping Federal Forestry Cooperation, 1945–1950

The aspirations and objectives of several groups helped shape federal cooperation with states and the private sector in the postwar era. Ellery Foster, research director for the International Woodworkers of America, proposed a three-point production and conservation program: technical and economic assistance to small operators, a national plan for forest regulation, and accelerated research to investigate the uses of waste wood materials. Foster argued that the union's program was a blueprint for reasonable prices, decent wages, good forestry practices.[5] Foster's scheme was in sharp contrast with other proposals that were afloat in the postwar era.

The National Lumber Manufacturers Association's (NLMA) peacetime program for federal assistance differed very little from its previous proposals. Early in 1946, the industry group recommended a maximum effort to "maintain and extend the cooperative principles" of the Clarke-McNary Act. The NLMA asked for the completion of the timber inventory; that "the maximum possible proportion of forest land" remain in private ownership; that the government increase funding for the Madison laboratory; and that Congress pass legislation "for protection against forest insects on all forests."[6] As the pace of economic activity quickened, the NLMA became more assertive in pursuing its version of federal cooperation, proposals that often ran counter to Forest Service recommendations.

While Watts was head of the Forest Service (1943–1952), the agency attempted to couple assistance to small forest landowners with federal cutting regulations. Because of its persisting suspicions about federal regulatory proposals and its domination by large capital groups, the NLMA and its regional affiliates were not enthusiastic about Forest Service assistance for small ownerships. Nevertheless, the Forest Service began to emphasize the importance of technical assistance to this class of owner. In 1947 Watts reported that these ownerships were "in an understocked condition," and although Norris-Doxey foresters had made "gratifying" progress, they had touched only a small part of "one of the toughest phases of the Nation's forest problem—the small woodlands."[7]

Assistant chief Richard E. McArdle detailed the Forest Service position on assistance to landowners in a policy statement to the Association of State Foresters in October, 1946. The offer of technical help to small forest owners "unquestionably" was the most important, because this group was the key to "present and future wood supplies."[8] Present federal programs, McArdle said, offered little help for small owners, most of whom could not afford to pay for technical assistance. The great need, McArdle told the state foresters, was "a program that will provide *on-the-ground* technical assistance to *individual landowners*." The choice, according to McArdle, was "not between public assistance and private assistance," but "between public assistance and almost no assistance."[9] Because "it would be . . . unwise" to offer assistance "to only one segment" of the forest products field, McArdle included large landholders in his scheme. These owners, he said, required "postgraduate advice" in specialized fields "and provisions should be made for it." But the "big parts" of the task both in money and in manpower were "the small landowners and the small processors."[10] McArdle's program for small operators would vastly expand the existing federal-state cooperative relationship.

The *Journal of Forestry* urged its readers to get behind McArdle's "imaginative approach," because it was at this level that forestry students must look for jobs, and small holders had the potential to produce most of the future supply of timber. To ready itself for this task, the Forest Service streamlined its technical assistance programs and placed all of its private cooperative activities in one administrative unit. J. A. Fitzwater, head of the state forestry division, argued that project foresters should be available to "small farm and nonfarm ownerships."[11]

In 1947, in response to an Agriculture Department request for long-range planning, the Forest Service listed "technical advice and assistance to small owners and operators" as its major consideration. The agency's plans called for an increase in the number of forest management specialists and more aggressive forestry extension programs. Although existing authority could handle some of the work, the service asked for new legislation "for technical assistance to nonfarmers," especially the small owners and processors.[12] The planning report included the conventional industry program, but its centerpiece was greater assistance to small ownerships.

The Forest Service lobbied hard for its planning proposal. When McArdle addressed state foresters in 1947, he praised federal-state forestry relations during the year, especially the agreement on a management assistance program for small forest owners.[13] But the more difficult struggle was getting an increasingly conservative Congress and the NLMA to support an ambitious proposal to increase federal assistance to small holders.

Richard Colgan, executive vice-president of the NLMA, attacked the Forest Service in 1947 for dissipating the public's money to serve its own purposes. Colgan criticized the agency's "top heavy" administration, with overhead "super-imposed on overhead," and high-paying office jobs that were "a serious drain" on funds and manpower that could better be used in the woods. He urged Congress to reduce the number of regional officers, to eliminate funds for expanding the national forests, and to discourage the Forest Service from blanketing the countryside with ideologies of control and regulation. However, the NLMA executive supported the full $9 million for fire protection and increases in funds for insect and disease control.[14]

Because of Colgan's testimony and the criticisms of some congress-men that confusion and costliness characterized farm forestry programs, the Forest Service changed the Norris-Doxey farm woodland service to a reimbursement basis in August, 1947. Under the new arrangement the service made agreements with cooperating state agencies to manage farm forestry programs. Charles A. Gillett, a forester with the American Forest Products Industries (AFPI), told the annual meeting of the Society of American Foresters (SAF) that more effort should be made to get state legislatures to increase their support for farm forestry.[15] There was good historical reason for the failure of states to provide management assistance—most state agencies had devoted their efforts to fire protection and small woodlot management had not been a major consideration.

The annual reports of the Forest Service in the late 1940s continued to emphasize the need to expand assistance to small woodland owners. These holdings included some of the most productive and accessible timberlands, which were "overcut and understocked," and constituted one of the "more formidable obstacles in private forestry."[16] Although federal programs like Norris-Doxey and extension forestry continued to grow, on-the-ground technical assistance to these owners remained limited.

In a brief history of management assistance programs in 1950, the Forest Service noted that its earliest efforts to encourage better forestry were aimed at large landowners. But the extension of management assistance to small woodland tracts, which had "suffered greatly from mismanagement and neglect," was the "big job."[17] However, the NLMA and other large industrial groups strongly opposed "subsidies" in the form of management assistance to a "single ownership" class.

Farm Forestry: The Early Years

The political battles at the national level over assistance to small land-holders tell only part of the story. At the end of the war the Forest Service made a strong case that small forestlands would be a critical factor in the postwar demand for forest products. What the service referred to as "nonindustrial private forestlands" by the 1970s had, in fact, been a matter of great concern to federal foresters for some time.

Long before Watts and his subordinates began to lobby for expanding aid to small owners, there had been fits and starts toward providing farm and other small landholders with management assistance. The more progressive state programs had engaged in limited work of this sort for some time. And although the federal effort to extend management and technical assistance to small ownerships dates to the earliest years of the Forest Service, it was not until the Great Depression that any substantial accomplishments occurred. During the 1930s several agencies extended forestry assistance to farm owners — the Civilian Conservation Corps (CCC) established demonstration tracts to show farmers how to manage their woodlands; the shelterbelt project created interest in tree planting on the Great Plains; and the Soil Conservation Service (SCS) promoted tree planting to curb soil erosion and to utilize better farm woodlands. Finally Congress passed the Norris-Doxey Cooperative Farm Forestry Act in 1937 to strengthen farm forestry extension work and provide farmers with low-cost planting stock. [18] The government used Norris-Doxey funds to establish "demonstration" projects until 1941, and then it used the appropriation exclusively for the shelterbelt project, still under the administration of the Forest Service. But the war brought changes; it closed the shelterbelt program and limited farm forestry assistance to marketing problems. [19]

Marketing assistance projects were part of the government's effort to boost lumber production during the war. Although less heralded than the Timber Production War Project (TPWP), Norris-Doxey cooperation required that states match the federal contribution. And when state agencies implemented these marketing programs, there was great variety. The Oregon forestry department aired woodlot marketing information over radio stations, and county agricultural agents publicized the service in their travels. In nearby Washington a similar program provided marketing assistance and advice for woodlot management. [20] Minnesota's forestry department provided marketing help for its farmers. The state's large number of small landholdings were especially suited to Norris-Doxey marketing assistance. The extraordinary demand for wood during the war encouraged the overcutting of small trees, a gloomy prospect for the future of forestry in the state. Although production doubled between 1939 and 1943, Minnesota still imported lumber for local use. Despite the increased demand, at the end of the war there was only one farm forester working in the southeastern (hardwood) part of the state. Effective management assistance for farm forestry was a post–World War II phenomenon in Minnesota.[21] Region 8 provided more marketing assistance for farm woodlot owners than any other section of the country, undoubtedly a reflection of the large acreage of private forestland in the South. The regional office distributed a manual to farm foresters who were directed to give advice *"with special emphasis on the marketing phase"*; to encourage farmers to cooperate in forest fire control; and to cooperate with state agencies in distributing planting stock.[22]

The Forest Service encountered difficulty in administering farm forestry programs in the South because a few state forestry agencies mismanaged the marketing assistance project. Assistant regional forester C. F. Evans told the Washington office that the Forest Service should never associate itself "irrevocably" with one state agency but "should hook up with the agency best equipped to do the work." When an agency failed to cooperate, Evans pointed out, the service should have other options.[23]

Raymond Marsh, an assistant chief of the Forest Service, thought cooperative arrangements with southern states — some with state foresters and others with the Extension Service — would pose problems for the future, although he found no evidence that extension or state foresters were more effective in administering farm forestry.[24] Marsh was one of several federal officials who were concerned about overlapping jurisdictions and tension between government agencies involved in common programs, that persisted well into the postwar era.

State contributions to Norris-Doxey work varied in the South. Eight of the eleven southern states established marketing projects during the war, but in Georgia management assistance for small holders did not come until the end of the decade, when the state legislature finally appropriated matching funds to employ farm foresters. However, the Georgia extension service operated several farm forestry demonstration projects, two of them among the first in the country.[25]

Florida's state forester, H. J. Malsberger, attributed the slow progress of southern forestry to the federal government's failure to provide "substantial public assistance" to aid private landowners. While state legislatures had been remiss in their obligations to private forest owners, in recent years federal funds had failed to meet existing state and private cooperative expenditures. He asked the public to fulfill its obligation to assist farm woodlot owners.[26]

The demand for Norris-Doxey marketing and management assistance was greater than the ability of federal agencies to meet the requests. As a consequence, there was a shift from intensive management projects to less concentrated programs that served more woodland owners. Finally, when the war in the Pacific ended, the secretary of agriculture transferred all Norris-Doxey SCS functions to the Forest Service. This move, an attempt to streamline farm forestry assistance under one agency, sharply increased Forest Service cooperative work.[27]

There were also many nonfarm forest owners who were not eligible for government assistance. Thus, as the economy returned to peacetime operation, the Forest Service recommended the extension of technical assistance to these landowners as well—the thousands of small holders who needed help "because few of them have special knowledge and skill in technical forestry."[28]

Farm Forestry Comes of Age

Despite financial problems and skeletal staffs in many states, considerable progress was made on small woodlots in the 1940s. A few states passed laws regulating the harvest of timber; a few state foresters turned their attention to tree planting and forest management; and the separation of state forestry departments into fire control and management sections also boosted woodlot forestry. But efforts to extend technical assistance to owners of small sawmills failed when important forest products groups opposed the measure.[29]

Forest Service assistance to small owners sometimes had contradictory results—good forestland valuable for agricultural production often was sacrificed for the latter, and farm forestry marketing assistance programs helped speed this process. On an inspection tour through Region 1, Fitzwater noted the paradox—the development of markets essential to the practice of forest management resulted in "destroying the forest" and thereby defeating forest management.[30] The success of marketing assistance programs for small owners, therefore, depended on proximity to markets, the kind and quality of timber, and the degree to which owners followed advice. The equation was not always a prescription for success.

In the Great Lakes states the regional forester's office advised close state supervision of its farm foresters because they were apt "to develop provincial outlooks." The regional forester urged state agencies to provide its foresters with proper training.[31] It is clear that the Forest Service maintained its customary supervisory role in administering Norris-Doxey programs.

When the Forest Service transferred Norris-Doxey assistance to a reimbursable, state-directed operation in 1947, some of the Forest Service regional offices objected. Thus when McArdle told A. R. Spillers, head of the cooperative forest management division, to speed-up the change to state administration in Region 6, McArdle suspected that the regional office "did not want to let go of these projects." State foresters in Oregon and Washington also perferred to see the work continued under federal direction. He told Spillers that Region 6 should stop "dragging its heels on the matter."[32]

One of the frustrating problems for state foresters was the limitations of field work. In Region 6, H. J. Andrews thought the Oregon forestry assistance program could be broadened if the Forest Service modified its rules to permit assistance to nonfarm owners. When Oregon's forestry department requested permission to use farm foresters to help enforce the state's forest conservation laws, the Region 6 office claimed the move would redound to the benefit of "Norris-Doxey work and to the state."[33] This effort indicates the great variety of small woodland assistance from one state to the next.

To streamline woodland management in Washington, the cooperating agencies agreed to coordinate the assistance programs. The Extension Service provided instruction in forestry, and the state's forestry agency furnished the "service principles." The extension forester was to have overall jurisdiction and direct the work of the farm foresters and administer the forestry projects.[34] Despite these efforts, the government never achieved the efficient coordination of Clarke-McNary and Norris-Doxey assistance programs for small forest owners.

When the Agriculture Department shifted to a reimbursement program, it also affected state civil service policies. In Oregon, which had an excellent retirement program, Norris-Doxey forestry was transferred to state administration, but in Washington, where there was no retirement plan, farm foresters convinced the state to place them under Extension Service supervision with federal civil service status.[35] The government dispensed federal matching funds under this arrangement through the forestry division, the money finally paying people who were technically federal employees. In this case, personnel satisfaction, not administrative efficiency or forestry requirements, prescribed the structure of small woodland forestry assistance.

Oregon and Washington confined their first farm forestry and woodlot assistance to the green lowlands of the Willamette Valley and Puget Sound. In the former, the valley's farm woodland supported stands of second-growth Douglas fir that could be easily logged and transported to market. The farm forester divided his time between assisting woodland owners and timber operators and worked closely with county agents to explain the program. The forester's major problem was the large area and the great number of ownerships under his jurisdiction.[36] When Congress passed the Cooperative Forest Management Act of 1950 and extended woodlot assistance to small nonfarm ownerships, the demand for technical help in Oregon increased. But most of the requests for small forest assistance still came from the western part of the state, and the state forester estimated in 1954 that only 3 percent of these owners were able to consult a farm or "service" forester.[37]

Similar circumstances prevailed in Washington, where farm forestry assistance spread from the Puget lowlands to the woodlands east of the Cascade Mountains. The state's forester reported in 1950 that small ownerships held the finest forestlands in Washington—the timber grew faster, and it was more accessible to markets.[38] But, as in Oregon, the numerous requests for assistance placed an impossible burden on the few farm foresters. In its biennial report for 1952 the Washington forestry division cited its biggest task—extending forestry assistance to private forest holdings of less than 120 acres. Under the Cooperative Forest Management Act of 1950, the state continued to administer farm forestry (now "service forestry") through cooperative agreements with the Extension Service and the Forest Service.[39]

At the end of the Second World War small farm woodland ownerships in Minnesota comprised 26 percent of the state's timberland area, most of it abused and neglected. Moreover, assistance to this class of owners was virtually nonexistent until the mid-1940s. Then in 1946 industrial organizations contributed $8,000 to the state forestry division to assist small forest owners in managing their woodlands. The state used the fund to establish a forest management service for owners of 1,000 acres or less, especially in southern Minnesota where the need was greatest.[40]

The Minnesota legislature stepped up its reforestation work in 1947 when it authorized the forestry division to produce planting stock for use on privately owned lands. By 1954 the forestry division employed six trained foresters to assist the state's small holders in 1954, and still the demand for services exceeded the state's ability to handle all requests.[41] When Minnesota entered into agreement with the Soil Bank Conservation Reserve Program in 1956, the state's private forest management service had a well-established technical assistance program for forest landowners.

Farm Forestry in the South

Nearly 60 percent of all industry-owned woodland in the United States is located in the South. When Walter H. Meyer of the Yale School of Forestry visited the region in 1958, he reported that industrial foresters had made "great strides" during the preceding ten years. This kind of praise for industrial forestry in the South was not new. Raymond E. Marsh had reported in 1947 that large owners in the South led other sections of the country "by a wide margin" in their use of good cutting practices.[42] But this appraisal of forest practices on the larger holdings did not extend to small ownerships.

In six southeastern states—Tennessee, Georgia, Florida, Alabama, Mississippi, and Louisiana—two-thirds of the forest holdings were in tracts of less than 5,000 acres. And farmers, many of them with marginal operations, were the most important ownership group in this class. The attempt to introduce good forestry to these owners began with the marketing programs under the Norris-Doxey Act and expanded in the postwar era to include technical assistance as well.[43] But this barely scratched the surface, because there were more than one-half million farm woodland owners in the region.

Promoting good forest management on the small woodlands of the South was a challenge for both federal cooperative programs and state forestry agencies. Most forestland not protected against fire was in the

South, and to compound this difficulty southern state forestry agencies had serious weaknesses. C. F. Evans told William Greeley that state foresters were anxious to promote forestry work, but few of them had the staff "to plan, direct, and supervise work on the scale demanded by their present opportunities."[44] And despite Forest Service attempts to streamline overlapping federal programs in the region, the old difficulties persisted.

The most perplexing problem was the jurisdictional battle between the Extension Service and Norris-Doxey assistance programs. Agencies in virtually every state struggled over the allocation of funds, project boundaries, and the management of farm forestry work. When Oklahoma's state forester asked permission to use Norris-Doxey foresters for fire protection, Fitzwater thought it would establish a bad precedent, because many states "would be delighted to see our ND foresters shifted to a strong fire protection approach."[45] As with other matters, the regional staff had the responsibility for making local decisions, but within the Forest Service guidelines for that particular program.

The state of Georgia was an anomaly in its assistance to farm woodland owners. It had the first Norris-Doxey "forest farmer" demonstration project in the United States, but the project ceased in 1942. Not until 1949 did Georgia again enter into a Norris-Doxey agreement with the Forest Service.[46] Rural poverty and an excessively penny-conscious legislature kept state appropriations for forestry at a minimum in the immediate postwar years. But material conditions—the increasing commercial value of Georgia's forestland—soon brought a dramatic transformation in legislative attitudes towards forestry.

Georgia's investment in federal forestry programs, of course, directly influenced the degree of federal assistance. In 1946 Georgia qualified for fewer federal matching dollars than most southern states, despite the fact that it ranked first in the production of naval stores, produced large quantities of pulpwood, and was second in the South (and fourth nationally) in milling lumber. Table 3 shows the amount of money appropriated from different sources for forestry in five southern states.[47]

But legislative priorities changed rapidly. The postwar building boom, the expansion of pulpwood production, and refinements in the development of pressed wood materials placed a premium on the rapid growth of trees. Requests for planting stock began to outpace the capacity of southern nurseries, and large landholders increased their pressure on state and federal foresters for technical assistance.[48] Georgia forestry was in the center of this transformation from a backward and devastated woodland environment to a leader in commercial forest products.

Despite a laggard state legislature, reforestation work in Georgia made some progress in the late 1940s. The state forestry office filled orders for planting stock, usually to landowners with only a few acres to plant. And because it operated on a skimpy budget, the agency limited its forestry assistance to owners of 150 acres or less. Finally a group of civic and business organizations pressured the legislature to expand the state's forestry capability, especially in fire protection. In January, 1949, the legislature established an official forestry board, the Georgia Forestry Commission.[49] The state was about to enter the modern era of cooperative forestry assistance. The new act removed the state forester's appointment from the governor's jurisdiction. The new five-member commission was responsible for selecting the state forester. The legislature also established a statewide system of fire

Table 3: Funds Available for all Forestry Purposes, by Source, in Five Southern States, 1946. (dollars per thousand acres of forestlands)

State	State	Federal	County	Other	Total
		Source of Funds			
Alabama	$28.50	$12.20	$ 3.00	$ 2.00	$43.00
Florida	15.00	17.50	13.00	—	45.50
Georgia	6.70	8.40	9.00	0.40	24.50
South Carolina	59.00	30.50	—	—	89.50
Louisiana	18.80	12.80	—	5.00	36.60

control that covered all forested lands outside the corporate limits of towns and cities.[50] A banner legislative year, but more was to come.

The biggest change was in funding for forestry work. Georgia increased its appropriation for the forestry commission from $173,350 in 1949 to $890,000 for 1950, which vastly accelerated federal programs in the state. Although most of the increased funds went to fire protection, the state also broadened its management, reforestation, and educational activities. But a critic noted in 1953 that the state's management assistance still "was little more than a service to small landowners for marking and estimating volumes of timber."[51]

At the onset of the 1950s, Georgia's forestry agency suffered from administrative inefficiency — a common bureaucratic malaise during periods of rapid growth. But it was a state with a great opportunity to extend its technical assistance programs to private forest owners. Moreover, these woodlands, especially along the coastal plain, were some of the most productive timber-growing areas in the nation.[52] Given the remarkable recuperative powers of Georgia's forests and the focus of ownership in the hands of relatively small ownerships, the future of the state's forestry seemed promising.

Although the Georgia Forestry Commission established "complete forest management" as one of its main objectives, commission policy limited assistance to 150-acre plots, or a maximum of four days a year with one landowner. Still, the workload was stupendous; the forestry commission estimated in 1950 that each forest management specialist was responsible for an average of 2.6 million acres. Table 4 shows the expansion of Georgia's management assistance program at the onset of the 1950s.[53]

In the next few years Georgia's forestry commission extended its management and marketing service to a greater number of small landholders. By the mid-1950s small landowners were still the "core of the forest management problem," but the state had made rapid strides in extending fire protection and management assistance to private owners. Increased funding for forestry work enabled the state to obtain federal assistance that it had been unable to attract in the past. Once Georgia made the breakthrough in state assistance to forestry, it became one of the most progressive of the southern states in its management programs.[54]

Summary

The powerful and well-organized forest products industry, always suspicious of federal assistance to small landholders, observed the postwar changes warily. The NLMA and its affiliates scrutinized federal policy carefully, fearful that an ambitious Forest Service would attach regulatory provisions to its cooperative assistance agreements. Trade officials favored assistance for research, insect and disease control, investigations into fire behavior, and help in seeking new marketing opportunities. But they looked critically at "subsidies" to small woodland owners and warned the public about such perceived threats as the creation of a wilderness system. And the industry made certain that the largest share of federal assistance still went to fire protection.

The postwar years posed different questions and raised new problems for federal and state forestry programs. The civilian demand for

Table 4: Growth in Georgia's Management
Assistance Program, 1949 and 1950

Activity	Year	
	1949	1950
No. of technical foresters spending 90 percent of time on private land management	3	8
Requests for assistance		
From landowners	362	694
From operators	109	224
Woodland owners advised	210	418
Acres of land owned	48,880	126,568
Woodland owners given assistance	143	184
Acres of land owned	11,826	16,918
Sawtimber marked for cutting (m.ft.b.m.)	12,206	16,508
Pulpwood marked for cutting (cords)	1,726	7,880

forest products, at a low ebb since the onset of the Great Depression, increased dramatically after 1945. A growing population and a modest prosperity (due to wartime savings) translated into lucrative investment prospects for long-term forest management. The increase in the practice of industrial forestry created new opportunities for expanding federal programs as forest owners became aware of the commercial value of their timberlands.

Farm forestry, especially as a practical field program, came to most states in the 1940s. This trend gained further momentum when Congress passed the Cooperative Forest Management Act of 1950 and extended assistance to all woodland owners and to processors of forest products. The rapid construction of forest products processing plants, especially in the South, and the bright future of forest products made woodlot forestry a viable alternative to a faltering cropland agriculture. Cotton and corn fields gave way to tree farms as farmers shifted to meet new marketing demands. But this transition also meant consolidation of ownerships and fewer people living in the countryside, and it was uncertain who would control the course of development and benefit from this new prosperity.

Chapter Twelve

The struggle to increase federal assistance for planting and management on smaller properties that emerged after 1945 involved progressively more complicated cooperative relations between the Forest Service and other federal and state agencies. Occasionally federal programs overlapped one another; some were attempts to rehabilitate impoverished rural areas; and still others tried to provide management and technical assistance to all ownership classes. These cooperative responsibilities were sometimes fragmented and random, and any attempt to place them in coherent and logical order could produce a similar result.

During these years the Forest Service extended its cooperative network to new federal agencies such as the Defense Department and a variety of poverty programs, and it expanded its work with traditional cooperators like the Soil Conservation Service (SCS) and the Extension Service. And federal forestry became involved in a myriad of new administrative responsibilities, some of them far removed from its organic roots. The growth of its administrative structure alienated groups like the National Lumber Manufacturers Association (NLMA), which feared that the Forest Service was more interested in extending its influence rather than carrying out its traditional cooperative mandates in fire protection, insect and disease control, and research. These antagonisms surfaced in legislative hearings over Forest Service participation in controversial programs and when the agency went before Congress for its annual appropriations.

Postwar Budget Battles and the Cooperative Forest Management Act

With the advent of a growing trend toward the right in American politics in the 1950s, legislative battles to fund forestry programs for small property holders assumed added dimensions. When the National Association of State Foresters (NASF) and the state extension services backed legislation in 1949 to raise the authorization for forest planting and management assistance to $2 million, the NLMA lobbied heavily against the bill. But a broad coalition finally pushed amendments through Congress raising the fire authorization to $20 million and $2.5 million in federal assistance to states in distributing planting stock. The Consulting Foresters Association and the forest industries defeated a measure that would have provided direct management assistance to small forest owners.[1] The increased authorizations represented a partial victory but also indicated that budgetary increases for assistance to this class of owners would be difficult in the years to come.

The NASF went before Congress again in 1950 to ask the lawmakers to extend management assistance to nonindustrial, nonfarm ownerships. Joseph F. Kaylor and Perry Merrill of the NASF met with Lyle Watts and Richard McArdle of the Forest Service, and representatives of the NLMA, the Southern Pine Association (SPA), and the consulting foresters to agree on a compromise proposal. After several key changes, the group agreed on a measure that permitted the Forest Service to cooperate with states to provide technical assistance to forest owners, operators, and the processors of forest products.[2] The compromise did not satisfy all parties. George Fuller of the NLMA, for example, called the measure "pump-priming" and said industrial owners, through exemplary forest practices, could accomplish the same task.[3]

Congress passed the resulting Cooperative Forest Management (CFM) Act in the fall of 1950. In essence, it expanded upon Norris-Doxey cooperation and extended management assistance to all classes of forest ownership and technical service to other operators. However, the Forest Service announced that it would give priority to small ownerships. The first year under the act service foresters marked, measured, and estimated the volume of trees in need of cutting, recommended harvest and logging methods, and offered advice in marketing forest products. Cooperating states were slower to hire specialists to advise small sawmill operators and processors, but by 1955 several states provided technical services to this group as well.[4]

Undoubtedly to placate private consulting foresters, the Forest Service directed its CFM field personnel to refer work to them whenever possible. Few consulting foresters competed with CFM personnel, but a group of influential forest consultants in Washington, D.C., had opposed the CFM program, and their opposition influenced others. Eliot Zimmerman, who helped administer CFM programs, recalled that this "extremely vocal" group accused the CFM foresters of "giving free services to potential clients of theirs." But most states restricted free services, and some of them contracted with private foresters to provide management assistance on private woodlands.[5]

Because of the expanded work under the CFM Act, the secretary of agriculture reorganized SCS and Forest Service activity at the state level. The secretary transferred all SCS farm forest programs to the Forest Service, which was to administer the projects through the office of the state forester until the latter was able to assume full responsibility. Although SCS personnel were responsible for the overall farm plan, state foresters were charged with forestry work.[6]

Industrial leaders were divided on the reorganization plan. Western Pine Association (WPA) forester Ernest Kolbe thought the move was "a step in the right direction" because "SCS was inefficient," but Clyde Martin of Weyerhaeuser disagreed. Farm forestry and overall farm management were one, he argued, and SCS foresters had handled the job well "without excess publicity."[7] As he had on previous occasions, Martin feared that the Forest Service would use the CFM programs as grist for its publicity mill.

The CFM Act quickened the bond between federal and state foresters and improved the technical competence of state employees. Although the Society of American Foresters (SAF) occasionally complained about political appointees, CFM field foresters held civil service appointments in most states by the 1960s.[8] And because there were no federal regulatory strings attached to CFM programs, the NLMA and its regional affiliates did not view CFM as a threat to industrial autonomy. But in an age where influence played an increasingly significant role in federal budgetary priorities, assistance programs for less powerful groups were always under attack.

The Struggle over Small Woodland Assistance

Some conservation organizations did not believe the CFM Act was sufficient to meet the burgeoning demand for forest products in the expansive postwar economy. For its part, the American Forestry Association (AFA) moved to reexamine the forest resource program it had adopted in 1946. Meeting in 1953 at Higgins Lake, Michigan, a group of "leading conservationists" proposed a five-point "blueprint" for forestry progress. While large industrial owners were managing their forests well, the Higgins Lake conferees reported, smaller forest owners lacked "sufficient knowledge of forestry principles to manage their properties efficiently." Small private holders, the Higgins Lake report continued, offered the "greatest" opportunity to increase forest production.[9]

Actually, the Forest Service had already initiated a major inventory, the Timber Resources Review (TRR), to investigate the productive condition of small forest ownerships. Commencing in 1952 several public agencies cooperated with the Forest Service in the field surveys. Although review drafts of the TRR findings were available by 1954, the forest products industries protested so strenuously that the report, *Timber Resources for America's Future,* was not published until 1958.[10]

Richard E. McArdle said the TRR findings showed clearly the need to intensify forest practices to meet future demand and pointed to small holdings as the ownership class in greatest need of assistance. To speed productivity on these lands, the Forest Service established the Small Woodland Ownership program, and in the fall of 1958 the agency conducted state and regional meetings to solicit advice on the scheme.[11] Following these meetings the Forest Service attempted to devise a small woodland assistance program, but after two years McArdle dropped the scheme because it was too expensive and controversial. The Forest Industries Council, a public relations and lobbying agency for major forestry corporations, had charged that the proposed "crash program" was "an unwarranted expenditure of public funds, in the form of subsidies and technical services."[12]

189

But the Forest Service continued to emphasize the contributions of small ownerships to future timber supplies. In a paper presented to the Fifth World Forestry Congress in 1960, Leonard Barrett outlined the most promising methods to build up inventories on small woodlands: (1) planting, (2) improving timber stands, (3) improving cutting practices, and (4) reducing losses from fire, insects, and diseases. Barrett noted that the quality of forestry practice in the United States improved with the size of ownership.[13] The TRR report and the Forest Service follow-up meetings, according to Barrett, called for a new approach to management assistance for small owners. In presenting the agency's latest thinking about the small forest problem to the World Forestry Congress, Barrett cited the need to gear programs on a practical basis, because of the variety of forest conditions across the country. There was no "simple solution."[14] This advice would test the administrative flexibility of the Forest Service during the next few years.

When the Forest Service conducted its grass-roots meetings, much of the testimony revealed a need for more on-the-ground assistance. There were complaints that federal programs were inefficient and poorly coordinated, and there were suggestions that the administration of forestry assistance be delegated to a single agency. Other priorities emphasized at the meetings included centralized marketing services, research tailored to the needs of small owners, and a plea for credit and insurance facilities.[15] These suggestions raised basic questions of policy and program direction for the Forest Service and challenged the priorities of industrial forestry organizations that sought different forms of management assistance.

Although the TRR study and the follow-up survey showed considerable support for expanding federal programs to small forest owners, the most powerful forest industry lobbying group, the NLMA, took a different view. Shortly after Congress passed the CFM Act, Richard Colgan, an NLMA vice-president, told a Senate committee that his organization opposed the expansion of state programs and that states should place limits on the "free service that may be provided to any one owner." But the NLMA did not have the field to itself. In 1954 Lowell Besley of the AFA told a House subcommittee that farm forestry and tree planting assistance had garnered "rich returns" because states now assumed more responsibilities for these programs.[16] For the remainder of the 1950s, the NLMA, the AFA, and other organized groups appeared before Congress to argue the merits (or demerits) of technical and trade assistance to small businesses.

In 1953 the NLMA urged Congress to reduce "other forestry appropriations . . . to offset increases . . . for cooperative fire protection and access roads." Two years later Kolbe advised the NLMA leadership to seek increases in appropriations for timber management on the national forests "at the expense of some unnecessary items." And in the budgetary battle for 1957, the *Denver Post* accused a congressional subcommittee of paying "too much attention" to special interest groups like the NLMA.[17] In its testimony, the NLMA had recommended that federal forestry functions be turned over to the states, a prominent theme during the 1950s.

The *Denver Post* attack, which charged the NLMA with "unenlightened self-interest," alarmed forest industry leaders. Fearful that such attacks would bolster the cause of small forest owners, A. Z. Nelson, the organization's forest economist, insisted that the Forest Service request for more funds for tree planting would "add additional subsidies to existing large subsidies" for small owners.[18] What Nelson and the major trade groups wanted were large subsidies for fire and insect and disease cooperation, minimal spending for other cooperative programs, and a shift in most forestry responsibilities to states, where the large forest products groups could more easily dominate.

The attacks on the Forest Service continued. Mortimer Doyle of the NLMA accused the federal agency of refusing "the advice and counsel" of the major industrial groups before sending its appropriation requests before Congress. In an analysis of the budget for state and private cooperation for 1960, the NLMA asked Congress to reduce the "subsidy" for Clarke-McNary fire cooperation. Whereas industry spokesman had bridled twenty years earlier when critics referred to the Clarke-McNary fund as a "subsidy," now they argued that the program had "accomplished much of its original purpose." The NLMA also labeled tree planting assistance to small owners as unnecessary, because private owners "have demonstrated that they will pay for planting their own trees."[19]

Emanuel Fritz, a veteran advisor to the NLMA and a professor of forestry at the University of California, Berkeley, spoke publicly and privately during this period about the need to eliminate "unnecessary" items in the Forest Service budget. Fritz thought that small holders would practice better management when markets made it profitable for them to do so, and he condemned the Washington habit of arrogating to itself all knowledge and technical ability. Like most industry leaders, Fritz did not believe the demand for forest products required such intense production on small forest properties. He told Colgan that the cost of planting and management cooperation was "inordinate," and aid to small owners was "premature."[20]

The Soil Bank Program

The NLMA also fought other federal landowner assistance programs during this time, even when the Forest Service was only minimally involved. One of these, the Department of Agriculture's soil bank program, was designed to remove cropland from production and to plant trees on the acreage. The system supposedly would reduce crop surpluses and serve as a conservation medium. But forest products leaders envisioned a much different scenerio. They feared that the scheme would erode ownership and place control of the land with state and federal authorities, and they chastised the administration and members of Congress for embracing the idea "almost overnight." Forest Service predictions of a prospective timber shortage, the NLMA charged in 1956, gave the soil bank plan legitimacy, but the planners had ignored the possibility of an excessive number of trees, and they seemed indifferent to its "economic and subsidy aspects."[21]

In a lengthy memorandum to Secretary of Agriculture Ezra Taft Benson, the NLMA warned that the soil bank program might contribute to the overproduction of timber. Then the NLMA got to the crux of the matter—farmers might demand "price supports on timber products as well as price supports on farm crops." Because there already was adequate forestland in the United States, federal foresters should reduce their reliance on "federal funds to solve state and private forestry problems."[22] The industry feared the soil bank plan because of its old concern for glutted markets and an excessive supply of standing timber. Private enterprise, forest products leaders insisted, was the best way to assure a sound forest economy. Objections such as these weighed heavily with members of Congress and shaped federal cooperative programs.

As the farm bill, with its soil bank proviso, made its way through Congress in the spring of 1956, Stuart Moir of the Western Forestry and Conservation Association (WFCA) urged the NLMA leaders to lobby hard to stave "off this threat to a stable forest economy." Leo Bodine of the NLMA's Washington office initiated a campaign to get the tree planting provision of the soil bank bill deleted. He informed member organizations that the measure was "potentially dangerous" to the forest products industry. The NLMA also issued a news release that criticized the farm bill because it would "burden farmers with more federal controls."[23] The NLMA also tried to enlist the support of the NASF. But Harry R. Woodward and other state foresters objected to the NLMA news release. Every "honest conservationist," he wrote the NLMA, backed the tree planting proposal because it would protect farmsteads and produce a forest crop in future years. Woodward thought there was "something dreadfully wrong" when public and industrial foresters told different stories to the public.[24]

When Congress included funding for the soil bank program in its general agricultural appropriations bill in 1956, the NLMA stepped up its opposition. The NLMA told Senator Carl Hayden that such federal farm subsidies were not "in the public interest." Better to balance the budget, "increase timber sales, build roads or aid research." The government, it said, was pulling tree farmers into the same "crop surplus morass" as the agricultural farmer.[25] But the farm bill of 1956, including its soil bank provision, became a reality.

The Forest Service and state foresters then worked out a tree planting agreement. McArdle asked industrial nurseries to make planting stock available because the soil bank program would need more stock than state nurseries could provide.[26] In the next few months the industry's loudest complaints about the soil bank program concerned the nursery and seed stock issue. Federal subsidies, it charged, gave public nurseries an unfair advantage over private ones. Industrial leaders also opposed subsidized reforestation and warned the public about federal control. But farmers and state foresters praised the program for helping to alleviate rural poverty.

Some industrial organizations attempted to influence state forestry agencies to refuse to participate in the soil bank program. In the

Pacific Northwest the influential WFCA advised its member states to act on their own initiative and avoid being put on the "dole." The WPA also thought states should reject federal contracts for growing "farm planting stock." In the South the SPA warned its members of the effect soil bank planting would have on traditional programs.[27] Most of the efforts to discourage states from participating in the soil bank tree planting program, however, were unsuccessful.

One state forester told an industry official that he signed the tree planting agreement because Forest Service personnel were always "reasonable and fair to deal with." The Minnesota Division of Forestry agreed to grow planting stock and provide technical assistance as part of its cooperation in the soil bank program. Frank Usenik, who worked in Minnesota's programs for private owners, remembers that soil bank funds helped expand the state nursery and reforest county, state, and private lands.[28] But, as they did elsewhere, private nurserymen objected to the Minnesota soil bank program because it competed with the private sector.

In anticipation of soil bank–tree planting activity, Minnesota added a third nursery in 1956, and the forestry division made plans to double its production during the next three to four years. The expanded capacity of the public nurseries angered private nurserymen who complained to Congress. But forestry division director, E. L. Lawson, wrote Minnesota Senator Hubert Humphrey that he was unaware of any "serious objections from commercial nurserymen." Although commercial nurserymen had raised questions in the past about unfair state competition, Lawson assured the senator that his agency had resolved these problems.[29]

When Congress terminated soil bank planting in 1962, the principle of planting trees on less-productive agricultural land lived on in a variety of Agricultural Conservation Programs (ACP), some of them originating in the Soil Conservation and Domestic Allotment Act of 1936. Although federal assistance in planting dates to the Clarke-McNary Act of 1924, it was not until the late 1930s that federal funds provided for a vast government planting program. In those banner years the Civilian Conservation Corps, the shelterbelt project, and a variety of relief agencies used tree planting to reduce unemployment. After the Second World War when there were no direct federal planting activities, cooperative assistance programs became the accepted practice again.

By the 1950s the SCS and ACP programs paid part of the planting costs for eligible landowners; the Pittman-Robertson Wildlife Restoration program assisted groups in planting trees for wildlife habitat; flood control agencies such as the Tennessee Valley Authority and extension foresters also provided some form of tree planting; and private groups like the Forest Industries Association promoted tree farms. All of these efforts had combined to offset the dramatic cutback in direct government planting.[30]

In states like Minnesota, where settlers had pushed into cutover regions with poor soil, cooperative tree planting programs were beneficial to small landowners. But the assistance came long after the lumbering era had ended. Unlike Wisconsin, which initiated an aggressive reforestation program in the 1930s, Minnesota's tree planting effort is relatively recent. And because of its early promotion of tree planting, Wisconsin's pine forests are in better producing condition today.[31]

Elsewhere, cooperative assistance programs also carried a large part of the responsibility for tree planting, especially in the South where this activity was most intense. The Forest Service reported that the number of trees planted between 1953 and 1958 had doubled, and public and private nurseries were hard pressed to meet the increased demand for planting stock. In the South the soil bank program accounted for about 77 percent of state forestry planting assistance, most of it extended to the owners of small properties.[32]

There is little doubt that the Conservation Reserve or soil bank projects contributed to the great expansion in planting in the late 1950s. In 1957 more than one billion trees were planted, most of them on land withdrawn from crop production under the Conservation Reserve system. Ten southeastern states planted 75 percent of the total for 1959. Georgia led all states in the number of trees planted, and soil bank funds financed more than half of that effort. It is estimated that the Conservation Reserve program underwrote 70 percent of the increase in the number of trees planted in the United States between 1957 and 1959.[33]

When Congress reduced soil bank appropriations, it had an immediate effect on tree planting on state and private land. From the banner years of 1959 and 1960, planting decreased 16 percent in 1961 and another 22 percent in 1962. Despite the decline in tree planting, the southeastern states still led the country in reforestation work in 1961 with 65 percent of the total acreage planted.[34]

Through the mid-1960s tree planting on private land remained fairly constant, and the leading states, both in nursery production and in putting trees in the ground, alternated between Georgia and Florida. But other states also made progress in reforestation. In Region 6, the chief forester praised Washington for its "pioneering work . . . in trying to solve" the state's reforestation problem. The Forest Service also assisted states in the production of genetically improved stock (authorized under Title IV of the Agriculture Act of 1956). Again, the state of Georgia was the pacesetter—taking advantage of the opportunity to produce more genetically improved planting stock than any other state.[35]

Cooperation and Rural Poverty

Although Congress justified soil bank and other cooperative tree planting assistance as measures to alleviate rural poverty, these were only token activities compared to the rural assistance programs that emerged in the 1960s. One of these was the John F. Kennedy administration's Rural Areas Development (RAD) program, initiated in 1961. The program paralleled the Multiple Use-Sustained Yield Act of 1960, which had directed the Forest Service to consider all potential uses in its management of the national forests. But RAD included an additional condition—the development of these resources for the benefit of rural communities.

The RAD program presented the Forest Service with new opportunities for cooperative forestry. And the Forest Service annual report for 1962 boastfully stated that all of its "management activities contribute . . . to the improvement of rural areas." Through the intelligent management of local forest resources, both rural communities and the future of forestry would benefit. Assistant Secretary of Agriculture John A. Baker told the Fifth American Forest Congress in 1963 that the CFM program also would contribute to RAD, because "it provides technical forestry service to America's small woodland owners."[36] In the next few years the Forest Service stressed the importance of CFM work to promote the RAD program.

Forest Service cooperation in rural development became more complex under Lyndon Johnson's Great Society program. And it added extra work for state foresters who had to attend endless meetings. Federal and state forestry representatives served on state rural action panels and worked closely with county and local planning groups.[37] The RAD projects required different forms of technical assistance depending on the section of the country. In the Pacific Northwest RAD development schemes emphasized recreation, but in the South where rural poverty was much more pervasive, the programs dealt with farm cooperatives, marketing assistance, and modernizing forest products operations.

In 1963 the Forest Service participated with the Extension Service, the SCS, and the Farmers Home Administration (FHA) in a conference in South Carolina to inform farm families about the opportunity to participate in RAD programs to alleviate rural poverty. In 1961 Alabama established its own state administration—Rural Resource Development—to improve the production, processing, marketing, and distribution of forest products. Several of the RAD projects required large, federally backed low-interest loans to forest products companies to rebuild plants and to modernize equipment. This led the state's development officials to describe progress under the RAD program as "most encouraging."[38]

Large landholders who wanted to develop the recreation potential of their forests also made inquiries to the Forest Service about RAD assistance. In one case, a north Georgia family holding 22,000 acres wanted "all the help from government possible" to build Swiss chalets, a chipping plant, recreational facilities, and motels and hotels. In another instance, a group of black businessmen, prompted by the closing of a box plant that put 200 people out of work, approached the Georgia Forestry Commission and the Forest Service for advice in developing a wood processing plant. Both agencies agreed to offer their services to assist with the latter project.[39]

Georgia's RAD programs included broad economic development plans for each county. Forest Service and state forestry officials advised county planners on the proper management of local forestlands, and when counties applied to the FHA for low-interest loans to fund development projects, foresters served as professional counselors for the FHA.[40] Most of these schemes involved the extension of loans to build forest products processing plants; RAD programs do not appear to have had a great impact on forest management work.

When the University of Georgia and the Georgia Mountains Association applied for funds to study the recreation potential of the northeast Georgia area, the Region 8 office gave its enthusiastic approval. Forest supervisor Paul Vincent pointed out that in its present condition, small-scale farming and forestry were the backbone of the "economically depressed" area. The study, he said, would help the Forest Service develop its recreation plans for the area, and the private and public development project would improve the local economy.[41] In short, the Forest Service would benefit and the scheme would contribute to the rehabilitation of a rural economy.

As programs and policies changed, RAD became more diffuse and lost some of its identity. In 1968 the Department of Agriculture emphasized a new "outreach" function, a change designed to bring "new directives and information" to rural development policy.[42] The "outreach" scheme never became a reality, because the incoming Richard Nixon administration reorganized the rural assistance programs. It dismantled some agencies altogether and reduced others to skeletal staffs — paper reminders of the Great Society programs of the Johnson administration. Even at its best, Forest Service participation in RAD was far removed from the practical accomplishments of soil bank and other assistance programs for small ownerships.

An adjunct of RAD that emerged in the 1970s was Resource Conservation and Development (RC&D), a program administered by SCS with the cooperation of the Forest Service and state forestry agencies. The purpose of RC&D was to enhance economic opportunity through technical and financial assistance. The program involved cost-share payments or loans to state and local governments to implement land use plans dealing with water-based recreation and wildlife, conservation, and sediment control projects.[43]

Federal Cooperation in the States

The extensive involvement of state forestry agencies in CFM, soil bank, RAD, and other cooperative programs placed a heavy workload on forestry staffs and strained state budgets. For the most part, the boom in building activity during the 1960s sustained state forestry departments in their efforts to gain increased appropriations for management assistance programs. And to take full advantage of federal assistance, states had to provide matching funds, a fact state forestry officials found useful, because they could argue forcefully for a larger state contribution by dangling the federal carrot before legislatures. But even in timber-dependent regions, cost-conscious legislators and temporary slumps in building activity sometimes curtailed programs.

In Oregon farmers and woodland owners had a variety of federal and state measures available to them by the 1960s. The Extension Service distributed pamphlets, conducted film and slide shows, and supported youth programs like the 4-H to advance forest management. Oregon's forestry department worked with soil conservation districts and the ACP to encourage forest production on privately owned woodlands, and the agency's "farm foresters" provided the technical forestry expertise for federal cooperative programs in the state. Included in these new responsibilities were market surveys for the increasing number of Christmas tree growers.[44]

When the legislature changed Oregon's timberland tax laws in 1961, landowners deluged state forestry officials with requests about the act. This workload increased in the wake of the Columbus Day storm in 1962, when landowners sought assistance in salvaging timber and in disposing of nonsalvagable debris before it became a fire and insect hazard. Then, in the midst of the clean-up effort, voters defeated an increase in the state's income tax, a move that forced the forestry department to eliminate four of its eight farm foresters.[45]

Difficulties other than natural disasters also hampered cooperative work in the Pacific Northwest. Stringent budgets in Oregon as well as Washington limited the effectiveness of the CFM programs. The Region 6 office reported in 1963 that CFM work "had not progressed as well as it might" because of budget limitations. But when the Oregon legislature restored the number of farm foresters to seven, the regional office commented that the CFM program in the state "has improved materially." By the end of the decade, Oregon's cooperative program employed twelve farm foresters, and the state of Washington operated with a similar number.[46]

However, the management assistance programs in the two states differed. Washington prohibited farm foresters from negotiating prices or contracts, and they could not scale forest products that were to be put up for sale. Otherwise their services were free. Oregon's forestry department also offered free services, but it directed farm foresters to devote their time to owners who followed the department's advice.[47] In each instance, however, the health of the forest products industry and the generosity of state legislatures determined the availability of assistance to small forest owners.

There were other variations in state CFM programs. In Minnesota the legislature limited assistance to landholders with 1,000 acres or less. And there were other forms of technical help available — Usenik, who worked for the Minnesota forestry division during this period, points out that the rapid expansion of federal programs in the 1960s actually increased the planning and technical assistance available to small ownerships. This aid expanded in the 1970s under the Forest Incentives Program, which permitted landowners to hire consultants through the state forestry agency.[48] Unlike Oregon and Washington, Minnesota's cooperative programs did not suffer sharp budget reductions during this period.

Most of Minnesota's forestry assistance work involved landholdings in the southeastern part of the state. In 1962 district foresters provided technical aid through a variety of cooperative programs — ACP, the Small Watershed Program, and the state's own watershed projects. Service foresters working on watershed projects surveyed the proposed watersheds, made recommendations for proper forest practices, and after the projects were approved, assured that landowners implemented the prescribed forest practices. A Region 9 assessment in 1962 praised Minnesota's foresters for their cooperation "with the several agencies and groups working on the small watersheds."[49]

The Minnesota forestry division also assisted the Agricultural Stabilization and Conservation Service (ASCS) in approving projects for planting. The landowner initiated the work through the local ASCS office, which contributed the funds for conservation projects. The ASCS and other cooperative programs established during the 1960s made it possible for the Minnesota forestry agency to service an increasing number of requests for assistance.[50]

Cooperative programs in the southern states differed from those in

Table 5: Timber Sources Review Report on Southern Forests

Type of Land	Number of Owners	Commercial Forest Land		Percent of Recently Cut Lands in High Productivity Class
		Acres	Percent	
Public	—	15,162,000	8.5	86
Private				
Large	164	26,365,000	14.8	81
Medium	1,424	20,607,000	11.6	63
Small	1,614,386	115,869,000	65.1	34

Percent of total pulpwood cut from different classes of ownership during 1950 in Region 8 States

Public	4
Pulp Company	13
Other Private 500 A	12
Other Small Private 500 Ap	71

the Pacific Northwest because of the South's heavy concentration of small ownerships. Moreover, the productivity of these holdings was a critical factor to the economic health of the region. The TRR reported that the "big job" in southern forestry was the small private holders who owned 65 percent of the commercial forestland, less than half of it in good productive condition.[51] (See Table 5.) In 1966 a forest researcher noted that it was the small owners of Louisiana and Georgia, who controlled three-fourths of the commercial timberland, who were the key to improving productivity.[52]

However, the heavy planting that took place in the South in the 1950s and early 1960s greatly increased productivity on small forestlands. In fact, a few large industrial groups and state foresters complained that the South was growing too much timber. But assistant regional forester Douglas Craig observed that the South was the only section of the country "in which we are getting this kind of talk." To counter such ill-founded information, Craig urged the region's division of information to "develop an active program" to inform the public about the nation's future timber needs.[53]

Southern states continued to expand their management assistance programs to private owners. Georgia, which was rapidly moving to the front in adopting industrially oriented forestry practices, passed legislation prohibiting the destruction of second growth during logging operations. And the increased acreage planted to trees required a more intensive forest fire protection system as owners realized the commercial potential of their growing stock.[54]

These were boom years for forestry in the southland, and Georgia, endowed with some of the best timber-growing conditions in the country, was one of the pacesetters. Such was the productivity of these forests that in 1964 a landowner completed a commercial pulpwood thinning of pine trees planted under the soil bank program in 1956. The Georgia Forestry Commission noted that it normally required twelve to fifteen years to grow a merchantable crop.[55]

Between 1961 and 1963 the Georgia Forestry Commission increased its expenditures for forest management. Although the amount was less than one-third of the money spent for fire control, the percentage increase for management assistance was much greater. Georgia state foresters also serviced ASCS, Conservation Reserve, FHA, Small Watershed, RAD, and the Georgia Crop Improvement Association's programs.[56] The forestry commission, moribund until after the Second World War, had come of age.

Because of the heavy demand for management assistance from small holders, in 1967 the Georgia Forestry Commission limited its aid to four days each fiscal year. But requests for technical help continued to increase. When Conservation Reserve contracts under the soil bank program began to expire in the late 1960s, the forestry commission assisted owners with production and income plans. Commission foresters also provided technical aid for the Naval Stores Conservation Program, a federal activity soon to be transferred to the state. The naval stores project covered fifty-three counties involving eighteen commission foresters in 1972; by 1979 the program had been cut back, and the state employed only four foresters who worked mostly with gum operators.[57]

The Georgia Forestry Commission took full advantage of federal cooperative programs during the 1970s. The Forest Service granted a special commendation to the commission's Metro Forestry Program in 1971 for providing assistance to urban homeowners in Augusta, Columbus, Macon, and Savannah. The number of urban owners given management assistance reached an all time high in 1979.[58]

Summary

The southern states are unique in the rapid development of forestry programs since 1945. The aggressive reforestation that has occurred in the South in the last thirty years and the expansion of state assistance programs are responsible for the emergence of the region as a leader in forest products. The postwar building boom and the increased demand for wood materials made reforestation economically feasible, even on nonindustrial ownerships. Pressured by industrial forestry interests, state legislatures raised their appropriations for forest protection, management, and research; federal cooperative programs complemented this move.

By 1980 diminished stands of private timber along the California coast and in the Pacific Northwest and the proximity of southern producers to major markets had effected a dramatic shift in industrial forestry away from the Pacific coast. And the smaller southern forest owners made up most of the increase in production. The predictions of the AFA Forest Resource Appraisal in 1946—which pointed to the "striking" potential for improving small woodland production—became a reality in the South in the 1970s as large forest products corporations stepped up their investments in the region.[59]

This second southern logging frontier, however, is different from the first. Now heavily capitalized and mechanized operations and a tendency toward larger forest holdings are the order of the day. It remains to be seen if this rebirth in the southern forest products industry will be less disruptive to communities than the first. Meanwhile, in the Pacific Northwest with its private stands in various stages of restocking, the old pattern of mill closures, high unemployment, and devastated economies is being repeated.

But in the South and elsewhere, federal cooperative initiatives provided the stimulus for the great spurt in forestry activities on small ownerships. Material conditions in the 1950s and 1960s combined to make possible a variety of reforestation, management, and technical assistance programs to small landowners. Powerful trade groups like the NLMA generally got what they wanted as well—more money for research and for fire, insect, and disease protection. To a certain degree this fact may have lessened the industry's opposition to assistance for small landowners.

The federal forestry agency itself survived alive and healthy. The attacks of congressional budget pruners and industry leaders do not appear to have harmed the Forest Service. The agency had become involved in heady new cooperative ventures between 1955 and 1970; and the onset of the "Environmental Decade" proved to be an even greater moment to investigate new fields and opportunities.

Chapter Thirteen

Forest protection embraces a broad array of programs ranging from the oldest—cooperative fire protection—to the more recent but equally extensive efforts to protect forests against infestations of insects and diseases. Because these threats to commercial forests respect no property boundaries, protection programs have necessarily involved extensive cooperation among federal, state, and private owners. Historically, Congress charged the Forest Service with major responsibility only for fire protection, but its management of the national forests and its extensive liaison with state forestry agencies made the service a primary participant in insect and disease control programs as well.

Despite the growing emphasis on management assistance programs, fire protection remained the most important form of federal assistance to state and private forestry long after the Second World War ended. In fact, the great edifice of federal-state cooperation in forestry was first erected to protect forests from fire. In the years since the war there have been new technical and geopolitical dimensions to fire cooperation, and insect and disease infestations have occupied a greater share of attention. But the central role of fire protection was still the major thrust of the cooperative relationship.

The postwar era posed new problems for cooperative fire control because the federal government had terminated its wartime emergency funds. And while fire researchers raised questions about the efficacy of controlling *all* wildfires, burgeoning urban populations in southern California made it necessary to develop techniques for controlling *some* wildfires. The multiple ownership jurisdictions in southern California among federal, state, county, and private holdings required efficient administration and cooperation at all levels.[1]

Although federal appropriations for fire protection increased after 1945, state contributions far outstripped the federal increment. The Cold War years also brought new opportunities to fire protection programs in the form of national defense money to investigate mass fire behavior. Although this work took federal foresters far afield from their professional forestry training, the Forest Service used the opportunity to expand its fire-related programs, especially in research. In his classic study, *Fire in America,* Stephen Pyne concludes that for nearly twenty years "the specter of atomic warfare would be the ghost in the machinery of fire research."[2] During the budget-conscious Eisenhower years, however, the Forest Service welcomed the Office of Civil Defense contribution.

Although extensive Forest Service cooperation in insect and disease control is more recent, the effort in the last decades has expanded dramatically—just as federal assistance in fire protection has declined. The more intensive management of forest stands and an increased aesthetic value placed on urban forests have brought greater research and funding to manage insect and disease outbreaks. In this respect the Forest Pest Control Act of 1947 did for insect and disease control what the Clarke-McNary law did for cooperative fire protection. But pest control activity has involved much more *public* controversy than comparable efforts in fire protection.

Forging a Broader Protection Network

In 1945 the Forest Service reported that almost one-third of the private forestland in the United States was still in need of fire protection, most of it in the South. Although Congress raised the federal contribution from $5.3 million to $7.3 million in 1946, the increase fell far short of the figure officials projected for adequate protection. Congress raised the federal appropriation to its authorized ceiling of $9 million in 1948, and the Forest Service praised the states for "substantial progress" in extending their protection programs. In 1949 Congress began increasing the authorization on an incremental basis over the next several years to $20 million.[3] And, as was the practice in the past, major forest conflagrations spurred new organizational schemes or garnered more appropriations from Congress.

When disastrous fires in southern Maine in October, 1947, overwhelmed the state's protection forces, Congress authorized the formation of the Northeastern Forest Fire Protection Compact, the first of its kind in the United States. The compact was an agreement between the New England states and New York to coordinate the prevention and control of forest fires in the seven-state area. The member states agreed to develop integrated fire plans, provide mutual aid, and establish a central agency to coordinate activities. The compact permitted the participation of the Canadian provinces, and by 1970 both Quebec and New Brunswick had joined.[4]

Within six months after congressional approval, the agencies had formed the Northeastern Forest Fire Protection Commission. Arthur Hopkins, the commission's executive secretary in the 1950s, reported some "fumbling" at first, but eventually the member foresters established a training program for each state. An unexpected dividend, according to Hopkins, was a "marked improvement" in the control of small fires.[5] The success of this compact spurred similar efforts in other regions.

Other compacts also took on international overtones. Minnesota and the neighboring Canadian province of Manitoba developed a cooperative agreement to suppress forest fires along their common international boundary. The pact was an elaboration of a 1947 agreement between the Minnesota forestry division, the Forest Service, and the provincial forestry agency for Ontario.[6]

By 1956 Congress had authorized four interstate compacts; one of these was the Southeastern Interstate Forest Fire Protection Compact. The compact originated in a series of meetings in 1953 to seek ways to "stamp out the menace of wildfires in southern forests." After congressional approval and state ratification, the Conference of Southern Governors endorsed the first regional meeting in the South to publicize the effort to eliminate willfully set fires. Forest products leaders widely praised the "cooperative" venture to "push forestry ahead" in the southern states.[7] The extensive publicity literally made fire control a household word in the region, and undoubtedly made the public more conscious of the consequences of intentionally putting the torch to the woodlands.

The Forest Service provided important support for the interstate compacts. Regional foresters served as secretaries and provided technical guidance both to the Southeastern and South Central Interstate Forest Fire Protection Compacts. State and federal fire personnel also held joint training sessions in the control of large fires. The record shows that cooperating states used the mutual aid agreements in battling destructive fires along state boundaries and in providing equipment to adjacent states.[8] The establishment of a regional compact to control fires from the increasingly valuable forestland in the South followed a period of exceedingly high fire danger.

Although the southern states did not eliminate costly fires overnight, the strategies adopted in the 1950s marked the beginning of the expansion of the southern protection systems. The Cooperative Forest Fire Prevention Program (CFFP), a national publicity network, also focused attention on the southern fire problem. And the southern forest products industry, increasingly conscious of the reproductive potential of the southern forests, contributed liberally to publicize the fire prevention campaign.

In Georgia the cost of fire protection rose more than 150 percent between 1950 and 1957. The state's forestry commission doubled its field personnel during this period, improved its technical capability to attack fires, and by 1957 all of its fire crews were mechanized.[9] The use of bulldozers, graders, and other surplus military equipment in the relatively even terrain of the Southeast virtually eliminated the threat of major fires.

Smokey Joins the Fight

The most popular program to publicize the destructive effects of forest fires was the CFFP, a publicity venture that began as a wartime program to encourage public participation in protecting against fires. The Forest Service and the Advertising Council cooperated in promoting the CFFP, which added the "Smokey Bear" poster to its publicity retinue in 1945. In 1950 a bear cub was found wandering the wake of a large fire on the Lincoln National Forest in New Mexico. With the concurrence of the Advertising Council, the cub was transferred to the National Zoo in Washington, D.C., where he became a living symbol of forest fire prevention.[10] Only the live bear has changed in Smokey publicity since the 1950s, a credit to one of the most clever advertising gimmicks of modern times.

The CFFP directed its public relations work toward preventable fires. The agency attributed the success of the program to the cooperation of state forestry departments, "conservation organizations and millions of private individuals." While CFFP directors attributed improved techniques in detecting and controlling fires for some of "the excellent progress," the agency claimed for itself, Smokey Bear, and the local "Keep Green" programs credit for "fires that did not start."[11]

Smokey's relentless campaign moved to Canada in 1956 when the Forest Service, the National Association of State Foresters (NASF), the Advertising Council, and the Canadian Forestry Association approved an agreement to put Smokey's presence to work in that country. A children's book, *The Story of Smokey Bear,* was published in French, Swedish, and Norwegian; Smokey comic books were published in Spanish, and Cambodia copied a Smokey poster and used native animals to translate the fire prevention message.[12] By 1960 Smokey was an international figure.

In 1958 the CFFP granted the first of its "Golden Smokey" awards. Cited for their outstanding contributions were the Advertising Council, the American Forest Products Industries, the American Forestry Association (AFA), and a fourteen-year-old girl from Smokey's homeland, Capitan, New Mexico. The CFFP bought radio and television spots featuring Smokey and produced a fire prevention film, *Vision in the Forest,* featuring the Vaughan Monroe family.[13] The CFFP used other film and television stars to deliver Smokey's message, many of them addressed to youthful audiences. Opinion polls suggested that Smokey Bear was better known to children of the 1950s and 1960s than the president of the United States.

The CFFP pushed the Smokey campaign on several fronts. The Fairmont Foods Corporation offered Smokey Bear flashlights as a premium on containers of Fairmont ice cream; the Atlantic and Pacific Tea Company displayed Smokey posters in stores across the country; the Kellogg Company used a Smokey Bear mask along with a fire prevention message on the back of Kellogg's corn flakes and rice krispies' cartons; and the Keep Minnesota Green Committee built a thirty-foot statue of Smokey Bear at International Falls, Minnesota.[14]

Because of the peculiar fire problems in the South, the Forest Service and southern state foresters organized a Southern Cooperative Forest Fire Prevention program in 1958. The project focused on incendiarism and debris burning and adopted the slogan: "Every time a forest fire strikes, you get burned." However, because of the importance of prescribed burning in the region, the Southern CFFP was careful to distinguish between wildfire and prescribed burning. The Southern CFFP stressed the prevention of debris fires and incendiarism — the chief cause of fires in the region. [15]

Both in the national and regional programs, the Smokey Bear campaign relied heavily on contributed services and commercial groups (who, in turn, capitalized on the bear's popularity) to spread the fire prevention message. On Thanksgiving night, 1969, the General Electric Company presented a free (for CFFP) hour-long musical, *Ballad of Smokey the Bear,* narrated by James Cagney. And the bear was flexible. When "multiple-use" became the new forestry buzz word in the 1960s, Smokey emphasized the great diversity of values associated with the nation's forestlands. [16]

The Southern California Dilemma

To help the Forest Service keep abreast of the latest information on forest fires, state foresters collected a vast array of statistics on forest fires. The Forest Service used the data to formulate policy and to suggest model fire prevention legislation to state governments. And the federal agency could claim that it was making headway in extending fire protection to public and private forests. But the fire problem persisted, particularly in inaccessible reaches of the West and in southern California. [17]

There is little doubt that the fire regime in southern California posed the most difficult problem for cooperative fire protection programs. After the Second World War urban developments pushed into the rugged chapparal-covered slopes east of the coastal region. The prolonged dry summer seasons combined with the brushlike fuel build-up in the mountains to produce high fire-hazard conditions. To compound these difficulties, the population began to penetrate into lands adjacent to primary watersheds, areas covered with flash fuels.

The California forestry division, which was committed to protecting watershed, timber, and grazing lands, had divided its private lands into three zones: (1) heavily timbered lands and important watersheds, (2) lands important to the state with no Clarke-McNary participation, and (3) lands of local responsibility.[18] Because structural fires in southern California presented a threat to watersheds and forestland, the forestry division fought fires in all three zones.

County governments surrounding major population centers in California also played an important part in cooperative fire protection. After 1945 the state contracted with these counties to protect state lands within their jurisdictions. Some counties collected their own revenue for fire protection and then contracted with the state to do the work. They were called "inside" counties. Where counties had established an independent protection system under a fire warden (approved by the forestry division), they were dubbed "outside" counties. These latter jurisdictions presented the greatest challenge to effective cooperation.[19]

The Forest Service had great difficulty determining which "outside" counties qualified for Clarke-McNary funds. A joint state and federal report in 1952 indicated that many "outside" counties were heavily populated and, therefore, areas of critical fire danger. In Los Angeles County, on the other hand, expenditures exceeded the qualifying requirement by almost 500 percent.[20]

The Forest Service always encouraged agencies having jurisdiction over lands outside the national forests to bear a greater part of the protection costs. In a policy memorandum in 1952, the service contended that it carried too much of the fire control burden in southern California and that it wanted to negotiate with "agencies which are not meeting their full responsibilities."[21] But jurisdictional problems and disputes over protection responsibility continued to be a major headache for Forest Service administrators.

In 1956 the Forest Service regional office approached the California forestry division about fire protection on private land inside the boundaries of the national forests. Although these lands were the responsibility of the state, the Forest Service provided fire protection under a cooperative agreement. But the state was reluctant to pay the same protection costs for these lands as it did for areas outside the national forests under state protection. The Forest Service objected when the California fire plan for 1956 would continue this arrangement. But the service was careful to praise the forestry division plan for providing a 68 percent increase in cooperative funds.[22]

Still the fires raged. In 1956 an incendiary fire on the Inaja Indian Reservation burned nearly 44,000 acres, and one month later fires in the Santa Monica Mountains burned 38,000 acres and destroyed 120 dwellings. In the wake of these disasters, the Forest Service, state and local agencies, and Congress conducted investigations into the southern California fires. Federal fire attention was riveted to the region. Backcountry and suburb were joined, and it was incumbent on the miscellaneous fire jurisdictions to cooperate in prevention and control work.[23]

The emergence of this new wildland-urban fire regime fostered new cooperative ventures. And the Forest Service increased the federal contribution for fire protection in southern California to the point that the region consumed 25 percent of the national fire budget. The focus of most of this effort was mass fire, a phenomenon that gained importance with the development of nuclear weaponry and the firestorms that might occur in the wake of such a war. But the association between forest fire protection and civil defense was fortuitous in the eyes of officials who wanted to boost their fire research budgets. Operation Firestop—a cooperative field experiment conducted in 1956 by the Forest Service, civil defense contingents, and state and county fire services—was one of these ventures. DeWitt Nelson, the director of California's Department of Natural Resources at the time, called the experiment in mass fire behavior "one of the biggest cooperative projects I've ever seen."[24] The three-month summer operation marked the beginning of more formal and extended financial ties to national defense.

Destructive forest fires continued to spur advances in agency cooperation. When fire disaster struck southern California again in 1970 (and similar conflagrations in other regions taxed federal and state protection forces), Congress voted funds for research into fire planning and communication. Federal forestry's Riverside Laboratory projected a five-year study to apply available information to the fireline. FIRESCOPE, an integration of federal, state, and local protection agencies, centralized the coordination and logistics of fire control efforts. FIRESCOPE treated all fire phenomenon alike, whether wildland or urban, and it provided a coordinating vehicle for other disasters as well.[25] In some respects, FIRESCOPE was a modernized, systems approach to cooperative fire control — the present-day form of an idea that originated with the Western Forestry and Conservation Association (WFCA) in 1909.

When protection officials raised the question of appropriations for Clarke-McNary fire cooperation, southern California served as both metaphor and model. Kenneth Pomeroy, the chief forester for the American Forestry Association (AFA), criticized President Richard Nixon's revenue sharing plan in the early 1970s, because it would "result in less fire money in the most critical area — southern California." After he retired as director of natural resources, Nelson used examples from southern California to plead for more federal fire protection funds. Population increases, "urban sprawl into the forest and watershed lands," and the public demand for more of the "amenity resources" called for a larger federal commitment to cooperative fire protection. Moreover, fire was ambulatory and was "frequently followed by floods, landslides, accelerated erosion, property destruction, and stream degradation."[26] Although Nelson magnified his description to fit the entire nation, it was more appropriate to the consequences of fire in southern California.

Recent Developments in Cooperative Fire Protection

Military interest in mass fire and the civilian concern for wildland fire in the 1950s and 1960s introduced the Forest Service to cooperation in rural fire protection. But these ties were informal and lacked congressional authorization until 1972, when Congress passed the Rural Community Development Act that provided federal assistance for a Rural Community Fire Protection Program. In 1978 the Cooperative Forestry Assistance Act formalized the program for rural fire protection.[27] The concept now has legitimacy within the purview of other Forest Service cooperative programs, and its ties to military interests have been sharply reduced.

Funding for rural fire protection is through the annual agricultural appropriation acts. State foresters, who serve as the formal grantees, treat the federal grants as "pass through" funds to be distributed to rural fire departments. State forestry agencies require that rural fire departments match these subgrants on a 50-50 basis. The funds are used to organize new departments, train personnel, and purchase equipment. The Federal Excess Property Program supports the equipment phase of the cooperative relationship.[28]

Since the early 1960s the Forest Service has participated in a cooperative fire study that extends beyond the United States. When the Food and Agriculture Organization of the United Nations established the North American Forestry Commission in 1960, it set in motion a series of continental forestry meetings. In 1971 the commission established the Fire Management Study Group, whose main objective has been "to promote mutual assistance among the three participating countries." The study group's main contribution to the exchange of information is its excellent publication, *Forest Fire News*.[29] Despite different administrative structures in Canada, the United States, and Mexico, the organization provides a meeting ground for the leaders of the three forest fire control communities.

By the end of the 1970s, Forest Service fire protection programs were in retreat. The statutory establishment of federal fire protection in 1911 had expanded to a size that even its most visionary proponents could not have anticipated. By the post–World War II era state agencies had assumed a larger responsibility for protecting state and private lands. Finally, the Cooperative Forest Management Act of 1978 allowed the federal government to withdraw its funds when they were no longer needed, a reversal of nearly seventy years of federal-state cooperation.[30] Program funding peaked in 1979 and then declined sharply. The cooperative activity that had done so much to strengthen the Forest Service and grant professional legitimacy to forestry was now being diminished or absorbed into broader programs.

But cutbacks in Forest Service funding for fire protection do not mean that its role in assistance programs has diminished. In fact, the more intense management of industrial forestlands and the effort to increase productivity on small woodlands brought the agency expanded cooperative opportunities in pest and disease assistance, watershed management programs, and the transfer of its research expertise to state agencies and private operators. And under the multiple-use concept, the service established liaison with public and private agencies not directly associated with the forest products industry.

The Forest Pest Control Act

Since its inception, the Forest Service has participated in cooperative insect and disease control programs. Although other government agencies held the statutory authority for conducting research and eradication work, the Forest Service usually was involved because of its responsibilities for the national forests and its working relationships with state forestry agencies. But its work languished until the 1930s when the Civilian Conservation Corps (CCC) enabled the Forest Service to participate in projects to control white pine blister rust and other forest plagues. The agency increasingly viewed this work as a major part of responsible forest protection.

Immediately following the Second World War, industrial groups and the AFA stepped-up their campaign for larger federal appropriations to control insects and diseases — deemed by some "more destructive than fire" to commercial timber stands. The AFA's forest resource appraisal of 1946 observed that some states had passed legislation to control epidemics, but there were no uniform patterns to coordinate operations or for sharing costs.[31] Administrative structures complicated the matter, because the Bureau of Entomology and Plant Quarantine (BEPQ) directed insect work, and the Bureau of Plant Industry, Soils, and Agricultural Engineering (BPI) handled tree diseases.

The federal government's long fight against the white pine blister rust was a precedent for other insect and disease control programs. Because of the variety of ownerships in the pine forests of the Rocky Mountain and Pacific Coast regions, Congress passed the Lea Act in 1940 to unify and coordinate blister rust control projects irrespective of property boundaries. And because the Lea Act was popular, western forest industry leaders like Stuart Moir wanted Congress to extend control programs to other pests, such as the pine beetle.[32]

Public foresters and industry officials in the Pacific Northwest were active in the move to improve the coordination of activities to protect forests from insect damage. Early in 1945, regional trade leaders and representatives of public agencies met in Portland and agreed on a call for "cooperative insect control legislation" based on the Clarke-McNary or Lea Act principle.[33] Western forestry interests who were concerned about insect damages to timberland property would benefit the most from the pest control legislation.

In the spring of 1946 the National Lumber Manufacturers Association (NLMA) and its regional affiliates lobbied aggressively for the passage of Senate Bill 1963, which authorized the Department of Agriculture to cooperate with states and individuals to carry out forest and insect disease control programs. The NLMA drew attention to the report of the Joint Congressional Committee of Forestry in 1941, which had recommended the extension of the Clarke-McNary Law "to provide for cooperative protection against forest insect and diseases." Paul Keen, an entomologist who worked in support of the bill, thought that the type of legislation "made very little difference" as long as it provided for the cooperation of federal, state, and private agencies.[34]

Supporters of the forest pest control bill differed over methods of funding. Moir thought the bill had "some bugs in it," and Keen feared that a strict 50-50 federal-state match would prevent the BEPQ from acting quickly to control sudden outbreaks of insects. But the main task, Moir pointed out, was to get a bill through Congress, because the bug problem was "as important to the pine region as is fire prevention."[35] Despite Moir's sense of urgency, the bill did not pass during the 1946 session.

Congressmen introduced companion forest pest control bills, similar to the 1946 version, in both houses early in 1947. George Fuller, a vice-president with the NLMA, thought the measures would pass easily because "the Forest Service is in perfect agreement with industry in this legislation." Richard Colgan of the NLMA testified in behalf of the bills and the Southern Pine Association (SPA) joined with the Western Pine Association (WPA) to file briefs favoring the legislation. Finally, both houses approved a consolidated measure, and the president signed the Forest Pest Control Act, which recognized a federal responsibility for forest insect and disease protection on all classes of ownerships.[36]

The Forest Pest Control Act offered federal technical and financial assistance to state forestry agencies to detect and control outbreaks of insects and diseases. As they had with the Clarke-McNary Act twenty-three years earlier, industry leaders cooperated with the Forest Service to lobby the measure through Congress. The responsibility for insect and disease control was to be a cooperative undertaking involving several federal agencies, including the Forest Service and its office of pest control. In 1953 a federal reorganization plan transferred the blister rust control program from the BEPQ to the Forest Service.[37] But this was only half the battle; there remained the task of getting Congress to fund programs in the field.

Funding and Cooperation in Pest Control

The struggle for pest control appropriations was similar to the annual battles for the Clarke-McNary fire protection program. When a spruce budworm outbreak occurred in the West in 1949, the WFCA and the WPA urged Congress to pass a deficiency bill to support a control program. "The bugs just don't wait to do their job until after Congress has appropriated money," Moir wrote the leadership of the NLMA. But some industry leaders, like A. J. Glassow, general manager of the Brooks-Scanlon operations in Bend, Oregon, questioned the need for more money to fight the spruce budworm epidemic while "many of us are trying to get the Federal Government to cut down on expenditures."[38]

There was no single formula for cooperation in forest pest control. W. L. Popham, as assistance chief in the BEPQ, outlined a variety of cooperative programs for the WFCA in December, 1949. In the case of a tussock moth outbreak in Idaho in 1947, he pointed out, Congress appropriated funds to match the state's contribution, and the BEPQ assumed responsibility for the technical phases of the program. The Forest Service cooperated with Idaho's forestry agency to direct the field operations.[39]

But when a spruce budworm epidemic occurred in Oregon in 1949, the Oregon forestry department assumed responsibility for the infestation on state and private lands, and the Forest Service took charge on federal and intermingled private lands. The cooperating agencies, Popham emphasized, strived to distribute funds equally to all the ownerships involved. The pest control act, he said, provided flexibility—"It is now up to us to see that the job is done in a business-like manner."[40]

Forestry agencies in Oregon and Washington carried out aerial surveys beginning in 1947 to locate and determine the extent of spruce budworm damage. The surveys, conducted during the summer months when damage was easily detected, included all forested areas in Region 6 and made it possible to compile a long range profile of forest insect behavior in the Pacific Northwest.[41]

The largest recorded infestation of spruce budworm occurred in 1950. But budworm activity has varied in Oregon and Washington; surveys showed no budworm damage in Oregon between 1964 and 1969, but infestations reappeared in 1970 and have continued to cause defoliation periodically ever since. Budworm damage in Washington has fluctuated even more. The Forest Service used DDT in its early spraying programs, but when the government banned the insecticide in 1972, the agency turned to other chemicals like Malathion (1965), Zectran (1971), SEVIN 4 oil (1976), and Orthene (1978).[42]

The spruce budworm was only one of many insects that threatened commercial forests in the Pacific Northwest. When a bark beetle infestation struck Englemann spruce in northern Idaho and western Montana in 1952, the cooperating groups drafted a program to halt the outbreak. They assessed the extent of beetle damage (which followed a major blowdown two years earlier) and planned a gigantic salvage operation that required the building of logging roads and a spraying program.[43] In major infestations such as the bark beetle outbreak of 1952, Congress usually made emergency funds available to allow the federal agencies to cooperate in protection work.

The forest products industry and the BEPQ established a cordial and close working relationship following the passage of the pest control act. The NLMA urged forest owners to "expand their cooperation" with the bureau to help develop adequate detection programs, and the bureau, in turn, thanked industry associations for "their keen interest in forest insect problems."[44] This mutual confidence is no mystery. Forest owners wanted government assistance to protect timberland from pest damages, and for its part the BEPQ relied on these groups to pressure Congress to provide funds for research and control work. It was a replay of the old Clarke-McNary game.

The forest industry also sought more funds to protect the national forests from insects and diseases. At a congressional hearing in 1953 Ernest Kolbe told the committee that forest insects were the "number one problem in the forests of the western United States," and he pointed to the sizable contributions of the state and private sector as good reason for federal cooperation in emergency situations.[45] Trade officials also emphasized the disparity between the state and private contribution and the federal allocations for insect and disease control.

When the government transferred forest insect and disease work in the Forest Service in 1954, the agency announced that it intended to administer its new responsibilities in ways similar to the arrangements for fighting forest fires. At a joint policy conference, a Forest Service spokesman said that the plan "should be based upon maximum cooperation"; that cooperation should involve federal, state, and private agencies; and that the federal government provide employees with training to report infestations.[46]

Secretary of Agriculture Charles F. Brannan established an advisory committee of Forest Insect and Disease Consultants to make recommendations for federal control programs. The committee included virtually every group interested in insect and disease work—chemical companies, the forest products industry, forest entomologists, state and urban foresters, and an industrial forester. When the Forest Service created its new Division of Forest Pest Control in 1956, the agriculture secretary established a "Pest Advisory" group of twelve members. But neither the Forest Service nor the secretary of agriculture consulted the group, and, according to committee member Kolbe, it was "deliberately relegated to the bone-yard."[47]

Despite occasional differences over the administration of pest programs, the Forest Service was able to expand its cost-share activities with state forestry agencies. In the late 1950s the service sprayed huge acreages with DDT to reduce spruce budworm damage in Arizona, Maine, Minnesota, and Oregon. The Forest Service pointed out to its critics that it worked with the U.S. Fish and Wildlife Service and state fish and game agencies to minimize damage from spraying operations, and in 1958 it cited a "cooperative" study to indicate the safety of the DDT applications.[48] This instance points to the difficulty with agencies that monitor their own programs, especially controversial ones involving the spraying of DDT.

During the 1960s the Forest Service cooperated with several federal agencies to monitor the effects of spraying programs on wildlife. But it continued to use pesticides and insecticides not specifically forbidden by the government. In its annual report for 1964 the Forest Service informed the public that the "buildup of residue in fatty tissues is a temporary condition" in animals like deer and elk.[49] Finally, an aroused public, spurred to action in 1962 by the publication of Rachel Carson's *The Silent Spring,* pressured the service to reevaluate its use of chemicals in insect and disease control programs. In this long and bitter controversy, the agency usually has aligned itself against citizen groups who wanted to prohibit or substantially reduce the use of potentially harmful sprays.

Regional Agreements and Compacts

Although federal research was an integral part of insect and disease control, forest products industries and state agencies conducted research of their own. The Georgia Forest Research Council, established in 1953, cooperated with the Georgia School of Forestry, the Forest Service, and industry to conduct insect and disease studies in the Southeast. In 1962 industry groups formed the Southern Forest Disease and Insect Research Council with the responsibility to allocate grants to southern universities to investigate disease and pest control.[50] The council played an important role in funding insect and disease studies, especially as the South entered the era of modern commercial forestry.

In the Pacific Northwest public and private agencies established the Northwest Forest Pest Action Committee to develop cooperative strategies to control insect and disease outbreaks. Its membership included every important forestry interest in the region—the WFCA, the Weyerhaeuser Timber Company, the Industrial Forestry Association, and federal and state forestry agencies. The committee represented commercial forestry interests in the Northwest, and, as such, it established a liaison between chemical companies and regional research agencies.[51]

Some interstate fire protection compacts included provisions that extended protection to the control of insects and diseases. The South Central States Forest Protection Compact cooperated in pest and disease programs in addition to its function as a regional fire organization. But the southeastern states compact restricted member states to fire protection.[52] Outbreaks of diseases and insects, however, galva-

220

nized southeastern land managers into action. And the southern pine beetle was the most important catalyst to organized action.

A recent study has referred to the southern pine beetle as "the most destructive insect killer of pines in the southeastern United States." Although recorded information about outbreaks dates from the late eighteenth century, it was not until the 1960s that public agencies began compiling reasonably accurate data. Larger and better-equipped pest control agencies and improved survey techniques have produced valuable information about the pine beetle.[53] This intensified effort to control the pine beetle has paralleled the reemergence of commercial forestry in the South and the broadening of the region's protection systems.

The fight to control the southern pine beetle has required extensive cooperation between state forestry agencies and thousands of private landowners. When an outbreak occurred, action committees informed the public through radio programs and newspaper articles and drafted control measures for the infested areas. These committees existed for the duration of an epidemic, that is, until it had been controlled or simply run its course. After the pine beetle had ravaged North Carolina in 1955, the Forest Service reported three years later that it had been "completely controlled."[54]

But not for long. In 1962 the service reported that timber losses to "the southern pine beetle were particularly severe." After a fourteen-month effort against an infestation in Georgia, Governor Carl Sanders announced that the outbreak "has been brought under control." The Region 8 office added its praise for the state's effort: "The control of the Southern Pine Beetle by the Georgia Forestry Commission is the most outstanding example of a State forestry agency effectively controlling this insect of any such outbreak in the South." To direct the pine beetle protection work and to help obtain federal support, the Georgia agency established an insect and disease advisory committee.[55]

Despite extensive projects involving the use of chemicals and the removal of infected trees, the outbreaks of the southern pine beetle have continued. When infestations broke out, state agencies and private owners availed themselves of the latest Forest Service control methods. But the most impressive phenomenon so far has been the pine beetle's cyclical behavior—when beetle activity diminished in

1978, the federal government provided no funds for suppression projects for 1979. Southern officials expected state salvage procedures to be sufficient to suppress the low rate of pine beetle damage.[56]

But the restless pest was at work again in 1980 when the Region 8 office reported that Georgia was "in the midst of a southern pine beetle outbreak." And in 1981 Forest Service staff entomologists said that the infestation had killed enough timber to build 34,500 homes. Despite these repeated outbreaks, control methods today differ little from those recommended twenty years earlier—salvage removal, chemical control, and better management of timber stands.[57]

Blister Rust and Tussock Moth Battles

When federal officials recognized that white pine blister rust required silvicultural treatment, they shifted responsibility for the program to the Forest Service in 1953. The agency appointed Warren Benedict, who had been in charge of eradication activity under the old entomology bureau, to direct the work. At first blister rust control was a separate activity, but an administrative reorganization in 1956 integrated the work with the newly created Division of Forest Pest Control.[58] The move marked a historic transition for the blister rust control program—it no longer stood alone as the single activity of its principal administrators.

When the transfer from the BEPQ to the Forest Service took place, the costs of the blister rust control program were immediately apparent to foresters in the Pacific Northwest. The Bureau of Land Management (BLM), for instance, limited its control effort on the Oregon and California railroad lands in western Oregon to timber having a certain commercial value. For other landownerships, the departing BEPQ drafted levels of program activity, depending upon the financial resources available.[59]

The transfer of blister rust control to the Forest Service caused some friction. At one point a BEPQ project leader hinted that the new administration was unwilling to plant white pine on land within established control units, thereby cancelling years of hard work and expense in establishing rust free zones. For its part, the Forest Service cited the lack of seed for white pine planting stock and problems with disease in its nurseries.[60]

The effort to protect against fire and insects and to control the white pine blister rust involved extensive cooperation between several ownerships in the Pacific Northwest. Although many of the blister rust control units embraced large areas of federal lands, these sections often intermingled with private holdings. And because the blister rust eradication program involved the large scale destruction of *Ribes* (the secondary host and carrier of the parasitic fungus), the cooperation of state agricultural agencies was necessary to prohibit the distribution of domestic *Ribes* to farmers within the boundaries of the blister rust control units.[61]

Although the eradication campaign has been successful in the eastern pine regions, rust damage throughout the western white pine range and the sugar pine of Oregon and northern California is still severe. However, genetics programs are producing rust-resistant stock, and the species is beginning to develop a natural immunity to the fungus. Benedict, whose professional career parallels the federal blister rust control program, concludes that white pine will survive this alien importation, "helped along by human effort."[62] But it is still not clear whether the genetics program will be any more effective than the massive *Ribes* removal projects of the Depression years. Perhaps time and the survival of fungus-resistant trees will provide the answer.

In recent years the Forest Service has been embroiled in a controversy involving the use of DDT to combat the Douglas fir tussock moth in the Pacific Northwest. The moth, a native to western North America, has experienced periodic explosions that have defoliated Douglas fir, white fir, and grand fir forests. Under the cooperative funding arrangements of the Forest Pest Control Act, the Forest Service carried out periodic DDT sprayings of these pests until the government banned the chemical in 1972.[63] Even then, use of the chemical was not forbidden under all circumstances.

When an outbreak of the tussock moth spread through eastern Washington, northeastern Oregon, and adjacent Idaho forests in the early 1970s, the U.S. Department of Agriculture applied to the Environmental Protection Agency (EPA) for permission to use DDT. When the EPA granted the emergency authorization for the use of DDT, it authorized the Interagency Douglas fir Tussock Moth Steering Committee to direct the spray plans. As part of its emergency permit, the Forest Service, the Bureau of Sports Fisheries and Wildlife, and state agencies developed a monitoring plan to study the effects of DDT on the environment.[64]

The Oregon Department of Forestry offered assistance to more than 200 small woodland owners whose lands were infested with the tussock moth. State foresters determined the volume of salvagable timber, provided owners with sample logging contracts and lists of loggers and mills, and gave each landowner an information sheet about government cost-share programs. The department also kept forest industry landowners informed and supplied with maps and data to assist in salvage work.[65]

At the time of the tussock moth outbreak in the early 1970s, the Forest Service argued that DDT was the only insecticide capable of controlling the pest on a large scale. With the support of state and industrial foresters the Forest Service was able to marshall powerful forces in favor of the use of DDT at a series of EPA hearings. The EPA discounted the arguments of critics who said the moth would soon run its course. The Forest Service applied the DDT in June, 1974, as part of the 1974 Cooperative Douglas fir–Tussock Moth Control Project.[66]

Because of the variegated ownership pattern in the infested area, the federal government assumed all charges for treating federal lands, but federal and state agencies and private landowners shared the cost for spraying state and private lands on a 50-25-25 arrangement. The spraying has effectively controlled the tussock moth infestation for the present, and the monitoring report contends that the impact of DDT was of very short duration. Critics say that results do not lend themselves to measurement because of the long-term effects of DDT on the biological chain.[67]

Summary

With the intensification of commercial forestry in the South and the increased attention paid to commercial stands of timber since the Second World War, fire and insect and disease control have assumed greater importance. Although forest fire protection will be required as long as humans use the woodlands, the threat of major conflagration in many sections of the country is a creature of the past. The technical

224

capability is now available in most areas to contain fires while they are small. Trial and error, large federal assistance programs, and an intense effort at the state and regional level have made this possible. Equally important, the undertaking has been truly cooperative, and it was the landholder's concern for protecting forest investments and a cooperative federal bureau that pointed the way.

Much the same can be said for the effort to protect forests from epidemics of insects and diseases. The rising costs of chemicals and the persisting controversy surrounding their use have done little to diminish the importance of protecting forests from excessive insect and disease damage. Moreover, all ownership classes — federal, state, and private — have cooperated through regional compacts and agreements and support for research programs to manage forest pests. Some of the technical means to combat forest pests have brought land managers face-to-face with an aroused public, skeptical about the application of certain kinds of herbicides and insecticides. Forest pest control is still a hot item of daily discussion — in newspapers and magazines, in legislative halls, and most of all in courts of law.

Chapter Fourteen

Ever since George Perkins Marsh raised the issue in his 1864 study, the scientific community in the United States has been interested in the relation between forest environments and the frequency and volume of flooding. Franklin Hough's early reports discussed the question, and natural scientists in the late nineteenth century associated the Mississippi River floods with the cutover pine lands in the Great Lakes states. And the debate over floods and forests was critical to the passage of the Weeks Act in 1911. In subsequent years Forest Service and industry spokesmen stressed the association between mountainsides denuded by fire and the rapid runoff of water in their appeals for fire protection appropriations.

The federal government became increasingly involved in watershed management as the twentieth century progressed. But the Great Depression was the catalyst for Forest Service involvement in surveys and investigations of watershed problems. Immediately after the Second World War, the agency joined with the Soil Conservation Service (SCS), the Agricultural Research Service, the Army Corps of Engineers, and other government agencies in watershed projects. These included cooperation in hundreds of Small Watershed Programs; in large-scale river basin development schemes; in the far-reaching Yazoo–Little Tallahatchie project; and several emergency flood situations.

The Small Watershed Program

In the early twentieth century the Forest Service cooperated in reconnaissance surveys in California and elsewhere to study flood control and watershed problems. But the agency did not become involved in flood and erosion control until the advent of the emergency programs in the 1930s. The Flood Control Act of 1936 and its many successors were responsible for the direct participation of the agency on a vastly expanded scale.[1] These early flood control measures limited the federal forester's role to surveys and investigations; actual forestry work on the watersheds was a post–World War II development.

In 1944 Congress amended its flood control legislation to authorize rehabilitation work on eleven watersheds—a move that initiated the great river basin development projects of the postwar era. Congress expanded the agency's authority again in 1954 to include flood prevention work on farmland outside the river basin projects. Known as the Small Watershed Program (PL-566), Congress designed the legislation to help local organizations carry out flood prevention tasks on watersheds not exceeding 250,000 acres. The program covered structural flood control measures, upstream watershed protection, and livestock control.[2] These projects filled the void between water-related conservation practices on individual ownerships and the large downstream basin development projects.

Under the Small Watershed Program, the Forest Service worked closely with the SCS and the Agricultural Research Service and the Army Corps of Engineers. The Forest Service cooperated with state agencies, and where the programs involved private forestland, state foresters assumed responsibility for the field work. By 1956 these projects included forest resource planning for the lower Mississippi River tributaries, the Columbia River basin, and elsewhere. The service also agreed to conduct studies of the Corps of Engineers' surveys of the Delaware River basin and to investigate the Bureau of Reclamation's plans for the Upper Colorado River Storage Project.[3]

Congress also appropriated funds for several watershed demonstration projects in 1953. Authorized for a five-year period, the funding was similar to the Small Watershed Program, but its duration was limited. The SCS initiated the demonstration projects on selected watersheds "to show what upstream watershed treatment can do in preventing floods and controlling sediment." The work involved the cooperation of state forestry officials and local sponsors. Although tree planting was important, the cooperating agencies also offered technical forestry assistance and participation in cooperative fire protection to landowners.[4] Congress disbanded the pilot demonstration project in 1958 when its legislative authorization expired.

Clearly, these federally funded projects provided an opportune moment for the Forest Service to extend its cooperative network to new fields. The Corps of Engineers and developers who promoted these schemes wanted the backing of as many agencies as possible to increase the likelihood for federal funding. The Forest Service willingly offered its expertise and support to these projects.

Forest Service–SCS-State Cooperation

The Forest Service and the SCS did not always function smoothly together, and their experiences in the watershed demonstration projects were no exception. Regional Forest Service officials and representatives from the Washington office held an important three-day meeting early in 1954 to discuss cooperative relations with the SCS for participating in the demonstration pilot program. Several of the regional foresters complained that the agriculture secretary's delegation of authority was unclear and that more definitive criteria were needed to clarify the responsibilities of each party.[5] Such complaints were not new, but the fact that both agencies attempted to clarify their responsibilities probably helped smooth relations for the duration of the program.

There were similar problems with interagency cooperation in the Small Watershed Program. In North Carolina the state forester complained that the SCS office wanted to do all the planning work, including woodland management. The state forestry agency, which had assigned a watershed forester to each project, appealed to the Region 8 office and got results. The assistant regional forester met with the appropriate North Carolina agencies and worked out an agreement that delegated all of the forestry activities on the PL-566 projects to the forester's office. But the Region 8 office also noted that Washington SCS officials had encouraged its field personnel to take over all farm planning work, and unless the Forest Service intervened, "the situation is going to grow increasingly worse at the field level."[6] The incident suggests that the Forest Service was quick to take offense when others challenged its turf.

But when Region 8 appealed to the Washington office about the aggressive designs of the SCS, it came up empty-handed. Warren T. Murphy, in charge of flood prevention and river basin programs, praised the regional office for working out an agreement in North Carolina, and he advised that such matters "be worked out in the field." He confirmed assistant regional forester Douglas Craig's suspicions that Washington would accept "our comments . . . rather coolly."[7]

When Region 8 became embroiled in another confusing case involving the PL-566 program in Arkansas, the office kept the matter at home. Watershed foresters in the state charged that the SCS had drafted forest management plans without seeking the cooperation of the state forestry agency. Harley Janelle, who toured the Arkansas projects for the Forest Service, reported that the administration of the state's watershed projects was inefficient and arbitrary and that SCS field personnel refused to cooperate or share details of their farm planning work with their counterparts in the Arkansas forestry agency.[8] Unlike the easy conciliation achieved in North Carolina, the Arkansas situation was more difficult. Yet Region 8 officials did not press Washington on the issue. Chastened once was enough!

The Arkansas situation contrasts sharply with cooperation on watershed projects in Minnesota. Forest Service inspectors praised the supervision and technical assistance Minnesota foresters provided to farmers, and it applauded the state for attempting to train its personnel in watershed management and hydrological principles. And the reports singled out for special commendation the state's cooperation with other agencies in the Small Watershed Program.[9] Minnesota's state foresters assisted in surveys of proposed watersheds, and once the SCS approved the projects, the state forestry division saw that cooperating landowners carried out the prescribed forestry practices. Officials usually selected badly eroded land for project work because state foresters and SCS personnel considered these lands critical sources of sedimentation and the rapid runoff of water.[10]

The Georgia Forestry Commission participated in several planting projects under the Small Watershed Program. State foresters cooperated with the soil conservation districts to provide management assistance for watershed projects. In 1964 the commission produced a film that emphasized the contributions watersheds made to community health and welfare, and in the early 1970s the forestry commission cooperated in a unique urban-centered project on the Bull Creek watershed adjacent to the city of Columbus. State foresters developed work plans, planted critical areas, and provided management assistance to landowners. [11]

Georgia's experience also shows the gradual dissolution of the Small Watershed Program in recent years. As part of a nationwide effort to reform state projects, the SCS and the Forest Service reviewed the program in Georgia. The investigation showed that "almost universally" accomplishments fell short of the original objectives. The review team advised administrators to reinventory critical areas and to close projects where programs were unworkable. Carl Hoover, who worked in watershed programs for many years, believes the budget-cutting that took place did little harm because watershed needs are not as critical today as they were ten years ago. [12]

For its part, the commission reasoned that its decision to cut back the PL-566 program was sound. Commissioners complained of "the constraints and restrictions" built into the program that made it difficult to achieve "significant accomplishment." Despite these cutbacks in the PL-566 program, the Georgia Forestry Commission continued to emphasize that forest management plans should include "maintaining, enhancing and rehabilitating the soil resource, protecting the water resource, and improving the productive capabilities." The commission recommended that prescribed burning be restricted to noncritical slopes, that tree planting take into consideration erosion control, and that all harvesting plans be designed to protect and enhance watershed stability. [13]

Large River Basin Projects

Comprehensive, large-scale river basin development originated in the flood control legislation of the late 1930s and early 1940s. The establishment of the Federal Inter-Agency River Basin Committee in 1943 assured that forestry would be an important part of the planning process. The committee's first action organization was the Columbia

River Basin Inter-Agency Committee; in later years it established a Missouri Basin Inter-Agency Committee and a Pacific Southwest Inter-Agency Committee. In 1950 President Harry S. Truman requested interagency participation for river basin planning in the New England and New York area and for the Arkansas–White and Red River basins.[14] The latter two proposals were similar to earlier schemes for river basin development, now more than a decade old.

Federal efforts to ameliorate the lower Mississippi River problem after the disastrous floods in 1927 led to a series of Army Corps of Engineers surveys and subsequently the first great multipurpose river basin project—the Tennessee Valley Authority (TVA). Most development plans, however, were less ambitious. The Arkansas–White-Red River (AWR) basin project was one of these.[15] As it did for other projects, the cooperating agencies emphasized the social and economic benefits that would accrue to residents of the AWR area through the planned development of the basin's resources.

The AWR Basins Inter-Agency Committee directed each of the participating agencies to submit detailed studies of their phase of the investigation. The committee also made plans to mail accounts of its meetings to the governors of states within the project area—Arkansas, Louisiana, Oklahoma, Texas, New Mexico, Colorado, Kansas, and Missouri. The Department of Agriculture established a small coordinating group (the USDA Field Committee) to advise its representative on the AWR Inter-Agency Committee.[16]

Despite the fact that the AWR study was primarily a fact-finding operation, cooperating agencies did not submit preliminary reports until the summer of 1954. In the interim the project went through several changes. Because of friction between federal departments, a Bureau of the Budget inquiry led to the appointment of a presidential arbiter and majority rather than unanimous decisions.[17] It is clear from the intervention of the budget office that interagency cooperation in the AWR investigation was not smooth.

The Department of Agriculture made other changes in the summer of 1953 and gave administrative responsibility for flood prevention programs and river basin investigations to the SCS. The Forest Service, however, retained responsibility for the forestry aspects of the program. In addition, the Forest Service placed flood prevention work with the Branch of State and Private Forestry and transferred responsibility for surveys from experiment station directors to regional forest-ers.[18] The administrative reshuffling would seem to indicate both in-terdepartmental friction and problems between agencies in the same department.

The AWR forestry report recommended the obvious: (1) protec-tion from fire, insects, and diseases; (2) planting; (3) good forest prac-tices; (4) proper range management; and (5) coordination of all activi-ties to maintain favorable watershed conditions. The report advised that the forestry program be implemented over a twenty-year period, although only a small part of the project was to be completed by that time. Although the AWR plan projected an increase of about three-quarter million acres in forestland, it did not consider this a major land-use shift, and it did not anticipate a major change in forest ownership.[19] The report estimated the cost of the program for all ownership classes, and it suggested three categories for project priori-ties: (1) "feasible and desirable" recommendations that could be car-ried out within a reasonable period of time; (2) recommendations that deserved further study; and (3) ideas that have been considered but show no promise.[20]

The AWR Inter-Agency Basins Committee disbanded when it is-sued its final report. Its forestry recommendations were passed on to federal and state agencies; thus, the direct recommendations of the forestry study, as with state and federal planting and forest rehabilita-tion work, were carried out under other authorizations. Although the Forest Service annual reports refer to the progress of other interagency basin studies, there are no further references to the AWR report. Un-like the TVA, the AWR basins sprawled over a vast countryside and did not present a tight political unit when it came to congressional logrolling. The AWR never achieved the status of a full-fledged ac-tion project.

Yazoo — Little Tallahatchie

The Yazoo — Little Tallahatchie (Y-LT) Flood Prevention Project was one of the most extensive flood and erosion control schemes ever undertaken. The work on the Yazoo and Little Tallahatchie water-sheds in Mississippi involved the Forest Service, the SCS, the Agri-cultural Stabilization Conservation Service (ASCS), Conservation

232

Reserve, and local farmers. State and federal planners initiated the project in 1947 and the field work continued to 1982. The objective of the program was to prevent overgrazing and incendiary fires in the two watersheds and to reforest critically eroding lands. Like other flood control programs, the Yazoo work was closely tied to economic rehabilitation.[21] The Mississippi Forestry Commission, industrial forestry associations, and federal and state agencies fully supported the project.

Timberlands comprised about half of the Y-LT watersheds, but farmers in the area thought of their forests only as poor grazing land and as a source of firewood.[22] The Forest Service and other cooperating agencies, therefore, confronted a gigantic selling job—convincing people to adopt ways that were new and contrary to conventional practice. The prevailing folk wisdom among landowners was to treat any obligation to society as "socialism," and rehabilitating worn-out land was expensive and lacked glamor.

The first phase of the Y-LT rehabilitation project included fire control, roadbank stabilization, tree planting, and brush dam construction. By 1956 the Mississippi Forestry Commission had extended fire protection to all counties within the watershed, and the Corps of Engineers had completed four dams on the tributaries to the Yazoo and planted over 10 million pine seedlings on reservoir lands. The newly created Tallahatchie Research Center—a branch of the Southern Forest Experiment Station and the Agricultural Research Service—conducted investigations to resolve problems associated with the Y-LT project.[23] The flood control and land rehabilitation effort was one of a kind in terms of providing assistance in the field and distributing planting stock to private landowners.

The Tallahatchie Research Center was a vital part of the Y-LT project. It conducted planting studies to improve the survival and growth of pine seedlings under adverse conditions. It studied the effectiveness of tree planting to reduce surface runoff and assessed the growth characteristics of the four major southern pines under different soil conditions. Equally important for the social implications of the project, the center changed its research emphasis from farm forestry investigations to studies in watershed hydrology and soil moisture and expanded its research in marketing and production economics.[24] The latter undoubtedly reflected the growing value of the restocked lands.

For its contribution to the project, the Forest Service relied heavily on its public information apparatus. And after ten years of public relations work, the Forest Service estimated that no area of its size had ever been subjected to such an intense "barrage of conservation propaganda." Although the SCS and the Mississippi Forestry Commission put out a constant stream of information, project foresters kept up the most sustained attack against the conventional way of doing things. The ten years of "educational activities" included more than 3,000 news articles, presenting an equal number of motion pictures, approximately 1,100 public talks, radio and television programs, and more than 300 "show-me" trips.[25]

And the propaganda campaign worked. According to Y-LT project manager, Victor B. MacNaughton, the landowner's changed attitude toward his woodland "has made the accomplishments on-the-ground possible." The educational work had created an atmosphere in which "a landowner literally cannot afford *not* to practice forestry." Investors, with an eye to the commercial potential of southern forestland, were buying up old farms and availing themselves of liberal government planting and assistance offers.[26] But MacNaughton ignored the likelihood that sharp-minded investors might view the combination of cheap land and federal assistance programs too good to pass up.

MacNaughton's planting report for 1963 recalled "the 1958 days of 'Wine and Roses' for forestry" on the Y-LT—24 million trees planted, landowners clamoring for technical assistance, and a new forest products plant under construction. "The future was bright and everything set for a forestry GO unlimited." But Y-LT landowners planted only 9 million trees five years later, the forest products plant had reduced the radius of its wood procurement area, and the pulp and lumber market was "soft." Field foresters learned, MacNaughton pointed out, "that trees merely as soil stabilizers without their economic sex appeal lost much of their attraction to land owners." Then, to make matters worse, the worst fire season in a decade struck the project area.[27]

The gloomy market conditions for 1963 did not improve much the following year. Although Y-LT planting increased, "public faith" in the future of forest products, MacNaughton reported, "is still not restored." He also pointed to other trends in the project area—a declining population and larger individual ownerships. But the "paramount problem" was the need for more marketing outlets for forest products; public interest in forestry, MacNaughton indicated, "had cooled in direct proportion to the availability of forestry markets."[28]

By 1965 prospects had brightened. The Georgia-Pacific Plywood Company began construction of a plywood mill at Louisville, Mississippi, and the International Paper Company announced plans for a pulp and paper mill near Vicksburg. The likelihood of additional mill construction prompted MacNaughton to dub 1965 as "the year the mills came to Mississippi":

There is still poverty here and conservation still costs money to start, but there are encouraging signs. Most houses are now painted and many are built of brick. Improved pastures are common; the bare ground is disappearing except at spring plowing in the bottoms; the per capita income is climbing; hundreds of lakes and ponds now dot the landscape, offering recreational opportunities besides doing their job in flood control. A great pulp mill on the Tennessee River already eyes the half-million acres of pine plantations, while Greenwood and Columbus are considered potential sites for new mills.[29]

As the decade rang to a close, MacNaughton thought that the Y-LT project had proved that pine trees had the ability to heal gullies, although their future commercial value was less obvious. And, Mac-Naughton noted, foresters had persisted with their planting operations in the face of severe obstacles. "Like the prophets of old," the Y-LT director exclaimed, "the foresters promised that industry would come after the trees were here. And, finally it came to pass!"[30] When U.S. Plywood–Champion Papers selected Oxford as the site for its new flakeboard plant, the region had achieved parity in its plant requirements. But the harvest of the Y-LT forests raised old questions about other forest industry frontiers.

MacNaughton questioned the ability of the Y-LT plantations to provide long-term stability in his 1967 report. Although forestland values were booming and "forestry has honor and status today on the Yazoo watershed," MacNaughton wondered about "tomorrow and the tomorrows to come?" Would the new growth "suffer the same fate as the original one with the accompanying destruction of land and economy?" Whether the Yazoo hills would again become the "hapless victim of the voracious dollar" would depend on a "wisdom and un-

235

derstanding" seldom displayed by industry and landowner.[31] The project head suggested that it would be difficult to maintain the watershed gains made in the past twenty years.

MacNaughton put the Y-LT case bluntly. Forest Service success with small woodland owners "has been small," and these difficulties were compounded in Mississippi where small ownerships occupied some of the most erosive soils in the country. "Whatever the cost," he concluded, "this is a battle Mississippi can't afford to lose."[32] The Y-LT situation was not unique; the increase in the productive potential of the Yazoo pineries paralleled developments in virtually every southern state. It is to MacNaughton's credit that he raised the important questions at least five years before the first sizable harvests on the Y-LT watersheds.

When the federal government attempted to divest itself of the Y-LT project, it encountered problems. Mississippi's state forester did not want the program transferred to his agency because of the expense. So the work remains a federal undertaking, although the Mississippi forestry agency has agreed to assume responsibility for the project in 1985. Federal foresters working on Y-LT lands are being transferred where budget limitations permit. Don Pomerening, who recently retired from the Forest Service and who worked in Mississippi from 1952 to 1962, describes the Y-LT project as "another very successful story."[33]

Charles Shade, who is public affairs officer and one of the last of the Forest Service staff associated with Y-LT, attributes the success of the project to the cooperating agencies and landowners. Although the economic benefits of the project are difficult to calculate, Shade believes Mississippians are better off today than they were forty and fifty years ago — "No longer are dreams washed away with the land." Professor Michael V. Namorato, in a recent history of the project, concurs: "Today, there is no doubt whatsoever that the Y-LT as a whole and the Forest Service particularly have made a significant contribution to improving the local economies of the areas under its jurisdiction."[34]

Emergency Flood Control Work

The Flood Control Act of 1950 also authorized the Department of

236

Agriculture to use its flood prevention funds for watersheds where natural disasters, usually floods or fires, had created potentially hazardous conditions. In 1956, for instance, the Forest Service broadcast nearly 300,000 pounds of grasses and other seeds on 60,000 acres of burned-over land. Because of its peculiar fire and flood conditions, southern California received most of these emergency appropriations.[35]

The government also used the emergency funds to clear channels, to construct debris basins, and for road drainage work. The Forest Service carried out fill and roadbank repairs to prevent potentially erosive material from washing into stream channels, and it cooperated in the construction of debris catchment basins on the Los Angeles River project. In this instance, the Forest Service used helicopters to install prefabricated channel stabilization structures, thus eliminating the need to build access roads to the area.[36] Although most of the emergency work was done in southern California, other areas applied for assistance in the wake of excessive fire damage.

When fires burned large acreages of the South in 1963, Forest Service deputy chief W. S. Swingler ordered emergency work to begin immediately. Because emergency programs required the approval of the SCS, Swingler urged the regional forester to cooperate with the conservation agency and with state foresters. He also advised the Region 8 office to consult with the Southeastern Forest Experiment Station regarding the appropriate grasses or mustard seed to be sown.[37]

In some instances, as with the severe California floods of 1969, Congress appropriated supplemental funds. To implement the rehabilitation work, the Forest Service cooperated with federal, state, and local agencies to fertilize large acreages already seeded to grass, to reforest more than 2,000 acres, to carry out rodent control and brush seeding activity, and to construct fences to control grazing.[38] In practice, a fine line separated emergency flood prevention activity from the more conventional work associated with the interagency basin and small watershed programs.

The unique problems associated with fire and flooding in southern California have attracted scientific attention since the late nineteenth century. The rugged topography, long and hot dry season, and highly combustible fuels have produced an extremely dangerous fire regime. And once fire has ravaged the terrain, there is little vegetative cover to inhibit soil erosion and to prevent the rapid runoff of winter rains. Therefore, flood control efforts always have focused on manipulating the vegetative cover to increase filtration into the soil and to reduce runoff. Under these conditions, fire control and flood prevention serve the same purpose, a phenomenon that has applied in other regions of the United States as well.[39]

And watershed protection, always important to southern California, was chiefly responsible for the early public support for forest reserves in the region. Shortly after Congress passed the Forest Reserve Act, the Southern California Academy of Sciences and the Los Angeles Chamber of Commerce formed the Forest and Water Society of Southern California to focus public attention on the need to protect the area's watershed resources. To convince others of the association between fire and flood, supporters of the reserves pointed to the disastrous fire that burned over the northern San Gabriel Range in 1884 and the catastrophic flooding of agricultural land that followed.[40]

The problem of fire and flood in southern California has persisted as it has nowhere else in the country. In the Copeland report of 1933, E. I. Kotok, who spent much of his forestry career in California, argued that fire protection was the basic requirement for a healthy watershed. Beginning in 1947, the California Division of Forestry cooperated with the California Forest and Range Experiment Station in watershed management research on the San Dimas Experimental Forest. After several years of collecting hydrologic data, the forestry division recommended that watershed management research should focus on watershed hydrology, the management of vegetation on upland slopes and in riparian zones, and the treatment of recently burned watershed.[41]

Forest Service cooperation in watershed projects was not limited to flood and erosion control. In 1956 the agency conducted a study with the Army Corps of Engineers and the SCS of the Yazoo Backwater Project, a combination levee and drainage reclamation system designed to create more agricultural land in the southern part of the Mississippi Delta. The project involved the construction of approximately 100 miles of levee along both banks of the lower Yazoo River and a series of pumping plants and flood gates to provide drainage. The joint study projected income differences in converting land from "inferior" forest production to commercial agricultural crops but anticipated that the net return for row crops would be "much greater than the net return from woodland." And higher profits in agricultural production would "tend to accelerate the conversion of woodland to other crops."[42] But, like the AWR investigation, state and private interests determined to what extent the Forest Service study would be implemented.

Summary

Although the Forest Service cooperated in PL-566 projects, watershed protection, and interagency river basin studies, Congress did not authorize the service to initiate these programs. The Army Corps of Engineers and regional development groups were responsible for most of the large river basin studies. The initiating groups then invited the Forest Service, the SCS, and other agencies to assist in the survey and field work. The Small Watershed Program was a different matter. Sponsoring agencies initiated the PL-566 projects, usually through the SCS, but occasionally through the Forest Service (and then the SCS). The Forest Service, of course, was interested in promoting these initiatives, because the work normally involved tree planting as a soil erosion and flood prevention measure.

When Congress passed the Cooperative Forest Management Act of 1950, the Forest Service listed watershed management as one of its program objectives. Emergency measures to prevent flooding, however, marked the only situation in which the service acted directly to initiate programs of this kind. The Forest Service is responsible for both emergency and regular flood and erosion control activity on the national forests and on other forest lands. But its participation in small watershed projects involved nonfederal, private holdings, except in the West where the work, by contrast, was almost exclusively on federal land. Each project required extensive liaison with federal and state agencies and with private landowners.

The watershed projects were a mix of administrative opportunism and legitimate flood and erosion control work. Certainly, the porkbarrel politics associated with water projects is reflected in some of the cooperative watershed work of the Forest Service. The waste and duplication of some of the interagency river basin projects are well known, as are the tendencies of federal agencies to bring in as many groups as possible to convince congressional committees of the multiple benefits associated with a particular program. On the other hand, the Forest Service participated in legitimate and beneficial watershed protection, both through the Small Watershed Program and emergency projects. And, despite the population decline and tendency toward larger landownerships in the Yazoo–Little Tallahatchie watershed, that project may turn out to be the most socially legitimate of its kind.

Chapter Fifteen

Since the early 1960s Congress has enacted a multitude of forestry-related measures that have deeply influenced Forest Service administrative jurisdictions, policies, and programs. This increased workload includes: (1) an expanded liaison with other agencies in the Department of Agriculture, (2) the growth of urban and community forestry programs, (3) greater attention in the late 1970s to small forest ownerships, (4) the establishment of federal incentive programs to increase forest production, and (5) the congressionally mandated work associated with environmental legislation.

This period also was one of continuing interagency conflict — between the Forest Service and other bureaus in the Department of Agriculture and with other agencies. The Forest Service also carried out a major restructuring of its state and private forestry work, and by the 1980s it began implementing presidential directives to shift most of this responsibility to state jurisdiction. Two major pieces of legislation — the Resources Planning Act (1974), and the cooperative Forestry Assistance Act (1978) — added to the administrative confusion of these years. The planning act reintroduced federal foresters to resource management concepts first touched upon in the 1930s, and it compounded the volume of administrative paperwork.

Forest Service administrators complained about added responsibilities and shrinking agency budgets. One retiree warned in 1975 that state and private work was being shortchanged to the benefit of the national forests. Richard McArdle observed in 1982 that presidential administrations and Congress had heaped new responsibilities on the

Forest Service without increasing its funds. Potentially more harmful, he reflected, was the effort to reduce appropriations for the agency's state and private forestry and research offices. But McArdle thought the service still was on better terms with state forestry agencies and the forest industry than it had been for three decades. [1]

There is little doubt that federal policies have greatly strengthened state forestry agencies, and that Forest Service relations with the forest products industry are more amicable. But whether this sense of good will and common ground has led to more socially productive and responsible forestry policies is still open to question. Many federal and state foresters argue that the programs and policies of the last twenty years have diffused and fractured the cooperative relationship. [2] The increased complexity in the number and scope of Forest Service activities in recent years is partly responsible for this confusion as is a persisting undercurrent of disagreement among service personnel about cooperative work.

From the end of the Second World War until the mid-1970s, federal assistance for state forestry programs enjoyed a period of almost uninterrupted expansion. In fact, the proliferation of commissions, administrations, interagency agreements, and cost-share programs brought periodic departmental and legislative efforts to streamline channels of authority and responsibility. This chapter outlines the more significant programs, policies, and legislation that have influenced cooperative work since the mid-1960s and the efforts by Congress to impose an efficient means for funding and assessing these programs. Powerful forces in the economy — presidential budgeting needs and the priorities of the multinational forest products corporations — also weighed heavily in determining Forest Service relations with states and the private sector.

Administrative Coordination and Restructuring
of Cooperative Assistance Programs

The Forest Service, the Soil Conservation Service (SCS), and the Extension Service have clashed for several decades over the administration of forestry programs. Since the establishment of the SCS in the Department of Agriculture in the 1930s, secretaries of agriculture have repeatedly attempted to end the jurisdictional infighting; agreements have been made and updated; but the problems have not disappeared—the expansion and addition of new federal programs in the 1950s and 1960s and the persistence of old rivalries are responsible for much of this.

In 1966, in what has been called the Tripartite Agreement, the secretary of agriculture clarified the responsibilities of the SCS, the Extension Service, and the Forest Service in administering forestry responsibilities through state agencies. The agreement established the USDA Forestry Planning Committee to coordinate interagency activity and encouraged the states to form similar committees. The agencies revised the agreement in 1974, but problems persisted. In 1975 the State and Private Forestry Advisory Committee (serving under the secretary of agriculture) urged the secretary to "foster a more unified team approach" between the Extension Service and the Forest Service on "cooperative forestry matters."[3]

Finally Secretary of Agriculture Bob Berglund ordered a major revision and expansion of the 1966 accord. The secretary's memorandum of 1978 added several new agencies as signatories to the USDA Interagency Agreement on Forestry. The secretary also directed the state committees to include all forestry cooperators to "clarify responsibilities" of USDA agencies in the protection, development, management, and use of "privately owned forest resources; urban forestry; wood processing and utilization; technology transfer; incentives and related activities." Its grand design was "to foster a high level of cooperation" among federal agencies and their cooperators at the state and local level.[4]

The Committee of State Foresters (a USDA advisory committee authorized under the Cooperative Forestry Assistance Act of 1978) reported in 1982 that not all of the interagency friction had been resolved. The committee complained that the USDA had authorized the SCS to spend $10 million to provide forestry advice to owners of critically eroding land at the expense of Forest Service assistance to private landowners. State foresters, the committee pointed out, had "a delivery mechanism to provide such service"; therefore, funding the SCS scheme merely duplicated existing programs.[5]

Interagency bickering dates at least to the second decade of the twentieth century when the Extension Service became actively involved in cooperative forestry. The emergence of the SCS in the 1930s added another Department of Agriculture agency in the same line of work. Overlapping jurisdictions, struggles for the control of programs, and limited funds for cooperative forestry assistance have contributed to this long-standing friction. One retired Forest Service officer, Edward C. Crafts, observed in 1975 that the Forest Service and SCS had a "straight-out conflict" over providing assistance to farmers and small landowners. "It is still happening." This sort of competition, he said, was "bureaucracy at its worst."[6]

The Forest Service initiated administrative changes of its own to streamline and improve the efficiency of its assistance programs. The agency put into effect a major reorganization in the East and South in 1966 when it removed state and private forestry activities from the jurisdiction of regional foresters and transferred these responsibilities to newly appointed area directors. The service established area offices in Upper Darby, Pennsylvania, and Atlanta, Georgia. The area offices were to devote their attention "to cooperative forestry programs and to non-Federal forest resources" in thirty-three states, most of them east of the Great Plains. They were charged with responsibility for developing rural economies, reducing poverty, restoring the quality of the "rural, urban, and suburban environment," and a host of other duties.[7] The charge to area directors reads as if it were intended to cover the entire spectrum of human endeavor, including civil defense activities.

To accomplish these goals, area directors assigned Forest Service specialists to work with state foresters, industries, and conservation organizations. The federal agency provided the financial aid and technical expertise, and the consultants served as members of the state forester's staff. The centerpiece for the overall program to reach state and private forestlands, however, rested in formal cooperative agreements with the states.[8]

Effective July 1, 1971, the Forest Service ordered "a major organizational change" in the two area offices to "foster inter-disciplinary team approaches" in the protection, management, and use of state and private lands. The administrative restructuring accorded "broad, mission-oriented responsibilities" to three assistant directors who, according to the plan, would provide better technical assistance to cooperators.[9] Although the agency described the new arrangement as a major innovation, its practical effect was to streamline lines of authority and broaden the ability of the service to offer technical assistance.

Delivering the Goods

In the mid-1970s the Forest Service adopted a new linguistic term— "delivery systems"— to describe its cooperative work in state and private forestry. In lay terms, this meant providing financial and technical assistance to state and private cooperators as expeditiously as possible. In a major policy statement issued in 1974, the service defined its mission in state and private forestry as providing "national leadership" in protecting, managing, and the use of state and private lands. The Forest Service listed the following as principal state and private forestry activities: (1) increasing wood production; (2) planning and development of land and water resources; (3) transferring technology to states and private users; (4) controlling pests and pollution; (5) coordinating the use of chemicals; (6) greater environmental quality in forestry; (7) protecting rural areas from fire; and (8) responsibilities related to emergencies, rural development, and specialized employment. [10]

An important administrative concern for the Forest Service during the 1970s was a broad area defined as technology transfer— the total process of providing state agencies, processors of forest products, and private landowners with the latest research findings and technical advice. In 1971 the General Accounting Office (GAO) reported that the Forest Service did not make the best use of its research, nor did the agency have established procedures for feeding field information back to research officials. The report concluded: "The Forest Service does not have adequate assurance that optimum benefits are obtained." [11]

The Forest Service acted promptly to implement the GAO recommendations. The agency explored new arrangements in the Southeast to make its research programs more responsive to forest industry needs and to provide users with access to research findings. The plan included improved communications among Forest Service regions, areas, experiment stations, universities, and state and local forestry officials. The Forest Service believed the changes would "improve the uniform and widespread use of research results." [12]

To further speed the process of getting research results into use, the

Forest Service conducted an agency-wide "National Research Implementation Workshop" in Atlanta, Georgia, in January, 1973; chartered a Workshop Steering Committee "to monitor and stimulate action"; and issued progress reports on workshop recommendations. [13] That Congress and presidential administrations were beginning to examine more closely the budget for state and private forestry assistance assured that monitoring of the GAO recommendations would continue.

In 1975 the State and Private Forestry Advisory Committee informed Forest Service chief, John McGuire, that getting research knowledge applied was "a continuing challenge" and that much new information was not reaching users. One year later the Office of Audit praised the Forest Service for "substantial efforts towards improving their operations" in getting research findings applied in the field, for "a more formal coordination between State and Private Forestry area offices and Research stations," and for improving communications within the Forest Service to carry out these responsibilities. The minor criticisms in the report included recommendations to improve the dissemination of research materials in the field, particularly to nonindustrial woodland owners. [14]

"Technology transfer" occupied much of the attention of Forest Service administrators in the late 1970s. McGuire established a Technology Transfer Staff Group in 1978 charged with responsibility for coordinating technology transfer at all levels of administration. The Forest Service followed this with a technology transfer workshop to inform agency personnel about the authorities, the latest developments, and the problems associated with identifying and getting information to users in the field. Workshop participants discussed problems of accountability, "vested interests" as barriers to effective work, coordination between administrative agencies, budget "constraints," and the need for better communications. [15]

At least one state, California, listed technology transfer as a major responsibility along with forest management, forest products utilization, urban forestry, and rural fire protection. The California agency cited "knowledge dissemination" and its "utilization" as the key to the quality and efficiency of its programs. The present "state of the art" in forestry research and its "delivery" to private interests, the

246

California Department of Forestry contended, was critical to effective technology transfer. [16]

By the late 1970s technology transfer had become a popular "buzz word" for a wide variety of Forest Service policies and programs. At the same time the Washington office showed an increasing inclination to cloak its memoranda and policy statements in the arcane jargon of "systems" administrators, a development that must have confused cooperators at the state and local level. The publication in July, 1981, of Technology Transfer Staff Group activities is a good example of this tendency. The author of the report provided definitions for frequently used words and terms to "minimize potential confusion over meanings and interpretations."[17] The "definitions," if anything, confuse rather than clarify matters for lay readers.

The 1981 study praised the Forest Service for being "ahead of other Federal agencies in institutionalizing" technology transfer; the service was "setting the pace" in the field. It singled out for special commendation administrative innovations, the drafting and distribution of planning guides and slide-tape presentations, and the emphasis on technology transfer work in management reviews. The report concluded that the technology staff group had accomplished 80 percent of its objectives and had raised the "visibility" of technology transfer as an important part of its activities. [18]

Assistance to Urban Forestry

In the early 1970s Congress increased its support for urban and community forestry projects when it authorized the Forest Service to assist in municipal management programs. The new policy permitted federal cost-sharing to states with urban forestry programs (although it limited such aid to technical assistance). Successful programs in Atlanta, Georgia, and St. Louis, Missouri, spurred Congress to adopt the urban forestry measure. *American Forests* praised the "great potential" of federal support for urban forestry in assisting cities and towns in the proper use of shade trees and ornamental shrubs. The magazine noted that "only a few" urban communities had trained personnel at their disposal. [19]

Despite the enthusiasm of federal foresters and the success of a handful of innovative programs, local inertia and increasingly tight-fisted federal budgets limited urban forestry projects during the 1970s. Then, in the 1980s, the federal government shifted an even greater financial responsibility to local governments. The USDA Advisory Committee on State and Private Forestry charged in 1978 that federal financial and technical assistance to states for urban forestry should be expanded. The committee noted that increasing the forestry consciousness of urban dwellers would ultimately benefit federal forest management programs.[20]

At the close of the 1970s the state of California had one of the more comprehensive urban forestry programs in the United States. According to Region 5 forester, Zane Smith, the California Urban Forestry Act of 1978 was largely responsible for making urban forestry an ambitious outreach scheme designed to assist every major population center in the state. During the first years of the expanded program, the California forestry department negotiated several lump sum grants involving federal, state, and private funding. To publicize the urban forestry scheme, the department of forestry published a "how-to" pamphlet—*The Hip-Pocket Urban Tree Planter*—to suggest ways to finance urban projects.[21]

The California urban forestry program covered a broader array of assistance than the federal plan. Because federal guidelines limited aid to technical assistance, the state forester's office had to take great care in determining what qualified for federal funds. To oversee the administration of the program, the 1978 state law called for the establishment of an urban forestry advisory committee. The main thrust of the California urban forestry measure was to encourage citizen involvement in local projects and to create jobs in tree maintenance and related activities.[22]

California's participation in urban forestry was part of a broader reorganization of forestry department responsibility. Community groups and public agencies developed pilot projects in Oakland, Needles, Los Angeles, and San Francisco. The state agency used the results of these projects to develop its statewide urban forestry program. According to Lloyd Forrest, head of the Forest Improvement Program of the California Department of Forestry, one of the most successful pilot projects was the Oakland Tree Task Force, a grass-roots effort initiated by a community organizer, Isabel Wade.[23]

Minnesota also expanded its urban forestry program at a similar juncture in state and federal affairs. The Minnesota Forestry Division provided technical assistance in urban forestry for several years, but in 1979 the division added three full-time urban foresters to its staff with the assistance of Forest Service matching funds. In the next two years urban specialists consulted with more than 200 communities about tree planting and maintenance, landscape planning, urban wood utilization, and urban development and multiple-use management.[24]

But urban forestry projects in California, Minnesota, and elsewhere confronted increasingly restricted budgets in the 1980s. USDA advisory committees on forestry regularly addressed the issues of support for urban and community forestry. In April, 1980, the advisory committee warned that urban forestry lacked firm political and budgetary support. When the incoming Reagan administration began to wield an even heavier axe on domestic spending programs, the Committee of State Foresters opposed cuts for urban forestry assistance. The committee urged state foresters to work with congressional contacts to underscore the importance of the program.[25]

California, of course, launched its urban forestry program in the midst of a growing protest over rising property taxes; finally voter resentment led to a successful statewide initiative restricting the ability of local governments to raise revenue. This move came in the midst of increasingly limited federal and state matching funds for local forestry projects; henceforth, the success of urban forestry programs in the state will depend on matching grants to citizens and business groups who have developed a working cooperation with a local forestry agency representative.[26]

Nonindustrial Forestlands

A good case can be made that the most significant of all Forest Service assistance programs in the last forty years has been the agency's effort to increase productivity on privately owned nonindustrial timberland—most of it located east of the Mississippi River. At the end of the Second World War Lyle Watts and Richard E. McArdle pointed out that the success of this ownership class was central to the future supply of forest resources. In a 1947 planning memorandum the Forest Service listed small holders as a primary consideration for assistance, and its annual reports for the late 1940s continued to call for greater aid to small woodland owners.[27]

The passage of the Cooperative Forest Management Act in 1950, the establishment of the soil bank program later in the decade, and other technical assistance measures in the 1960s boosted production on small ownerships. Although a variety of forestry incentive plans emerged in the late 1960s and early 1970s, emphasis on the timber-growing capacity of nonindustrial private forestlands diminished. But a major report to the National Commission on Materials Policy in 1973 again focused attention on this ownership class. Authored by Edward P. Cliff, a retired chief of the service, the study emphasized the importance of small forestlands and the need for more technical assistance and incentives to their owners. "Existing programs," Cliff emphasized, "are totally inadequate."[28]

Congress passed a series of incentive measures in the next few years. Then, in response to President Jimmy Carter's environmental message of May, 1977, the USDA initiated a comprehensive study of cooperative forestry work. The investigation emphasized the significance of small forestlands to the future requirements of the wood-using industries.[29] The resulting USDA report, *The Federal Role in the Conservation and Management of Private Nonindustrial Forest Lands,* recommended improved education—"a prerequisite to gaining wide participation in other programs"—to provide small landowners with a more rational basis for managing their woodlots. The study urged that public agencies make a greater effort to assure the availability of technical service, that federal cost-share incentives and educational and technical assistance programs be increased, and that state forestry planning be encouraged.[30]

The USDA study reached these conclusions in the midst of a sharp increase in inflation and mounting pressures to curb federal expenditures for domestic programs. In 1975 the State and Private Forestry Advisory Committee noted that the Office of Management and Budget had encouraged the Forest Service to drop federal participation in cooperative forestry programs in states capable of financing their own projects. The committee opposed such cutbacks because most states were not able "to do the full job alone," and assistance to private landowners should be considered an investment "benefitting the public."[31]

An overheated economy and dramatically rising lumber prices spurred interest in improving production on small forest landownerships. The National Association of State Foresters (NASF) and the Forest Service conducted several regional meetings in 1979 to define the "needs and priorities" of small forest landowners. Dubbed the Private Nonindustrial Forestry Project (PNIF), the meetings led to the publication of four regional reports and a national conference "to bring it all together" in late 1979.[32] Several Carter administration officials addressed the Washington, D.C., conference, including Secretary of Agriculture Bob Berglund and Assistant Secretary for Natural Resources and Environment M. Rupert Cutler.

Secretary Berglund told the conferees that nonindustrial forests provided "the only real opportunity" to increase significantly the nation's forest resources. To assure an adequate timber supply, the secretary recommended revised land tax policies (because of escalating land values), full implementation of the Resources Planning Act, and maintaining support for technical assistance to small landowners.[33] Berglund made these remarks at a time of declining federal support for research and state and private forestry programs and rising state budgets and taxpayers revolts in California and elsewhere.

Although the PNIF regional reports differed in emphasizing the importance of small woodlot forestry problems, Rexford A. Resler, an executive with the American Forestry Association (AFA), listed the most important priorities in the regional summaries: (1) tax relief; (2) greater technical assistance and expansion of research; (3) better marketing information; (4) expansion of financial assistance programs such as cost-share and forest incentives; (5) improved protection from fire and pest problems; (6) more frequent resource inventories; and (7) a widespread fear of excessive regulation.[34] But, Resler noted, the "tight budget climate" would make it unrealistic to expect the Forest Service and the Department of Agriculture to advocate tax incentives and other financial inducements to increase productivity on small forest ownerships. The AFA executive advised that a broad coalition of forestry interests was needed to improve the "financial climate for sound forest management."[35]

Forest Service chief Max Peterson, who participated in the conference, thought federal foresters "had better tools to work with" than ever before to resolve the dilemma of "nonindustrial private land management." The competition for funds would be keen, but the "potential" for improving aid to small holders was great. His remark about the struggle for federal funds was prophetic, for by the 1980s mounting federal deficits prompted annual reexaminations of domestic spending programs. In 1982 the Committee of State Foresters emphasized that state and private forestry funding, especially assistance to small forest owners, should have a "high priority" in budgeting, because this class of ownership would "be a major supplier of timber in the future."[36]

In October, 1983, Thomas Borden, president of the Society of American Foresters and the state forester for Colorado, told the annual meeting of professional foresters that federal efforts to shift the financial burden for state and private forestry to states were "terrible." The "chronic problems" of funding research, technical advice to small landholders, and other state and private programs had worsened in the early 1980s. Politicians, he charged, operated on the "simplistic philosophy that trees will be here tomorrow" without regard for proper investment in forest management.[37]

Federal Incentives for Private Forestry

Some of the cooperative assistance plans to aid small landholders date to the rehabilitative legislation of the New Deal. Direct financial outlays to farmers and small landholders to encourage good forest management was first attempted through the Agricultural Conservation Program (ACP) under the Soil Conservation and Domestic Allotment Act of 1936. The ASCS administered the ACP funds through county agents for reforestation and timberland improvement. In the early 1970s the ASCS redirected its programs, including forestry, toward long-range objectives. The agency changed its entitlement projects to Rural Environmental Assistance Programs (REAP).[38]

One of the most ballyhooed programs to increase timber production on small forest ownerships since 1973 has been the Forestry Incentives Program (FIP). The program provides federal cost-share support from 50 to 75 percent for owners of less than 500 acres, with the requirement that the acreage have the potential to grow a certain volume of timber. The Forest Service provided the technical background, the ASCS determined eligibility and made payments to applicants, and state forestry agencies and private consultants carried out the on-the-ground technical assistance to the landowner.[39]

During its first year of operation federal cost-share expenditures totaled $8.3 million for planting and timber stand improvement on 257,000 acres. Program administrators spent two-thirds of the money in the South, the regional imbalance due to a funding formula that favored eastern states. The average federal cost-share per landowner was about 73 percent, most of it for holdings of less than 100 acres.[40]

In 1975 Congress raised the FIP appropriation from $12 million to $15 million and for the remainder of the decade the program expanded slowly. But the USDA State and Private Forestry Advisory Committee criticized the inadequate federal support for FIP, "the only significant economic incentive available to encourage landowners to make needed forestry investments." At the same time, the committee worried that FIP was becoming a substitute for ACP forestry work, that the two programs were "cumbersome" and inefficient and not responsive to landowners' needs.[41] The program, the committee hinted, had hidden dangers; it had the potential to undermine traditional programs, and shifting federal winds, in turn, could eliminate the incentive policy altogether.

The State and Private Forestry Advisory committee repeatedly urged that FIP and ACP payments be exempt from ordinary income for tax purposes. Taxing incentive programs like FIP, the committee claimed, was "counterproductive." Congress should adopt tax investment incentives that would encourage small landowners to make a commitment to "continuing timberland productivity." The Committee of State Foresters also recommended revised tax laws to encourage forest production. Finally, the revenue act of 1978 (amended in 1979) exempted cost-sharing payments for capitalized reforestation expenditures from an owner's gross income.[42]

The state of Minnesota, with more than $5 million acres of forestland in small ownerships, was an active cooperator in several federal assistance programs. The Minnesota Department of Natural Resources offered technical aid and advice through its private forest management program. Its cooperation in direct financial assistance included FIP and ACP, both administered by ASCS to assist forest ownerships in need of reforestation. In 1981 the state legislature appointed a committee to develop a comprehensive forest management plan and to examine all state programs that involved federal cooperation, including FIP and ACP.[43]

In addition to administering FIP and ACP assistance, the California Department of Forestry has operated a state-financed variation of FIP, the California Forest Improvement Program (CFIP). Funds generated from timber sales on state forestlands support the incentive measure. It provides financial aid to qualified owners of less than 5,000 acres of forestland for reforestation, precommercial thinning, and other cost-effective measures. The purpose of CFIP is investment in timberland to increase the volume of forest products, an objective that is consistent with the production-oriented federal FIP.[44]

The actual cost-share rate under CFIP depends on the project and the landowner's situation. Owners of less than 500 acres qualified for a 90 percent rate provided they met other eligibility requirements. The slump in the forest products economy in the early 1980s decreased the revenue available to CFIP, and the California Department of Forestry was forced to eliminate the positions of three foresters working in the program. But the overall cost-effectiveness of CFIP and its potential to boost timber production has made it a popular program with the California legislature.[45] At the present time California operates federal forestry assistance programs—FIP and ACP—and its own CFIP with sharply reduced funds.

By early 1982 FIP assistance to small landholders was in jeopardy. Although the maximum acreage restriction was raised to 1,000, budget-conscious congressional committees began to look more critically at state and private forestry funding, including FIP. The Committee of State Foresters pointed out that if Congress deleted the FIP funds, the nation would lose "reforestation momentum." The program still operates, although on a reduced scale. Federal appropriations for FIP dropped from $15 million to $12.5 million in 1980 and have remained at that level.[46]

There were several other federal assistance programs to help nonindustrial forest owners and small manufacturers in the 1970s. All were production oriented—some to increase forest growth, others to eliminate waste in manufacturing, and still others to provide producers and manufacturers with more accurate marketing information. New environmental requirements increased the difficulty of harvesting timber on small tracts, a problem especially serious in the East. In response to this, the Forest Service inaugurated its Improved Harvesting Program (IHP), a plan to provide technical assistance to timber harvesters to help them make a profit and also meet environmental requirements. The IHP, according to administrators, urged the maximum use of all materials in felled timber.[47]

The escalating price of standing timber during the 1970s also contributed to an intensified effort to reduce manufacturing waste. The Forest Service established the Sawmill Improvement Program to help manufacturers reduce waste in converting sawtimber into lumber (or, in the program's jargon, to increase the mill's "lumber recovery potential"). Because of rising energy costs, the Forest Service also has offered technical advice on the use of forest resources for fuel. Under the "Wood for Energy" project, a federal initiative to meet consumer and commercial demands for wood fuel, the service provided harvesting assistance to woodland owners who were seeking market information.[48]

On the Legislative Front

Since 1970 several important legislative initiatives have deeply influenced federal forestry assistance. These measures have accelerated changes that have taken place over the last several decades—shifting technical and financial responsibility for state and private forestry work to state organizations (with the Forest Service maintaining oversight of programs that include federal funds). Improvements in state forestry organizations predate the Great Depression, but the growing professional stature of these agencies is largely a post–World War II development. The move toward federal block grants in recent years has speeded up this trend, requiring states to show only general competence, a plan of action, and a financial match to receive federal funds. But two pieces of legislation—the Forest and Range Land Renewable Resources Planning Act (RPA) of 1974, and the Cooperative Forestry Assistance Act of 1978—have had the greatest effect on Forest Service work with states and the private sector.

The RPA, according to one authority, was the first "comprehensive legislative reconsideration" of Forest Service activities since the early twentieth century. The measure had its roots in the market-oriented needs of the forest products industry, which, in the face of escalating timber prices and restricted use designations on public land, wanted the assurances of a steady supply of timber. The RPA, which represented a renewed interest in broad-scale resource planning, was an amendment to the McSweeney-McNary Forest Research Act of 1928. A major purpose of the RPA was to provide states with the most recent data on forest resources as a basis on which to judge timber management programs and to guide investment decisions in management and manufacturing.[49]

To some, this was a move to protect congressionally designated re-forestation funds from presidential impoundment; to others, the measure was assurance that the Forest Service would establish clear and distinct long-range management goals. But the RPA was more — it stepped up the modernizing and centralizing tendency toward planning and computerized models. It also multiplied the volume of paper work for officials in federal and state agencies. The RPA was "landmark legislation" because it required the Forest Service "to provide a plan of action for Federally-funded forestry activities." And it involved state foresters from the beginning.[50]

Some state foresters feared that the Forest Service would use the first RPA report to document national forest requirements to the detriment of its other responsibilities. The Advisory Committee on State and Private Forestry pointed out that the RPA would "improve the scope and quality" of information about private forest ownerships. To speed this process the committee advised the Forest Service to work directly through governors' offices and state universities to compile its data.[51]

The RPA state assessments also figured in the move to adopt block grants to states for cooperative programs. The block grants represented a turn away from the project formula for cooperative assistance funding to providing money for total programs based on state planning assessments. When Congress amended the RPA in 1976 with the National Forest Management Act, it further emphasized the importance of state planning in the inventory and assessment procedure that was so critical to the block grant scheme.[52]

At its first meeting in 1978, the Committee of State Foresters encouraged states to adopt forest resource planning to produce data for the RPA surveys and to provide a framework for annual budgets and block grant payments for cooperative programs. Under this arrangement the Forest Service would establish the minimum requirements for the RPA assessments and the consolidated payments plan. The block grant approach was advisory, not mandatory, and the committee recommended that the Forest Service implement the consolidated payments approach without penalizing states operating under the old project formula procedures. But, the committee noted, states using the new method "would get more flexibility in their use of Federal funding." At subsequent meetings, the Committee of State Foresters urged the Forest Service to guide the allocation of funds to states based on their resource plans.[53]

When the Reagan administration assumed office in 1981, forty-seven states were participating in forest resource planning. As more states adopted forest resource plans, most of them opted for consolidated payment grants rather than the traditional project format for funding. Great pressure was put on states to adopt forest plans, although the option to fund programs on a project basis still existed. However, by 1982 state foresters feared that federal budget cuts for Forest Service state and private forestry activity were "diluting" state forestry planning activities. According to the Committee of State Foresters, a disproportionate share of federal funds was being allocated to the national forests at the expense of state and private forestry assistance.[54]

The USDA published its first RPA survey in 1977 and the second in 1981. The most recent report emphasized the importance of previous assessments of forest resources — past surveys helped guide and develop public and private forestry policy, defined problems, stirred public interest, and provided a firm basis for shaping forestry programs. The 1981 study was concerned with "prospective trends" in the demand and supply of the forest, range, and water resource and, like the first report, was production-oriented.[55]

One of the major problems in compiling these lengthy assessments of the nation's renewable resources was the nature of the data. To minimize duplication and to assure greater reliability for these decennial projects, the federal agencies involved formed an interagency agreement that provided for cooperation in surveys, inventory appraisals, and planning associated with renewable resources.[56] This undertaking involved liaison that reached from federal and state agencies to the local level. The county SCS technician and service forester were as important to the reliability of the data as those who designed the computerized models in Washington, D.C.

When the next RPA assessment is compiled at the end of the 1980s, there will be a more reliable basis to judge its significance for state and private forestry programs. However, the massive inventories of forest resources in the 1981 report undoubtedly provided valuable information to guide investment decisions in timberland and forest products manufacturing. Regional assessments of present and future hardwood and softwood resources provide the necessary data to determine where and when to build forest processing facilities. But its utility to the vast majority of small holders is more questionable.

The editors of the 1981 RPA report indicated that the present span of time between inventories was too long to "adequately monitor changes taking place in timber resources." In some states, the report noted, timber harvesting has increased as much as 40 percent over a ten-year period. The editors suggested that the surveys be accelerated and intensified to meet the needs of those who depend on updated and accurate data. The Advisory Committee on State and Private Forestry made a similar recommendation four years earlier.[57]

Another legislative act that has shaped federal cooperative assistance in recent years is the Cooperative Forestry Assistance Act (CFA) of 1978. The measure complemented the Resources Planning Act of 1974 and authorized the Forest Service to cooperate with state forestry agencies to implement programs affecting "nonfederal forestlands." The act states that the secretary of agriculture, in consultation with the Committee of State Foresters, shall establish general requirements for state forest resource programs, including the apportioning of funds. The CFA placed under one legislative umbrella virtually all of the provisions for federal-state cooperation and cost-sharing in forestry that had been covered under traditional programs like Clarke-McNary and Cooperative Forest Management. Rupert Cutler, an assistant USDA secretary, said the CFA "redefines and reinforces Federal-State relationships."[58]

The 1978 law also integrated a private organization—the NASF—in the development of federal programs because the state

258

foresters' organization selected the seven-member Committee of State Foresters. The secretary of agriculture also encouraged the formation of committees in each state to feed information to the national committee. Finally, the CFA authorized financial and technical assistance to states to help in gathering and formulating data for state forestry plans.[59] The cooperative act of 1978 built upon the directives set forth in the RPA and encouraged states to shift from project to block grant funding. Again, no coercion, but a more than subtle persuasion to move states in the direction of federal objectives.

Federal Forestry and Environmental Legislation

Several other programs and policies have shaped state and federal forestry relations during the last twenty years. The National Environmental Policy Act (NEPA) of 1969 required every federal agency to prepare environmental impact statements on all legislative proposals and federal actions that significantly affect the quality of the environment. Environmental impact assessments did not become an important factor in planning until the mid-1970s when environmental groups began to file legal challenges to resource development projects.

Complementing NEPA and involving USDA cooperation were the clean air act amendments of 1970 and 1977, the Federal Water Pollution Control Act of 1972, and the Clean Water Act of 1977. The latter two pieces of legislation introduced the point versus nonpoint strategies for controlling water pollution and involved forest land managers and the forest products industry. The clean water legislation of the 1970s, in fact, had a greater impact on forest management activities than any other federal environmental statute. From time to time the USDA advisory committee on state and private forestry urged the Forest Service to take a more active role in working with the Environmental Protection Agency (EPA) to meet environmental requirements.[60]

Some state foresters feared that the EPA might preempt what they deemed traditional forestry responsibilities in environmental matters. To prevent this from happening, the state foresters wanted the Forest Service to secure specialists and become more "actively and aggressively involved," especially in water pollution matters. For its part, the USDA advisory committee urged the Forest Service to work with the EPA to emphasize the "desirability of education and incentives as being more effective than regulation." State foresters, who were in the forefront of much of the controversy, usually had Forest Service support in their efforts to limit the EPA tendency toward regulation.[61] William Greeley, who had preached the virtues of voluntarism and persuasion, would have been pleased. Whether "education and incentives" are effective regulators, however, is another issue.

The environmental legislation of the 1970s increased the workload and responsibilities of federal and state foresters and further crowded office filing space. Forest Service administrators complained that the agency had to struggle with new assignments without corresponding increases in funding or personnel. The combination of resource planning, environmental impact statements, roadless area review assessments, and its more conventional state and private forestry responsibilities strained the agency's administrative duties at the same time that its budget was coming under increasing attack. One has to sympathize with Donald Pomerening, who worked as an administrator in the Washington office during this period. After seven or eight years at the task, he recalls: "I got sort of burned out on the job, tired . . . my responsibilities increased so much . . . [that] I asked for a transfer to anyplace that they would send me."[62]

Summary

The relationship between federal and state agencies in forestry cooperation today is largely administrative. The onset of block grants and the establishment of state forest resource plans has placed the Forest Service in the role of general overseer of broad planning and program objectives rather than its more conventional one of specific project and program direction. These developments, combined with an increased professionalism in the state agencies and diminished federal support for state and private forestry, will likely contribute to greater autonomy for state forestry agencies in the future.

The 1980s differ from earlier decades in other ways. Whereas the federal government instituted social and economic rehabilitation programs of great magnitude during the 1930s, the current trend is to dismantle or downplay policies that have even a faint resemblance to Depression-era programs. And by contrast with the 1930s, in the recession of the early 1980s, Congress placed further limits on state and private forestry cooperative assistance programs. And there were no emergency funds to take up the slack. These circumstances underscore the obvious — that cooperative forestry is in the midst of a transition, with state agencies assuming the bulk of the responsibility for forestry work on state and private lands.

Epilogue

Today the federal government provides the private sector with a variety of goods and services, especially in the form of technical assistance, that safeguards industrial property and enables the business community to make decisions with a greater degree of predictability. The general public, through federal tax and income policies, provides the financial backing to carry out these measures. This system of public support for private enterprise evolved gradually and reached maturity when industrial trades organized on a national basis to bring greater influence on the federal legislative process. Public and private officials cooperated in a common effort to integrate and rationalize private business activity with government policy. The natural resource industries — coal, oil, steel, and lumber — pioneered in establishing this relationship between the public and private sector.

Because it was one of the first major resource industries in the United States, the forest products trade provides excellent insights into the developing liaison between the private sector and a related federal agency (in this case, the Forest Service). And for most of the twentieth century important natural resource industries like lumber have enjoyed congenial relations with the federal government. Forest products leaders have been largely successful in convincing legislators that federal support for private policy would serve the national (and public) interest. Federal foresters, with a few conspicuous exceptions, have concurred in this belief. Congressional legislation in the twentieth century has slowly and steadily integrated this relationship into the national polity.

263

When Congress first began establishing scientific bureaus in the late nineteenth century, federal administrators developed close working relationships with related private groups. The private sector valued the federal bureaus for their scientific expertise and marketing information, and these same private organizations provided valuable lobbying support for government administrators seeking funds to expand federal research and assistance programs. These shared interests and objectives have deeply influenced Forest Service cooperative policy. Although some have criticized this relationship, it has dominated the character of federal-private activity for most of the twentieth century.

There are other important considerations that must be recognized in analyzing the development of federal forestry programs. The economic imperatives of market capitalism — in this case the material conditions surrounding the forest products trade — have determined the thrust of the cooperative relationship. Forest Service proposals went no further than powerful interests in the lumber trade permitted. And in many instances the private sector initiated these moves. For their part, however, most federal foresters shared a common vision with progressive industry leaders about the general objectives of cooperative policy. When the market was down or pending material shortages threatened the industry, Forest Service and lumber spokesmen went before Congress to ask for federal assistance. With few exceptions, public and private leaders normally spoke with one voice.

In establishing its cooperative assistance programs, congressional leaders (with the approval of lumber industry officials) developed a policy of allocating administrative responsibility to state forestry agencies. The state bureaus and departments, in turn, served as the administrative conduit for federal funds. There was nothing sentimental or romantic about this development; trade leaders wanted to assure that the government distributed its cooperative assistance funds with a minimum of federal requirements. Once industry officials gained their objectives in Washington, D.C., it usually guaranteed that state agencies would administer the programs in similar fashion: Which is to say that industrial conditions have determined the kind and quality of federal resource programs.

Because of the different forest ownership classes in the United

States, the dissemination and practice of scientific forestry have been by nature a cooperative affair. Fire protection was the first and most obvious arena for federal and state land managers and private landowners to cooperate on a broad scale. In this case, private forest owners who wanted to protect their valuable stands from the ravages of fire provided the initiative for the formation of the first timberland protective associations.

The findings of state forestry investigating commissions in Maine, New York, and Pennsylvania prompted these eastern states to pioneer in establishing regularized procedures for protecting forest properties from fire. But federal participation in cooperative fire protection did not gain statutory recognition until the enactment of the Weeks Law in 1911 (although the Forest Service had signed a few agreements with railroad companies before the passage of the act). Since the establishment of the Weeks Law programs, however, federal assistance to states and private landowners has expanded to include a wide variety of forestry-related activities — research, reforestation, insect and disease control, marketing assistance, and virtually every other arena of utilitarian and commercial interest to forest owners and industrial processors.

This expansion serves to reemphasize the signal feature of federal assistance in forestry — its close relation to the economic health and market conditions of the forest industry. The trade organizations and industry leaders who helped shape federal policy sought legislative programs and supported projects to meet the needs of private timber holders and lumber processors. For their part, most Forest Service officials agreed that the health of the lumber and forest products industry should be potent factors in legislative considerations. Federal forestry cooperation, therefore, always involved more than the disinterested dissemination of scientific knowledge to forest owners and industrial processors. Hard-fought political struggles in the federal congress and in state legislatures determined the direction and content of Forest Service cooperative policy.

The evolution of the lumber and forest products economy and the development of federal cooperation in forestry are closely related. The industry had no organizational base until after the Civil War. Then, as industrial capitalism matured and became more closely integrated in the last quarter of the nineteenth century, lumbermen formed regional and national trade associations to represent the industry at the federal level. It is no accident that the vast expansion of federal forestry activity and the formation of the first nationwide lumber trade organization, the National Lumber Manufacturers Association (NLMA), occurred simultaneously. During these years the industry sought tariff and tax adjustments, fire protection assistance, the relaxation of the antitrust laws, additions to the forest reserves, and other policies designed to alleviate the strains of a highly speculative and unstable business climate. In cooperation with industrial leaders, the Forest Service developed programs to address these requests. In many respects, the service was more willing than a budget-conscious Congress to serve the lumberman's and timber owner's needs.

The industrial interests that influenced the direction of federal cooperation also limited its field of operations. Cooperative work extended only as far as congressional authorizations and appropriations would allow. And in some instances Congress authorized but never appropriated funds to carry its programs into action. As with other important natural resource industries, lumbermen and their allied groups exercised a powerful influence in the nation's capital, both extending and proscribing federal cooperation. Although there were occasional differences between the Forest Service and the private sector, the relationship for the most part has been cooperative rather than adversarial.

Federal forestry programs have attempted to meet most of the critical needs of the private sector. Whether the programs provided fire protection and assistance for insect and disease control or federal cooperation in forestry research, they served to integrate private ends with public policy and to provide public funds to achieve those goals. And no two people provided a more articulate rationale for integrating public and private policy than E. T. Allen and William B. Greeley.

Edward Tyson Allen was a pioneer in laying the basic strategy for cooperative fire protection. As early as 1912, he told a lumbermen's meeting that trade associations were uniquely fitted to collect and disseminate information "for educating the public." Forest preservation, Allen observed, was a "cooperative enterprise" that involved federal and state forestry agencies and private landowners; the great task was to convince the public to support cooperative forestry programs on a scale commensurate with its own interest.[1] Better than any other individual, Allen outlined the industry's version of a practical, working basis for cooperation, and he helped give that definition meaning through newspapers and other public forums.

But the person who had the greatest influence in shaping the federal government's cooperative forestry policy in the twentieth century was William B. Greeley. Although he argued the industry's view, he was certain that this would ultimately benefit the public. The key to a stable national forestry policy, he insisted time and again, rested upon close cooperation between the public and the forest industry. Federal policy should avoid discord and strive to assist lumbermen achieve efficient and stable operations through a helpful and cooperative spirit. A healthy industry, Greeley thought, would bode well for future generations.[2] Under Greeley's influence federal legislative and regulatory programs usually originated as part of a collaborative effort between industry and federal forestry leaders.

On occasion, and especially during periods of social crisis like the Great Depression, there were serious challenges to the prevailing view of cooperation. During the 1930s the Forest Service and the forest products industry carried on a running debate over the nature of federal cooperation. Chief Forester Ferdinand Silcox and his successor, Earle Clapp, demanded requirements in good forestry practices from the industry in exchange for the expansion of cooperative assistance. When Silcox drew attention to the social consequences of the lumbermen's activities and demanded some form of regulation, industry leaders accused the Forest Service of advocating "socialist" policies and called for greater cooperative incentives with no regulatory strings attached. Allen, Greeley, and others charged that the Forest Service was tending toward dictation and deviating from its tested and proven policy of cooperation. During the Second World War, however, the government dropped the regulation debate and provided many of the economic incentives the industry sought.

Social programs have been a prominent part of Forest Service administration since the New Deal emergency projects of the 1930s. The Civilian Conservation Corps (CCC) and other work relief programs vastly expanded Forest Service administrative responsibilities and its cooperation with federal and state agencies. Although Congress terminated most of these with the onset of the war crisis, other watershed rehabilitation and subsidy schemes took their place in the postwar era. But budget conscious congresses and powerful influences in the nation's capital limited these grand conservation and development plans. And major industrial groups like the NLMA were always on hand to assure that an ambitious Forest Service did not attach regulatory strings to its cooperative assistance agreements.

With the growing demand for forest products after the Second World War, industrial leaders pushed for expanded cooperative assistance programs for forest products research, insect and disease control, investigations into fire behavior, and more help in marketing their goods. At the same time, the NLMA and its successor, the National Forest Products Association (NFPA), viewed more critically what it termed "subsidy" programs to assist small woodland owners and to alleviate rural poverty. Congressional budgetary debates during the 1950s and 1960s sometimes pitted groups like the National Association of State Foresters and the Society of American Foresters against the NFPA and its industrial allies.

In the postwar years the southern states, endowed with some of the best timber-growing conditions in the country, took advantage of a variety of federal planting assistance programs to embark on an aggressive reforestation effort. These activities are responsible for the reemergence of the South as a leader in the manufacture of forest products. The postwar liquidation of the old growth stands along the Pacific coast and the proximity of the South to major markets have effected a shift in the center of industrial forestry activity from the Pacific Northwest to the Southeast. Large and well-funded state forestry agencies have accompanied the return of the region as a major factor in forest production.

Federal cooperation in forestry, therefore, has always been closely linked to the priorities and economic condition of the forest products industry. Equally important, as Greeley repeatedly insisted, government assistance was necessary to place the forest products business on a "regime of continuous production."[3] For people like Greeley, a close working relationship between federal forestry and the private sector was necessary to bring this about. Greeley was less mindful of protecting the public's interest because he was certain that it coincided with those of the private sector.

Others were more skeptical, although their margin of disagreement with Greeley was not great. In 1915 chief forester Henry Graves

argued that government must "aid constructively in solving industrial problems." He believed that "cooperation between public and
private agencies" would be a potent factor in solving economic problems and promoting the "common welfare." But Graves insisted that
cooperation between the public and private sectors must seek "broad
public benefits."[4] For Graves and other like-minded federal foresters
who followed, the problem for the Forest Service was to maintain a
"constructive" attitude toward industry while it protected the interests of the public. Subsequent Forest Service heads—particularly
Robert Y. Stuart, Lyle Watts, and Richard McArdle—struggled to
protect the agency's independence in policy matters. To Silcox and
Clapp, however, the issue was less complex—the industry should be
forced to accept its social responsibility; regulatory requirements
attached to cooperative programs, they believed, would accomplish
that objective.

To industry leaders, Silcox and Clapp were disrupting traditional
forms of cooperation between the public and private sector. And,
although these spokesmen insisted that the Forest Service keep politics out of its decision-making, the policies that emerged were explicitly political. Trade officials argued that cooperation was a two-way
street and that the Forest Service must incorporate the industry's
viewpoint in its policies. Or, as an NLMA official warned on one occasion, "the November elections will determine in large part just how
cooperative the approach to problems is to be." The "cooperative
approach," the industry leader reasoned, implied "teamwork and uni-
ty" and avoided any reference to regulation.[5]

It is this mix of political pressures and obligations that has shaped
Forest Service cooperation. Its programs, like the work of other federal agencies, will accomplish no more than congressional and state legislative politics permit. This sensitive political framework limits
Forest Service options and denies the agency the freedom to pursue
initiatives other than those sanctioned under the watchful eye of
powerful Washington lobbyists. The story presented here traces the
successful implementation of cooperative policies and discusses some
of the agency's initiatives that were proscribed because they were
opposed by influential groups in the nation's capital.

Forest Service cooperation was much more than the selfless sharing
of scientific expertise in forestry; it involved the dissemination of in-

formation and financial assistance to promote one of the country's basic industries. The successes and failures of Forest Service cooperative programs are part of the larger history of the development of the forest products industry and the evolution of the modern industrial economy.

Notes

Chapter One

1. Harold K. Steen, *The U.S. Forest Service: A History* (Seattle: University of Washington Press, 1976), p. 8; William N. Sparhawk, "The History of Forestry in America," U.S. Department of Agriculture (hereafter USDA) *Trees: Yearbook of Agriculture* (Washington, D.C.: Government Printing Office, 1949), pp. 703–704; Henry Clepper, *Professional Forestry in the United States* (Baltimore: Johns Hopkins University Press, 1971), p. 15.
2. Samuel Trask Dana and Sally K. Fairfax, *Forest and Range Policy: Its Development in the United States,* 2d ed. (New York: McGraw-Hill, 1980), p. 25; Steen, *U.S. Forest Service,* p. 8.
3. Clepper, *Professional Forestry,* p. 16; Frank J. Harmon, "Remembering Franklin B. Hough," *American Forests* 86 (Jan., 1977):34–37, 52–53; Franklin B. Hough, "On the Duty of Governments in the Preservation of Forests," in *Conservation in the United States: A Documentary History,* ed. Frank E. Smith, 1 (New York: Chelsea House, 1971), p. 688.
4. Harmon, "Remembering Franklin B. Hough," pp. 49–51; Sparhawk, "History of Forestry in America," pp. 704–705; Steen, *U.S. Forest Service,* pp. 10–13.
5. Harmon, "Remembering Franklin B. Hough," pp. 49, 51–52; Franklin B. Hough, *Report upon Forestry,* 1 (Washington, D.C.: Government Printing Office, 1878), pp. 8–15.
6. Steen, *U.S. Forest Service,* p. 17. Hough received a special award for his

reports in 1882 at an international geophysical congress in Venice. See Harmon, "Remembering Franklin B. Hough," p. 52.

7. Andrew Denny Rodgers, *Bernhard Fernow: A Story of North American Forestry* (Princeton, N.J.: Princeton University Press, 1951), p. 52.

8. Dana and Fairfax, *Forest and Range Policy,* p. 42; Clepper, *Professional Forestry,* p. 20; Sparhawk, "History of Forestry in America," p. 705.

9. Reports and clippings relating to the first annual convention of the American Forestry Congress, Apr., 1882, in Records Relating to the First Convention of the American Forestry Congress, 1882, Record Group 95, Records of the Forest Service, National Archives and Records Service (hereafter cited as NA/RG95); William G. Robbins, *Lumberjacks and Legislators: Political Economy of the U.S. Lumber Industry, 1890– 1941* (College Station: Texas A & M University Press, 1982), p. 19; Dana and Fairfax, *Forest and Range Policy,* pp. 42–43.

10. Ralph W. Hidy, Frank Ernest Hill, and Allan Nevins, *Timber and Men: The Weyerhaeuser Story* (New York: Macmillan, 1963), p. 130; USDA, Division of Forestry, *Annual Report* (1883):447–448.

11. Samuel Trask Dana, *Forest and Range Policy: Its Development in the United States,* 1st ed. (New York: McGraw-Hill, 1956), p. 83; Sparhawk, "History of Forestry in America," p. 705. For an account of Egleston's ineptitude, see Clepper, *Professional Forestry,* p. 20.

12. Steen, *U.S. Forest Service,* pp. 23–24; Rodgers, *Bernhard Fernow,* pp. 113, 196–197; Division of Forestry, *Annual Report* (1886):166.

13. Division of Forestry, *Annual Report* (1886):149, 166; Dana and Fairfax, *Forest and Range Policy,* p. 51.

14. Dana and Fairfax, *Forest and Range Policy,* pp. 162–165.

15. Division of Forestry, *Annual Report* (1886):149, 162–165.

16. Division of Forestry, *Annual Report* (1892):314. Also see Charles Mohr, "The Interest of the Individual in Forestry in View of the Present Condition of the Lumber Interest," *Proceedings of the American Forestry Congress, 1888* (Washington, D.C.: Gibson Brothers, 1889), pp. 36–41.

17. Sparhawk, "History of Forestry in America," p. 705; Rodgers, *Bernhard Fernow,* pp. 115–116; Dana, *Forest and Range Policy,* pp. 98–99.

18. Sparhawk, "History of Forestry in America," p. 706; Dana and Fairfax, *Forest and Range Policy,* pp. 55–56; Hidy, Hill, and Nevins, *Timber and Men,* p. 136; Henry Gilbert White, "Forest Ownership Research in Historical Perspective, *Journal of Forestry* 48 (Apr., 1950):262; Rodgers, *Bernhard Fernow,* p. 199.

19. Steen, *U.S. Forest Service,* pp. 28–30; Dana and Fairfax, *Forest and Range Policy,* pp. 58–59.
20. Roderick Nash, *Wilderness and the American Mind,* rev. ed. (New Haven, Conn.: Yale University Press, 1967), pp. 134–136; Dana and Fairfax, *Forest and Range Policy,* p. 59.
21. Bernhard Fernow to H. G. deLotbiniere, Mar. 6, 1897, Letters Sent by the Division of Forestry, NA/RG95–2; Rodgers, *Bernhard Fernow,* pp. 223–224.
22. John Minto to Gov. William P. Lord, Oct. 25, 1897, in box 1, John Minto papers (hereafter cited as Minto Papers), Oregon Historical Society, Portland; *Report of the Secretary of the State Board of Horticulture on Forestry and Arid Land Interests* (1889), in box 1, Minto Papers.
23. Steen, *U.S. Forest Service,* pp. 34–36; Dana and Fairfax, *Forest and Range Policy,* pp. 60–62; Hidy, Hill, and Nevins, *Timber and Men,* p. 292; Bernhard Fernow, "Letter to the Editor," *American Forests* 2 (1896):45.
24. Division of Forestry, *Annual Report* (1886):166, 171, (1892):313.
25. Ibid. (1886):178–179, 181, (1889):282.
26. Steen, *U.S. Forest Service,* pp. 23–24; Division of Forestry, *Annual Report* (1889):273–275, 282–283, 291.
27. See the following requests to the division: H. A. Stahl to B. E. Fernow, May 12, 1896, A. R. Starkey to Fernow, May 11, 1896, C. I. Millard to Fernow, Nov. 4, 1892, and A. W. Stedman to Fernow, Mar. 28, 1892, all in Letters Received by the Division of Forestry, 1888–1899, NA/RG95–1.
28. Stanley Doggett to E. B. [*sic*] Fernow, July 11, 1896, and G. F. Steele to Fernow, Jan. 18, 1894, ibid.; Division of Forestry, *Annual Report* (1892):293, (1893):303.
29. Division of Forestry, *Annual Report* (1891):192, (1892):294, and (1893):304.
30. Steen, *U.S. Forest Service,* p. 37; Division of Forestry, *Annual Report* (1886):162, (1891):191.
31. Division of Forestry, *Annual Report* (1897):141, 144.
32. Ibid. (1886):179–180, (1892):309.
33. Ibid. (1889):295; Rodgers, *Bernhard Fernow,* pp. 235–236.
34. Clepper, *Professional Forestry,* pp. 28–29.
35. M. Nelson McGeary, *Gifford Pinchot: Forester-Politician* (Princeton, N.J.: Princeton University Press, 1960), pp. 11–12; Harold T. Pinkett, *Gifford Pinchot: Private and Public Forester* (Urbana: University of Illi-

nois Press, 1970), p. 71; William B. Greeley, *Forests and Men* (New York: Doubleday, 1951), p. 59.

36. The report by Gunn, Richards and Company, "Forest Service," is quoted in McGeary, *Gifford Pinchot,* p. 94.

37. Gifford Pinchot, *Breaking New Ground* (New York: Harcourt, Brace, 1947), pp. 140–147.

38. Division of Forestry, *Annual Report* (1889):94, (1900):105; USDA, Bureau of Forestry, *Annual Report* (1902):109; Pinchot, *Breaking New Ground,* p. 141.

39. Pinkett, *Pinchot,* pp. 48–49; Steen, *U.S. Forest Service,* p. 55; Dana, *Forest and Range Policy,* pp. 119–121.

40. Bureau of Forestry, *Annual Report* (1903):498–499.

41. J. Girvin Peters, "The Possibilities and Limitations of Government Cooperative Work with the Private Owner," paper presented to the Society of American Foresters, Dec. 22, 1904, filed in "Administration-Office of Cooperation," Records of the Office of State and Private Cooperation, 1896–1908, NA/RG95–68.

42. Ibid.

43. For a brief description of the work of the Service Committee, see *Preliminary Inventories: Records of the Forest Service* (Washington, D.C.: National Archives and Record Service, 1969), p. 4; minutes of the Service Committee, Dec. 31, 1903, NA/RG95–8.

44. Minutes of the Service Committee, Apr. 18, 1903, NA/RG95–8.

45. Pinkett, *Pinchot,* pp. 51–52; Division of Forestry, *Annual Report* (1900):103; Bureau of Forestry, *Annual Report* (1901):329, (1902):110.

46. These included vastly expanded cooperative relations with states, discussed in Chapter Three.

47. Division of Forestry, *Annual Report* (1899):95, (1900):107; Bureau of Forestry, *Annual Report* (1901):332, (1902):111, (1904):197; Pinchot, *Breaking New Ground,* pp. 149–150.

48. Division of Forestry, *Annual Report* (1899):97, (1900):106; Bureau of Forestry, *Annual Report* (1901):333; Gifford Pinchot, *Practical Assistance to Tree Planters,* USDA, Division of Forestry, Circular No. 22 (Washington, D.C.: Government Printing Office, 1899), pp. 10–11.

49. George L. Clothier, "The Possibilities and Limitations of Government Cooperative Work with the Private Owner," paper presented to the Society of American Foresters, Dec. 22, 1904, filed in "Administration-

Office of Cooperation," NA/RG95–68. Clothier's paper was appended to a paper by J. Girvin Peters. See n. 41.

50. Ibid.; USDA, Forest Service, *Annual Report* (1906):29.

51. USDA, Forest Service, *Annual Report* (1906):30–31; Wilmon Droze, *Trees, Prairies, and People: A History of Tree Planting in the Great Plains States* (Denton: Texas Women's University Press, 1977), pp. 39–44.

52. Pinchot, *Breaking New Ground*, p. 239; Bureau of Forestry, *Annual Report* (1901):331–332, (1902):111; Forest Service, *Annual Report* (1908):28; Pinkett, *Pinchot*, p. 97.

53. Forest Service, *Annual Report* (1905):202; Bureau of Forestry, *Annual Report* (1902):111.

54. Raphael Zon, "Plan for Creating Forest Experiment Stations," May 6, 1908, unpublished report filed in Research Compilation File, NA/RG95–115; Zon, "The Search for Forest Facts," *American Forests* 36 (July, 1930):421–423; Norman J. Schmaltz, "Raphael Zon: Forest Researcher," *Journal of Forest History* 24 (1980):27.

55. Zon is quoted in Schmaltz, "Zon," pp. 29–30; "Reports—Products, 1909–1912," in Records of the Office of the Chief, 1908–1947, NA/RG95–4.

56. Gifford Pinchot, *Practical Assistance to Farmers, Lumbermen, and Other Owners of Forest Lands*, USDA, Forest Service Circular No. 21 (Washington, D.C.: Government Printing Office, 1898), p. 1. Also see Pinchot, "Work of the Division of Forestry for the Farmer," *Yearbook of the Department of Agriculture* (Washington, D.C.: Government Printing Office, 1898), pp. 297–308.

57. Steen, *U.S. Forest Service*, p. 92; minutes of the Service Committee, Dec. 31, 1903, and Dec. 12, 1908, NA/RG95–8.

Chapter Two

1. Dana and Fairfax, *Forest and Range Policy*, pp. 3–4; Nash, *Wilderness and the American Mind*, pp. 44–66.

2. B. E. Fernow, *Report upon the Forestry Investigations of the Department of Agriculture, 1877–1898*, U.S. Congress, House Doc. no. 181, 55 Cong. 3, 1899, p. 167.

3. For a discussion of the function of trade associations in the lumber industry, see John H. Cox, "Trade Associations in the Lumber Industry of the

Pacific Northwest, 1899–1914," *Pacific Northwest Quarterly* 41 (1950): 285–311, and Robbins, *Lumberjacks and Legislators,* pp. 34–43.

4. National Industrial Conference Board, *Trade Associations: Their Economic Significance and Legal Status* (New York: National Industrial Conference Board, 1925), p. 15; Cox, "Trade Associations in the Lumber Industry, 285; Arthur Robert Burns, *The Decline of Competition: A Study of American Industry* (New York: McGraw-Hill, 1939), p. 40.

5. Nelson C. Brown, *The American Lumber Industry: Embracing the Principal Features of the Resource, Production, Distribution, and Utilization of Lumber in the United States* (New York: John Wiley and Sons, 1923), p. 232; Thomas R. Cox, *Mills and Markets: A History of the Pacific Coast Lumber Industry to 1900* (Seattle: University of Washington Press, 1974), pp. 255, 277; Charles A. Gillett, "Citizens and Trade Associations Dealing with Forestry," in *Fifty Years of Forestry,* ed. Robert K. Winters (Washington, D.C.: Society of American Foresters, 1950), p. 288; Clepper, *Professional Forestry,* p. 198.

6. Robert K. Ficken, *Lumber and Politics: The Career of Mark Reed* (Seattle: University of Washington Press, 1979), p. 21; "Historical Data," Nov. 1, 1937, box 155, National Forest Products Association Records (hereafter cited as NFPA Records), Forest History Society, Santa Cruz, Calif.; Dana, *Forest and Range Policy,* pp. 171–172; Pinchot, *Breaking New Ground,* pp. 294–295.

7. Dana and Fairfax, *Forest and Range Policy,* pp. 111–112; "Lumbermen Favor Forestry," *American Forests* 9 (Apr. 1903):204; "American Forest Congress," *American Forests* 11 (Jan., 1905):11; "Resolution Adopted by the National Hardwood Lumber Association," May 24, 1907, "Resolution Adopted by the National Lumber Manufacturers Association," June 15, 1907, both in box 61, American Forestry Association Records (hereafter AFA Records), Forest History Society, Santa Cruz, Calif.

8. Clepper, *Professional Forestry,* pp. 198–199.

9. Quoted in *American Forests* 7 (June, 1901):146; Gifford Pinchot, "The Forester and the Lumberman," *American Forests* 9 (Apr., 1903):176–177; Bureau of Forestry, *Annual Report* (1903):498; Forest Service, *Annual Report* (1906):39, (1909):34.

10. Brown, *American Lumber Industry,* pp. 255–256; *Timberman* 1 (April, 1900):13, (June, 1900):12, 2 (Aug., 1901):5, 29.

11. *Timberman* 1 (June, 1900):12, 8 (Mar., 1907):47, 10 (Oct., 1909):19;

American Lumberman (Mar. 9, 1907):24; *Pacific Lumber and Trade Journal* 14 (June, 1908):22.

12. The following sources provide only a partial listing of the mounting numbers of publications that focus on the economic and political origins of the conservation movement. Samuel P. Hays, *Conservation and the Gospel of Efficiency: The Progressive Movement, 1890–1920* (Cambridge, Mass.: Harvard University Press, 1959); Elmo Richardson, *The Politics of Conservation: Crusades and Controversies, 1897–1913* (Berkeley: University of California Press, 1962); Gabriel Kolko, *The Triumph of Conservatism: A Reinterpretation of American History, 1900–1916* (New York: Macmillan, 1963); Robert H. Wiebe, *The Search for Order, 1877–1920* (New York: Hill and Wang, 1967); James Weinstein, *The Corporate Ideal in the Liberal State* (Boston: Beacon Press, 1968).

13. Earle Clapp, a long-time Forest Service official and acting chief from 1939 to 1943, said this was true of forest conservation once the forest reserves were centered in the Department of Agriculture. Clapp to Henry A. Wallace, Feb. 8, 1940, container 10, official file 1c, Franklin D. Roosevelt Papers (hereafter FDR Papers), Franklin D. Roosevelt Presidential Library, Hyde Park, N.Y.

14. Division of Forestry, *Annual Report* (1886):155–156.

15. J. E. Defebaugh, "Relation of Forestry to Lumbering and the Wood-Working Industries," *Proceedings of the American Forestry Association* (1893):150–152.

16. Pinchot, "The Forester and the Lumberman," p. 176; Royal S. Kellogg, "The Rise in Lumber Prices," *American Forests* 12 (Feb., 1906): 68–69.

17. *American Lumberman* (Sept. 28, 1908):29; *Timberman* 11 (Sept., 1910): 19, 11 (July, 1910):19.

18. Ernest Bruncken, "Private Forestry and Taxation," *American Forests* 9 (Oct., 1903):509; Steen, *U.S. Forest Service*, pp. 92, 130; Alfred Gaskill, "How Shall Forests Be Taxed," *American Forests* 12 (Jan., 1906):119.

19. *Forty Years of Western Forestry: A History of the Movement to Conserve Forest Resources by Cooperative Effort, 1909–1949* (Portland, Ore.: Western Forestry and Conservation Association, 1949), pp. 8–10; E. T. Allen is quoted in the *Timberman* 11 (Aug., 1910):35; National Lumber Manufacturers Association, *Annual Report* (1910):15–17, (1912):23, 25.

20. Gifford Pinchot, "Forestry on Private Lands," *Annals of the American Academy of Political and Social Science* 33 (1909):493.

21. Dana, *Forest and Range Policy,* p. 174; Steen, *U.S. Forest Service,* p. 93.

22. J. Cox, "Trade Associations in the Lumber Industry," p. 308; *American Lumberman* (Sept. 12, 1908): 29, (Dec. 5, 1908):31.

23. Transcript of organizing meeting of the Western Forestry and Conservation Association," box 1, Western Forestry and Conservation Association Records (hereafter WFCA Records), Oregon Historical Society, Portland; *Pacific Lumber and Trade Journal* 14 (Feb., 1909):17; *American Lumberman* (Mar. 13, 1909):35; *Timberman* 11 (Jan., 1910):19.

24. J. Cox, "Trade Associations in the Lumber Industry," pp. 294–295; Steen, *U.S. Forest Service,* pp. 110–111; Ralph C. Bryant, *Lumber: Its Manufacture and Distribution* (New York: John Wiley and Sons, 1922), p. 327.

25. U.S. Congress, *Congressional Record,* 60th Cong., 1st sess., Jan. 30, Feb. 4, 1907, pp. 2020–2021, 2200.

26. Charles Edward Russell, "The Mysterious Octopus: The Story of the Strange and Powerful Organization That Controls the American Lumber Trade," *World Today* 21 (1921):1735–1750; "Speech of Elias M. Ammons before the Colorado Assembly in Reply to Mr. Pinchot," in *Congressional Record,* 61st Cong., 2d sess., May 19, 1910, p. 6530; ibid., 61st Cong., 3d sess., Mar. 1, 1911, p. 3774; ibid., 62d Cong., 2d sess., May 16, 1912, pp. 6531, 6539, 6544, 6547.

27. Pinkett, *Pinchot,* pp. 81–84; McGeary, *Gifford Pinchot,* pp. 88–90.

28. Minutes of the Service Committee, Mar. 3, 1907, Dec. 12, 1908, NA/ RG95–8; John Ise, *The United States Forest Policy* (New Haven, Conn.: Yale University Press, 1920), p. 288.

29. Pinchot, "The Forester and the Lumberman," pp. 177–178; *Timberman* 13 (Dec., 1911):52–53.

30. *West Coast Lumberman* 29 (Dec., 1915):42; "Reports to Officers and Committees of the Third Annual Meeting of the West Coast Lumbermen's Association," 1913, in box 1, West Coast Lumbermen's Association Records (hereafter, WCLA Records), Oregon Historical Society, Portland; *Timberman* 16 (Aug., 1915):30.

31. *Timberman* 10 (June, 1909):19, 13 (Nov., 1911):19; *West Coast Lumberman* 25 (Dec., 1913):30, 42.

32. *Timberman* 16 (Aug., 1915):27–28, 30–34; *West Coast Lumberman* 28 (Aug., 1915):24–25.

33. William B. Greeley, *Some Public and Economic Aspects of the Lumber Industry*, USDA Report No. 14, 1917, pp. 3–4, 13.
34. Ibid., 13–15.
35. Ibid., 99–100.

Chapter Three

1. Joseph S. Illick, "State Forestry," in *Fifty Years of Forestry*, pp. 222–225; Ralph R. Widner, ed., *Forests and Forestry in the American States: A Reference Anthology* (Washington, D.C.: Association of State Foresters, 1968), pp. xix–xx.
2. Harmon, "Remembering Franklin B. Hough," p. 52; Sparhawk, "History of Forestry in America," p. 705.
3. Illick, "State Forestry," pp. 224–225; Sparhawk, "History of Forestry in America," p. 704; Widner, *Forests and Forestry*, p. xx; Dana and Fairfax, *Forest and Range Policy*, pp. 43–44.
4. Eliot Zimmerman, "The History of State and Private Forestry" (manuscript in Forest Service, Region 8, State and Private Forestry Office, Atlanta), p. 4; Fernow, *Report upon the Forestry Investigations*, p. 172; Widner, *Forests and Forestry*, p. xx.
5. Widner, *Forests and Forestry*, pp. 8–9.
6. C. Raymond Clar, *California Government and Forestry from Spanish Days until the Creation of the Department of Natural Resources in 1927* (Sacramento: Department of Natural Resources, 1959), 1:96–127.
7. Ibid., 156–160; Fernow, *Report upon the Forestry Investigations*, p. 183.
8. Widner, *Forests and Forestry*, pp. xx, 30–33, 56–58; Illick, "State Forestry," p. 225.
9. Fernow, *Report upon the Forestry Investigations*, p. 181.
10. Illick, "State Forestry," p. 224; Fernow, *Report upon the Forestry Investigations*, pp. 180–181; Zimmerman, "History of State and Private Forestry," p. 8.
11. Elizabeth Bachman, *A History of Forestry in Minnesota with Particular Reference to Forestry Legislation* (St. Paul: Department of Conservation, 1965), pp. 5–10.
12. Ibid., p. 10; Fernow, *Report upon the Forestry Investigations*, p. 185.
13. Bachman, *History of Forestry in Minnesota*, pp. 10–14.
14. Widner, *Forests and Forestry*, pp. 25–29; Fernow, *Report upon the Forestry Investigations*, pp. 177–180, 183; Sparhawk, "History of Forestry in America," p. 706.

15. Zimmerman, "History of State and Private Forestry," p. 8; Widner, *Forests and Forestry*, p. 483.

16. Rodgers, *Bernhard Fernow*, pp. 193–194.

17. Zimmerman, "History of State and Private Forestry," p. 5; Clepper, *Professional Forestry*, p. 233.

18. Pinchot, *Breaking New Ground*, pp. 49–50; Widner, *Forests and Forestry*, p. 201; Fernow, *Report upon the Forestry Investigations*, p. 180.

19. Pinchot, *Breaking New Ground*, p. 50; Clepper, *Professional Forestry*, pp. 33, 36–37.

20. Division of Forestry, *Annual Report* (1893):325.

21. Fernow, *Report upon the Forest Investigations*, pp. 24–25.

22. Division of Forestry, *Annual Report* (1892):317; George P. Ahern to Bernhard Fernow, Mar. 20, 1891, in "G. P. Ahern, U.S.A., 1894–1898," Letters Received by the Division of Forestry, 1888–1899, NA/RG95–1.

23. Illick, "State Forestry," pp. 226–227; Clepper, *Professional Forestry*, pp. 85–87.

24. Division of Forestry, *Annual Report* (1892):319.

25. Ibid. (1900):103–104; Bureau of Forestry, *Annual Report* (1903):498; Pinkett, *Pinchot*, p. 52.

26. Division of Forestry, *Annual Report* (1899):94; Bureau of Forestry, *Annual Report* (1902):123, (1903):508–509.

27. Bureau of Forestry, *Annual Report* (1904):174; Widner, *Forests and Forestry*, pp. 553–554.

28. Bureau of Forestry, *Annual Report* (1903):498; Clar, *California Government and Forestry*, 1:172–173, 193–197.

29. Clar, *California Government and Forestry*, 1:199–204.

30. Bureau of Forestry, *Annual Report* (1904):171–172; California, *Report of the State Forester* (1906):15, in Forestry Reports, Miscellaneous, 1906, California State Archives, Sacramento.

31. California, *Report of the State Forester* (1906):21; Clar, *California Government and Forestry*, 1:207.

32. Bureau of Forestry, *Annual Report* (1904):171; Clar, *California Government and Forestry*, 1:206.

33. The California Board of Examiners is quoted in Clar, *California Government and Forestry*, 1:206.

34. Forest Service, *Annual Report* (1906):23, (1908):30–31.

35. Ibid. (1908):30–31, (1909):30–31, (1910):47–48; Dana and Fairfax, *Forest and Range Policy,* pp. 288–289. The Wisconsin report is in Alfred K. Chittenden, *The Taxation of Forest Lands in Wisconsin* (Madison: Democrat Printing Co., 1911).

36. Washington State Forestry Association, First Annual Meeting, Jan. 9, 1897, U.S. Forest Service Clipping File, Forest History Society, Santa Cruz, Calif. (hereafter FHS clipping file). This file, put together during the early years of the Forest Service, provides published accounts of service activities between 1890 and about 1910.

37. Washington, *Report of the State Fire Warden for the year 1905 to the State Board of Forest Commissioners* (1905):7.

38. Ibid., pp. 8–11; George Thomas Morgan, Jr., "The Fight against Fire: Development of Cooperative Forestry in the Pacific Northwest, 1900–1950" (Ph.D. diss., University of Oregon, 1964), p. 67.

39. Widner, *Forests and Forestry,* pp. 173–174; Morgan, "The Fight against Fire," pp. 71–73.

40. Washington, *Report of the State Fire Warden* (1907):6–7; Widner, *Forests and Forestry,* p. 174.

41. Morgan, "The Fight against Fire," pp. 72–73; Washington Forest Fire Association, *Annual Report* (1908):10–11, in "State and Private Forestry," Office of State and Private Forestry, U.S. Forest Service Region 6, Portland, Ore.

42. E. O. Siecke, "The Development of Oregon's Forest Policy," *Commonwealth Review* 1 (1916):189–199; Morgan, "The Fight against Fire," p. 70; Widner, *Forests and Forestry* pp. 169–170.

43. Morgan, "The Fight against Fire," pp. 61–64; *Timberman* 6 (Aug., 1904): 37.

44. Siecke, "Development of Oregon's Forest Policy," pp. 191–192; Oregon, *Annual Report of the State Forester* (1935):8–9.

45. Lawrence Rakestraw, "The West, States' Rights, and Conservation," *Pacific Northwest Quarterly* 48 (1957):92; Oregon, *Report of the Oregon Conservation Commission* (1909):35, (1910):9.

46. According to E. T. Allen, the testimony of Smith C. Bartrum, a Forest Service employee attached to the national forests in Oregon, was critical to the enactment of the state's forestry law of 1907. See Morgan, "The Fight against Fire," p. 86.

47. Ibid., pp. 58–59; Widner, *Forests and Forestry,* pp. 168–169.

48. E. T. Allen to E. Pendleton Herring, June 22, 1930, in E. T. Allen Papers, Oregon Historical Society, Portland.
49. Treadwell Cleveland, Jr., "Forestry on Private Lands," circa 1910, "Management — Private Ownership," NA / RG95 – 64; *New York Times,* Aug. 23, 1910.
50. Peters, "The Possibilities and the Limitations of Government Cooperative Work with the Private Owner," pp. 13–14.
51. Forest Service, *Annual Report* (1909):31–32.
52. Ibid. (1910):47–48.

Chapter Four

1. Minutes of the Service Committee, Oct. 12, Nov. 3, 1910, NA / RG95 – 8.
2. Pinchot, "Forestry on Private Lands," p. 4; Henry Graves, "Public Regulation of Private Forests," *Annals of the American Academy of Political and Social Science* 33 (1909):23.
3. "Government and Private Cooperation in Compilation of Forest Fire Data," May 3, 1909, and "States Cooperate with Forest Service to Obtain Forest Fire Statistics," June 26, 1909, both in "News Items, May-June, 1909," News Articles and Press Releases, NA / RG95 – 51.
4. Minutes of the Service Committee, Jan. 20, 1909, NA / RG95 – 8; "Lumbermen's Associations Cooperate with Forest Service in Fire Patrol," June 17, 1909, in "News Items, May-June, 1909," News Articles and Press Releases, NA / RG95 – 51.
5. "Lumbermen's Associations Cooperate with Forest Service in Fire Patrol," June 17, 1909, in "News Items, May-June, 1909," News Articles and Press Releases, NA / RG95 – 51; *American Lumberman* (Aug. 21, 1909):37.
6. *American Lumberman* (Aug. 21, 1909):38; Morgan, "The Fight against Fire," p. 94.
7. *Timberman* 13 (Dec., 1911):50, 52.
8. "Suggestions by the United States Forester," *National Lumber Manufacturers Association: Official Report* 9 (1911):205 – 206.
9. Minutes of the Service Committee, Feb. 17, 1909, NA / RG95 – 8; "Railroads to Cooperate in Fire Control," *American Forests* 16 (June, 1910):375 – 376; Morgan, "The Fight against Fire," pp. 128–130; Forest Service, *Annual Report* (1912):77.

10. Steen, *U.S. Forest Service,* pp. 123–125; Dana and Fairfax, *Forest and Range Policy,* p. 111.

11. Morgan, "The Fight against Fire," pp. 138–140; Dana and Fairfax, *Forest and Range Policy,* pp. 111–112.

12. Steen, *U.S. Forest Service,* p. 129; J. Girvin Peters, "Cooperation with States in Fire Patrol," *American Forests* 17 (1911):383–384.

13. Memorandum for Mr. Graves, Apr. 20, 1911, and Henry Graves to Secretary of Agriculture, May 8, 1911, in "Policy—Weeks Law," Records of the Central Files of the Division, 1913–1944, NA/RG95–97.

14. Forest Service, *Annual Report* (1911):63, (1912):75–77; J. Girvin Peters, *Forest Protection under the Weeks Law in Cooperation with States,* USDA, Forest Service Circular no. 205 (Washington, D.C.: Government Printing Office, 1912), pp. 5–7.

15. Forest Service, *Annual Report* (1913):48.

16. Peters, *Forest Protection under the Weeks Law,* p. 8.

17. Forest Service, *Annual Report* (1912):76, (1913):47–48.

18. Peters, *Forest Protection under the Weeks Law,* p. 11; Forest Service, *Annual Report* (1913):48–49.

19. George H. Cecil to the Forester, Dec. 27, 1912, "Weeks Law Collaborators' Conference, January 9 and 10, 1913," NA/RG95–97.

20. Addresses by Representatives of States Which Are Prospective Cooperators under the Weeks Law, Jan. 9 and 10, 1913, pp. 153–154, in "Weeks Law, Department Bulletin No. 13," NA/RG95–97.

21. J. Girvin Peters, "Cooperative Fire Protection under the Weeks Law," Jan. 19, 1914, in "Weeks Law, Conferences, 1914," NA/RG95–97.

22. Weeks Law Circular Letter to District Foresters, Jan. 15, 1916, "P— Legislation, the Weeks Law," and L. H. Jones, acting solicitor, to the Forester, Sept. 17, 1914, "Weeks Law—Navigability—1914," both in NA/RG95–97.

23. Memorandum for Mr. Graves, Dec. 29, 1914, "P—Legislation, The Weeks Law," NA/RG95–97.

24. J. G. Peters to Austin F. Hawes, Apr. 2, 1913, and Hawes to Peters, Apr. 14, 1913, in "Weeks Law—Circular Letters—1913—General Instruction," NA/RG95–97.

25. Louis S. Murphy, acting chief of state cooperation to State Foresters, Aug. 18, 1914, and Murphy to W. G. Howard, Jan. 20, 1915, in "Weeks Law—Circular Letters—1914," NA/RG95–97.

26. E. W. Ferris to George H. Cecil, Feb. 17, 1915, "Weeks Law—Circu-

lar Letters—1915—1916," and J. G. Peters, "Federal and State Cooperation in Fire Protection," in "P—Legislation, The Weeks Law," NA/RG95–97.

27. Circular Letter to District Foresters, Jan. 15, 1916, in "P—Legislation, The Weeks Law," NA/RG95–97.

28. *Timberman* 13 (Mar. 1912):32J.

29. *West Coast Lumberman* 25 (Dec. 15, 1913):30, 42.

30. Ibid., 42.

31. Forest Service, *Annual Report* (1915):21, (1917):27, (1919):27.

32. Ibid. (1916):26, (1917):28.

33. Minutes of the Service Committee, Oct. 13, 1921, NA/RG95–8; Forest Service, *Annual Report* (1912):17.

34. Minutes of the Service Committee, June 6, 1924, NA/RG95–8.

35. Ibid., Feb. 17, 1922.

36. Ibid.; Forest Service *Annual Report* (1922):21; J. G. Peters, "Weeks Law Co-operation," *Proceedings of the Northeastern Forest Fire Conference* (1920):10.

37. Stephen J. Pyne, *Fire in America: A Cultural History of Wildland and Rural Fire* (Princeton, N.J.: Princeton University Press, 1982), pp. 143–160.

38. J. G. Peters, "Weeks Law Cooperation," Mar. 18, 1920, in "Weeks Law Collaborators Meeting—Albany, N.Y.—1920," NA/RG95–97.

39. J. G. Peters to District Forester, June 4, 1921, "Weeks Law—Circular Letters—1920," and State Cooperation under the Weeks Law, "Weeks Law—State Cooperation, 1923," both in NA/RG95–97; Zimmerman, "History of State and Private Forestry," p. 40.

40. Minutes of the Service Committee, Nov. 30, 1923, NA/RG95–8; J. G. Peters, memorandum for the files, Apr. 18, 1924, NA/RG95–97.

41. Zimmerman, "History of State and Private Forestry," p. 40.

42. *A National Plan for American Forestry*, Senate Doc. le, 73d Congress, 1st sess., Mar. 30, 1933, pp. 776–777.

43. Wilson Compton, "Forest Economics: Some Thoughts on an Old Subject," *American Forests* 25 (Sept., 1919):1337–1339.

Chapter Five

1. Bachman, *History of Forestry in Minnesota*, pp. 12–18.

2. Ibid., pp. 19–21. The new forestry laws of 1911 are printed in *Forestry: Sixteenth Annual Report of the Forestry Commissioner of Minnesota for the Year 1910* (St. Paul: Pioneer Co., 1911), pp. 50–55.

3. Minnesota Forestry Board, *First Annual Report of the State Forester* (1911):12–13; Bachman, *History of Forestry in Minnesota,* pp. 21–22.

4. Minnesota, *First Annual Report of the State Forester* (1911):13–14; Minnesota, *Annual Report of the Minnesota State Forestry Board* (1920):13.

5. Minnesota, *First Annual Report of the State Forester* (1911):14–15, 20; Minnesota, *Third Annual Report of the State Forester* (1913):61.

6. Minnesota, *Third Annual Report of the State Forester* (1913):62.

7. J. G. Peters to William T. Cox, Dec. 16, 1912, in Minnesota Department of Conservation, Minnesota State Archives, St. Paul.

8. Minnesota, *First Annual Report of the State Forester* (1911):21–22; *Second Annual Report of the State Forester* (1912):13; Bachman, *History of Forestry in Minnesota,* p. 23.

9. Minnesota, *First Annual Report of the State Forester* (1911):35, *Second Annual Report of the State Forester* (1912):13, *Fourth Annual Report of the State Forester* (1914):18.

10. Minnesota, *Fourth Annual Report of the State Forester* (1914):21–22; William T. Cox to Pentecost Mitchell, Feb. 12, 1912, in Minnesota Department of Conservation, Forestry Board, Minnesota State Archives (hereafter Forestry Board Correspondence).

11. J. H. Foster, Office Report Inspection of Federal Fire Cooperation: Minnesota, Aug., 1913, in "Weeks Law Inspection Reports," NA/RG95–97.

12. J. H. Foster to W. T. Cox, Apr. 21, 1916, and Smith Riley to Cox, Feb. 10, 1917, in Forestry Board Correspondence.

13. John McLaren, Weeks Law Inspection Report, Nov. 15, 1918, in ibid.

14. William Cox to E. C. Hurst, Mar. 10, 1919, J. Stahl to Cox, Feb. 12, 1919, and Cox to District Forester, Mar. 7, 1919, all in ibid.

15. William Cox to District Forester, Mar. 7, 1919, ibid.

16. Arthur Lee Cook, Minnesota: Report of Inspection, 1919, J. A. Mitchell, Inspection Report: Minnesota, Sept., 1920, and Sept., 1921, all in "Weeks Law Inspection Reports," NA/RG95–97.

17. J. G. Peters to William T. Cox, Feb. 16, 1921, Forestry Board Correspondence.

18. William T. Cox to Smith Riley, May 15, 1919, and Fred Morrell to Cox, May 24, 1919, in ibid.

19. Willis C. Hawley to Henry Graves, May 21, 1919, and Graves to Hawley, May 23, 1919, ibid.

20. Bachman, *History of Forestry in Minnesota*, pp. 30–32; William Greeley to William T. Cox, Jan. 5, 1922, in "Weeks Law Inspection Reports," NA/RG95–97, and Cox to Gifford Pinchot, Mar. 14, 1919, in Forestry Board Correspondence.

21. William Greeley to William Cox, Jan. 5, 1922, "Weeks Law Inspection Reports," NA/RG95–97.

22. Widner, *Forests and Forestry*, p. 503.

23. Morris S. Isseks, *History of State Administrative Agencies in Oregon, 1890–1910* (Portland: Works Progress Administration, 1939), p. 248; Widner, *Forests and Forestry*, p. 170; William G. Robbins, *The Early Conservation Movement in Oregon, 1890–1910* (Corvallis: Oregon State University Press, 1975), p. 21.

24. Oregon, *Report of the State Forester* (1912):18.

25. Ibid., 19–21.

26. Ibid. (1911):12–13, (1912):33–35.

27. W. B. Greeley, "Washington and Her Forest Industries," undated manuscript in box 16, William B. Greeley Papers, University of Oregon Library, Eugene; Widner, *Forests and Forestry*, p. 175.

28. *Fourth Annual Report of the Washington Forest Fire Association* (1911):8.

29. *Fifth Annual Report of the Washington Forest Fire Association* (1912):10–11; Washington, *Report of the State Forester and Fire Warden* (1912):20–21.

30. *Sixth Annual Report of the Washington Forest Fire Association* (1913):14–15; *Seventh Annual Report of the Washington Forest Fire Association* (1914):11.

31. Oregon, *Report of the State Forester* (1914):33; Siecke, "Development of Oregon's Forest Policy," pp. 194–195.

32. Oregon, *Report of the State Forester* (1911):14, (1913):16, (1914):30–32, (1918):6.

33. *Eighth Annual Report of the Washington Forest Fire Association* (1915):7; Washington, *Report of the State Forester* (1915):15–16, (1921):14–15.

34. Washington, *Report of the State Forester* (1921):14–15; *Annual Report of the Washington Forest Fire Association* (1921):15.

35. *Annual Report of the Washington Forest Fire Association* (1920):12–15; Washington, *Report of the State Forester* (1919):21–23; Widner, *Forests and Forestry*, p. 271.

36. Washington, *Report of the State Forester* (1921):19.

37. Oregon, *Report of the State Forester* (1919): 29–30; C. S. Chapman to J. F. Kimball, May 12, 1919, box 8, WFCA Records.

38. Central Oregon Fire Patrol Association to C. S. Chapman, Apr. 18, 1915, box 8, and F. A. Elliott to Chapman, July 21, 1923, box 12, both in WFCA Records.

39. Norman Jacobson, U.S. Forest Service Inspection Report of the Weeks Law Cooperative Patrol Work in the State of Oregon during the Season of 1916, and E. H. McDaniels, Inspection Report of Cooperation under the Weeks Law between the U.S. Forest Service and the States of Washington and Oregon, Season of 1924, both in box 9, WFCA Records.

40. Dana, *Forest and Range Policy*, p. 265; Clepper, *Professional Forestry*, pp. 109–110; Richard C. Ellis, "The Oregon and California Railroad Land Grant, 1866–1945," *Pacific Northwest Quarterly* 39 (1948):274–276; Oregon, *Report of the State Forester* (1920):34.

41. Report on O & C Protection, Calendar Year 1922, in "O & C Reports, 1915–1936," Records of the Office of the Chief, NA/RG 95–4.

42. Ibid.

43. Widner, *Forests and Forestry*, pp. 271–272; Washington, *First Report of the Department of Conservation and Development* (1922):4–5.

44. Washington, *Report of the State Forester* (1921):30–31; Widner, *Forests and Forestry*, p. 272.

45. Washington, *Nineteenth and Twentieth Annual Reports of the Forestry Division* (1924):38–41.

46. Oregon, *Report of the State Forester* (1919):33–35.

47. Ibid. (1920):42–55.

48. Ibid. (1922):25; Earl Pierce, "Clarke-McNary Cooperative Fire Control Allotments: Past-Present-Future," address to the Twenty-Fifth Annual Meeting of the Association of State Foresters, p. 62, box 216, Records of the National Association of State Foresters (hereafter NASF Records), Denver Public Library.

49. I. James Pikl, *A History of Georgia Forestry* (Athens: University of Georgia Press, 1966), pp. 9–10.

50. Ibid., 13.

51. J. G. Peters, "Forest Fire Protection in Georgia," *American Forests* 28 (Aug., 1922):457–458.

52. "Forestry as a Unit of State Government," undated manuscript,

pp. 13–14, files of the Georgia Forestry Commission, Macon; Pikl, *History of Georgia Forestry,* pp. 18–19.

53. Widner, *Forests and Forestry,* pp. 95–99; Forest Service, *Annual Report* (1916):25, (1917):27.

54. Forest Service, *Annual Report* (1920):26; Widner, *Forests and Forestry,* pp. 107–110.

55. Widner, *Forests and Forestry,* pp. 120–123.

56. Ibid., pp. 131–132.

Chapter Six

1. George T. Morgan, Jr., *William B. Greeley: A Practical Forester* (St. Paul: Forest History Society, 1961), p. 65; Greeley, *Forests and Men,* p. 110; David Mason to Charles McNary, June 16, 1924, McNary folder, file 310, David Mason Papers, Oregon Historical Society, Portland; *American Lumberman* (Apr. 19, 1924):56.

2. L. C. Boyle to Charles Keith, Nov. 14, 1917, box 110, NFPA Records; Melvyn Dubofsky, *We Shall Be All: A History of the Industrial Workers of the World* (Chicago: Quadrangle, 1969), pp. 349–375; Dana, *Forest and Range Policy,* pp. 204–205.

3. Wilson Compton, "The Price Problem in the Lumber Industry," *American Economic Review* 7 (1917):582–583; Wilson Compton to John H. Kirby, Nov. 18, 1918, box 110, NFPA Records.

4. J. Girvin Peters, "Cooperative Fire Protection under the Weeks Law," in "P—Legislation, The Weeks Law," NA/RG95–97.

5. Austin Cary, "How Lumbermen in Following Their Own Interest Have Served the Public," *Journal of Forestry* 15 (Mar., 1917):281–284; Burt Kirkland to Raphael Zon, Nov. 12, 1918, box 2, Raphael Zon Papers, Minnesota Historical Society, St. Paul.

6. *Southern Lumberman* 84 (June 30, 1917):20; "Editorial: Cut-Over Lands a National Problem," *American Forests* 23 (May, 1917):304–305; *Timberman* 19 (Aug., 1918):27–28.

7. Minutes of the Service Committee, Sept. 11, 1919, NA/RG95–8.

8. Henry Graves, "A National Lumber and Forest Policy," *Journal of Forestry* 17 (1919):351–356; Steen, *U.S. Forest Service,* pp. 142–143.

9. Graves, "National Lumber and Forest Policy," pp. 360–361.

10. Ibid., pp. 362–363.

11. *Lumber* 645 (Nov. 3, 1919):33, (Oct. 27, 1919):43.

12. *American Lumberman* (Nov. 1, 1919):57; *Timberman* 20 (Aug., 1919): 90–91, 93.

13. Royal S. Kellogg, "A Discussion of Methods," *American Forests* 25 (Aug., 1919):1282–1283; Compton, "Forest Economics," pp. 1337–1339.

14. "Forest Devastation: A National Danger and a Plan to Meet It," *Journal of Forestry* 17 (Dec., 1919):900, 911–912, 914. Henry Graves thought Raphael Zon had influenced the writing of the Pinchot report and that it was socialistic. For his part, Zon predicted that when the article appeared in print, "the feathers will begin to fly." See Steen, *U.S. Forest Service*, p. 178, and Zon to Earle Clapp, Nov. 4, 1919, box 2, Zon Papers.

15. Greeley, *Some Public and Economic Aspects of the Lumber Industry*, passim, and "Self-Government in Forestry," *Journal of Forestry* 18 (Feb., 1920): 103–105.

16. U.S. Forest Service, *Timber Depletion, Lumber Prices, Lumber Exports, and Concentration of Timber Ownership*, Report on Senate Resolution 311 (1920), pp. 64–65, 69–70.

17. Minutes of the Service Committee, Sept. 16, 1920, NA/RG95–8; Forest Service, *Annual Report* (1920):1–2, (1921):1–3.

18. George Dean, "A Brief Historical Review of the National Association of State Foresters," paper presented to the forty-eighth annual meeting of the National Association of State Foresters, box 420, NASF Records; J. G. Peters to William T. Cox, Nov. 5, 1920, Cox to Peters, Nov. 8, 1920, and Gifford Pinchot to Cox, Nov. 1, 1920, all in Forestry Board Correspondence; "State Foresters Demand Legislation," *American Forests* 27 (Jan., 1921):19; Gifford Pinchot to Girvin Peters, Sept. 21, 1920, Allen Papers.

19. William Greeley, "The Forest Service Plans for Cooperation with States," paper read at Atlantic City, N.J., Nov. 12, 1920, in box 4, Greeley Papers.

20. Dean, "Brief Historical Review"; William Greeley, "Wood For the Nation," address to the New York Lumber Trade Association, Jan. 28, 1921, box 4, Greeley Papers.

21. *American Lumberman* (July 17, 1920):69; E. T. Allen to R. S. Kellogg, Jan. 10, 1921, Allen to William Greeley, Sept. 16, 1920, and Allen to Harris Reynolds, Sept. 25 and 28, 1920, all in box 1, National Forestry Program Committee Records (hereafter NFPC Records), Cornell Uni-

versity Libraries, Ithaca, N.Y.; *Southern Lumberman* 97 (July 31, 1920):39–40.

22. Ralph S. Hosmer, "The National Forestry Program Committee," *Journal of Forestry* 45 (Sept., 1947):629–630; Greeley, *Forests and Men,* p. 103; E. T. Allen to R. S. Kellogg, June 1, 1921, box 1, NFPC Records. The legislative hearings and lengthy testimony on the various forestry policy bills are covered in detail in several sources. See especially Steen, *U.S. Forest Service,* pp. 179–188, and Robbins, *Lumberjacks and Legislators,* pp. 98–108.

23. E. T. Allen to William Greeley, Feb. 20, 1922, and Greeley to Allen, Mar. 4, 1922, both in box 2, NFPC Records.

24. U.S. Congress, Senate, Select Committee on Reforestation, *Hearings,* 67th Cong., 4th sess., passim.

25. Ibid., Nov. 22, 1923, pp. 1363–1373, 1384–1389; Allen memo to George Jewett, Dec. 10, 1939, box 4, WFCA Records.

26. R. S. Kellogg to Elwood Maunder, Oct. 31, 1962, Royal S. Kellogg— Letter File, Manuscripts Collection, Forest History Society, Santa Cruz, Calif.

27. Zimmerman, "History of State and Private Forestry," pp. 46–49; Cooperative Program of the Department of Agriculture under Sections 1–4 of the Clarke-McNary Law, May 25, 1925, in "SC—Clarke-McNary Law Program, General, 1924–1925," NA/RG95–97.

28. *American Lumberman* (June 14, 1925):36; *Lumber World Review* (Jan. 25, 1925):43; George Long to E. T. Allen, July 11, 1924, box 13, WFCA Records.

29. Minutes of the Service Committee, Jan. 4, 1923, NA/RG95–8; Morgan, "The Fight against Fire," pp. 168, 181.

30. William B. Greeley to Branch Chiefs, District Foresters, and Forest Supervisors, Apr. 4, 1924, Research Compilation File, NA/RG95–100.

31. Ibid.

32. Ibid.

33. Zimmerman, "History of State and Private Forestry," p. 48.

34. *West Coast Lumberman* 47 (Dec. 15, 1924):34.

35. Ibid.

36. Cooperative Program of the Department of Agriculture under Sections 1–4 of the Clarke-McNary Law, May 25, 1925, in "SC—Clarke-McNary Law Program, General, 1924–1925," NA/RG95–97; *West Coast Lumberman* 47 (Dec. 15, 1924):34, 53.

37. Fred Morrell to the Forester, Dec. 17, 1924, in "PC Clarke-McNary Law—Secs. 1–4—D-1—1924–1925," NA/RG95–97; Forest Service, *Annual Report* (1925):9.

38. Joseph F. Kaylor, "Farm Forestry," in *Fifty Years of Forestry,* pp. 261–263; Clepper, *Professional Forestry,* pp. 187–188.

39. Clepper, *Professional Forestry,* p. 189.

40. Minutes of the Service Committee, Jan. 19, 1922, NA/RG95–8.

41. Ibid.

42. Forest Service, *Annual Report* (1923):4; memorandum of Department Policy for Cooperation with States in Forestry, May 3, 1924, in "General," NA/RG95–4.

43. Minutes of the Service Committee, Apr. 16, June 12, 1925, NA/RG95–8.

44. *Lumber World Review* (Jan. 25, 1925):43; Kaylor, "Farm Forestry," p. 263.

45. Cooperative Program of the Department of Agriculture under Sections 1–4 of the Clarke-McNary Law, May 25, 1925, in "SC—Clarke-McNary Law Program, General, 1924–1925," NA/RG95–97.

46. Minutes of the Service Committee, June 2, Sept. 15, 1927, NA/RG95–8; Droze, *Trees, Prairies, and People,* pp. 44–45.

47. Forest Service, *Annual Report* (1927):8; (1928):13, 16; G. H. Collingwood, *The Practice of Forestry on Private Lands as Influenced by Forestry Extension,* USDA Circular No. 36 (Washington, D.C.: Government Printing Office, 1927), p. 1.

48. E. T. Allen to William Greeley, Dec. 6, 1924, box 9, WFCA Records; *West Coast Lumberman* 47 (Dec. 15, 1924):58. During these years other groups asked Allen to intercede to restore budget items. In one instance, the California Protective Association requested that Allen intervene to increase the appropriation for the forest experiment station at Berkeley. See William M. Wheeler to Allen, Dec. 30, 1925, box 12, WFCA Records.

49. William Greeley to E. T. Allen, Feb. 15, 1926, and Allen to A. W. Laird, Aug. 30, Laird to Allen, Sept. 1, and Allen to Laird, Sept. 15, 1926, all in box 13, WFCA Records.

50. E. T. Allen to William Greeley, Sept. 24, 1926, and Statement of Timberland Owners to the President, Oct. 7, 1926, ibid.

51. NLMA News Release, "Protecting a Great National Asset," Oct. 7, 1926, Ovid Butler to E. T. Allen, Oct. 19, 1926, George D. Pratt to the

President, Oct. 7, 1926, and William Greeley to Allen, Oct. 22, 1926, all in ibid. Also see, "Editorial: A Plea for 'Ultimate Economy,'" *American Forests* 22 (Nov., 1926):676–677, and "Cooperators Confer with President Coolidge to Cut Down Fire Loss," ibid., 679–680.

52. Forest Service, *Annual Report* (1928):12.
53. Henry Graves, "Federal and State Responsibilities in Forestry," *American Forests* 31 (Nov., 1925):677–686.
54. William Greeley, "Future Trends in National and State Forestry," in "Proceedings: Clarke-McNary Law Conference, Washington, D.C., October 15, 1926," NA/RG95–97.
55. E. E. Carter memorandum for Major Stuart, Apr. 22, 1927, in "Progress under Weeks Law," NA/RG95–97.
56. "Forest Fire Cooperation," Sept. 29, 1928, in "SC—Weeks Law—Allotments, Expenses," ibid.
57. Forest Service, *Annual Report* (1928):8; minutes of the Service Committee, Mar. 26, 1925, and Mar. 31, 1927, NA/RG95–8.
58. Orion Howard Cheney, "The New Competition in the Lumber Industry," in NLMA, *Annual Report* (1927):3; Wilson Compton, "Will the Lumber Industry Stand Up and Be Counted?" ibid., p. 2; Ward Shepard, "The Necessity for Realism in Forestry Propaganda," *Journal of Forestry* 25 (Jan., 1927):14–16, 19.

Chapter Seven

1. Steen, *U.S. Forest Service,* p. 101; Clepper, *Professional Forester,* p. 10.
2. Minutes of the Service Committee, July 1, 1909, NA/RA95–8; W. B. Greeley to the Forester, June 9, 1909, in "Forest Service Federal Cooperation, Personnel Reports, etc., 1908–1910," Correspondence of the Office of Federal Cooperation, 1908–1911, NA/RG95–67.
3. Dana and Fairfax, *Forest and Range Policy,* pp. 86–89; Steen, *U.S. Forest Service,* pp. 163–167.
4. Minutes of the Service Committee, Mar. 22, 1909, Aug. 9, 1911, NA/RG95–8; Forest Service, *Annual Report* (1913):30–31.
5. Forest Service, *Annual Report* (1923):33–35; American National Livestock Association, *Proceedings of the Sixteenth Annual Convention* 16 (1913):54–61; William Greeley, "Stabilizing Use of Public Ranges," address to the American National Livestock Association, Jan. 30, 1923, in box 4, Greeley Papers.

6. On the importance of lumber market statistics, see Wilson Compton, "How Competition Can Be Improved through Association," *Proceedings of the Academy of Political Science* 11 (1917):32–38; J. Cox, "Trade Associations in the Lumber Industry," pp. 285–311.
7. Steen, *U.S. Forest Service,* p. 111; D. F. Houston to the Secretary of Commerce, Mar. 22, 1917, box 1, WFCA Records.
8. Minutes of the Service Committee, Oct. 1, 29, Dec. 10, 1913, NA/RG95–8.
9. Ibid., Feb. 3, 1916; *Lumber* 67 (May 27, 1921):23, (June 3, 1921):11; Robert Himmelberg, *The Origins of the National Recovery Administration: Business, Government, and the Trade Association Issue, 1921–1933* (New York: Fordham University Press, 1976), p. 31. Clapp is quoted in the *National Lumber Bulletin* 2 (Mar. 5, 1922):5.
10. H. E. Burke, "My Recollections of the First Years in Forest Entomology," manuscript in the Office of Insect and Disease Control, State and Private Forestry, U.S. Forest Service, Region 6, Portland, Ore., pp. 1–3.
11. Ibid., p. 3; Steen, *U.S. Forest Service,* p. 282.
12. Minutes of the Service Committee, Feb. 9, 1910, Oct. 2, 1912, NA/RG95–8; Burke, "Recollections of the First Years in Forest Entomology," p. 22
13. Widner, *Forest and Forestry,* p. 105; Warren V. Benedict, *History of White Pine Blister Rust Control—A Personal Account* (Washington, D.C.: USDA, 1981), pp. 4–9, 24; Minutes of the Service Committee, Feb. 3, 1916, NA/RG95–8; Forest Service, *Annual Report* (1924):14.
14. Burke, "Recollections of the First Years in Forest Entomology," pp. 24–25; Forest Service, *Annual Report* (1921):16, (1922):18–19.
15. Steen, *U.S. Forest Service,* p. 113; William C. Tweed, *Recreation Site Planning and Improvement in the National Forest, 1891–1942* (Washington, D.C.: U.S. Forest Service, 1980), p. 5.
16. Tweed, *Recreation Site Planning,* p. 5; minutes of the Service Committee, Sept. 23, 1915, NA/RG95–8.
17. Tweed, *Recreation Site Planning,* pp. 6–7.
18. "National Forests Widely Used for Recreation," Jan. 19, 1917, Forest Service news release, in FHS clipping file.
19. Tweed, *Recreation Site Planning,* pp. 7–10.
20. Arthur H. Carhart, "Municipal Playgrounds in the Forests," July, 1919, Wallace Hutchinson, "Outdoor Life in Colorado's National

Forests," Jan. 29, 1920, Arthur Carhart, "Recreation in the National Forest," Sept., 1922, Allen Chaffee, "A Month in the National Forests," n.d., John D. Guthrie, "Oregon Forest Camps Popular with Tourists," May 10, 1923, Verne Rhoades, "Road Construction Aids Campers in North Carolina's National Forests," n.d., all in FHS clipping file.

21. A. S. Peck to Forest Supervisors, May 7, 1920, and Peck to the Forester, Nov. 23, 1920, NA/RG95–4; Steen, *U.S. Forest Service,* p. 158.

22. Tweed, *Recreation Site Planning,* pp. 12–13; Forest Service, *Annual Report* (1924):25.

23. *West Coast Lumberman* 27 (Mar. 15, 1915):34; Steen, *U.S. Forest Service,* pp. 139–140.

24. Minutes of the Service Committee, July 24, 1914, NA/RG95–8; Forest Service, *Annual Report* (1915):27.

25. Forest Service, *Annual Report* (1916):26–27, (1917):29.

26. Ibid. (1918):1–2, 29.

27. Minutes of the Service Committee, Nov. 30, 1917, June 13, 1918, NA/RG95–8; Forest Service, *Annual Report* (1918):30–31.

28. Minutes of the Service Committee, July 17, 1919, NA/RG95–8; Forest Service, *Annual Report* (1919):28–29, (1920):26–27.

29. William M. Wheeler to E. T. Allen, Dec. 30, 1925, box 12, WFCA Records; J. M. Pricehurd to William Greeley, Dec. 1, 1924, box 74, NFPA Records.

30. Wilson Compton to R. S. Kellogg, Dec. 19, 1925, and Arthur Upson to Kellogg, Dec. 23, 1926, both in box 3, NFPC Records.

31. Steen, *U.S. Forest Service,* pp. 140–141; minutes of the Service Committee, Apr. 9, 1926, NA/RG95–8.

32. Minutes of the Service Committee, Apr. 9, 1926, NA/RG95–8.

33. Forest Service, *Annual Report* (1928):1–2; Dana, *Forest and Range Policy,* pp. 225–226; James Fickle, *The New South and the "New Competition": Trade Association Development in the Southern Pine Industry* (Urbana: University of Illinois Press, 1980), p. 258; R. S. Kellogg to C. S. Chapman, Apr. 20, 1927, Earle Clapp to Kellogg, Jan. 5, Feb. 4, 1928, all in box 4, NFPC Records; Arthur C. Ringland to R. S. Hosmer, Dec. 15, 1927, box 1, Ralph S. Hosmer Papers, Cornell University Libraries, Ithaca, N.Y.

34. Fickle, *The New South and the "New Competition,"* p. 258; Raphael Zon to Glenn W. Herrick, Aug. 2, 1920, box 3, Zon Papers.

35. Dana and Fairfax, *Forest and Range Policy*, pp. 117–118; Clepper, *Professional Forestry*, pp. 232, 272; Greeley, *Forests and Men*, p. 93.

36. Greeley, *Forest and Men*, pp. 92–93; Portland *Oregon Journal*, Feb. 26, 1966; Fickle, *The New South and the "New Competition*," pp. 84–87.

37. J. G. Peters to W. T. Cox, May 29, 1917, and Peters, memorandum for the Forester, May 15, 1917, both in Forestry Board Correspondence.

38. A. F. Potter to W. T. Cox, Dec. 15, 1917, and Henry Graves to the Boy Scouts of America, May 9, 1918, ibid.

39. Henry Graves to W. T. Cox, June 8, 1918, D. R. Cotton to Cox, Aug. 20, Cox to Cotton, Aug. 27, Cotton to Cox, Sept. 20, and Cox to Cotton, Sept. 28, 1918, all in ibid.

40. Minutes of the Service Committee, May 5, June 2, 1927, NA/RG 95–8.

41. Forest Service, *Annual Report* (1927):1–2.

42. Lawrence W. Rakestraw, "Urban Influences on Forest Conservation," *Pacific Northwest Quarterly* 56 (1965):108–111; Ronald F. Lockmann, *Guarding the Forests of Southern California: Evolving Attitudes toward Conservation of Watershed, Woodlands, and Wilderness* (Glendale, Calif.: Arthur H. Clark Co., 1981), pp. 23, 89–92.

43. Minutes of the Service Committee, Aug. 9, 16, 1911, NA/RG95–8.

44. Ibid., Oct. 23, 1912.

45. Greeley, *Forests and Men*, pp. 202–204.

46. Forest Service, *Annual Report* (1925):4.

Chapter Eight

1. William Greeley to A. W. Greeley, Sept. 5, 1939, box 7, Greeley Papers.

2. U.S. Forest Service, *Lumber Production, 1869–1934* (Washington, D.C.: Government Printing Office, 1936), p. 74; Forest Service, Annual Report (1929):2, 6.

3. *American Lumberman* (Aug. 17, 1929):53–58, (Jan. 4, 1930):29.

4. Wilson Compton to the president, Apr. 2, and American Forestry Association to the president, Apr. 30, 1930, both in "National Timber Conservation Board," Presidential Papers, Hoover Papers (hereafter cited as PPHP), Herbert Hoover Presidential Library, West Branch, Ia.; Society of American Foresters, Report of Forest Policy Committee, Dec., 1930, box 69, Society of American Foresters Records (hereafter SAF Records),

Forest History Society, Santa Cruz, Calif. For a more detailed account of the Timber Conservation Board, see Robbins, *Lumberjacks and Legislators,* pp. 155–164.

5. Fred Morrell, "Report on Possibilities of Cooperative Management of National Forest and Private Lands," Oct. 31, 1931, in "Agriculture— Forest Service, Forest Management," PPHP; Robert Y. Stuart to Paul Redington, June 28, 1932, box 71, NFPA Records.

6. "Conclusions and Recommendations of the Timber Conservation Board," in "National Timber Conservation Board," PPHP.

7. George P. Ahern, *Deforested America* (Washington, D.C.: Privately published, 1928); "Editorial: 'Deforested America,'" *Journal of Forestry* 35 (1929):99. Gifford Pinchot wrote the foreword to the pamphlet and funded part of the costs of publication and distribution.

8. Wilson Compton, *Reforested America* (Washington, D.C.: NLMA, 1929); Clepper, *Professional Forestry,* pp. 143–145; minutes of the Forestry Committee of the West Coast Lumbermen's Association, July 2, 1929, box 2, WFCA Records.

9. "Forest Policy for the United States," circa 1939, box 69, SAF Records; Clepper, *Professional Forestry,* p. 144; John B. Woods, "The Forestry Situation in the U.S. Today and a Simple Workable Remedy," *Journal of Forestry* 28 (Nov., 1930):930.

10. William N. Sparhawk, "Problems in Determining the Economic Feasibility of Forest Use," *Journal of Farm Economics* (July, 1929):409–410.

11. Forest Service, *Annual Report* (1929):6, (1930):3.

12. Herbert A. Smith, "A Public Forest Policy," *Journal of Forestry* 28 (Nov., 1930):914, 916–917.

13. Ibid., pp. 919, 923–924.

14. Ward Shepard, "Cooperative Control: A Proposed Solution of the Forest Problem," *Journal of Forestry* 28 (Feb., 1930):113, 115, 120.

15. Franklin Reed to E. T. Allen, Jan. 15, 1930, Allen to Reed, Jan. 20, Allen to William B. Greeley, Jan. 20, and Greeley to George S. Long, Jan. 28, 1930, all in box 2, WFCA Records.

16. Fickle, *The New South and the "New Competition,"* pp. 117–119; "Conclusions and Recommendations of the Timber Conservation Board," in "National Timber Conservation Board," PPHP.

17. "Price and Production Stabilization Industry's Major Need," *American Lumberman* (Nov. 1, 1930):22; "Time to Balance Lumber Production against Demand," ibid. (Mar. 11, 1931):20; H. W. Cole, "A Program

for the Lumber Industry," *West Coast Lumberman* 58 (Feb., 1931):13, 59 (Apr., 1932):19; Wilson Compton, "Has Forest Conservation Created a False Alarm," *Scientific American* 145 (Dec., 1931):386–387; Raphael Zon to Charles L. Pack, Aug. 27, 1931, box 7, Zon Papers; Forest Service, *Annual Report* (1932):1.

18. *American Lumberman* (Apr. 25, 1931):26; J. P. Weyerhaeuser, address to the U.S. Chamber of Commerce, May 24, 1932, copy in folder 30, box 2, Mason Papers.

19. U.S. Congress, Senate, *A National Plan for American Forestry,* Senate Doc. 12, 73rd Cong., 1st sess., Mar. 13, 1933, p. x; Clepper, *Professional Forestry,* p. 146.

20. *National Plan for American Forestry,* pp. 60–61.

21. Ibid., pp. 62–63.

22. Wilson Compton, in "Comments on the Copeland Report," *American Forests* 39 (June, 1933):259; Ovid Butler, executive-secretary, AFA, Annual Report, 1933, box E-2, AFA Records; Henry Graves, in "Comments on the Copeland Report," pp. 258–259; Ward Shepard to Robert Stuart, Apr. 28, 1933, copy in box 7, Zon Papers.

23. Himmelberg, *Origins of the National Recovery Administration,* p. 182; Ellis W. Hawley, *The New Deal and the Problem of Monopoly: A Study in Economic Ambivalence* (Princeton, N.J.: Princeton University Press, 1966), pp. 36–43; *American Lumberman* (May 13, 1933):15.

24. Ward Shepard to Robert Stuart, Apr. 28, 1933, box 7, Zon Papers; Shepard to Franklin D. Roosevelt, May 29, 1933, container 8, Official File 1c, FDR Papers; Raphael Zon to Gifford Pinchot, May 23, 1933, box 7, Zon Papers.

25. Franklin Roosevelt to Henry Wallace, June 16, 1933, in Edgar B. Nixon, ed., *Franklin D. Roosevelt and Conservation,* 1 (Hyde Park, N.Y.: Franklin D. Roosevelt Library, 1957), pp. 181–182; Wilson Compton's testimony to the Forest Conservation Conference on Lumber and Timber Products Industries with Public Agencies (Oct. 24, 1933), pp. 24, 144–146, and (Oct. 25, 1933), pp. 232–236, copy in box 69, NFPA Records.

26. H. H. Chapman, "Second Conference on the Lumber Code," *Journal of Forestry* 32 (Mar., 1934):272–274; "Conference on Lumber and Timber Products Industries with Public Agencies on Forest Conservation," ibid., pp. 275–307; U.S. National Recovery Administration, "Amendment to Code of Fair Competition for the Lumber and Timber Products

Industry," in National Recovery Administration, *Codes of Fair Competition*, 8 (Washington, D.C.: Government Printing Office, 1934), p. 696.

27. Wilson Compton to Franklin Roosevelt, May 16, 1934, container 1, OF148, FDR Papers.

28. Steen, *U.S. Forest Service*, p. 227; J. J. Farrell to John W. Watzek, June 3, 1935, container 1, OF446, FDR Papers.

29. Minutes of the meeting of the Joint Committee of Conservation Conferences, Feb. 28, 1935, folder 32, box 2, Mason Papers.

30. Ferdinand A. Silcox, "Foresters Must Choose," address to the annual meeting of the Society of American Foresters, Jan. 29, 1935, published in the *Journal of Forestry* 33 (Mar., 1935):198–204.

31. Minutes of the Service Committee, Nov. 16, 1933, NA/RG95–8.

32. Steen, *U.S. Forest Service*, pp. 198–199; Clepper, *Professional Forestry*, pp. 149–150; William Greeley to Austin Cary, Apr. 24, 1934, box 7, Greeley Papers.

33. John B. Woods to David Mason, Aug. 9, and Mason to Woods, Aug. 14, 1935, folder 33, and Mason to Woods, Feb. 29, Mar. 16, 1936, folder 34, all in box 2, Mason Papers.

34. *West Coast Lumberman* 63 (Jan., 1936):24; F. A. Silcox to John B. Woods, Apr. 21, 1936, box 54, NFPA Records.

35. *Southern Lumberman* 156 (Apr. 15, 1938):24.

36. Ibid., 158 (Apr. 1, 1939):20.

37. John B. Woods to F. A. Silcox, Feb. 10, 1939, box 54, NFPA Records; *Southern Lumberman* 159 (Sept. 1, 1939):2.

38. Greeley, Forests and Men, p. 212; Forest Service, *Annual Report* (1938):16–17; (1939):2.

39. Forest Service, *Annual Report* (1939):3–14.

40. "The Forestry Situation in the South; Graphic Portrayal," memo from Secretary Henry Wallace to President Roosevelt, Jan. 5, 1938, and Roosevelt to Wallace, Jan. 28, 1938, container 10, OF1c, FDR Papers; Wilson Compton to Wallace, June 1, 1938, box 36, and Minutes of NLMA Conservation Committee, July 19–20, 1938, box 27, both in NFPA Records; E. T. Allen to George Jewett and C. S. Chapman, Sept. 7, 1938, box 4, WFCA Records.

41. U.S. Congress, *Hearings before the Joint Committee on Forestry. Forest Lands of the United States*, 75th Cong., 3rd sess., pt. 1, 1939, pp. 1715–1718, 1731, 1956–1959, 1966–1967.

42. U.S. Congress, *Report of the Joint Committee on Forestry. Forest Lands of the United States,* 77th Cong., 1st sess., 1941, pp. 20, 24, 26–33.

43. *American Lumberman* (Apr. 5, 1941):64; Wilson Compton, "We Have More Problems than We Have Answers; But We Are Finding the Answers," report to the Executive Committee, NLMA, May 14, 1941, p. 8, in box 145; William Greeley to E. T. Allen, June 20, 1940, and Allen to Greeley, June 16, 1940, both in box 61, all in NFPA Records.

44. Lawrence W. Hamilton, "The Federal Forest Regulation Issue," *Journal of Forest History* 9 (Apr., 1965):10; Clepper, *Professional Forestry,* pp. 155–156.

45. Dana, *Forest and Range Policy,* pp. 279–280; Steen, *U.S. Forest Service,* pp. 250–253.

46. C. Stowell Smith to Clyde Martin, Nov. 6, 1939, "Legislation—Forest Restoration Act (Individual Correspondence)," and E. W. Tinker, memorandum for Mr. Silcox, Nov. 1, 1937, "Programs—Public Welfare, 1937–1938 (Forerunner of Forest Restoration Plan)," both in NA/RG95–64.

47. E. W. Tinker to Harry C. Woodworth, Nov. 4, 1937, Tinker to Ward Shepard, June 8, and Shepard to Tinker, June 13, 1938, in "Programs—Public Welfare, 1937–1938 (Forerunner of Forest Restoration Plan)," NA/RG95–64.

48. Frank Heyward to C. F. Evans, June 21, 1938, and E. W. Tinker, memorandum for Mr. Kotok, Oct. 26, 1938, ibid.

49. G. B. MacDonald to Regional Forester, June 21, 1938, E. W. Tinker, memorandum for Mr. Kotok, Oct. 26, 1938, and Tinker to Fred R. Rauch, Dec. 28, 1938, ibid.

50. "A National Forestry Plan," Dec. 14, 1938, ibid.

51. William Greeley to E. W. Tinker, Dec. 30, 1938, ibid.

52. Clyde Martin, "Scope of Restoration Plan," *American Forests* 45 (Nov., 1939):530; C. Stowell Smith to Martin, Nov. 6, 1939, in "Legislation—Forest Restoration Act (Individual Correspondence)," NA/RG95–64; "Editorial: The Cooperative Forest Restoration Bill," *Journal of Forestry* 37 (Nov., 1939):835–836.

53. Herman H. Chapman, "Why the Cooperative Forest Restoration Bill Should Not Pass," *Journal of Forestry* 38 (Mar., 1940):231–234, and Fred Rogers Fairchild, "Comment," ibid., p. 240.

54. Henry B. Steer, "Forest Economics: With Special Reference to Stumpage, Log and Lumber Prices," *Journal of Forestry* 30 (1932):860.

1. Dana, *Forest and Range Policy,* p. 247; Franklin Roosevelt to Ovid Butler, Aug. 15, and Roosevelt to Miller Freeman, Sept. 6, 1932, in Nixon, ed., *Franklin D. Roosevelt and Conservation,* 1:119–120; W. G. Howard to Roosevelt, Dec. 28, 1932, container 1, OF149, FDR Papers.
2. Robert Y. Stuart, "The National Forests and Unemployment," Sept. 12, 1931, in "Management Plan R-2—Harney—Custer Working Circle," NA/RG95–64.
3. Ibid.
4. G. H. Collingwood, "Forestry Aids the Unemployed," *American Forests* 38 (Oct., 1932):550; R. L. Deering, "Camps for the Unemployed in the Forests of California," *Journal of Forestry* 30 (May, 1932):554–557.
5. Fred Morrell, "Some Financial Aspects of Cooperative Forest Protection," *Journal of Forestry* 30 (Mar., 1932):307–309.
6. The best scholarly study of the CCC is John Salmond's *The Civilian Conservation Corps, 1933–1942: A New Deal Case Study* (Durham, N.C.: Duke University Press, 1967).
7. Rexford Guy Tugwell, *The Democratic Roosevelt* (New York: Doubleday, 1957), p. 331.
8. Salmond, *Civilian Conservation Corps,* pp. 9–23.
9. Ibid., pp. 26–30. Congress did not establish the statutory CCC until 1937.
10. "Federal Forest Activities," *Journal of Forestry* 31 (May, 1933):506–507.
11. Clepper, *Professional Forestry,* pp. 129–130; Salmond, *Civilian Conservation Corps,* p. 121; William E. Leuchtenberg, *Franklin D. Roosevelt and the New Deal, 1932–1940* (New York: Harper and Row, 1963), p. 174.
12. E. T. Allen to Charles Lathrop Pack, Dec. 29, 1933, box 5, WFCA Records.
13. C. S. Cowan, "The CCC Movement and Its Relation to the Clarke-McNary Act," *Journal of Forestry* 34 (Apr., 1936):383–387.
14. Minutes of the Service Committee, Nov. 16, 1933, NA/RG95–8; C. F. Evans to the Editor, *Asheville Citizen,* Dec. 5, 1933, in "ECW Information, General, 1933," NA/RG95–144; A. K. Besley, memorandum for C. M. Granger, Apr. 23, 1935, and Granger, memorandum

for Besley, both in "ECW, Supervision, 'Cooperative Fire Fighting Agreement,' 1936," ibid.

15. S. B. Show to Chief, Forest Service, Dec. 21, 1936, L. C. Stockdale, to Chief, Bureau of Biological Survey, June 24, 1935, and H. C. Hilton, memorandum for Mr. Morrell, Feb. 17, 1936, in "ECW, Supervision, 'Cooperative Fire Fighting Agreement,' 1936," NA/RG95–144.

16. Minutes of the Service Committee, Nov. 16, 1933, NA/RG95–8.

17. G. H. Collingwood, "Forestry Conservation in the 75th Congress," radio talk to the National Farm and Home Hour, Jan. 27, 1937, in Public Relations, American Forestry Association, 1936–1944, California State Archives, Sacramento.

18. Salmond, *Civilian Conservation Corps,* p. 71; Guy D. McKinney to C. M. Granger, Nov. 8, 1934, in "ECW, Information, 1934," NA/RG95–144.

19. News Release, "CCC Erosion Camps to Plant 40,000,000 Trees in the Spring," Nov. 13, 1933, USDA, Office of Information, "Fire Toll in National Forests Held to Low Level This Year," Oct. 5, 1933, California Region—U.S. Forest Service, NEWS BULLETIN, n.d., in "ECW, Information, General, 1933," and John D. Guthrie, memorandum for Mr. Granger, May 8, 1935, in "ECW, Information, 1935," all in NA/RG95–144.

20. Director, Agricultural Experiment Station, Madison, to Robert Fechner, Dec. 15, 1934, in "Forest Service (Continuance of Soil Erosion Work)," E. W. Tinker to the Forester, Dec. 2, 1935, and Guy D. McKinney to Fred Morrell, Nov. 25, 1935, all in "ECW Information, 1935," all in ibid.

21. Fred Morrell to Regional Foresters, Jan. 10, 1936, in "ECW Information, January to June, 1936," ibid.

22. G. M. Conzet to A. G. Hamel, Sept. 19, 1933, and Conzet to Richard Bailey, Apr. 30, 1934, in Forestry Board Correspondence.

23. E. V. Willard, commissioner of conservation, to E. W. Tinker, June 30, 1934, A. G. Hamel to G. M. Conzet, Aug. 17, 1936, Lyle Watts to Forest Officers, Apr. 18, 1933, and CCC Conservation Work, June, 1933, to Sept. 30, 1937, all in ibid.

24. Bachman, *History of Forestry in Minnesota,* pp. 43–46.

25. Clar, *California Government and Forestry,* 2:221–231.

26. Ibid., pp. 233, 239–240.

27. Ibid., p. 243.
28. Widner, *Forests and Forestry,* p. 542; Clar, *California Government and Forestry,* 2:266.
29. Morrell, "Some Financial Aspects of Cooperative Forest Protection," 301–309; Pikl, *History of Georgia Forestry,* p. 28.
30. Pikl, *History of Georgia Forestry,* p. 27; B. M. Lufburrow, "Forest Protection Has Proven Profitable," *Proceedings of the Georgia Forestry Commercial Congress* (Savannah: Georgia Forestry Association, 1930), p. 28; A. B. Hastings to B. M. Lufburrow, May 10, July 22, 1929, and C. F. Evans, memorandum, Mar. 10, 1933, all in "C-M Law—Inspection—Southeastern States District (1928–1933)," NA/RG95–97.
31. Pikl, *History of Georgia Forestry,* p. 28; "Forestry as a Unit of State Government," p. 17, n.d., copy in files of the Georgia Forestry Commission, Macon.
32. *Report of the Commission, Department of Forestry and Geological Development to the Governor and General Assembly of the State of Georgia* (1933–1934):5; (1935–1936):5–6, in Georgia State Archives, Macon.
33. "What Conservation Workers Are Doing," *Forestry–Geological Review* 3 (July, 1933):1; Georgia Department of Natural Resources, *Biennial Report* (1937–1938):27–29.
34. "Forestry as a Unit of State Government," p. 17; Pikl, *History of Georgia Forestry,* p. 33; Georgia Department of Natural Resources, *Biennial Report* (1937–1938):31.
35. Georgia Division of Forestry and the U.S. Forest Service, *Forest Resources of Georgia* (1939):32, in Subject File, Forest History Society; B. F. Grant and A. E. Patterson, *Forest Facts for Georgia,* Forestry Bulletin no. 10 (1946), p. 18, copy in box 38, AFA Records.
36. Widner, *Forests and Forestry,* pp. 420–421, 474–475.
37. Oregon, *Report of the State Forester of Oregon* (1935):32–33, (1936):14.
38. Ibid. (1938):48, (1942):22.
39. Fred Morrell to Regional Forester, Apr. 9, 1935, G. D. Cook to Regional Forester, June 18, 1936, and J. W. Ferguson to Charles McNary, Feb. 14, 1938, Acc. No. 58816, RG95, Federal Records Center, Seattle.
40. Washington, *Eighth Biennial Report of the Division of Forestry* (1936): 24–25, 32–33.
41. C. J. Buck to Forest Supervisor, Oct. 30, 1937, Acc. No. 66751, RG95, Federal Records Center, Seattle.
42. Washington, *Eleventh Biennial Report of the Division of Forestry* (1942):21.

43. C. M. Granger to Robert Fechner, Jan. 18, 1935, "Forest Service (Charts Comparing Work)," NA/RG95–144; Salmond, *Civilian Conservation Corps,* pp. 122–123; Benedict, *History of White Pine Blister Rust Control,* pp. 34–37.

44. Salmond, *Civilian Conservation Corps,* p. 123.

45. E. W. Tinker to T. S. Goodyear, May 20, 1939, in "CCC Cooperation, Special R-1 to NEFE, 1939," NA/RG95–144.

46. Fred Morrell, memorandum for Mr. Silcox, Apr. 9, and Morrell to Regional Forester, Apr. 20, 1938, in "CCC Cooperation, Regions 1 to 10, 1938," ibid.

47. Fred Morrell, memorandum for E. W. Tinker, Mar. 29, May 18, 1939, in "CCC Cooperation, Special, R-1 to NEFE, 1939," ibid.

48. Salmond, *Civilian Conservation Corps,* pp. 37–38, 42, 84; Fred Morrell to C. H. Taylor, Sept. 14, 1935, in "Forest Service (Correspondence Relative to Questions of Employment, Complaints, etc., requesting reports)," NA/RG95–144.

49. Wilson Compton to G. H. Collingwood, Mar. 28, and William Greeley to Fred Morrell, Mar. 31, 1942, both in box 22, NFPA Records; Earl Morrell, memorandum for E. W. Tinker, Mar. 29, 1939, in "CCC Cooperation, Special, R-1 to NEFE, 1939," NA/RG95–144; Steen, *U.S. Forest Service,* p. 216.

50. *Report of the U.S. Forest Service Programs Resulting from the New England Hurricane of September 21, 1938* (Boston: Northeastern Timber Salvage Administration, 1943), pp. 3, 5–6; Dana, *Forest and Range Policy,* pp. 251–252.

51. *Report of the U.S. Forest Service Programs,* pp. 18–21; Earl S. Peirce, "Salvage Programs Following the 1938 Hurricane," p. iv, 1968, Regional Oral History Office, Bancroft Library, University of California, Berkeley.

52. *Report of the U.S. Forest Service Programs,* pp. 18–21; Peirce, "Salvage Programs Following the 1938 Hurricane," p. 8.

53. Forest Service, *Annual Report* (1939):14; Dana, *Forest and Range Policy,* p. 252; Peirce, "Salvage Programs Following the 1938 Hurricane," pp. 8–9.

54. News Release, "Program for Salvage of Storm Damaged Timber in New England Announced," Nov. 1, 1938, and Press Release, "Town Salvage Committees Announced by Federal Forester," Nov. 22, 1938, both in NA/RG95–19.

55. Restoring New England Forests, Jan. 18, 1939, Crosby A. Hoar, "Should Federal or State Governments Plan Conservation and Flood Control in New England," broadcast address, Feb. 14, 1939, and George R. Phillips to Saidie O. Dunbar, Feb. 17, 1939, all in "NET-SA, Information—Addresses, 1938–1939," ibid.

56. E. W. Tinker, memorandum for Mr. Silcox, Mar. 13, 1939, in "(NEFE-NETSA) General Inspection, 1938–1940," and Frank R. Tuthill, memorandum for State Project Director, Apr. 21, 1939, in "(NEFE) (NETSA) Soil Conservation Service, Cooperation," all in ibid.

57. E. W. Tinker to William H. Vanderbilt, Jan. 16, 1939, in "(NETSA) Information, Addresses, 1938–1939," ibid.

58. Wilson Compton to Federated Associations, July 8, 1939, box 55, NFPA Records.

59. "Forest Service and Lumbermen Confer on New England Salvage," *American Lumberman* (Sept. 23, 1939):43; Wilson Compton to James McNary, Sept. 13, 1939, and J. F. Campbell to Compton, July 19, 1940, both in box 55, NFPA Records.

60. *Report of the U.S. Forest Service Programs,* p. 174; Dana, *Forest and Range Policy,* p. 252.

61. *Report of the U.S. Forest Service Programs,* p. 59; Peirce, "Salvage Programs Following the 1938 Hurricane," p. 47; Harold C. Hebb to G. H. Collingwood, Aug. 13, 1943, box 55, NFPA Records.

62. Dana, *Forest and Range Policy,* p. 251.

63. Droze, *Trees, Prairies, and People,* pp. 219–220.

64. Ed Munns, memorandum for the Forester, Oct. 13, 1933, "Supervision, PSFP," Carlos Bates to the Forester, Aug. 1, 1934, "Shelterbelt, Organization, 1934–1936," both in NA/RG95–99; Droze, *Trees, Prairies, and People,* p. 64.

65. Droze, *Trees, Prairies, and People,* pp. 78–103.

66. Ibid., pp. 104–121.

67. Ibid., pp. 225–226; Dana, *Forest and Range Policy,* p. 251.

Chapter Ten

1. Forest Service, *Annual Report* (1940):1–2, 21.

2. Steen, *U.S. Forest Service,* p. 246.

3. Richard Polenberg, *War and Society: The United States, 1941–1945* (New York: Lippincott, 1972), pp. 5–13.

4. G. H. Collingwood to Earle Clapp, Mar. 19, and Clapp to Collingwood, Feb. 11, 1942, both in box 54, NFPA Records.

5. Earle Clapp to G. H. Collingwood, Feb. 11, 1942, ibid.

6. Clyde Martin to G. H. Collingwood, Jan. 29, Stuart Moir to Collingwood, Jan. 20, and Collingwood to Moir, Feb. 16, 1942, all in ibid.

7. William Greeley, "The War Job for Foresters," *American Forests* 48 (Apr., 1942):175; Greeley, *Forests and Men,* p. 216.

8. Earle Clapp to Claude Wickard, Dec. 27, 1941, in "National Defense," NA/RG95–4.

9. General Plan for a Forest Products Service (F.P.S.), July 10, 1942, box 27, NFPA Records.

10. Fickle, *The New South and the "New Competition,"* pp. 263–264.

11. M. L. Fleishel to the President, Dec. 10, 1942, and Government Control of Local Forest Enterprise, circa late 1942, both in box 27, NFPA Records.

12. Government Control of Local Forest Enterprise, and objections to Plan for a Forest Products Program of U.S. Forest Service, circa Feb., 1943, ibid.

13. Franklin D. Roosevelt to Mr. Nelson, Feb. 26, 1943, container 1, OF446, FDR Papers; text of White House statement issued to Associated Press, Feb. 26, Southern Pine War Committee to Southern Pine Manufacturers, Feb. 27, and Wilson Compton to Lumber and Timber Products War Committee, Feb. 27, 1943, all in box 27, NFPA Records; Fickle, *The New South and the "New Competition,"* p. 354.

14. J. Phillip Boyd to Lyle Watts, Jan. 28, 1943, "Cooperation—General, SCS-REA-FCA—1935–46," NA/RG95–64.

15. Ibid.

16. Ibid.

17. General Statement, Timber Production War Project, Apr. 15, 1943, ibid.

18. Summarized statement, Timber Production War Project, July 22, 1943, ibid. The state and private chief is quoted in Howard Hopkins, "Accomplishments of the Timber Production War Project," *Journal of Forestry* 44 (May, 1946):330.

19. National Lumber Manufacturers Association to Lumber and Timber Products War Committee, Aug. 9, 1943, box 55, NFPA Records; Howard Hopkins, "The Timber Production War Project," *Journal of Forestry* 42 (1944):790–791.

20. Hopkins, "Timber Production War Project," pp. 792–794.
21. Ibid., p. 795; Howard Hopkins to J. Philip Boyd, Dec. 15, 1943, in "Cooperation, Timber War Project (TPWP)—1943," NA/RG95–64.
22. W. S. Swingler, "The Project in the Northeast," *Journal of Forestry* 42 (1944):342; Corydon Wagner to Wilson Compton, Sept. 7, 1943, box 55, NFPA Records.
23. Wilson Compton to Corydon Wagner, Sept. 14, G. H. Collingwood to R. B. Parmenter, Oct. 13, and R. E. Broderick to Collingwood, Nov. 15, 1943, all in box 55, NFPA Records.
24. Harold C. Hebb to G. H. Collingwood, Feb. 15, and H. S. Crosby to Wellington R. Burt, Mar. 8, 1944, both in ibid.
25. Wellington R. Burt to G. H. Collingwood, Mar. 18, 1944, ibid.
26. R. M. Evans to Wilson Compton, June 20, 1944, ibid.
27. Hopkins, "Accomplishments of the Timber Production War Project," p. 330.
28. NLMA Position on HR 5973 and HR 5605, Apr. 23, 1946, box 55, NFPA Records.
29. Forest Service, *Annual Report* (1942):13.
30. Ibid. (1942):13, (1943):18; Pyne, *Fire in America,* pp. 370–371.
31. Forest Service, *Annual Report* (1942):18–19, (1944):9; Pyne, *Fire in America,* 371.
32. Report Covering Accomplishments under $2,300,000 War Forest Fire Cooperation Program on State and Private Forests, Jan. 20, 1944, in "Supervision, Reports—WFFC—1944," NA/RG95–4; Forest Service, *Annual Report* (1942):13.
33. Report Covering Accomplishments, Jan. 20, 1944, in "Supervision, Reports—WFFC—1944," NA/RG95–4.
34. Ibid.; Forest Service Report Covering Accomplishments under the $2,300,000 War Forest Fire Cooperation Program for the Protection of State and Private Critical Forest Areas during the F.Y. 1944, Oct. 4, 1944, and Brief Report of WFFC—Fiscal year ending 1944—Minnesota, July 31, 1944, both in ibid.
35. Forest Service Report, F.Y. 1944, and Report of War Forest Fire Cooperative Work in States within Region 8 during Fiscal year of 1944, July 28, 1944, both in ibid.
36. The War Forest Fire Program, State of Oregon, July 1 to Dec. 31, 1943, State of Washington, Report on WFFC Activities from July 1,

1943, to Dec. 31, 1943, and the War Forest Fire Cooperation Program in Region 6, Fiscal Year, 1944, Aug. 12, 1944, all in ibid.

37. Ibid.

38. Ibid.; H. J. Eberly, Report Governing $1,000,000 War Forest Fire Cooperation Program on State and Private Forests during Fiscal Year 1945, Oct. 19, 1945, in ibid.

39. *Thirty-Second Annual Report of the State Forester of Oregon* (1944):31; "Editorial," *American Forests* 49 (Oct., 1943):489; Wayne Coy to Franklin Roosevelt, May 16, 1942, in Nixon, ed., *Franklin D. Roosevelt and Conservation,* 2:551.

40. Washington, Division of Forestry, *Eleventh Biennial Report* (1942):30–32.

41. *Thirty-First Annual Report of the State Forester of Oregon* (1942):13–15.

42. H. J. Andrews to Lt. Col. Neil R. MacIntyre, Nov. 16, 1944, and Andrews to Commanding Officer, Northern Security District, Dec. 22, 1944, both in Acc. No. 66742, RG95, Federal Records Center, Seattle; Washington, Division of Forestry, *Twelfth Biennial Report* (1944):31.

43. H. J. Andrews to Col. Calley, Dec. 22, 1944, Acc. No. 66742, RG95, Federal Records Center, Seattle.

44. Clar, *California Government and Forestry,* 2:306–307.

45. Pikl, *History of Georgia Forestry,* pp. 39–40.

46. Widner, *Forests and Forestry,* pp. 421–423, 438–439, 445.

47. Ibid., pp. 466–467, 475, 488–489.

48. Fickle, *The New South and the "New Competition,"* pp. 354–361.

49. Steen, *U.S. Forest Service,* pp. 248–249; Forest Service, *Annual Report* (1942):11.

50. Forest Service, *Annual Report* (1944):25–26, (1945):32.

51. Ibid. (1942):14–15, (1943):22.

52. Ibid. (1943):22–23, (1944):17–20.

53. Ibid. (1943):22; Steen, *U.S. Forest Service,* pp. 253–254.

54. Wilson Compton, "Forest Conservation: A Task in Engineering and in Public and Private Cooperation," *Proceedings of the American Philosophical Society* 89 (1945):423–427.

Chapter Eleven

1. Forest Service, *Annual Report* (1943):6–7.

2. Ibid., 8, (1944):4, (1945):13–14.

3. Ibid. (1945):14–15; W. N. Sparhawk, "Forestry and Farm Relief," *United States Banker* (Mar., 1929):7–8, 30, copy in FHS clipping file.
4. "Report of the Forest Resource Appraisal," box 2, Greeley Papers.
5. Ellery Foster, "Lumber Snafu," *Journal of Forestry* (June, 1946):399–400.
6. NLMA Position on HR 5973 and HR 5605, Apr. 23, 1946, in box 55, NFPA Records.
7. Forest Service, *Annual Report* (1947):21–22.
8. R. E. McArdle, "Technical Assistance for Private Owners," *Journal of Forestry* 45 (Jan., 1947):36.
9. Ibid., p. 36.
10. Ibid., pp. 38–39.
11. "Editorial: Helping Owners of Small Forest Properties," *Journal of Forestry* 45 (Jan., 1947):1–2; J. A. Fitzwater, "The Present Situation in Cooperative Forest Management and the Job Ahead," paper delivered to the twenty-fourth meeting of the Association of State Foresters, Oct. 3, 1946, in box 216, NASF Records.
12. R. E. Marsh to Mr. Watts and Staff, Apr. 14, 1947, in "Supervision—Programs, Pattern for Agriculture, General, 1947," NA/RG95–99.
13. R. E. McArdle, "Progress in Federal and State Forestry Relationships during the Past Year," address to the twenty-fifth annual meeting of the Association of State Foresters, July 17, 1947, in box 216, NASF Records.
14. "Colgan Cracks Down on Forest Service," *Southern Hardwood Bulletin,* no. 10, May 10, 1947, copy in box 54, NFPA Records.
15. Charles A. Gillett, "Aids to Farm Forestry," pp. 221–222, in report from Proceedings of the Society of American Foresters' Meeting, 1947, in "General—P—Programs, Farm Forestry," NA/RG95–99; Forest Service, *Annual Report* (1948):36; R. E. Marsh, memorandum for the record, Oct. 2, 1947, in "Pattern for Agriculture, 1947," NA/RG95–99; Kaylor, "Farm Forestry," pp. 266–267.
16. Forest Service, *Annual Report* (1947):22, (1948):35–36, (1949):37.
17. Ibid. (1950):14–15.
18. Kaylor, "Farm Forestry," pp. 263–265.
19. Ibid.
20. Charles L. Tebbe to J. A. Fitzwater, Nov. 18, 1943, Dan D. Robinson, "Production of Farm Products for War," radio talk, Oct. 30, 1943, and

H. J. Andrews to Washington Forest Supervisors and Rangers, Jan. 31, 1944, all in "Regions 1 to 6, P—Programs, Farm Forestry, Marketing Assistance," NA/RG95–99.

21. J. A. Donery, "Forest Resources in Minnesota," *American Forests* (Jan., 1948):26; interview with Frank Usenik, Aug. 28, 1981.

22. Manual for Farm Foresters Assigned to the Cooperative Farm Woodland Marketing Project, Atlanta, Nov., 1942, in "P—Programs—Farm Forestry—Marketing Assistance—Region 8, 1942," NA/RG95–99.

23. J. A. Fitzwater to C. F. Evans, May 31, 1944, and Evans to Fitzwater, June 8, 1944, in "Region 8, P—Programs, Farm Forestry, Marketing Assistance, 1/1/44 through 12/31/44," ibid.

24. R. E. Marsh to Mr. Watts and Mr. McArdle, Nov. 20, 1944, ibid.

25. Ibid.; Pikl, *History of Georgia Forestry*, p. 33.

26. H. J. Malsberger, "How to Attain Our Objective," *Journal of Forestry* 42 (Aug., 1944):564–567.

27. Kaylor, "Farm Forestry," pp. 265–266; Forest Service, *Annual Report* (1946):16.

28. Forest Service, *Annual Report* (1946): 16–17.

29. Kaylor, "Farm Forestry," pp. 266–267; "Norris-Doxey Project Foresters Aid 14,200 Small Forest Owners in States," U.S. Forest Service News Release, Nov. 8, 1946, in "General—P—Programs, Farm Forestry, 1/1/48–12/31/48," NA/RG95–99.

30. J. A. Fitzwater to Regional Forester, Missoula, Mont., Nov. 15, 1946, and Fitzwater to Regional Forester, Denver, Nov. 14, 1946, both in "Supervision, 1946, Farm Forestry, R1 and R9," ibid.

31. A. G. Hamel to State Foresters and Farm Foresters, Feb. 13, 1947, in "Region 9—P—Programs, Farm Forestry—1947," ibid.

32. R. E. McArdle, memorandum for Mr. Spillers, Sept. 4, 1947, and P. D. Hanson to Chief, Forest Service, July 2, 1947, both in "Regions 1 to 6—P—Programs, Farm Forestry—1947," ibid.

33. R. E. McArdle to Regional Forester, Portland, Jan. 30, 1947, H. J. Andrews to Chief, Forest Service, Feb. 14, 1947, Thomas H. Burgess to Washington Office, Dec. 18, 1947, and A. R. Spillers to Burgess, Dec. 23, 1947, all in ibid.

34. Thomas Burgess to Division of Cooperative Forest Management, Washington Office, Dec. 7, 1948, in "Regions 1 to 6, P—Programs, Farm Forestry, 1948," ibid.

35. Thomas Burgess to the Chief, Forest Service, Apr. 15, Burgess to C. W. Smith, Mar. 3, and M. M. Bryan to the Record, Nov. 16, 1948, all in ibid.

36. Oregon, *Biennial Report of the State Forester* (1946):32–35.

37. Ibid. (1954):50–52.

38. Washington, Department of Conservation and Development, *Fifteenth Biennial Report* (1950):70–71.

39. Ibid., *Sixteenth Biennial Report* (1952):40, 63–64.

40. Donery, "Forest Resources in Minnesota," pp. 26–28; Bachman, *History of Forestry in Minnesota,* p. 54.

41. Bachman, *History of Forestry in Minnesota,* pp. 54–55, 61, 67.

42. Clepper, *Professional Forestry,* pp. 252–254; Walter H. Meyer, "Impressions of Industrial Forestry in the Southeastern United States," *Journal of Forestry* 58 (Mar., 1960):179–187.

43. "Farm Forestry in the Sixth District," *Monthly Review: Federal Reserve Bank of Atlanta* 32 (May 31, 1947):57–61.

44. Forest Service, *Annual Report* (1946):15; C. F. Evans to W. B. Greeley, Nov. 24, 1947, box 11, Greeley Papers.

45. D. W. Watkins to C. F. Evans, May 21, and Charles H. Flory to R. E. McArdle, July 5, 1945, both in "Region 8 — Programs, Farm Forestry, 1945," and Glen Durrell to J. Herbert Stone, Oct. 10, Stone to Chief, Forest Service, Oct. 23, and J. A. Fitzwater to Stone, Nov. 1, 1946, all in "Region 8 — Programs — Farm Forestry, 1946," NA/RG95–99.

46. Pikl, *History of Georgia Forestry,* pp. 33, 45.

47. Ibid., p. 42.

48. C. F. Evans to W. B. Greeley, Nov. 24, 1947, in box 11, Greeley Papers; Pikl, *History of Georgia Forestry,* pp. 43–44.

49. Pikl, *History of Georgia Forestry,* p. 44.

50. "Forestry as a Unit of State Government," n.d., pp. 22–23, in files of the Georgia Forestry Commission, Macon.

51. Ibid., pp. 24–25; L. A. Hargraves, "The Georgia Forestry Commission—Objectives, Organization, Policies, and Procedures" (Ph.D. diss., University of Michigan, 1953), pp. 163–164.

52. A. E. Patterson, "A Brief Examination of the Forest Resources of Georgia," paper read to the Association of American Geographers, Southeast Division, Athens, Dec. 2, 1949, in Subject Files, Forest History Society; *Georgia Forest Facts* (Washington, D.C.: American Forest Products Industries, 1952), p. 4, in ibid.

310

53. Georgia Forestry Commission, *Forward in Forestry: Biennial Report of Progress* (1949–1950):23, 25–27.

54. Georgia Forestry Commission, *Forestry for a Greater Georgia: Biennial Report of Progress* (1951–1952):20, and its *Trees for Georgia: Biennial Report of Progress* (1953–1954):30; Pikl, *History of Georgia Forestry*, p. 50.

Chapter Twelve

1. Zimmerman, "History of State and Private Forestry," pp. 85–86; USDA, Agriculture Information Bulletin, No. 83 (1952), *Highlights in the History of Forest Conservation*, p. 17.

2. Zimmerman, "History of State and Private Forestry," pp. 88–89; *Highlights in the History of Forest Conservation*, p. 17.

3. Zimmerman, "History of State and Private Forestry," pp. 89–90.

4. Forest Service, *Annual Report* (1951):54–55, (1952):38, (1955):8, (1956):10.

5. Ibid. (1952):38; Zimmerman, "History of State and Private Forestry," pp. 92–93.

6. Minutes of meeting of Executive Committee, Association of State Foresters, Washington, D.C., May 31–June 1, 1951, in box 216, NASF Records.

7. George Fuller to members, Conservation Committee, NLMA, Feb. 20, 1951, Ernest L. Kolbe to Fuller, Mar. 1, 1951, and Clyde S. Martin to Fuller, Feb. 26, 1951, all in box 10, NFPA Records.

8. Clepper, *Professional Forestry*, pp. 100–101.

9. "A Proposed Program for American Forestry," *American Forests* 59 (Aug., 1953):25, 32–33.

10. Steen, *U.S. Forest Service*, pp. 286–289; Richard McArdle to Leo V. Bodine, Oct. 14, 1955, in box 25, NFPA Records; U.S. Forest Service, Region 6, "Questions and Answers on the Small Forest Ownership Program," Aug. 21, 1958, manuscript in box 3, Stuart Moir Papers, Oregon Historical Society, Portland.

11. "Questions and Answers on the Small Forest Ownership Program"; Thomas Burgess to Stuart Moir, Sept. 5, 1958, both in Moir Papers.

12. "Questions and Answers on the Small Forest Ownership Program," Moir Papers; Zimmerman, "History of State and Private Forestry," p. 99; "Recommendations Regarding Small Forest Ownerships," approved by Forest Industries Council, Jan. 30, 1961, in U.S. Forest

Service file, Keep Oregon Green Association Collection, Oregon Historical Society, Portland.

13. Leonard I. Barrett, "Special Problems of the Small Forest Owners in the United States," paper presented to the Fifth World Forestry Congress, Aug. 29–Sept. 10, 1960, in box 3, Moir Papers.

14. Ibid.

15. Ibid.

16. Richard Colgan, Testimony before the Senate Committee on Agriculture and Forestry, n.d., copy in box 96, NFPA Records; "Where AFA Stands: Besley Scores Proposed Budget Cuts for Cooperative Forestry Activities," *American Forests* 60 (Mar., 1954):8.

17. NLMA to Federated Associations, Jan. 14, 1953, and Ernest L. Kolbe to A. Z. Nelson, May 9, 1955, both in box 8, NFPA Records; *Denver Post,* Feb. 27, 1957.

18. A. Z. Nelson to Ernest L. Kolbe, Mar. 18, and Kolbe to U. R. Armstrong, Apr. 2, 1957, both in box 8, NFPA Records.

19. Mortimer B. Doyle to Bernard L. Orell, Apr. 15, 1958, box 28, and Ralph D. Hodges, Jr., to Senator Carl Hayden, May 27, 1959, box 8, both in ibid.

20. Emanuel Fritz, "Forest Service and Cooperative Forestry," *American Forests* 64 (June, 1958):4, 49–50; Fritz to Richard Colgan, Feb. 13, 1957, box 8, NFPA Records.

21. Charles A. Gillett to A. Z. Nelson, Dec. 15, 1955, and Leo V. Bodine to NLMA Board of Directors, Jan. 20, 1956, both in box 10, NFPA Records.

22. Leo V. Bodine to Ezra Taft Benson, Jan. 18, 1956, ibid.

23. Stuart Moir to Leo V. Bodine, Mar. 1, Bodine to Federated Associations, Mar. 7, 1956, and NLMA News Release, n.d., all in ibid.

24. Harry R. Woodward to A. Z. Nelson, Mar. 17, and Nelson to Woodward, Apr. 20, 1956, both in ibid.

25. Ralph D. Hodges to Senator Carl Hayden, May 27, 1959, box 8, ibid.

26. E. L. Peterson to Leo V. Bodine, July 18, and Richard E. McArdle to W. S. Bromley, Aug. 17, 1956, both in ibid.

27. Stuart Moir to WFCA Trustees, Sept. 19, F. H. Raymond to Ernest Kolbe, Sept. 26, and V. W. Cothren to Otto Lindh, Dec. 5, 1956, all in ibid.

28. L. T. Webster to Ernest Kolbe, Oct. 1, 1956, in ibid.; Minnesota Divi-

sion of Forestry, Department of Conservation, *Biennial Report* (1959): 1–2; Frank Usenik to the author, Sept. 5, 1981.

29. E. L. Lawson to Perry Merrill, June 6, 1956, Lawson to Senator Hubert Humphrey, Apr. 5, 1957, Lawson to Paul W. Kunkel, Mar. 21, 1962, and Emil Kukachka, memorandum on Nursery Operations, July 10, 1963, all in Conservation, Forestry Division, Minnesota State Archives, St. Paul.

30. Roland Rotty, "Forest Planting in the United States: 1951 and Some Comparisons with Past Years," unpublished data in "Source Data for Summary of Forest Planting in the United States," NA/RG95–97.

31. Frank Usenik to the author, Sept. 5, 1981.

32. Forest Service, *Annual Report* (1958): 1, 3.

33. Ibid. (1959):20; Georgia Forestry Commission, *Annual Report* (1960): n.p.; Oregon, *Biennial Report of the State Forester* (1962):18.

34. Forest Service, *Annual Report* (1961):23, and (1962):7–8.

35. Ibid. (1963):27, (1964):2, (1965):33, (1967):23, (1968):33; E. H. Marshall to L. T. Webster, Sept. 16, 1964, in Title 4 file, State and Private Forestry Office, U.S. Forest Service, Region 6, Portland, Oreg.

36. Forest Service, *Annual Report* (1962): 1; John A. Baker, "Resources and the Rebirth of Rural America," address to the Fifth American Forest Congress, Oct. 29, 1963, in Fifth American Forest Congress folder, Keep Oregon Green Association Collection.

37. Forest Service, *Annual Report* (1964): 15; comments on Major General Forestry Assistance Activities, Apr. 23, 1964, memorandum, in box 3, Acc. No. 70A699, RG95, Federal Records Center, Atlanta.

38. Fay Bennett to J. K. Vessey, Oct. 28, 1963, summary of conference on Farmer Cooperatives and Job Training, Sept. 22–27, 1936, and Alabama Rural Areas Development Newsletter, Feb., 1964, all in box 3, Acc. No. 70A699, RG95, Federal Records Center, Atlanta.

39. J. F. Renshaw to R. A. Jiles, Jr., Apr. 16, Nathan Byrd to Renshaw, Apr. 24, D. A. Craig to Ray Shirley, Jan. 23, Shirley to Craig, Feb. 4, Craig to Shirley, Apr. 6, and Shirley to Craig, Apr. 13, 1964, all in box 5, ibid.

40. Paul Y. Vincent to S. L. Vanlandingham, Dec. 6, 1963, Feb. 4, 1964, and Ellery Foster to Gordon E. Reckford, Jan. 14, 1964, all in ibid.

41. Paul Vincent to Regional Forester, Aug. 17, 1962, in ibid.

42. Forest Service, *Annual Report* (1968):32.

43. Richard L. Knox to Dennis Roth, July 1, 1983, in History Section, U.S. Forest Service, Washington, D.C. (hereafter History Section); USDA, *Land Use Planning Assistance Available through the United States Department of Agriculture* (Washington, D.C.: Government Printing Office, 1974), p. 28.

44. Oregon, *Biennial Report of the State Forester* (1962):17, 30–31.

45. Ibid. (1964):17; Cooperative Forest Management: Annual Narrative Report for 1964, Aug. 13, 1964, copy in Title 4 file, State and Private Forestry Office, U.S. Forest Service, Region 6.

46. Cooperative Forest Management: Annual Narrative Report, F.Y. 1963, Aug. 20, 1963, Aug. 13, 1964, Aug. 3, 1965, and Cooperative Forest Management: Interim Narrative Report, Feb. 3, 1969, all in ibid.

47. E. H. Marshall to Chief, Forest Service, Aug. 24, 1972, in Acc. No. 148808, RG95, Federal Records Center, Seattle.

48. Frank Usenik, interview with the author, Aug. 28, 1981.

49. Bachman, *History of Forestry in Minnesota,* p. 89; Paul J. St. Amant to Edward L. Lawson, June 7, and L. J. Ashbaugh to St. Amant, June 7, 1962, and Resume of Federal Aid Programs of the Division of Forestry, July 17, 1963, memorandum, in Department of Conservation, Forestry Division, Minnesota State Archives.

50. Clarence Prout to R. O. Lee, Aug. 12, 1964, in Department of Conservation, Forestry Division, Minnesota State Archives; Minnesota Department of Natural Resources, *Biennial Report* (1972):50.

51. The TRR figures are cited in State and Private Forestry in Region 8, Aug., 1957, memorandum in State and Private Forestry Office, U.S. Forest Service, Region 8, Atlanta.

52. George W. Abel, "The Complexities of Modern Forest Management in the South," *Proceedings of the Fourth Insect and Disease Work Conference* (1967), copy in the Minnesota State Archives.

53. D. A. Craig to J. K. Vessey, Sept. 14, 1963, in box 1, Acc. No. 73A514, RG95, Federal Records Center, Atlanta; "History of the Georgia Forestry Commission," p. 13, unpublished draft filed in Georgia Forestry Commission, Macon.

54. Georgia Forestry Commission, *Biennial Report of Progress* (1954):31, and (1960):n.p.

55. Ibid. (1964):n.p.

56. Ibid. (1963):n.p., (1964):n.p.

57. Ibid. (1967):n.p., (1970):n.p., (1972):12, (1979):13.

58. Ibid. (1971):12, (1972):9, (1979):11, 14.

59. "Report of the Forest Resource Appraisal," box 2, Greeley Papers.

Chapter Thirteen

1. Pyne, *Fire in America,* pp. 407–410.

2. Ibid., p. 480.

3. Forest Service, *Annual Report* (1945):29, (1946):14–15, (1948):38– 39.

4. Austin H. Wilkins, "The Story of the Maine Forest Fire Disaster," *Journal of Forestry* 46 (1948):568–573; Forest Service, *Annual Report* (1950):9; Dana, *Forest and Range Policy,* pp. 309–310; Zimmerman, "History of State and Private Forestry," pp. 87–88; Pyne, *Fire in America,* p. 357.

5. Arthur S. Hopkins, "Interstate Forest Fire Control," address to the National Association of State Foresters, Oct. 5–7, 1954, copy in box 216, NASF Records.

6. Bachman, *History of Forestry in Minnesota,* pp. 67–68.

7. Forest Service, *Annual Report* (1956):12–13; "Southern Fire Conference," *American Forests* 62 (Mar., 1956):18–19, 57–58; First Annual Meeting: Southeastern States Forest Fire Compact Commission, Oct. 25, 1955, in box 2, Acc. No. 66A1274, RG95, Federal Records Center, Atlanta.

8. Forest Service, *Annual Report* (1957):3; Sixth Annual Meeting, Southeastern States Forest Fire Compact Commission, Dec. 1, 1960, in box 2, Acc. No. 65A20, RG95, Federal Records Center, Atlanta.

9. Area and Cost Revision, 1957, State of Georgia, in box 1, Acc. No. 66A1274, RG95, Federal Records Center, Atlanta.

10. Zimmerman, "History of State and Private Forestry," p. 103; Pyne, *Fire in America,* pp. 176–177.

11. Forest Service, *Annual Report* (1955):10, (1956):13, (1959):22.

12. Ibid. (1955):10, (1958):5.

13. Ibid. (1958):5, (1956):13.

14. Highlights of the 1954–1955 CFFP campaign, 32nd Annual Meeting of the National Association of State Foresters, Oct. 5–7, 1954, in box 216, NASF Records.

15. Pyne, *Fire in America,* p. 178; Forest Service, *Annual Report* (1959):22, (1961):24; Walter Ahern, "The Southern CFFP Program," paper pre-

sented to the 21st Annual Southern States Forest Fire Control Conference, May 24–27, 1960, in box 1, Acc. No. 66A1274, RG95, Federal Records Center, Atlanta.

16. Forest Service, *Annual Report* (1963):28, (1967):21; John Beale, "Cooperative Forest Fire Prevention," report to the 38th Annual Meeting of the National Association of State Foresters, Sept. 13–15, 1960, in box 216, and E. M. Bacon, "Remarks on State and Private Forestry," report to the 47th Annual Meeting of the National Association of State Foresters, n.d., in box 2, both in NASF Records.

17. Forest Service, *Annual Report* (1962):5, (1963):28.

18. DeWitt Nelson, *Management of Natural Resources in California, 1925–1966,* an interview with Amelia R. Fry (Santa Cruz, Calif.: Forest History Society, 1976), p. 173; James K. Mace, "Rural Fire Protection in California," *Journal of Forestry* (Apr., 1950):264.

19. County-State Cooperation in Fire Control, memorandum prepared for joint meeting of county and state forestry personnel, Aug. 16, 1951, in Forestry, July–December, 1951, California State Archives, Sacramento.

20. Report of Inspection and Audit of Forest Service and Outside Counties, Jan. 17–25, 1952, in ibid.

21. Policy Covering Cooperative Protection Agreements between the U.S. Forest Service, Other Federal Agencies, States, Counties, Timber Protective Associations and Other Land Owners, circa, 1952, memorandum in Forestry, California State Archives.

22. Assistant Regional Forester to Supervisors, Oct. 1, 1956, in box 16, Acc. No. 59-A-710, RG95, Federal Records Center, San Bruno, Calif.

23. Pyne, *Fire in America,* pp. 404–409.

24. Ibid., p. 421; Nelson, *Management of Natural Resources in California,* p. 125.

25. Pyne, *Fire in America,* pp. 320–321.

26. Kenneth B. Pomeroy, "Roadblock or Detour?" *American Forests* 77 (July, 1971):5; DeWitt Nelson, "Why CM-2 Needs a Boost," ibid., 75 (June, 1969):52.

27. Pyne, *Fire in America,* pp. 293, 357, 455, 464; Zimmerman, "History of State and Private Forestry," pp. 106–107; USDA, Forest Service, *How the Rural Community Fire Protection Program Can Help You,* publication No. FS-312 (Washington, D.C.: Government Printing Office, 1978), p. 3.

28. Briefing Paper: Rural Fire Prevention and Control, Aug. 7, 1981, p. 1, Office of Cooperative Fire Protection, U.S. Forest Service, copy in possession of the author.

29. James Sorenson, *Seventeen Years of Progress through International Cooperation* (Atlanta: U.S. Forest Service, Southeastern Area, State and Private Forestry, 1979), pp. 5–9, 14.

30. Pyne, *Fire in America,* pp. 293, 357; Briefing Paper: Rural Fire Prevention and Control, p. 2.

31. John B. Woods, "Report of the Forest Resource Appraisal," 1947, p. 11, in box 5, Greeley Papers.

32. Benedict, *History of White Pine Blister Rust Control,* pp. 37–38, 46–47; Stuart Moir to G. H. Collingwood, June 17, 1945, in box 78, NFPA Records.

33. Report of Forest Insect Control Conference, Portland, Feb. 26, 1945, in box 7, NFPA Records.

34. Forest Conservation Division, NLMA, to Federated Associations, Mar. 8, Stuart Moir to G. H. Collingwood, Mar. 2, and Paul Keen to Moir, Feb. 26, 1946, all in ibid.

35. Stuart Moir to R. A. Colgan, Mar. 29, 1946, ibid.

36. George M. Fuller to H. V. Simpson, Feb. 14, 1947, statement by Richard A. Colgan, NLMA, before the Subcommittee of the House Agricultural Committee, Apr. 28, 1947, and Ed. R. Linn to H. C. Berckes, Feb. 22, 1947, all in ibid.; *Highlights in the History of Forest Conservation,* p. 16.

37. Benedict, *History of White Pine Blister Rust Control,* p. 46.

38. Stuart Moir to George Fuller, Dec. 22, 1949, Ernest L. Kolbe to A. J. Glassow, Jan. 9, and Glassow to Kolbe, Jan. 11, 1950, all in box 7, NFPA Records.

39. W. L. Popham, "Development of the Cooperative Effort in Forest Pest Control," *Journal of Forestry* 48 (May, 1950):321–323.

40. Ibid.

41. USDA, Forest Service—Pacific Northwest Region, *Budworm Activity: Oregon and Washington, 1947–1979* (1980), p. 8.

42. Ibid.

43. "Spruce Beetle Outbreak in Forests of Northern Idaho and Western Montana," U.S. Forest Service Press Release, Jan. 29, 1953, in box 7, NFPA Records.

44. Resolution Adopted at the 42nd Annual Conference of the Western

Forestry and Conservation Association, Portland, Nov. 28–30, 1950, in box 3, WFCA Records; Henry Bahr to Avery Hoyt, Jan. 14, and Hoyt to Bahr, Feb. 7, 1952, both in box 20, NFPA Records.

45. Leo V. Bodine to Ernest Kolbe, Feb. 2, Kolbe to E. C. Rettig, Feb. 4, 1953, and statement by Kolbe on Need for Funds to Battle Forest Insects in the West and in the Nation, May 25, 1953, all in box 7, NFPA Records.

46. Minutes of Meeting: Industry–Forest Service Policy Conference, July 8, 1954, in box 29, ibid.

47. Ernest L. Kolbe to Truman W. Collins, Feb. 14, Kolbe to A. Z. Nelson, Aug. 3, 1956, and Kolbe to Nelson, July 24, 1957, all in box 7, ibid.

48. Forest Service, *Annual Report* (1958):6–7.

49. Ibid. (1959):24, (1963):29, (1964):19.

50. Georgia Forestry Commission, *Biennial Report of Progress* (1954):10–11; Abel, "Complexities of Modern Forest Management in the South," p. 14.

51. Minutes of the Annual Meeting, Northwest Forest Pest Action Committee, Nov. 1, 1954, Acc. No. 46460, RG95, Federal Records Center, Seattle.

52. James W. Craig to Charles A. Connaughton, Mar. 25, 1955, in box 2, Acc. No. 64B105, RG95, Federal Records Center, Atlanta.

53. Terry S. Price and Coleman Doggett, *A History of Southern Pine Beetle Outbreaks* (Macon: Georgia Forestry Commission, 1978), pp. 1–2, 5.

54. Fred Whitefield to Charles Connaughton, Mar. 16, 1955, and Status Insect Control—Region 8—F. Y. 1959, both in box 2, Acc. No. 64B105, RG95, Federal Records Center, Atlanta.

55. Forest Service, *Annual Report* (1962):6; Georgia Forestry Commission, *Annual Report* (1963):n.p.

56. USDA, Forest Service, *Evaluating Control Tactics for the Southern Pine Beetle: Symposium Proceedings* (January 30 to February 1, 1979), Southeastern Area, State and Private Forestry, Technical Bulletin 1613, p. 1; USDA, Forest Service, *Forest and Insect Disease Conditions in the South, 1978,* Southeastern Area, State and Private Forestry, Forestry Report SA-FR4 (Sept., 1979), pp. 3–4.

57. William Hoffard, "Biological Evaluation of Southern Pine Beetle Infestations on West Point Lake, Forest Insect and Disease Management," Report No. 80-1-16, June, 1980, in U.S. Forest Service, State and Pri-

vate Forestry Office, Atlanta; USDA, Forest Service, *Direct Control Methods for the Southern Pine Beetle,* Agriculture Handbook No. 575 (Mar., 1981), p. 3.

58. Benedict, *History of White Pine Blister Rust Control,* p. 46.

59. T. M. Tyrrell to Alex Jaenicke, Mar. 25, and C. P. Wessela to W. V. Benedict, May 6, 1953, both in Acc. No. 46460, RG95, Federal Records Center, Seattle.

60. T. H. Harris to J. Herbert Stone, Aug. 21, and Stone to Harris, Aug. 27, 1953, ibid.

61. Benedict, *History of White Pine Blister Rust Control,* p. 1; W. V. Benedict to L. B. Loring, Feb. 18, Loring to Benton Howard, Mar. 18, and J. Herbert Stone to James F. Short, Apr. 1, 1960, all in Acc. No. 33613, RG95, Federal Records Center, Seattle.

62. Benedict, *History of White Pine Blister Rust Control,* p. 44.

63. Oregon, Department of Forestry, *Biennial Report* (1964):10.

64. C. M. Hofferbert to Forest Supervisors and District Rangers, R-6, Mar. 7, 1974, in Acc. No. 58653, RG95, Federal Records Center, Seattle.

65. C. F. M. Narrative Report by Bob Bourhill, Service Forester, Northeastern Oregon District, n.d., in Acc. No. 148808, RG95, Federal Records Center, Seattle.

66. USDA, Forest Service—Pacific Northwest Region, *Environmental Monitoring Program: 1974 Cooperative Douglas Fir–Tussock Moth Control Project* (Portland: n.p., 1981), pp. 5–6.

67. Ibid., pp. 6, 8.

Chapter Fourteen

1. Dallas M. Lea and C. Dudley Matson, *Evolution of the Small Watershed Program,* USDA Agricultural Economic Report No. 262 (Washington, D.C: Government Printing Office, 1974), p. 1.

2. Forest Service, *Annual Report* (1955):9; Lea and Matson, *Evolution of the Small Watershed Program,* pp. 1–2; William Murray to Dennis Roth, June 21, 1983, in History Section.

3. Forest Service, *Annual Report* (1956):11.

4. Charles Connaughton to Iris Blitch, Aug. 9, 1954, and Frank Albert to Forest Supervisors, Jan. 26, 1955, both in box 2, Acc. No. 64B105, RG95, Federal Records Center, Atlanta; Forest Service, *Annual Report* (1955):9, (1956):11, (1957):4–5.

5. D. M. Ilch to the Record, Feb. 1, 1954, in box 2, Acc. No. 64B105, RG95, Federal Records Center, Atlanta.

6. D. A. Craig to J. K. Vessey, Nov. 18, 1959, and Harley Janelle, memorandum to Craig, Nov. 25, 1959, both in ibid.

7. D. A. Craig to J. K. Vessey, Nov. 18, Vessey to Chief, Forest Service, Dec. 16, 1959, and Warren T. Murphey to Regional Forester, Region 8, Feb. 5, 1960, all in ibid.

8. D. A. Craig to Arkansas State Forester, Mar. 4, 1960, and Harley Janelle, Field Review of PL-566 Projects — Arkansas, Feb. 3–4, 1960, both in ibid.

9. Paul J. St. Amant to Edward L. Lawson, June 7, and St. Amant to L. J. Ashbaugh and Karl Davidson, June 7, 1962, both in Department of Conservation, Forestry Division, Minnesota State Archives, St. Paul.

10. Resume of Federal Aid Programs of the Division of Forestry, July 17, 24, 1964, and Cooperative Forestry Programs, Dec., 1959, all in ibid.

11. Georgia Forestry Commission, *Annual Report* (1960):n.p., (1964):n.p., (1972):13.

12. Resource, Conservation, and Development — PL-566 Review, Georgia Forestry Commission, Oct. 28, 1981, draft copy in U.S. Forest Service, Region 8, State and Private Forestry Office, Atlanta; interview with Carl Hoover, June 14, 1982.

13. Resource, Conservation, and Development — PL-566 Review, Georgia Forestry Commission, Oct. 28, 1982.

14. *Highlights in the History of Forest Conservation,* pp. 17–18.

15. Gilbert F. White, *Strategies of American Water Management* (Ann Arbor: University of Michigan Press, 1969), pp. 35–36.

16. H. D. Burke, Summary Brief of AWR Study, July 1, 1954, in box 4, Acc. No. 66A1275, RG95, Federal Records Center, Atlanta.

17. Ibid.

18. Ibid.

19. Ibid.

20. Ibid.

21. E. R. DeSilvia to Jamie L. Whitten, Nov. 2, 1956, in Forestry Activities: Yazoo–Little Tallahatchie Flood Prevention Project, Miss., records held by the History Section; interview with Carl Hoover, June 14, 1982.

22. E. R. DeSilvia to Jamie Whitten, Nov. 2, 1956, in Forestry Activities: Y-LT Project.

23. FP—Programs—Flood Prevention, Little Tallahatchie Work Plans, F.Y. 1949, and E. R. DeSilvia to Jamie L. Whitten, Nov. 2, 1956, both in ibid.

24. Annual Report: Y-LT Project, F.Y. 1958, in ibid.

25. Annual Report: Y-LT Project, F.Y. 1958, in ibid.

26. Victor B. MacNaughton, "Something of Value," reprinted from the *Southern Lumberman* (Dec. 15, 1956), copy in ibid.

27. Y-LT Project: Annual Planting Report, 1962–1963, and Annual Report: Y-LT Project, F.Y. 1963, both in ibid.

28. Y-LT Project: Annual Planting Report, 1963–1964, and Annual Report: Y-LT Project, F.Y. 1963, both in ibid.

29. Annual Report: Y-LT Project, F.Y. 1965, in ibid.

30. Y-LT Project: Annual Planting Report, 1966–1967, in ibid.

31. Y-LT Project: Annual Report, 1967, in ibid.

32. Ibid.

33. Interview with Carl Hoover, June 14, 1982; interview with Don Pomerening, Mar. 18, 1982.

34. Charles Shade to the author, Oct. 5, 1983; Charles I. Shade, "In Mississippi, Trees Heal the Land and Provide a Growing Future," reprinted from *Southern Lumberman* (Dec., 1982), copy in possession of the author; Michael V. Namorato, "A History of the U.S. Forest Service's Role in the Yazoo–Little Tallahatchie Flood Prevention Project, 1932–1975," manuscript, in USDA, Forest Service, Southern Region office, Oxford, Miss.

35. Forest Service, *Annual Report* (1956):11, (1957):5.

36. Ibid. (1958):7, (1959):25, (1961):27.

37. W. S. Swingler to Regional Forester, Apr. 26, 1963, in box 10, Acc. No. 66A1276, RG95, Federal Records Center, Atlanta.

38. Forest Service, *Annual Report* (1969):50.

39. Pyne, *Fire in America,* pp. 29–33, 61.

40. Lockmann, *Guarding the Forests of Southern California,* pp. 91, 99, 108.

41. E. I. Kotok et al., "Protection against Fire," in *National Plan for American Forestry,* 2:1396–1397; State of California, Department of Natural Resources, Division of Forestry, Cooperative Forest Management Research, May 15, 1956, memorandum in Forestry, California State Archives, Sacramento.

42. P. H. Russell to R. H. Wells, Mar. 19, 1957, box 12, and Report on Present and Anticipated Agricultural Conditions: Yazoo Backwater

Project, Yazoo River Basin, Miss., Apr., 1957, box 2, both in Acc. No. 66A1275, RG95, Federal Records, Atlanta.

Chapter Fifteen

1. "Retiree Newsletter No. 78," June 7, 1982, in History Section.
2. William Murray to Dennis Roth, June 21, 1983, and Donald Pomerening to Roth, July 1, 1983, both in ibid.
3. Richard L. Knox to Dennis Roth, July 1, 1983, and report of the State and Private Forestry Advisory Committee, Apr. 3, 1975, both in ibid.
4. Secretary's memorandum no. 1933—revised, Oct. 24, 1978, in ibid.
5. Summary minutes, Committee of State Foresters, Mar. 11, 1982, in ibid.
6. Edward C. Crafts, *Congress and the Forest Service, 1950–1962,* interviewed by Amelia R. Fry (Berkeley: Bancroft Library, University of California, 1975), p. 9.
7. National Association of State Foresters, unpaginated loose-leaf notebook (hereafter, NASF notebook), in History Section; USDA, Forest Service, Northeastern Area, State and Private Forestry, *Meeting the Challenge of Change* (circa, 1966), p. 1, in Subject File, Forest History Society Library.
8. *Meeting the Challenge of Change,* pp. 1–2; USDA, Forest Service, *Introduction to S&PF* (circa, 1972), p. 16, in Subject File, Forest History Society Library, Santa Cruz, Calif.
9. USDA, Forest Service, Northeastern Area, State and Private Forestry, *Design for the Future: An Inter-Disciplinary Team Approach to Mission-Oriented Objectives* (circa, 1971), pp. 1–2, in ibid.
10. USDA, Forest Service, *The Forest Service Mission in State and Private Forestry* (Nov., 1974), pp. 1–8, in ibid.
11. Comptroller General of the United States, Report to the Congress, *The Forest Service Needs to Ensure That the Best Possible Use Is Made of Its Research Program Findings* (Jan. 6, 1972), pp. 1–3, in U.S. Forest Service, Office of State and Private Forestry, Washington, D.C. (hereafter S&PF).
12. "Plan for the Application for Research Findings and Better Communications between Research Users and Scientists," in ibid.
13. Memorandum, John R. McGuire to Regional Foresters, Directors, Area Directors, and Washington Office Division Directors, May 14, 1974, in ibid.

14. Report of the State and Private Forestry Advisory Committee, May 16, 1975, in History Section; USDA, Office of Audit, "Audit Report: Forest Service Research/State and Private Forestry — Research Dissemination and Application as of July 20, 1976," in S&PF.

15. John R. McGuire to John C. Barber et al., Nov. 18, 1976, and "Technology Transfer in the Forest Service: A Background Paper," Jan. 11, 1979, both in S&PF.

16. "Cooperative Forest and Fire Staff: A Synopsis of Activities and Major Issues," Nov., 1980, memorandum in California Department of Forestry Office, Sacramento.

17. USDA, Forest Service, *Milestone: Technology Transfer in the Forest Service, Report on Technology Transfer Staff Accomplishments and Evaluation, 1978–1981* (Washington, D.C.: USDA, 1981), pp. 4–6.

18. Ibid., 7, 13.

19. NASF notebook; *American Forests* 78 (Jan., 1972):7.

20. USDA Advisory Committee on State and Private Forestry, Nov., 1978, in History Section.

21. Zane C. Smith, Jr., to Chief, U.S. Forest Service, Aug. 30, 1979, in California Department of Forestry Office, Sacramento; California Department of Forestry, *The Hip-Pocket Urban Tree Planter* (Sacramento: n.p., 1979), pp. 10–16.

22. Smith to Chief, U.S. Forest Service, and memorandum, California Department of Forestry, Urban Forestry Advisory Committee, July, 1979, both in California Department of Forestry Office.

23. *Urban Forestry* (USDA—Forest Service, Region 5, 1980), p. 5.

24. Minnesota Department of Natural Resources, *Biennial Report* (1980–1981):33.

25. Report of the Advisory Committee on State and Private Forestry, Apr., 1980, and report of the Committee of State Foresters, Mar. 5, 1981, both in History Section.

26. *California Urban Forestry Grant Program* (Sacramento: California Department of Forestry, 1980), pp. 1–3.

27. U.S. Forest Service, *Annual Report* (1945):13–14, (1947):22, (1948): 35–36, (1949):37; McArdle, "Technical Assistance for Private Owners," p. 36; R. E. Marsh to Mr. Watts and Staff, Apr. 14, 1947, in "Supervision—Programs, Pattern for Agriculture, General, 1947," NA/RG95–99.

28. USDA, Forest Service, *What the Forest Service Does* (Washington, D.C.:

Government Printing Office, 1970), pp. 2–3; Edward P. Cliff, *Timber: The Renewable Resource* (Washington, D.C.: Government Printing Office, 1973), pp. 5-1 to 5-9.

29. USDA, Interagency Committee Report, *The Federal Role in the Conservation and Management of Private Nonindustrial Forestlands* (Jan., 1978), pp. i–ii.

30. *Federal Role in the Conservation,* pp. 59–60

31. Report of the State and Private Forestry Advisory Committee, May 16, 1975, in History Section.

32. USDA, Forest Service, *Proceedings of the National Private Non-Industrial Forestry Conference,* General Technical Report, WO-22 (May, 1980), pp. 1–2.

33. Ibid., pp. 3–5.

34. Ibid., pp. 79–81.

35. Ibid., pp. 82–83.

36. Ibid., pp. 87–89; summary minutes, Committee of State Foresters, Mar. 5, 1981, and Mar. 11, 1982, in History Section.

37. *Portland Oregonian,* Oct. 18, 1983.

38. Dana and Fairfax, *Forest and Range Policy,* p. 284.

39. Thomas J. Mills, *Cost Effectiveness of the 1974 Forestry Incentives Program,* USDA, Forest Service, Research Paper RM-175 (Oct., 1976), pp. 1–2.

40. Ibid., pp. 3, 5; report of the State and Private Forestry Advisory Committee, May 16, 1975, in History Section.

41. Report of the State and Private Forestry Advisory Committee, May 16, 1975, Dec. 30, 1977, Apr. and Nov., 1978, in History Section.

42. Ibid., Dec. 30, 1977, Apr., 1978, Mar. 6, 1980, and Apr., 1980; *The New Reforestation Tax Incentives* (Washington, D.C.: Forest Industries Committee on Timber Valuation and Taxation, 1981), pp. 3–4.

43. *Minnesota Forests* (Summer, 1981):3, 8; Minnesota Department of Natural Resources, *Biennial Report* (1978–1979):30, (1980–1981):32.

44. Tess Smith and Andrew Chapman, *Landowners Guide to the California Forest Improvement Program* (Sacramento: California Department of Forestry, 1980), pp. 6–8.

45. Ibid., pp. 8–13; phone conversation with Tom Randolph, service forester, California Department of Forestry, Oct. 21, 1983.

46. *Forestry Cost-Share Assistance for the Forest Landowner* (Washington, D.C.: Government Printing Office, 1981), n.p.; report of the Committee of State Foresters, Mar. 11, 1982, in History Section; phone conversation

with John VanCalcar, state conservation program specialist, Portland, Oct. 21, 1983.

47. Report of the State and Private Forestry Advisory Committee, May 16, 1975, in History Section; Cooperative Forestry and Fire Staff: A Synopsis of Major Issues, Nov., 1980, memorandum in California Department of Forestry Office.

48. USDA, Forest Service, *The Sawmill Improvement Program* (Washington, D.C.: Government Printing Office, 1975), n.p.; report of the Advisory Committee on State and Private Forestry, Apr., 1980, in History Section.

49. Dana and Fairfax, *Forest and Range Policy*, pp. 323–324; USDA, *The Nation's Renewable Resources—An Assessment, 1975*, Forest Resources Report No. 21 (June, 1977), pp. 224–225; USDA, Forest Service, *An Assessment of the Forest and Range Land Situation in the United States*, Forest Resource Report No. 22 (Oct., 1981), p. v.

50. Dana and Fairfax, *Forest and Range Policy*, pp. 325–327; NASF notebook, n.p.

51. *Assessment of the Forest and Range Land Situation*, pp. vi–vii; report of the State and Private Forestry Advisory Committee, May 16, 1975, and May 26, 1975, in History Section.

52. Report of the State and Private Forestry Advisory Committee, May 26, 1976, and Apr. 26, 1977, in History Section.

53. Ibid., Mar. 7, 1979, Mar. 6, 1980.

54. Ibid., Mar. 5, 1981, Mar. 11, 1982.

55. *Assessment of the Forest and Range Land Situation*, pp. vi–vii.

56. Ibid., pp. 327–328.

57. Ibid., p. 330; report of the Advisory Committee on State and Private Forestry, Apr. 26, 1977, in History Section.

58. John McGuire to governors, n.d., in report of the Committee of State Foresters, Mar. 6, 1979, in ibid.; *Proceedings of the National Private Non-Industrial Forestry Conference*, p. 114.

59. John McGuire to governors, n.d., in report of the Committee of State Foresters, Mar. 6, 1979, in History Section.

60. Dana and Fairfax, *Forest and Range Policy*, pp. 235–237, 246–255; report of the State and Private Forestry Advisory Committee, May 16, 1975, in History Section.

61. Report of the State and Private Forestry Advisory Committee, May 16, 1975, and May 26, 1976, in History Section.

62. Richard C. McArdle, "Newsletter No. 78," June 7, 1982; *History Line* (Fall, 1980):5; Donald Pomerening, interview with author, Mar. 18, 1982.

Epilogue

1. *Timberman* 13 (Mar., 1912):32J; *West Coast Lumberman* 25 (Dec. 15, 1913):30, 42.
2. William B. Greeley, *Public and Economic Aspects of the Lumber Industry,* pp. 3–4, 13–15, 99–100.
3. William Greeley to A. W. Greeley, Sept. 5, 1939, box 7, Greeley Papers.
4. *West Coast Lumberman* 29 (Nov. 15, 1915):39.
5. Leo V. Bodine to S. V. Fullaway, Jr., July 5, 1952, box 28, NFPA Records.

Index

American Forestry Congress, 4, 7,
34
American Forests, 157; involved in
policy debate, 89; praises federal
support for urban forestry, 247
American Lumberman, 123, 151–
152; applauds Theodore
Roosevelt, 24; and conservation,
26; and tariff, 27; praises
Clarke-McNary, 94
American National Livestock Asso-
ciation, 107
American Protective League, 117
Andrews, Christopher C., 40; as
U.S. minister to Sweden and
Norway, 37; on development of
forestry in Minnesota, 37, 67
Andrews, H. J., 178; as Region 6
forester, 166
Antitrust investigations, 28
Appalachian Forest Reserve, 17, 23
Appalachian National Park Associa-
tion, 54
Arizona, 17
Arkansas: and forestry commission,
38; as big lumber producer, 80;
fire protection in WW II, 167;
and Small Watershed Program,
229
Arkansas-White-Red River (AWR)
basin project, 231; Inter-agency
Committee, 231–232; forestry
report, 232
Army Corps of Engineers, 226–
227, 231, 238–239; Y-LT
work, 233
Article X of the Lumber Code Au-
thority, 129, 130
Ashe, W. W., 98
Ashland, Oregon, 118
Association of State Foresters, 72,

136, 172; endorses Forest Res-
toration Plan, 135
Atlanta Chamber of Commerce, 81
Atlantic and Pacific Tea Company,
209
Austria, 17

Baker, John A., 196
Ballad of Smokey the Bear, 210
Ballinger, Richard, 106
Bankhead, John H., 133–134
Bark Beetle, infestations of, 147,
218
Barrett, Leonard, 190
Bates, Carlos, 153
Baudette-Spooner fire, 67
Benedict, Warren, 222–223
Benson, Ezra Taft, 192
Berglund, Bob, 243, 251
Berlin Mills, 89
Besley, Lowell, 190
Bessey, Charles E., 40
Biltmore Estate, 39
Biological Survey, 115, 153
Black walnut, use of, 117
Blodgett, John W., 93
Bodine, Leo, 193
Borden, Thomas, 252
Bowers, Edward A., 7
Boyd, J. Philip, 159, 160; as head
of lumber production in WW II,
159; as Weyerhaeuser official
during WW II, 169
Boyle, L. C., 86
Boy Scouts of America, 117
"Brains trusters," 138
Branch of Research (Forest Service),
113; created, 17
Brannan, Charles F., 219
Brewer, William, 2, 3
British Columbia, 47

Mitchell, J. A., 70
Moir, Stuart, 157, 193, 215–217
Monroe, Vaughan, 209
Montana, 40, 47, 58
Morrell, Fred, 121, 124, 142,
  148–149, 153
Muckrake writers, 28
Muir, John, 24
Multiple Use–Sustained Yield Act
  of 1960, 196
Munns, Ed, 121, 129, 153
Murphy, Warren T., 229

Namorato, Michael V., 236
National Academy of Sciences, 7
National Association of State For-
  esters (NASF), 92, 187, 193,
  209, 251, 268
National Commission on Materials
  Policy, 250
National Environmental Policy Act
  (NEPA) of 1969, 259
National Forest Management Act of
  1976, 256
National Forest Products Associa-
  tion (NFPA), 268
National Forestry Program Com-
  mittee, 89, 92, 114
National Grange, 5
National Industrial Recovery Act
  (NIRA), 128
National Lumber Manufacturers
  Association (NLMA), 26, 59,
  85, 87, 92, 99, 108, 114, 123,
  125, 130, 133, 142, 151, 156,
  162, 173, 184, 186, 188, 190,
  193, 204, 216, 217–218, 266,
  268–269; and railroad issues,
  22; endowment to Yale University, 23; and Bureau of Forestry, 23; and Forest Service, 24;

supports American forest policy,
  88–89; lobbies for research bill,
  115; peacetime program for
  federal assistance, 171; criticizes
  Cooperative Forest Management
  Act, 187; seeks reduction in
  Clarke-McNary fire fund, 191;
  advises Ezra Taft Benson, 192
National Park Service, 112, 165;
  established, 110
*National Plan for American Forestry,
  A,* 127
National Recovery Administration
  (NRA), 88, 123, 126
National Wholesale Lumber Deal-
  ers Association, 23
National Wool Growers' Associa-
  tion, 107
National Zoo (Washington, D.C.),
  208
Native Americans, 20
Naval Stores Conservation Pro-
  gram, 202
Nelson, A. Z., 191
Nelson, DeWitt, 212–213
Nelson, Donald, 156–157, 159
New Deal, 134, 138–139, 141,
  154, 252, 267
New England, 1, 54; development
  of municipal forests in, 119
New England Forest Emergency
  Organization (NEFE), 150
New England hurricane of 1938,
  120, 149–152, 154
New Hampshire, 52, 54
New Hampshire Forestry Commis-
  sion, 43
New York, 37; forestry organiza-
  tions, 34; creates forestry agen-
  cies, 35; establishes Adirondack
  and Catskill preserve, 35; re-

338

Pennsylvania Bureau of Forestry, 38
Pennsylvania Forestry Association,
35, 38
Peters, J. Girvin, 14, 63, 87, 91,
117; directs cooperative fire protection, 55; attends New England collaborators' conference,
57–58; and protective associations, 58; inspects Great Lakes
states, 62; as judge of state cooperation, 64; praises William
Cox, 68
Peterson, Max, 252
Pinchot, Gifford, 26, 41–42, 91,
93, 94, 106, 107, 113, 121,
130; appointed Division of Forestry chief in 1898, 11–16;
Circular No. 21, 13; as modernist, 14; and collaborators, 15;
and private sector, 18; and
NLMA, 23; and National
Wholesale Lumber Dealers
Association, 23–24; on forest
conservation and lumber industry, 25; and tariff, 27; and lumber industry, 27; and press releases and newspapers, 29; and
Heyburn's attacks, 29; fired in
1910, 29; and Biltmore forest,
39; creates Division of State and
Private Forestry, 48; and fire and
cooperation, 51–52; as Pennsylvania forester, 82; chairs SAF
policy committee, 89–90; in
Pennsylvania governor's race,
90; on regulation, 90; opposes
national parks, 110
Pittman-Robertson Wildlife Restoration program, 195
Poland, 155

Pomerening, Donald, 260;
appraises Y-LT project, 236
Pomeroy, Kenneth, 213
Popham, W. L., 217
Portland, Oregon, 24, 89, 118
Potter, Albert, 119
Prairie States Forestry Project, 149
Pratt, Joseph H., 62
Preus, J. A. O., 72
Private Nonindustrial Forestry
Project (PNIF), 251
Protective associations, 51
Progressivism: and conservation
movement, 28
Puget Sound, 179
Pyne, Stephen: *Fire in America*, 62–
63, 206

Railroad companies, 9
Rakestraw, Lawrence, 46
Reagan administration, 249, 257
Reclamation Service, 18
Reconstruction Finance Corpora-
tion, 150
Reed, Franklin W., 126
Region 1, 163, 177
Region 5, 248
Region 6, 164, 178, 196, 218
Region 7, 152
Region 8, 164, 198, 221–222,
228–229, 237; and marketing
assistance for farm woodlot own-
ers, 176
Region 9, 200
Research, 112–113, 167
Resler, Rexford A., 251
Resource Conservation and De-
velopment (RC&D), 198
Resources Planning Act of 1974,
241, 256, 258